Abrm Davenport

TO JOSEPH B. HOYT, OLIVER HOYT, WILLIAM HOYT, GEORGE W. QUINTARD, EDWARD A. QUINTARD, NATHANIEL WEED, AND JAMES H. HOYT, SONS OF STAMFORD, THIS HISTORY OF THE TOWN WHICH THEIR ENTERPRISE HAS DONE SO MUCH TO HONOR, IS GRATEFULLY DEDICATED BY

THE AUTHOR.

LIST OF PORTRAITS.

---

* For our beautiful Frontispiece from a portrait, now owned by Rev. J. S. Davenport, of New York, the author is indebted to the kind offices of A. B. Davenport, Esq., author of the Davenport Family.

CONTENTS.

APPENDIX.

PREFACE.

After my Introductory Chapter, which is largely prefatory, there is need of but a very brief, formal preface. My dedication expressed my sense of obligation to seven of the sons of Stamford, without whose pecuniary aid the publication of the work must have been deferred. To another son of the town, whose name I must not give, I am under the same obligation. To many others of our citizens my obligations cannot be forgotten, as long as the record remains which they aided me in making, or while my long subscription list reminds me of their interest in my work. To all these, I now gratefully submit this History of the beautiful town, which I know they delight to honor.

In doing so, I could wish its omissions and its faults were fewer; yet I am most of all content, that whatever of either are noticed, were unavoidable. For one omission, rendered necessary both by the size and the expense of the volume, and still more by the merits of the subject itself, demanding fuller and more careful treatment, I trust my readers will find the best possible compensation in the forthcoming STAMFORD SOLDIERS' MEMORIAL.

Of its mechanical execution, the History will speak for itself. For the few typographical errors here found, the considerate reader will surely find large amends in the general accuracy of the work; and both the author and his townsmen have just occasion for pride, that our local press has been able to send forth so large a volume, to which so few exceptions can be taken.

If nothing further is done, in this contribution to our local history, the author is happy to submit these first fruits, at least, of the full harvests of these two hundred and twenty eight years.

HISTORY OF STAMFORD.

CHAPTER I.

INTRODUCTORY.

Not two and a quarter centuries have passed since the region in which the beautiful village of Stamford now lies, was a savage wilderness. No foot of white man, unless it may have been that of some adventurous explorer, had ever treaded its solitary paths. The same blue waters mirrored as now the same gently retreating hill-sides, but they had never photographed as now the cottages and spires of a civilized and Christian people. Overlooking the quiet Rippowam harbor were the same hills as now; the softly rounded Noroton, towards the rising sun, the higher central Mataubaun, (the morn revealer,) stretching far up towards the north, and the lowlier, yet no less lovely ridge to the west, behind which the setting sun went to his rest for the night. The "Myanos" and Noroton rivers, larger then than now, unhindered by dam, coursed their roaring or babbling way beneath the tufted foliage of the primeval forest into the sunny waters of the sound; while the rippling Rowalton separated these realms of the jealous Rippowam from the hunting grounds of the lordly Mahackeno. No where from the Rowalton to the Mianus, and from the southern waters along the "four hour's walk" towards the dreaded forests of the fierce Mohawks, could one rest his eye upon either the presence or trace of the pale face or his work.

Bears growled where now the hum of industry is heard. Wolves roamed and howled amid thickets which no woodman's axe had ever invaded. Wild birds amid their leafy bowers sang their carols to wild beasts in their leafy lairs. No voice of man had for once awaked the echoes of these hills and glens, save when some Indian lover wooed to his side the dark eye of his heart, or when the proud warrior of some savage clan rang ont the defiant warwhoop of his great wrath.

Here had lived and loved, only another race. Here and there, nestling amid ledges and between over-arching trees, was an Indian's home—a wigwam as rude in its structure and finish as the untutored savage who had built it. A few brawny red men with their "dusky mates" and bright-eyed little ones, numbering in all, not to exceed some three hundred souls, were the sole human tenants on this soil. Nor were even they its permanent possessors. Their sagamores, Ponus and Wescussue, held the undisputed title to all the land, and in their paternal condescension, they meted out for the season to their loyal subjects, such patches as they could plant with corn or beans. Of course there was no general tillage of the ground. The utmost ingenuity of Indian art had no conception of the plow, and could furnish but a sorry substitute for even the white man's axe and hoe and spade.

Nor had the still waters of either Rippowam or Toquam harbor, yet felt the keel of civilized commerce. The light bark canoe had for many generations been wont to shoot swiftly from point to point across the shallower indentations of the coast, while the huge trunk of some lofty forest oak, excavated by tedious scraping with shells and sharpened flint stones aided by the skillful use of fire, had supplied the aborigines with their only safe transport for the rougher sea voyage. At intervals of long period, the waters of the sound had been the theater of fierce and bloody sea-fights. Not in gallant and gigantic ship, moved at the commander's will by steam or sail, but in these rude monarchs of Indian sea-craft, driven with mightiest stroke of well-trained oar against each other, in fearfully frightful and fatal encounter. One such naval engagement had crimsoned our harbor with savage blood, just before the white man for the first time entered its glassy waters.

Nor had the sharp crack of the hunter's rifle, nor the roar of modern artillery, ever yet disturbed these solitudes; though instead, the twang of the sounding bow and the sharp whizzing of the winged arrow had often brought to the ground the eagle in his loftiest flight, or cut short the swiftest footed wild deer in his race.

Here everything was in its rudest dress—hillside and glen, forest tree and mossy rock, wavy margined coast and arbored, murmuring stream, all were as nature made and meant them—all as their untutored and unambitious occupants had left them. All attempts at improvement by the rude savage had only marred the native beauty they had invaded. The homes here built, the paths here opened, all changes here made, begun and ended still in forest homes and paths and change. Nature mainly held her own against the utmost of all that Indian art and industry could do.

And still no intelligent and cultivated eye could have gazed upon this uncultivated domain, without being struck with its singular and quiet beauty. There was not in it the stirring grandeur of Alpine scenery, nor yet the sublime immensity of the prairie's stretch; but there was something which while it might move the beholder less would not fail to please him more. Rarely, on earth, do pleasant hill-sides sweep up more gracefully from heaven-penciled waters, and still more rarely, do hill and lowland and vale blend in pictures of more pleasing loveliness.

So felt even the Indian, as his sharp eye swept over the broad landscape from his outlook on his favorite Mataubaun; and so thought the weary pilgrims of another race as they came to find on this coast the future homes of their own and their children's children.

The Indian passed away, and with him perished the story of his race. All their tender loves and all their stern revenges; every adventure of chieftain or of subject; noble deeds of affection and of heroism, all alike unrecorded, have gone forever into an oblivion from which no pen of historian can recover them.

The last faint traces which his departing footsteps left, are all that remain to witness to the Indian's power and skill.

The white man came. In defiance of the savage race on these borders of a frowning wilderness, in the midst of blood-thirsty beasts of prey, he was forced to seek his home. He counted and accepted the cost. He set up the altars of his faith. He taught the wilderness to bud and blossom; and bud and blossom and fruitage he turned to his use. He made of the forest tree his comfortable house. The virgin soil answered his call, and loaded his table with her fruits. Idle water streams soon leaped upon his water wheels, and with tireless gladness helped on his course. The patient genius of education took his little ones in care, and taught their young minds to plan and their hands to execute new triumphs in his progress.

The old forests and all the profitless savagery of Indian life soon gave way, and farms and schools, industry and thrift, civilization and religion, homes of comfort and of elegance attested the presence of the more intelligent, and permanent race.

For two hundred and twenty-six years that race have now on this ground plied their intelligence, their invention, their industry and their skill. Six or seven generations of their children have here grown up, borne their part in the great work of man on earth, and left the accumulating treasures of their career as a precious legacy to the generation which now have occasion to rejoice in the succession.

And why may we not, why should we not gather up the lessons which those busy years can furnish? Who would refuse to trace the record which Providence has here drawn? Who withhold from the hardy pioneers who inaugurated, and from the wise and valiant men who have transmitted with the added luster of their own bright fame, this noble inheritance to us? Surely, not the worthy sons of names so worthy. Surely, not the natives of other towns, who have been drawn hither by the charms or the promises of good which their earlier homes could not offer, and who are now gathering here the fruits of a prosperity which others sowed. Every just, every filial, every honorable son or citizen of Stamford must respond to the claim which his native or adopted town has to a permanent and instructive memorial. It were as undutiful, as it is unjust to the departed generations, to refuse such a tribute. No pains should be deemed too costly, which can secure it.

It was such a feeling which moved the author, some dozen years ago, to examine the records of the town to learn if they offered sufficient material towards such a work. Though very imperfect, almost illegible in some places and defaced or totally wanting in others; though exceedingly meager everywhere, except in recording the annual lists of town officers, from selectmen down to the key-keeper of the town pound, there still seemed enough of the earlier records left to justify the attempt. Thanks to the providence of our town officers twenty-five years ago, by whom the mutilated aud rapidly wasting remnants of the old records were carefully arranged and bound together for preservation.

This township, whose story for two and a quarter centuries I have undertaken to tell, occupies about one-third of that seacoast parallelogram which stretches off from the southwest corner of Connecticut. By the original grant, made over by the Indians, it must have covered nearly that entire parallelogram, together with a parallel strip lying on the north of it and now owing allegiance to the Empire State.

But by the excision of several portions of the tract, the Stamford to which my research is mainly limited, has come to occupy the central part of the first grant—a tract now, not far from ten miles in length from N. N. W. to S. S. E.; and on an average about seven miles in width, on a line running a little to the South of West. It is bounded on the north-north-west by the towns of North Castle and Poundridge; on the east-north-east by the towns of New Canaan and Norwalk; on the south-south-east by Long Island Sound, and on the west-south-west by Greenwich.

This entire tract has a gentle slope towards the south-south-west, and its surface is made up of a not ungraceful succession of ridges having the same general direction, yet of the greatest possible variety of length and contour, yet gradually lifting themselves to greater elevations towards the north, where the central one has by common consent won the distinction of our High Ridge. Meandering among these ridges, as if to carve the surface into forms of most pleasing variety, we find the Mianus and its main tributary on the north-west; the old Indian Rippowam, and now, from its English use, the Mill river, with its eight serviceable branchlets draining ten times as many hill-sides and rippling through many a pleasant vale; the shorter Noroton, laughing its joyous way down through the defiles in the north-east part of the town, to the open plains we call New Hope, and thence toying its playful way around the eastern base of our Noroton hill, into the smooth waters of its own lovely bay; and next, and still less, the gentle brooklets ever to be dishonored by their late born names, Stoney Brook and Good Wife, yet ever to be used for bounding and draining the gentle slopes whose waters find their beds; and last, as if to warn us that we must find our eastern frontier somewhere, the prosy Five Mile, whose beauties and whose uses, we are doomed to share with our Norwalk neighbors towards the east.

Of all the hills and valleys and plains bounded and separated by these brooks and streams, the time would fail me to write. To be known, they must be seen; and, seen in the freshness of their summer dress, they will be felt to be a goodly sight. Whoever scans them, clothed with the variegated hues of the early autumn, will call them pleasant and beautiful.

A very accurate eye and a sober judgment the topographist had, who wrote of this town a quarter of a century ago:

"This is a pleasant and fertile township; rich in the resources of agricultural opulence, abounding in the means of subsistence, with the advantages of a ready and convenient market. The surface of the town is undulating, exhibiting a pleasant diversity of moderate hills and valleys. The soil is a rich gravelly loam, adapted to both tillage and grazing."

Somewhat more enthusiastic was the estimate of its topography, in some favored localities, of the very celebrated Dr. Dwight, who traveled over large portions of our broad land that he might observe and note their excellences or their defects. His judgment is worth transcribing for this preliminary chapter of our history:

"There are three uncommonly interesting spots in this township; one on the western side of the harbor which is called the Southfield, a rich and beautiful farm.

"Another is a peninsula on the east side of the harbor, Shippan, the property of Moses Rogers, Esq., of New York. This also is an elegant and fertile piece of ground. The surface slopes in every direction, and is encircled by a collection of exquisite scenery. The Sound and Long Island beyond it, with a gracefully indented shore, are directly in front; and both stretch westward to a vast distance, and seaward till the eye is lost. On each side, also, lies a harbor, bounded by handsome points.

"A train of groves and bushy islands, peculiarly pleasing in themselves, increase by their interruptions, the beauty of the waters. The farm itself is a delightful object, with its fields neatly inclosed, its orchards and its groves.

"Here Mr. Rogers has formed an avenue a mile in length, reaching to the water's edge. At the same time he has planted on the grounds surrounding his house, almost all the forest trees which are indigenous to this country. To these he has united plantations of fruit trees, a rich garden and other interesting objects so combined as to make this one of the pleasantest retreats in the United States.

"The third, named the Cove, is on the western side of Noroton river. On this spot, in very advantageous situations, have been erected two large mills for the manufacture of flour, and a small village or rather hamlet for mechanics of various kinds. The view of the harbor in front, the points by which it is limited, the small but beautiful islands which it contains, the Sound, the Long Island shore, a noble sheet of water in the rear, the pleasant village of Noroton, and the hills and groves in the interior is rarely equalled by scenery of the same nature, especially when taken from a plain scarcely elevated above the level of the ocean."

Such is the testimony of Dr. Dwight, to the beauty of these three still noticeable points in the topography of the town.

Nearly fifty years have passed since that judgment was penned; and during this period the progress of settlement or of improvement has added many a locality, whose natural or cultivated beauty equals or exceeds these. Whoever traverses this tract from east to west, over almost any one of our roads will find himself frequently surprised by a sudden view of some charming landscape—whose beauty is only enhanced by the silvery edging of its southern front. Such views one will be glad to linger upon, from our Richmond, and Strawberry, and Noroton, and Summer, and Ox ridge elevations, near the Sound; and from Fort and White hills, from Hunting and Davenport and Long and High ridges, further to the north. And besides these, a score of other summits might be named, each one of which is itself a gem set in the coronal of our summer landscape, yet most of all delightful for what it shows us, of the broad panorama in which it lies.

But what gave the name STAMFORD to this township? In his centennial address, delivered here in 1841, the Rev. Mr. Alvord, who had evidently spent no little time in his historical inquiries, gives this explanation of the name. "Our fathers in changing the name," from Rippowams, the Indian name, "called the town after Stamford in England, which place was doubtless the former residence of some of them." This is a most natural conclusion, and one which we shall be able, neither to prove or disprove.

But if it was true, that an English town gave name to the New England settlement, it would yet be a question which of the three places in the mother land, should have the honor. It might have been the Stamford Bridge, in Yorkshire, on the Derwent, a place famous for that successful contest in which Harold utterly defeated the insolent Norwegian invasion. The orthography of the name, as reported by Hume is precisely that which we find on our earlier records; it is not so remote from the theatre of the good Mr. Denton's earlier ministerial labors, as not, for some reason or other, to have been chosen as a fitting name for the new settlement. Or it may have been that other

Stamford of England, on the extreme western borders of Worcestershire, as the Connecticut town was, on the same extreme of New England. We know not but the very loveliness of this beautiful town of the charming Teme, may have been seen or fancied to belong, in its elements at least, to the new township on the margin of the New England Rippowam. Good authority, at a later date, has told us that "the situation of Stamford is delightful." And still again, "it would be utterly impossible through the medium of words, or at least any words which I can select, to give an idea of the lovely country where I was born and reared." And yet once more, we have the same enthusiastic admiration expressed by the same gifted pen. It is the hearty and affectionate tribute of the talented Mrs. Sherwood—her skillful photograph of the dearest scenes of her childhood, in which she would commend to all her readers "the lovely parsonage of Stamford, the elegant home in which I was born." And surely no one who has an eye for the lovely and beautiful in landscape, will deny that some future Mrs. Sherwood may, with equal truth, so daguerreotype the charms of more than one home in the Stamford, yet to be, here in this Southwestern corner of Connecticut. But, perhaps, as has been generally supposed, the name comes from the Stamford of Lincolnshire. That, also, was a border town, and like this, on the Southwestern extreme of the county. And there are, possibly, other local and historical reasons which may seem to indicate this as the original, to whose scenery or to the affection of whose dutiful children, our New England Stamford owes its name.

As to the English homes of our settlers, our utmost diligence has failed to trace a single family to the Lincolnshire Stamford. Indeed, but one of the earlier names of our pioneers, has been found on any of the Stamford records we have seen. The Browns, a name, universal almost as the Smiths, were early in the ancient English Stamford of Lincoln. And they were also of no little repute. Their monuments still speak of their fame. The church of All Saints, standing on the north side of the Red

Lion Square, in the old English town, was the gift of John Brown, who was an alderman of the city in 1462; and in the St. Mary's can now be seen brass figures of William Brown and his wife. A hospital, also, founded in the reign of the third Richard, is still a monument here to the humanity of this William Brown.

Not far from this Stamford, on the borders of Leicestershire, Mr. Denton had his nativity, and spent his earlier years; and it is not improbable that some feature of the place made so favorable impression on his boyhood, that when he came to stand, in manhood, at the head of this yet nameless settlement, he could find no fitter or worthier name for the place which he intended to make the home for his old age.

But sometimes the subtlest of influences establishes a new empire, to which the most trifling occurrence, a mere slight resemblance even, shall give its name. So, doubtless it was some slight feature of many of the townships in New England, which led to the selection of their names,—their peculiar water margin, their running streams, their hills, or valleys, or plains; and the same unimportant hint which settled the choice of the founders, settled also the name assigned to the town thus founded.

I confess myself to have been not a little surprised by Simpson's engraving of the Lincolnshire Stamford. It is found in Allen's History of the County of Lincoln. It is a southerly view of the old town, and the first impression it gave me was that of a veritable prototype of the modern Connecticut Stamford, as seen from the south-west.

The two landscapes are strikingly alike. The five steeples or towers are almost literally reproduced in the modern engraving of the modern Stamford. A large castellated mansion towards the right of the old picture, occupies nearly the position of the Noroton Hill residences, on our map; and the almost involuntary decision was, there need be no wonder why the founders called these hills and wooded slopes another Stamford.

Nor was the resemblance scarcely less, in the engraving found in Britton's "Beauties of England and Wales." The landscape seemed the same. Hills and intervales wore the same contour, and were cleaved by not dissimilar river beds. And if the self same mold gave form and feature to the two, why should not the same express them both?

But how completely, a careful study of these pictures of the English Stamford, would dispel the illusion that they designed to illustrate the trans-Atlantic town.

The artificial of the two is all unlike. The architecture of the one antedates by long centuries the other. The institutions and customs which the one illustrates, are equally antiquated and foreign to the other. Long ages of time and a wide ocean in space must certainly separate them.

Witness those huge uplifted arms of that slow grinding windmill, and you need not ask them if their unwieldy and unsightly aerimotion belongs to the age or to the neighborhood, even, of the modern cis-Atlantic town.

Witness those circular arches and wavy moldings of that old Benedictine convent, which plainly tell of an age far earlier than the very oldest of the many styled architecture of the Connecticut town. Witness those ancient monasteries and friaries, in which, ages before the white man had even found the site of the new Stamford, there must have been gathered successive generations of men who practiced or simulated the holiest self-denials of the Christian life. Witness, too, those mouldering ruins, that tell us the presence here, in ages long since gone by, of the old Roman and his power; and those other dismantled halls, where other generations were trained in all the most courtly and elegant culture of that early age.

This English Stamford dates from a very early period. Henry Huntington gives us our first account of it. As early as Bladud, one of the British kings of the ninth century, it was a place of some note. The Romans called it Durobevia, from the rocky ford over the Welland here. The Saxons translated the same feature into their language, and called it the Stane-ford or rocky ford which in the progress of orthographic change has come to be Stamford. Our first spelling of the modern names, it will be seen, is Stanforde; and we may, without serious misgiving, accept as its prototype, the ancient Stanforde in the Wapentake of Ness.

We have already alluded to the local records from which a portion of these details are drawn. But quite as fortunate is it, that so many of the papers of the town have been preserved by the care of the state. But for the aid of these papers, now arranged and indexed in the state library in Hartford, but few of the older towns of the state could furnish material for an intelligible record of their local history. Certainly, Stamford, one of the oldest of these towns, is greatly indebted to this state providence for many of the records which this history preserves.

Next to these sources of our history, stand the ecclesiastical records of the First Church and those of the Middlesex Church and Society, (Darien); the former commencing with Dr. Welles' ministry in 1747, and the latter with the organization of the Society in 1739.

It must always be regretted that the records of the First Church, down to the settlement of Dr. Welles, are not to be recovered. The Society records of that period are identical with such town records as are preserved, and are scarcely less valuable to the history than those of the town itself.

Next in value are those faithful transcripts of the records of the New Haven colony, from 1638 to 1649, and from 1653 to 1665, published by C. J. Hoadly, Esq., State librarian; and a like faithful transcript of the Connecticut colony records, from 1636 to 1677, executed by J. Hammond Trumbull, Esq, Secretary of State. Nor should the old Dutch records of the New Netherlands be lost sight of in this research. Of the history of this region, anterior to the date when our colonial records begin, and of the earlier conflicts with the Aborigines, they give us many facts and hints of great interest.

Besides these, which have the force of original records, we find of great service to the satisfactory elucidation of our local history, such works as Trumbull's Connecticut, which abounds in material for its earlier periods, and the later work of Hollister which brings the collection down almost to the present date. Hall's Norwalk, Mead's Greenwich, Prince's and Thompson's histories of Long Island, and Bolton's thorough work on Westchester County, have also great value, treating as they do of localities whose earlier history was so inwoven with ours. Nor are the printed histories of our revolutionary period to be overlooked in this list of authorities. Especially are we indebted to the local records supplied by Hinman in his report of the part which Connecticut bore in that contest; and scarely less to the faithful account which Sabine gives us of the opposers of the war. Still more important are the contemporaneous records, collected at such cost of time and money in the American Archives.

In family history and genealogy, much use has necessarily been made of Savage's great thesaurus of abbreviated genealogical lore; and for reporting the prominent family of which it treats, no work or works could readily take the place of Mr. A. B. Davenport's "Davenport Family."

Besides these sources of our history, the author has had free access to several of our best historical libraries, from which have been drawn many of the facts here recorded. Especially is he indebted for this indulgence granted him, at the Yale College Library and that of the New Haven Colony Association, in New Haven; at the State Library and the Connecticut Historical Society, in Hartford; at the Astor and Merchants and New York Society Libraries, of New York city; and at that of the Long Island Historical Society, in Brooklyn, N. Y.

CHAPTER II.

THE SETTLEMENT.—1640-42.

In the spring of 1640, a company of dissatisfied and restless men in Wethersfield, were anxious to end the contentions and feuds which for four or five years had rendered their home in that new colony comfortless and unprofitable. The reasons for that distracted condition, among a band of men who had left the father land not six years before, to seek a quiet and peaceful home for themselves, may never be fully made known. Certainly no contemporaneous record which I have been able to find has reported them. But, both the town records, and those of the Connecticut colony, which then included only the three settlements at Windsor, Hartford, and Wethersfield, agree in representing the Wethersfield disagreement so positive as not likely to be harmonized, as long as the spirited factions should remain together. So thought the Peace Commissioners who went down from Hartford to see if the peace could be preserved. So decided the Church Committee from Watertown, who had been sent out into the wilderness to look after the brethren who had so recently emigrated from their company. So decided, also, that princely pioneer among our Connecticut worthies of that age, the Rev. Mr. Davenport, who had gone up from New Haven to see if fraternal counsel would not restoré harmony to that disturbed community; and so believed the discerning men among the contestants themselves. Their judgment accepted the judicious advice of Mr. Davenport, and they proceeded to arrange the terms of a peaceful separation.

The church at Wethersfield had only seven voting members,

six who had come from Watertown, and one who had joined them. Four of them were on one side in the controversies which had divided the people, and three on the other, but the latter constituted the majority of the community. As a peace measure the majority of the church agreed to emigrate with the minority of the planters; while the majority of the planters conceded them the right of taking with them the records, and so transferring their church organization to the new field.

But whither should, or could they go? All the region to the west of them, until they should reach the Dutch settlements in New Netherlands was as yet an unbroken wilderness. To the south, at New Haven, and down the river at Saybrook, new settlements were just established, but offered no inducements to so large a company of emigrants as they would muster. On the Sound, at Guilford, Milford, Fairfield, and Stratford, companies of pioneers were just breaking ground for the sites of their new colonies. Everywhere else the wilderness and savage held sway.

But Mr. Davenport, who had advised the separation, though the enterprise of the young colony to whose success he had so largely contributed, was prepared to offer them a place for a home. The New Haven colony, in its zeal to maintain an equal footing with the Connecticut colony, whose seat was at Hartford, had just made a purchase, through their agent, Capt. Nathaniel Turner, of that tract which lies to the west of the present town of Norwalk. This they offered to the waiting company at Wethersfield. The Committee appointed by that company, accepted the purchase, and soon the arrangements were completed for the formal occupation of the place. The following record of the decision of the General Court of New Haven, held the 14th of ninth month, 1640, exhibits the title under which the colonists were to take possession of their new domain:

"Whereas, Andrew Ward and Robert Coe of Wethersfield were deputed by Wethersfield men the 30th of the 8th month, commonly called October, 1640, to treat at New Haven, about the plantation lately purchased by said town called Toquams, which being considered of it was agreed upon by the said court and justices aforesaid that they shall have the said plantation upon the terms following: first, that they shall repay unto the said town of New Haven all the charges which they have disbursed about it, which comes to thirty-three pounds as appears by a note or schedule hereunto annexed; secondly, that they reserve a fifth part of said plantation to be disposed of at the appointment of this court to such desirable persons as may be expected, or as God shall send hither, provided that if within one whole year such persons do not come to fill up those lots so reserved that then it shall be free for the said people to nominate and present to this court some persons of their own choice which may fill up some of those lots so reserved if this court approve of them; thirdly, that they join in all points with this plantation in the form of government here settled, according to agreement betwixt this court and Mr. Samuel Eaton about the plantation of Totokett. These articles being read together with Mr. Samuel Eaton's agreement in the hearing of the said parties or deputies, it was accepted by them and in witness thereof they subscribed their names to the articles in the face of the court."

Thus were the founders of Stamford supplied with a place for their future residence. Providence had opened it as a refuge for them; and they gladly fled to it. They hoped to find in their new home, equally, freedom from the tyrannous rule under which they had been exiled from the land of their birth, and from the petty annoyances which had tried their patience and their temper in their brief sojourn on the banks of the Connecticut. Few pioneers among the emigrants from the old world to this, had been more severely tested than they had been; and we may be assured that they hailed with no common satisfaction the pleasant and quiet retreat to which they had been thus conducted.

The story of their introduction to their new home, the company they constituted, the community they established, the plans they made and matured, their trials and their triumphs, let it be our present business to learn. Reverently and dutifully let us ask after the men, who in times of great trial, through days and years of weakness and suffering, of hope deferred and pressing fears, sustained themselves in the great work of laying deep and broad foundations for the permanent prosperity of their children's children in this new world.

The following passage, providentially saved from the first book of the Stamford records, will introduce us to these men. Defaced as it is in some places, and wanting as it is in others, we may well be thankful that so much of it remains. It is the most effectual key we have to the earlier portion of our history. We will transcribe what remains of it, as a perpetual witness to some of the earliest and most vital facts of the story we are to trace. The portions of the record now effaced, which are supplied, will be included in parentheses. The remainder of it is the literal record as it was made by the original recorder himself. The first paragraph, which is a mere title, was evidently inserted after the name of the settlement had been changed, though written by the same hand which made the record following it. These earliest records are all in the handwriting of Richard Law.

1640-41. A town bo(ok of the) freeholders of the towne (of Stamford as it) was afterwards called, but now Rippowam, contay(n)in(g the acts) and conclusions of the companie of Wethersffeld men, to (begin a) removal thither this winter. And also their most matteriall acts and agreements, touching the place how they came by it, theire rat(es) and accounts, theire divisions and grants of land, and records of every man's land, and passages of land from one to another.

First these men whose names are underwriten have bound thems(elves) uuder the paine of forfiture of 5 lb a man to goe or sende to Ripp(owan) so begin and psecute the designe of a plantation there by ye 16th o(f) may next, the rest, theire familyes thither by ye last of novembe(r) 12 months, viz.

Ri Denton	Ri Gildersleue	Tho Weekes	Sam Sherman
ma mitchell	Edm Wood	Jon Wood H	Hen Smith
Thur Rainor	Jo Wood	Jer Jagger	Vincint Simkins
Robt Coe	Jer Wood	J Jisopp	Dan Finch
And Ward	Sam Clark	Jo Seaman	Jo Northend 20

And whereas the purchase of the place and vewing of it first mayde by our frends of new hauen and we stand indebted to them for it: it (is) ordered at the same time That 100 bushells of corne at 35 a bushell be paid in towards it we raised and sent them as followeth, m(r) ma mitchel

	bu. p.		bu.				
Sergt. M. M.	14.3	Jo. Reynoulds,	3.2	Jo. Northend.	2.3	Tho. We(eks),	2.2
T. Rainer,	5.3	Jo. Whitmore,	3.1	Jonas Wood, H.	2.3	Jer. (Wood)	2.1
Mr. Denton,	4.1	Ro. Bates,	3.1	Edm. Wood,	2.2	Th(o Morehouse),	2.1
And. Ward,	4.1	Ri. Crab,	3.1	Jon Wood,	2.2	(Ro Fisher)	2.0
Ro. Coe,	4.1	Sa. Sherman,	3.1	Sam. Clarke,	2.2	(Jo. Jissop,)	2.0
Ri. Gildersleue,	4.0	Jef. Firries,	3.1	Fra. Bell,	2.2	(Hen. Smith),	1.3
Ri. Law,	3.2	Dan. Finch,	3.0	Jer. Jaggar,	2.2	(Vincint), ——	1.3
				*Jo. Not or M M,	2.1	Jo. Seaman,	1.3
	40.3		22.3		20.1		16.1

40.3
22.3
20.1
16.1
100.0

Of the above list, all the names appear on our subsequent records, excepting that of "Jo Nott." Though John Nott did not settle in the town, he is at this late date worthily represented in the seventh generation by Samuel Nott Hyde, Esq., son of Lucretia Nott, daughter of Samuel Nott, D. D. as in note.

Of the thirty men above named, only twenty-eight came to Stamford in the summer of 1641, as the record immediately following the list shows. On the 19th Oct. of that year they were notified by a "sufficient warning, to come in," to make choice of those who should administer the affairs of the new colony. Mr. Denton, Mathew Mitchell, Andrew Ward, Thurston Rainer, and Richard Crab were this provisional government. Their commission, given by that pure democracy then assembled, made them in all essentials the authoritative rulers over the people. Enough of the record remains to show what their prerogatives were: to order the common affairs or intended plans of the people, and to determine the differences that shall arise; and "settle them according to equity, peace, law and convenience." That they were not unequal to the honor put upon

*This is undoubtedly that of John Nott, of Wethersfield, who for some reason did not come to Stamford. His family remained in Wethersfield for two generations. His grandson, Abraham, went to Saybrook, where his son Stephen was born in 1728. This Stephen was the father of Samuel, D. D., so long the patriarch of Eastern Connecticut, and also of Eliphalet, D. D., so long and so successfully the president of Union College.

them, and that the people did not find their trust betrayed, the progress of our history will show.

The next item on the records of special interest to us in determining who the settlers of the town were, and how they sought the interests and rights of each other in the very beginnings of their civil arrangements, is the account of the first assignment of lands to the settlers. The entire list of names is preserved on the records, though portions of the statement of the principles on which the appropriation is made are indistinct:

"Also this is to be noted, that in a full meeting of the company that was intending to come hither the same spring that we came, every of those TWENTY-EIGHT men aforementioned and John Jisop were severally considered of and what quantity of (land) was meet for every man determined of—the man under consideration absenting himself while his case was in hand, and so successively; and when he was called in again and demanded if so much gave him content, and so contentment and satisfaction was by every one of these men acknowledged; and they set down these numbers of acres of marsh and upland after the same proportion as followeth:

	Acres.		*Acres.*		*Acres.*		*Acres.*
Math. Mitchell,	28	Jo. Renoulds,	11	Jonas Wood H.	08	Jer. Wood,	6
Thurston Rainer,	20	Jo. Whitmore,	10	Jo. Northend,	08	Thos. Weeks,	6
Mr. Denton,	14	Ri. Crab	10	Jer. Jagger,	07	Jo. Seaman,	6
And. Ward,	14	Jeff- Firries,	10	Edm. Wood,	07	Ro. Fisher,	5
Ro. Coe,	14	Ro. Bates,	10	Jon. Wood, O,	07	Jo. Jissop,	5
Ri. Gildersleue,	13	Sam. Sherman	10	Sam. Clark,	07	Hen. Smith,	3
R. Law,	11	Dan. Finch,	09	Fra. Bell,	07	Vincint, ——	3
				Tho. Marshall,	07		
							276

The above record is authoritative as to who the first twenty-nine landholders of Stamford were. The last name on the list undoubtedly should be SIMKINS, as it is found among the twenty who were bound to each other to begin the settlement, according to agreement with the New Haven colony. We shall now proceed to ascertain, as far as the record will enable us to do so, the other names which during the following season, were added to the twenty-nine. The following record is still legible in the original manuscript of the first recorder:

"And in town meeting, Dec. 7, was there granted, besides house lots as other men had, Tho. Armitage, ten acres; Jo.

Ogden, ten acres; Wm. Mayd, (Mead), five acres; with woodland as chosable as those above.

"Also to these men, besides, house lots as others, (Joh)n Stevens, Tho. Pop, Tho. Hyoute, Hen. Akerly, Jo. Smith, senr., Jo Smith, jun., (John Ro)ckwell, Jam. Pyne, Dan Scoffeld, & Jo. Coe; every of them two acres (homelot) and three acres woodland in the field now to be inclosed."

The above record makes the resident landholders, by Dec. 7, 1641, to be forty-two. Immediately following the last record, are these:

"(Oc)tober 1642, in a general town meeting was given these, foll(owing), these lots as other men, marsh & woodland, viz: ( )ine, Jo. Underhill, eight acres; to Robert Hustice seven acres; ( ) acres; Jo. Miller, five acres, to Jo. Finch, six acres; ( )ree acres; & to every of them woodland after the same pro(portion, & to Willi)am Newman two acres marsh & three acres woodland.

"( )ember 1642, was granted these men every man (a house lot &) land in the field to be inclosed, viz: Jo. Lum, Jam. Sw(ead), ( ), Symon Seiring, & to Jonas Weede a house and (pasture lan)d in the field to be inclosed. ( ) Pierson, Jo. Towne & Wm. Graves have had every one (a house lot) & Tho. Slawson house lot and three acres in the field [ ] and eight men are freeholders as above."

We have already seen whom on their arrival the founders of the town selected to arrange and administer their affairs. But very few other records of this early date are preserved. Yet, these few are of the more value, since they serve to exhibit to us the most we can know of these worthy men. In November, 1641, they made a second election of seven men for townsmen, viz.: "Math. Mitchell, Thurston Raynor, And. Ward, Jo. Whitman, Ri. Law, and Ri. Crab." Their official work is defined to be, "to order town occasions."

It will be noticed that but six of the seven men are named in this list, and the omission of one name may be most exactly illustrative of the men and the times. By reference to the first appointment made in October, the name of Mr. Denton will be found first on the list. It will be marked by still another token of honor. The others are all recorded with their christian names; he alone with the title of Master. He was their MINISTER. Was it not tacitly understood that his voice was to be heard in all matters that concerned their welfare, or that of their families? Was there any need, therefore, of making a formal enrolment of his magisterial name, when the very name to them had a leader's and master's authority?

Another "general town meeting" is held in December, 1641. Enough of the record remains be show that the business of the meeting was to secure a suitable fencing "of fields for the freeholders." So much of both margins is gone as to render it difficult to recover the precise terms on which the fencing was to be done, but enough is left to show that each man's part of the work was to be determined by his share of the land to be inclosed—a certain number of "rodd for every acre he hath then, well [made] and sufficient." The fence was to be done "by the first day of April, 1642, and whosoever hath [not completed his] fence according to this order by that time shall forf[iet] shillings for every rod." Ri Guildersleeve and Ro Bates were appointed to view the fence after the first of April, and report all defaults, if any, to the "men chosen for town occasions, [under penalty] of forfeiture of five shillings a man if they do no[t]."

To secure passable roads we find this decree of the town passed. It was probably done before any of the last transactions recorded.

"It was ordered, That whereas every man may count [all as his] Right before his lott to the middle of the street to be his, [but the trees he may] fall for his own use, if he like not to let them stand so [ ] the ground and clear the way of them, and if do not f[all them and clear] the way of them, to forfite for every tree not so fallen [ ] two shillings six peence."

Immediately following the above is this record: "It was ordered by those that were now come that Matthew Mitchell and Fra. Bell shall lay out house lots and order the man [ner of assigning them]; rectify what is amiss and consider what allowance [is to be made for] holes, etc., not fit to be measured for land and to measure [their lots for) every man at two pence a acre, or three shillings a house lot."

Another public concern of these pioneers, and one which required their first attention, was the establishment of a grist mill. Probably the measures for doing this were taken before they left Wethersfield. We find, duly recorded, the entire transaction, a specimen of which must be recorded in these pages as illustrative of the age to which it belongs. The formal order is passed as early as September 1641, to build at a common charge a mill. The frame and body of the mill was to be made by "Samuel Swane," for "51 li.; and the other parts by those of the town that were fit to do such work." It seems that the mill was built and "set a going," but that during the year it was sold to Thurston Rainer and Francis Law for £74 10s.

It also appears that an agreement was made with Math. Mitchell and Jo. Ogden for building a dam, of which the town agreed to bear the charge. In January after these arrangements were made, it would seem that either by fire or freshet, or both, "the mill and the dam were brought to nought." It further is probable from the record, that the town were responsible for the mill, as they were to have the use of it until the "somer," (summer) of 1643. On the destruction of the property a rate bill is made out, of five shillings an acre, and twelve shillings a house lot, to meet the loss by this calamity. This assessment list is a curiosity, and if carefully preserved should be engrossed for perpetual preservation on our pages. In addition to the mill account there is also connected with it a charge for what in the record is called the "Capt. house." As many of the charges are considerably obliterated, a single specimen of one less defaced than the most of them, is here inserted. A modern accountant might use a smoother and more graceful chirography, but would fail of making a more exact balance of the account. The selected specimen is that which stands second on the list:

T. Rainer debtor for lose by mil 44.9 Capt. house 22s. purchase. mil 18.12.6 all wch 21.19.3 due to him.
paid the Char. mil 7.18.8 Capt. house 34.8 last Char. 24s. 6d. S. Swain 171.00.0—all 27.17.10 towne owes him 5.17.7.

Whoever will take the trouble to effect the reductions necessary to the solution of the above problem will find the account accurate. In the same way, the charges are made and the credits are given through the entire list, with a single exception. In the charges against Capt. John Underhill, no mention is made of the item found in the other accounts of the "Capt. house." The presumption therefore is, that the military chieftain of our Stamford pioneers, was excused from the charge for the support of the Stamford fortress, since he was expected to discharge his duty to the community in another way.

This account, which seems to have been made out in January 1642, has charges against fifty-two persons. As the margin on which the names occur is entirely gone from the second page of the charges, only twenty-four of the parties are reported in the regular account. Besides these, four other names casually occur in the accounts. The only name which does not already appear on our list of the settlers, is that of Samuel Swane.

There is probably but one more record, now preserved, which can assist in confirming the accuracy of our list of the pioneers of the Stamford settlement. That was made in the fall of 1641, and is even more defaced than those we have already examined. It is thus introduced:

"It was ordered that [ ] should be made for defraying [town] charges."

Then follows an almost unintelligible statement of the nature of the charges and the principles upon which they are to be adjusted. Enough remains of the records to show that the charge made by the New Haven "friends" who had secured for them the territory, had never been paid in full. It also appeared that a difference was made between the Wethersfield men who came to Stamford with the first company and those who did not come, so that it was agreed "to lay 3s. 8d. an acre on marsh and house lott, upon the company that came from Wethersfield, and 3s. 5d. an acre upon the rest."

"The account, very short, yet wee hope, plainly, now followeth, with the sd rate included in the ballance of every particular, but that it may be somd [summed] up, it is drawn in two [parts]."

A single specimen of these charges and credits will here be given, drawn up so as to show what is meant by the "two parts" above.

T. Rainer For bill charges 85s. 6 for 5 3-4 bush 17s. 3 for 1-2 that he paid at W. 22s. 6 all makes 6. 5. 3	For rate now 3. 18. 10 for so much due at w. 2s. 3 To recv. of S. C. 21s. 1 of Jer. Wood 19. 9d J Renoude 3s. 6 all makes up 06. 5. 5

Then follow similar accounts with all the parties concerned in the transaction.

On this record occurs the name Jam. Pine, which is probably the James Pyne on the former list. The names which are found here are all of them reported already in the preceding lists of the settlers.

This adds to the list of our pioneers, all but one of whom were land owners for the second year of the colony, seventeen new names, making in all fifty-nine. No other record reports any additional distribution of land to the settlers. A few more certainly received their lands in the mutual distribution, as is evident from the records of several house lots still preserved. But their names can probably never be recorded.

No fuller list of these settlers down to the end of 1642 can now be hoped for, but the record thus transcribed is authorative as to the presence here, thus early, of the following worthy list—our roll of pioneers. Twenty of them, by the opening of the summer of 1641, had already doubtless planted themselves near each other in their pioneer tabernacles, on a sinuous path between Noroton and Tomuck, now Richmond Hills, winding its way around ledges and knolls since then removed, and avoiding more than one pathless swamp, where we now have our most solid and right lined thoroughfare. Thirty-eight more of them, drawn by the good report which had gone back from those who had thus made proof of the goodly land, had followed, and were here to spend the ninth month of the second year of the colony. Fifty-nine, at least, of these sturdy men, with their wives and little ones, braved in their extemporized homes, the colds and storms of the winter of 1642. How many others, and who, were counted worthy to share with them the honors of that bold adventure, we may never know. We have gratefully recorded these names, that we may know whom we honor as we shall trace the growth and fair fame of the town they thus came to found. They will appear in our third and fourth chapters, with such record as we shall be able to make of their origin and their families.

LIST OF PIONEERS TO THE END OF 1642.

1. Mathew Mitchel,
2. Thurston Raynor,
3. Rev. Richard Denton,
4. Andrew Ward,
5. Robert Coe,
6. Richard Gildersleve,
7. Richard Law,
8. John Reynolds,
9. John Whitmore,
10. Richard Crabb,
11. Jeffry Ferris,
12. Robert Bates,
13. Samuel Sherman,
14. Daniel Finch,
15. Jonas Wood, H.,
16. John Northend,
17. Jeremy Jagger,
18. Edmond Wood,
19. Jonas Wood, O.,
20. Samuel Clark,
21. Francis Bell,

31. John Ogden,
32. William Mead,
33. John Stevens,
34. Thomas Pop.
35. Thomas Hoyt,
36. Henry Akerly,
37. John Smith, sen.,
38. John Smith, jr.,
39. John Rockwell,
40. James Pyne,
41. Daniel Scofield,
42. John Coe,
43. John Underhill,
44. Robert Hustis,
45. John Holly,
46. John Miller,
47. John Finch,
48. George Slawson,
49. William Newman.
50. John Lum,
51. James Swead,

22. Thomas Morehouse,
23. Jeremiah Wood,
24. Thomas Weeks,
25. John Seaman,
26. Robert Fisher,
27. Joseph Jessup,
28. Henry Smith,
29. Vincent Simkins,
30. Thomas Armitage,
52. Simon Hoyt,
53. Simon Seiring,
54. Jonas Weed.
55. —— Pierson,
56. John Town,
57. William Graves,
58. Thomas Slawson,
59. Francis Yates.

CHAPTER III.

NOTES ON THE SETTLERS AND THEIR FAMILIES.—1640–2.

In this chapter we shall indicate the proprietors of the town, who were here before the end of 1642, with such account of their origin and families as we have been able to secure. The record against each name will furnish, usually, the evidence for its presence here. The list has been made with all possible care, that we might know who and what kind of men were the founders of the town.

Possibly a few other names should have been included as worthy a place on the list, and possibly some of these were of persons too transiently here to be counted among those who so worthily laid the foundations of our community.

AKERLY, HENRY, received Dec. 7, 1641, two acres, homelot, and three acres of woodland. Savage makes him at New Haven in 1640. The Colony Records mention him there, as rebuked for "building a cellar and selling it without leave" in April of that year. Hinman supposes he came with Underhill and Slawson, while our record makes him precede them nearly a year. He was a house carpenter and farmer. His death is recorded here, June 17, 1650. This name on the records is spelled as above, and also, Akerlye, Ayckrily, and on the inventory of his estate, which was witnessed Jan. 4, 1658, Accorley. His widow, Ann, is said to be 75 years old in 1662. This name is, perhaps, now represented by Ackley.

ARMITAGE, THOMAS, received ten acres of land, Dec. 1641. According to Savage, he belonged to Lynn, Mass. He came from Bristol, England, in 1635, in the ship James, with the Rev. Richard Mather and others, and removed in 1637 to Sandwich, Mass., whence he came to Stamford as above. From Stamford he soon went with Underhill and company to Oyster Bay, L. I. In 1647 he appears on the list of the Hempstead settlers.

BATES, ROBERT, came from Wethersfield, with the first colony, and is on the list of the thirty who paid one hundred bushels of corn to the New Haven "friends," who had surveyed and transferred the territory to them. His lot in Wethersfield, which was thirty and a third rods in width, containing 182 acres, was sold in 1641 to William Gibbons. His death is recorded, at Stamford, June 11, 1675. His will, probated Nov. 1, 1675, makes bequests to his son John, his daughter Mary Ambler and son-in-law John Cross. He bequeathed certain negroes, who are to be made free at 40 years of age.

BELL, FRANCIS, is on the list of the twenty-nine settlers, who were assigned land in 1640, when he received seven acres. As his name does not appear on the Wethersfield records with the other Stamford settlers, it is probable he was still quite young. He became prominent here, and has been fully represented in every generation since, in descendants both of his own and of other names. His wife Rebecca died here, in 1684, and he, Jan. 8, 1690. His son Jonathan was the first child born in the town, and his birth was in 1641. Mrs. Bell's clothes, of which the inventory is on record, Book 1, Page 12, were by the husband's order, divided equally between the two daughters, Rebecca Tuttle and Mary Hoyt. The inventory of Lieut. Francis Bell, dated Jan. 1689, is found on page 116, of 1st Book of Records, amounting to £317 12s. His will, on record at Fairfield, dated 3, 24, 1689, makes bequests to his son Jonathan, grand-son Jonathan, Mary Hoyt, grand-daughter Hannah, and "grand-daughter Rebecca, whom he had brought up," and to his daughter Tuttle's four sons, Jonathan, Simon, William, and Nathaniel.

CLARK, SAMUEL, came with the company from Wethersfield, and is on each of the first three lists made at the time of the settlement. He received seven acres of land. Savage supposes he was at Milford in 1669, thence removing to Hempstead, L. I.; that he married Hannah, daughter of Rev. Robert Fordham, and was living in New Haven in 1685.

COE, JOHN, son of Robert, received, Dec. 7, 1641, two acres, houselot and three acres wood land. He was born in England, Norfolk county, in 1622, and he came with his father to Watertown, thence to Wethersfield, and thence to Stamford. He soon went to Hempstead, L. I., thence to Newtown, and afterwards to Greenwich in 1660. He was one of the purchasers of Rye; but returned to Long Island where he was apappointed a Magistrate by the Connecticut Colony. He had five sons; John, Robert, Jonathan, Samuel, and David. In 1651 he sold his house and homelot to Elias Bailey.

COE, ROBERT, was born in Norfolk county, England, in 1596, and came in the Francis to Watertown, Mass., in 1634. He was admitted freeman at Boston, Sept. 3, 1634, and is enrolled among the settlers of Watertown, the same year. He brought with him his wife Ann, aged thirty-three years, and three children; John, aged eight years, Robert, aged seven, and Benjamin, aged five. In 1635 he went to Wethersfield where he remained until the settlement of Stamford. In the first division of land here he received fourteen acres, which would indicate a high standing among the settlers. He was one of the members of the Wethersfield church. While here, he once, at least, represented the town in the general court of New Haven. He went with Mr. Denton and his colony in 1644 to Hempstead, L. I. His son Robert went to Jamaica in 1656. Here he was a man of distinction. He was the deputy from the town to the general court of Connecticut in 1656, and was Sheriff of the county from 1669 to 1672. His son Benjamin went with the father to Hempstead, whence he went to Jamaica where he had a family. His descendants have been both numerous and respectable. A record of the Coe family was prepared by Rev. D. B. Coe, D. D., of New York, and printed in 1856.

CRABB, RICHARD.—His name first appears on the roll of the general meeting of the freemen, at Hartford, for the election of magistrates, Jan. 16, 1639; and April 9, 1640, he is present as deputy, and must have been a man of some note. He came to Stamford with the company from Wethersfield, and is on the list of those who paid the hundred bushels of corn to the New Haven Colony, and of those to whom the first assignment of land was made. He received ten acres. His land must have been assigned him west of the present limits of the town, as he is spoken of subsequently in the records, as belonging to Greenwich. His position is sufficiently attested by his appointment on the first provisional government of the colony. In 1658, we find him making trouble in the church. He seems to have become a quaker, or at least, to have harbored quakers and kept quaker books. He could not agree with the church in their opinion of the sanctity of the Sabbath, and spoke disparagingly or contemptuously of the ministry. Mr. Bishop, the pastor of the church became discouraged, and we find Mr. Crabb, the offender, brought into court for trial. He was fined to pay £30 to the jurisdiction, and give bonds in £100, for his good behavior, and also to make public acknowledgment at Stamford to the satisfaction of Francis Bell, and those others whom he had wronged. In 1660 the constables of Stamford are desired to use their endeavors to arrest the person of Richard Crabb, of Greenwich.

DENTON, REV. RICHARD, came with his parishioners from Wethersfield. His name heads the first list of the new colony, and stands third on the list of those who paid for surveying the tract. He received fourteen acres, only two of the settlers exceeding him in the assignment of land. Mather makes him to have been a minister at Halifax, Yorkshire, England. In 1644 he took quite a large company of the Stamford settlers and went to Hempstead, on Long Island. See Biographical Sketch.

FERRIS, JEFFREY, made freeman in Boston in 1635, came with the first settlers, is on the list of those who paid for the survey, and received ten acres at the first assignment of land. Savage says he was from Watertown, Mass., where he was made freeman, probably May, 6, 1635, whence he came to Wethersfield. He sold his lot in Wethersfield, of 45 acres, to John Deming. He came with the first colony from Wethersfield, and in 1656 is one of the eleven Greenwich men who petitioned to be accepted under the New Haven jurisdiction. His will, found on the probate records at Fairfield, is dated Jan. 6, 1664. He wills to the four boys he brought up, ten pounds sterling a piece, if they live with any of his children until they are eighteen years old, the money then to be put out for them until they are twenty years of age. His will names also his wife Judy, son James, son Jonathan Lockwood, and Mary Lockwood, son Peter's three children, and son Joseph's two. Judy Bowers, his widow, receipts for her widow's portion, Mar. 6, 1667. His marriage contract with his wife Susannah, widow of Robert Lockwood, of date May 28, 1661, pledges certain legacies to the children of Robert Lockwood, deceased, and mortgages his Greenwich lands and "housings." He died in 1666. The name Ferris is from Leicestershire, house of Feriers, from Henry, son of Gualchelme de Feriers, to whom William the Conqueror gave large grants of land in the three shires of Stafford, Derby and Leicester.

Tradition invests the emigration of this family to this country with the hues of romantic adventure—the ancestress, high born, following her plebeian lover out into this western world, to share with him here the fortunes which English aristocracy would not allow there.

FINCH, DANIEL, made freeman in Boston, 1631, and enrolled same year among Watertown settlers. In 1636, he was constable in Wethersfield, whence he came with the Stamford settlers, 1641, and is on each of the three first lists of the colony. He received nine acres in the first distribution of land. Savage supposes he was from Watertown, Mass., and that he came in the fleet with Gov. Winthrop; that he was made freeman May 18, 1631; that he went to Wethersfield in 1635 or '36, where he was constable in the latter year. He also makes him remove in 1653 to Fairfield, where he married, Dec. 25, 1657, Elizabeth, widow of John Thompson, and died March 1667. His marriage agreement with Elizabeth Thompson is on the probate records at Fairfield.

FINCH, JOHN, is assigned by the town in October 1642, six acres, with marsh and upland as the other men. He died here in 1657. He sold his house and homelot in 1653 to Richard Ambler. The inventory of his estate, Book 1, page 66, bears date 9th of 12th mo., 1658.

FISHER, ROBERT, was here early, if not with the first colony. He had land assigned him by the town, as appears from the testimony of Thomas Morehouse, Mar. 17, 1649, in which he says that John Whitmore sold to his son John, the land which was Robert Fisher's, by gift of the town.

GILDERSLEEVE, ROBERT, came with the first company from Wethersfield, and is on each of the first three lists of settlers. He received, in the first distribution of land, thirteen acres. In 1664 he went to Hempstead. His lot in Wethersfield, which was thirty-seven and a half rods wide, containing 255 acres, was sold to John Talcott in 1643. He and his son are accepted freemen in the Connecticut colony from Hempstead, in 1664. Before coming to Stamford, while in Wethersfield, he was "convicted" before the general court of Connecticut for "pernitious speeches," tending to the detriment and dishonor of the

Commonwealth, fined £20, and bound over under a bond of £20. In the colony records this name is spelled Gyldersly. In 1636 he is appointed with John Plum, by the general court of Connecticut, to survey the inventory of John Oldham, and perfect the same to submit it to the court at the next session. The same restlessness which made him dissatisfied at Wethersfield, seems to have affected him in Stamford. He soon went with Mr. Denton's company to Hempstead, L. I. While here he once represented the town in the general court at New Haven.

Graves, William, received a house lot in the distribution of Nov. 1642; he lost his wife Sarah, here in 1651, and his son Benoni, in 1657. In a deed of land to William Newman in 1657, he is said to be of Newtown, L. I.

Holly, John, was here, as present records show, as early as 1647. Wm. H. Holly, Esq., copied from the records several years ago the birth of John, son of John Holly, in Oct. 1642, which would suggest that the family may have been here even so early. He purchased land on the 26th of 12th month, 1647, of William Newman; and from that date his purchases of real estate are numerous. He was a noted man, and much in the public service. In 1679, he gave his house and lot to his son Samuel, and land to his son John, reserving to himself and wife, half the fruit of the orchard. He also gave land at the same date to his son Increase. In his will on record at Fairfield, his legatees are his wife Mary, and his children John, Samuel, Increase, Elisha, Jonathan, Elizabeth Turney, Bethia Weed, Hannah Hoyt, and Abigail. See Biographical Sketch.

Hoyt, or Hyatt, Thomas, received three acres of woodland. This name was spelled very variously on the records—Hoyette, Hyat, Hyot, Hioute, Hout, Hoyt, Hoight, Hayt, Hiat, Hoit, and Hoyte. Thomas "Hyat" died here in 1651. I suppose him and Simon to be the ancestors of the Stamford Hoyts. The inventory of his estate was rendered in court in 1662, amounting to £132 2s. 3d. The court gave to the widow her third, and made Cornelius Jones administrator, to divide the rest among the six children. The administrator was so well pleased with the case, as to take for his wife the widow Elizabeth, and their marriage is on record, 1. 8. 1657. The children are recorded as giving receipts to their father-in-law Cornelius Jones, as follows: Caleb, Dec. 23, 1661; Ruth, then become Mrs. John Wescot, Feb. 9, 1667; Rebecca, 13. 8. 1674, for twelve pounds, eleven shillings seven pence; Thomas, 21. 8. 1674, a like sum; and Deborah gives similar receipts, 30. 9. 1669. These receipts are for their several portions of their father, Thomas "Hiat's" estate. John "Hiat," of "Younkers," N. Y., gives receipt, July 6, 1689, for twenty pounds, current pay to the said Cornelius Jones, his father-in-law. After careful collation of names, I am unable to distinguish among the settlers the two family names, Hoyt, and Hyatt. Within twenty-five years of the settlement I find these different ways of spelling the same name. On page 113 and 114, Records No. 1, the estates of both Thomas Hyatt and Simon Hoyette are receipted for by the heirs of both. In these receipts we have the following different spellings: Hoyt, 1662; Hiat, 1669; Hoyte, 1661; and the promiscuous entry of these receipts for the two estates would seem to indicate that they belonged to the same family. Joshua, son of Simon, spells his name Hyot. When the name became settled in its two leading forms, Hoyt and Hyatt, as distinct family names, I hardly think the records will show.

Hoyt, Simon, was probably here with the first settlers. I take the liberty of entering his name in one of the places whose name has been effaced by time. He died here in 1657, and his name occurs quite often on the records of the town. The inventory of his estate is on record, dated Oct. 9, 1657, and amounting to 225 pounds. After his death, his widow Susanna, it appears, married a Bates. His children, as indicated by receipts given for their portions of the father's estate, were: Joshua, Moses of Westchester, John, Samuel, Benjamin, Mrs.

Samuel Finch, and Mrs. Samuel Firman. In the distribution of the estate of their mother, then Susanna Bates, Feb. 1, 1674, besides the above names, appeared also that of Thomas Lyon, who probably had married one of her daughters.

HUSTED, ROBERT, was one of the company who received land in Oct. 1642. He had come from Mount Wollaston, now Braintree, Mass. He is probably the father of that Robert Hustis who, according to Bolton's Westchester, went from Fairfield to Westchester in 1654. His will, dated July 8, 1652, makes bequests to his son Angel, of all his lands in Greenwich, with housings; to his son Robert all his lands in Stamford, with cattle and housings; to his wife a maintenance and other bequests; and to his daughter Ann, ten pounds. In 1654, his widow Elizabeth, by will makes bequests to her son Angel of Greenwich; to Robert of Stamford, and to her daughter Ann, the wife of Richard Hardy. In the will of Robert the name is Husted, and in that of the widow the name is written Hustis and both are equally distinct, and that they refer to the same family, is also, as clear as the form of the name. The names of the children are also changed from Husted to Hustis, though in the second will the name is spelled both Hustes and Hustis.

JAGGER, JEREMY, came with the first company from Wethersfield, and is on each of the first three lists of the colony. He received, in the first distribution of land, three acres. His name occurs frequently in the early records of the town. He was engaged before the settlement of the town in the service of the Connecticut colony, in the expedition against the Pequods. Here his services were of good account, and thirty-four years later the general court of Connecticut, in reward for his merit in the service, gave his three sons twenty acres of land a piece. In 1655 we find him petitioning to have his fine remitted. The court granted the request as long as he "carry it well." An inventory of his estate, prized by Richard Law and Francis Bell, Dec. 11, 1658, was given in upon oath by Elizabeth, wife of Robert Usher, May 19, 1659, amounting to

£472 and 17s., a large estate for those days. It is on record at Fairfield. His executor seems to have been Robert Usher, as receipts to him are on record from two of his sons, Jeremy and John, for their full portions of their father's estate. He died in 1658. An account of his sympathy with those who were disaffected towards the New Haven colony will appear in its appropriate place.

JESSUP, JOHN came with the first colony from Wethersfield, and is on each of the first three lists of the colony. He received, in the first distribution of lands, five acres. In 1664 he represented Westchester in the Connecticut Assembly. His name is spelled on our records, Gesseppe, Giseppe, Gesoppe, Gishop. John Jessup was in Hartford, 1637, Wethersfield, before 1640, Stamford, 1641, Long Island about 1654, representative from Westchester, 1664, and back on the Island again, 1673. This name is thought to have come from Yorkshire, England. (See Gen. Reg., Vol. X., page 358.)

LAW, RICHARD, came with the first settlers from Wethersfield, is on the second and third lists of the settlers, and received, at the first assignment of land, eleven acres. He married Margaret, daughter of Thomas and Frances Kilborn, of Wethersfield, who was born in 1612. Mr. Law is not on the Wethersfield records as a landholder, like the most of the settlers who came with him. But he is reported in the colonial records, in 1638, when he is appointed with George Huberd, from Wethersfield, to trade in beavers with the Indians, on the Connecticut river. No other Wethersfield man was to do so, under penalty of five shillings "per pounde, to be paide pr. evry pounde they soe trade." He is also reported in the case of the estate of John Oldham, as indebted to it £6 4s. 11d. A further account will be given of him in the chapter devoted to biography.

LUM, JOHN, was here in 1642, and received a houselot in the distribution of that date.

MAYDE, (MEAD) WILLIAM, received, Dec. 7, 1641, five acres houselot, with woodland. The wife and son of William Mead died here in 1658. I think this William must have been the father of the family of this name in Greenwich, though his descendant, the late Major D. M. Mead, author of the History of Greenwich, supposes his ancestor to have emigrated from England about the year 1642, a year later than our William is enrolled among the Stamford settlers.

MILLER, JOHN, received from the town in October 1642, five acres, houselot and marsh and upland, as the other men. This name is on Chapin's list of the Wethersfield colony, where he was in 1630. He died soon after coming to Stamford, in 1642, leaving three sons, according to the inventory of his estate, recorded 12, 24, 1665, John, Jonathan, and Joseph. His widow married Obadiah Seeley. His son John was granted land here in 1667, and proposed freeman in 1669. In 1697 he and his two brothers are named in the patent of Bedford.

MITCHELL, MATTHEW, came with the settlers from Wethersfield. His name stands next, on the first list of the colony, to the minister's, and heads both the next two lists. He paid about three times as much as any other of the settlers towards the survey of the land, and received twenty-eight acres in the first distribution of the land. His land in Wethersfield, which seems to have been, in extent, much larger than that of the other proprietors, excepting one, was subsequently divided into four farms, and was taken by the Graves, Gershom Bulkely, John Hollister, and Robert Rose. He came in 1635, so Savage, with Rev. Richard Mather, in the James. He was of Bristol, and brought with him two sons, David and Jonathan. He was successively at Concord and Springfield, where he signed the compact with Pynchon in 1636. In 1659 he was in Wethersfield. He is returned to the court in Hartford, in 1640, as for the town of Wethersfield, but he is found "incapable of the place," lying under censure of the Court. In June of this year, at the meeting of the General Court in Hartford, it is recorded that "Mr.

Michell for undertaking the office of town clark or recorder, notwithstanding his uncapableness of such office by censure of courte, he is fyned to pay to the county twenty nobles." It is also added: "that party of the town of Wethersfield who chose the said Mr. Michell to office, notwithstanding the censure of the courte, are fyned to the county five pounds." Under date of July 2d, we find this record: "Mr. Mytchell hath this day returned into court his acknowledgment to Mr. Chaplin, and for that, with other considerations, for former extraordinary chardges which he had formerly borne for public service at the forte, the court have remitted his former censure." His will, proved June 16, 1646, makes bequests to his son Jonathan, daughters Susanna and Hannah, son David and his wife. See Biographical Sketches.

MOORHOUSE, THOMAS, is on the list of those who shared in the first distribution of land, and received seven acres. In 1649 he was here, as appears from his testimony in court. Savage makes him in Fairfield in 1653. His will and inventory are on the Fairfield Records, Sept. 11, 1658. His wife Isabel, is mentioned in the will, and children, Hannah, Samuel and Thomas, the last of whom was to be paid his portion in four years; Mary in five years, and so each child one year later; and if any of them die before 17, their part to be divided, if unmarried.

NEWMAN, WILLIAM, hath assigned to him by the town, in Oct., 1642, two acres marsh and three acres woodland. In 1659 complaints having been made to the court in New Haven respecting the "sizes of shoes," the court hearing that William Newman had an instrument which he had brought from England which "was thought to be right to determine this question, did order that the said instrument should be procured and sent to New Haven, to be made a "Standard" which shall be the rule between buyer and seller, to which it is required that all sizes be conformed." Mr. Newman was evidently a man of note in the young colony, and once represented the town in the General Court. Savage supposes he may have removed to Narragansett after 1669. In 1676 William Newman, planter of Stamford, sells to John Austin, "taylor" of Stamford some land. His will, dated 7. 9. 1673, makes his legatees, his wife Elizabeth, and his children, Thomas, Daniel, John, ——, Elizabeth, and Hannah. It also mentions his brother John.

NORTHEND, JOHN, came with the colony from Wethersfield, and is on each of the first three lists of the settlers. He received in the first distribution of the lands eight acres.

OGDEN, JOHN, received, Dec. 7, 1641 ten acres houselot, with woodland, like the first company. In 1642 he agreed with Gov. Kieft, of New York, to build a stone church for twenty-five hundred guilders. In 1644 he was a patentee of Hempstead, L. I. In 1651 he was living in Southampton, where he was chosen an assistant. He is named in the Royal Charter of 1662. He went into New Jersey with Gov. Carteret, and was a representative from Elizabethtown in the first assembly of that province in 1668. In a deposition made by Richard Webb, Nov. 22, 1667, John Ogden is called son of John Budd.

Richard Ogden, brother of the above, went to Fairfield where he became a man of note. His descendants have been numerous and respectable.

PIERSON, ——, received in the distribution of Nov., 1642, a houselot. The christian name is obliterated, but that of Henry is given to the Pearson who emigrated with Mr. Denton in 1644. A Jacob Pearson (Pierson) was among our land-holders in 1661.

POP, THOMAS, received Dec. 7, 1641, a houselot, with woodland the same as the first company. This name should probably be Pope; and he probably went soon after the colony settled here over to Hempstead.

PYNE, JAMES, received Dec. 7, 1641, two acres, houselot, and woodland the same as the first company. He went to Hempstead, L. I., and was accepted as freeman from that town of the Connecticut Colony in 1664. John Pine bought land in Hempstead, L. I., of Robert Dean, of Stamford, in 1684.

RAYNOR, THURSTON, came with the first company from Wethersfield. His name on each of the first three lists stands next to Matthew Mitchell. In the first distribution of lands he received twenty acres. He sold his lot in Wethersfield which contained 330 acres to Richard Treat. Drake's Founders of New England reports him as passenger in the Dlizabeth, of Ipswich, the last of April, 1634, Suffolk county, at the age of forty, with his wife Elizabeth, aged forty-six. His children, as reported on the passenger list, were Thurston, aged thirteen; Joseph, eleven; Edward, ten; Elizabeth, nine; Sarah, seven; and Lydia, one. Previously to coming to Stamford he had represented the town of Wethersfield in the Connecticut Colony at Hartford. We learn from the colony records that he was fined both in 1637 and '38, for failing to appear in court at the appointed hour. On reaching Stamford he was appointed to the New Haven court with senatorial honors. This distinction places him among the foremost of our pioneers. From Stamford he went to Southampton, L. I., where he was held in honor. His will was made in Southampton in 1667, and in it, his wife is called Martha. She was, probably, a second wife.

RENOULDS, JOHN, appears on the list of the settlers of Wethersfield, from which place he probably came with the first settlers of Stamford. His name is on the second and third lists of the colonists. He received in the first allotment of land, eleven acres. Sarah Reanolds, his wife, probably, died here in 1657.

ROCKWELL, JOHN, received, Dec. 7, 1641, two acres, homelot and woodland, as the first company. He probably went to Rye, where he died in 1676. John Rockwell, probably the same as the above, was here in 1656, as his testimony in court of that date witnesses. In 1669 he sold land to Daniel Wescott, the deed being witnessed by Clement Buxton and Matthew Bellamy. In the same year he sells his house and homelot to Daniel Weed. John "Keeiler," son of Ralph, formerly of Norwalk, married, June 18, 1679, Hittabel, daughter of John Rockwell, formerly of Stamford. (See Hall's Norwalk). This John Rockwell is supposed by Savage to have been a son of William of Windsor, who was born in England, and who married Sarah Ensign in 1651. In town meeting, Feb. 14, 1667–8, it was voted that John Rockwell, sen., shall have liberty to mow and have the grass of the meadow upon Noroton Islands, as long as he shall live in Stamford. Rockwell Ridge is a locality often referred to in the records of the town.

Scofield, Daniel, received, Dec. 7, 1641, two acres, homelot and woodland, as the first company. He died in 1671. His children were Daniel, John, Richard, Joseph, Sarah the wife of John Pettit, and Mary. His widow Mary, became the third wife of Miles Merwin. The son Joseph suffered so much from hardships in King Philip's war as to lose his life in 1676, giving his estate to his brothers and sisters. His will, dated Sept. 4, 1664, gives to his wife one-third the estate, with use of the house for her life time; to his daughter Sarah, five ponnds; and to her two children five pounds; and to the other four children, Daniel, John, Jeseph, and Mercy, the rest of the estate, His wife and two of the sons, Daniel and John, were made executors.

Seaman, John, came with the first company from Wethersfield. His name is on each of the first three lists of the colony, and he received in the first distribution of land three acres.

Seiring, Simon, appears on the records, in 1642, as landholder, where his name is spelled Cymon. He is reported on the list of those who went, in 1644, with Mr. Denton to Hempstead, L. I., and no further trace of the name is found.

Sherman, Samuel, came with the first settlers from Wethersfield. His name appears on each of the first three lists of the new colony, and he received, in the first distribution of land, ten acres. He and Richard Gildersleeve had a lot together in Wethersfield, which Capt. John Talcott bought. He was a man of some note, as appears from his appointment as assistant in the New Haven court, in 1662, and his re-appointment the next two years; and also to the General Court of Connecticut, after the union of the town colonies, in 1665. He sells land here in 1664 to John Chapman. In 1672 he is found with the company who founded Woodbury. His children, born in Stamford, according to Cothren's list, corrected by Mr. Savage, which ought to be correct, were: Samuel, b. Jan. 19, 1641; Theophilus, Oct. 28, 1643; Mathew, Oct. 21, 1645; Edmund, Dec. 4, 1647; John, Feb. 8, 1651; Sarah, Feb. 8, 1654; Nathaniel, Mar. 21, 1657; Benjamin, Mar. 29, 1662, and Daniel, whom careful Mr. Judd made David, Apr. 15, 1665. Cothren supposes he married Sarah Mitchel in England, which Savage does not credit. In his sale of house and land in 1654, he is said to be "now living in Stratford." In leaving Stamford he probably took every member of his family, as the name does not subsequently occur on our records. The descendants of this pioneer of Stamford have numbered many very eminent men, among whom are now in active service, Senator Sherman,[3] of Ohio, and the nervous and irresistible General Wm. Tecumseh Sherman.

Simkins, Vincent, came with the first company from Wethersfield. In Chapin's "Glastenbury for Two Hundred Years," this name is given as Smiking. It appears on each of the first three lists of the colony, excepting the surname is omitted in the third list, where Vincent ——— is assigned three acres, and is the last on the list. This christian name is in some places Vincen. His widow probably married William Oliver. Her name was Mary, as appears from the sale of the Simkins place to John Holmes in 1671. The inventory of his estate was presented to the New Haven Court of Magistrates in May 1656, having been prized by John Holly and John Waterbury in Stamford in November 1653. His wife was daughter of Henry Akerly, of Stamford. He had two sons, Daniel and John. Daniel appears among the settlers of Bedford, N. Y. He was in Stamford in 1669, '70; and sold here in 1682. John sold his land in Stamford and removed soon after his father's death, which took place in 1653.

Slawson, George, came probably from Sandwich, Mass., with Thomas Armitage, in 1642. He appears in our account of the first church of the town as a leading member, and he was also evidently a man of note in civil life. I suppose him to have been the representative from the town in 1670. He had three children as appears from his will, dated Dec. 16, 1694, Eleazer, John, and a daughter who married John Gould. He died Feb. 17, 1695. His son John married in 1663, Sarah Tuttle, of New Haven, and had a son John born in 1664, and Jonathan in '67. The wife of this John was killed Nov. 17, 1676, by her brother, Benjamin Tuttle, who was executed for it the following June. He then married a second wife, Elizabeth Benedict, and had a daughter Mary and a son Thomas. He died in 1706. He was doubtless the ancestor of the present Slason families in town.

Slawson, Thomas, in November or December, 1642, received a houselot, and three acres "in the field," besides. Savage says he did not stay long in Stamford.

Smith, Henry, came with the first company from Wethersfield. His name, is on each of the first three lists of the new colony, and in the first distribution of land he received three acres. Whence he came to Wethersfield is not known. He was promoted for freeman in 1670, and died in 1687. He had a son John, mentioned in his will, and a daughter Rebecca, who married, July 2, 1672, Edward Wilkinson, of Milford, and a daughter Hannah, who married a Lawrence.

Smith, John, sr., received, Dec. 7, 1641, two acres, houselot, and woodland the same as the first company. He and his son John went to Hempstead, Long Island. Smith, John, jr., received, Dec. 7, 1641, two acres, houselot, and woodland as the first company. In 1675, John, jr., in a deposition, gives his age at 60 years, and says that while in Stamford he was called Rock John Smith, for distinction.

STEVENS, JOHN, received, Dec. 7, 1641, two acres, houselot and woodland as the first company. The descendants of this pioneer have been quite numerous.

SWAIN, SAMUEL, in Sept. 1862, is engaged to build at the common charge of the townsmen, a mill, as appears from a record of that date, and his name occurs later in the records. This is probably the same "Leeiftenant Swain," who in 1654, was ordered to suspend further work on the mill he was then engaged in building in Norwalk. If he had a family here we have no record to show.

SWEAD, JAMES, received a houselot in the distribution of Nov. 1642. Of this family name our records give us Henry, as holding land here in 1650, bounding that of Richard Hardy. The name is there spelled Swede.

TOWNE, JOHN, received in the distribution of Nov. 1642, a houselot.

UNDERHILL, CAPT. JOHN, had assigned to him in Oct. 1642, houselot, eight acres, and woodland as the others. He was made a freeman in Boston in 1631. This most famous of our Stamford settlers will have a more extended notice among the Biographical Sketches, in its proper place.

WARD, ANDREW.—This name appears in the first record of the "Corte holden at Newtown, 26th April, 1636." He was one of the five worthies, who thus had in their hands the destinies of the new settlement at Newtown, (Hartford), and so, those of the state. The record states that he had been dismissed from the church of Watertown in Mass., on the 28th of May last, and he with his associates are authorized to renew the covenant. He continued a member of the court until Sept. 1639. At the session held Oct. 1639, he is nominated by the court to be presented for the vote of the county for magistrate in April next.

In 1637 he is reported in the records of the General Court, as collector of Wethersfield and he doubtless came to Stamford with the Wethersfield settlers. His name is on each of the first three lists of the pioneers, and during his life here he was a prominent man. He was chosen magistrate for the colony in 1646 to represent it in the higher branch of the New Haven court. His will, still found on record in Fairfield, bears date, June 8, 1659, and makes bequests to his wife Esther, son John, daughter Sarah, daughter Abigail, and his two youngest sons Andrew and Samuel. It is stated also that his other children had received their portions. From this pioneer of the town have descended eminent names. Henry Ward Beecher gets his middle name from him, and his daughter Mary was grandmother of President Aaron Burr.

WEED, JONAS, came to Watertown in 1631 where he was made freeman, and thence to Stamford in 1642. He died here in 1676. His will, on record at Fairfield, dated Nov. 26, 1672 makes his legatees, his wife Mary; and his children, John, Daniel, and Jonas; Mary, wife of Geo. Abbot; Dorcus, wife of Jas. Wright; Samuel; John Rockwell for Elizabeth; Sarah; and Hannah, wife of Benjamin Hoyt. His administrators were his wife Mary, and his sons Daniel and John. The widow died in 1690. His son John Married Joanna, daughther of Richard "Westcoat." The son Jonas married Nov. 6, 1670, Bethia, daughter of John Holly, and to him the father gave in 1671 the house where he was then living. The descendants of this Jonas Weed have been very numerous here, and they have, also, always been among our prominent citizens.

WEEKS, THOMAS, went from Wethersfield to Hadley and returned to Wethersfield, from which place he probably came with the first company of settlers to Stamford. His name is on the second and third lists of the colonists, and he received in the first distribution of land six acres. In 1666 he probably was in Huntington, L.I., as the grant made in that year includes his name. Savage makes him of Oyster Bay before 1654. where he died in 1671, leaving children, Thomas, John, Rebecca, Martha, Elizabeth, Mary, and Sarah. This name is variously spelled Weeks, Weekes, Wickes, Wicks, Wyx, and Wix.

WHITMORE, JOHN, came with the first company of settlers from Wethersfield. His name is on the second and third lists of the colonists, and he received, in the first distribution of lands, ten acres. His lot in Wethersfield, of 54 acres, was sold to Richard Treat. He was murdered by the Indians, here, in 1648. The inventory of his estate, £217 4s. 2d., was presented at the Court of Magistrates in New Haven, May 26, 1656, and had been made Dec. 8, 1648, and prized by Robert Hustis. and Jeffry Ferris. He was held in honor, while living here, having represented the town in the New Haven Court. His children, Savage thinks, were all born in England—Thomas, born about 1615; Francis, born about 1625; John, born about 1667; Ann, born about 1621; and Mary, about 1623.

WOOD, JONAS, sen., came with the first company of settlers from Wethersfield. His name is on each of the first three lists of the colonists, and he received in the first distribution of land, eight acres. He was among the settlers of Springfield, in 1636, from which place he went to Wethersfield. In 1648 he brings an action against Thomas Newton, of Fairfield, when he is reported as from Long Island. In 1654 he was in Southampton, L. I,, as appears from an action against him in the Court of Magistrates at New Haven. In that action he is called Hallifax Jonas, by Richard Mills, of Stamford, in his testimony. In 1658, Jonas Wood, (O), and Jonas Wood, (H), both of Huntington, L. I., agents for the inhabitants of the same, desire to join with this colony, (New Haven). In May 1662, on the petition of Huntington, L. I., he is appointed by the general court in Hartford, the first townsman and custom-master. He became, on Long Island a man of some prominence. His name heads the list of those to whom the town of Huntington was granted in 1666.

WOOD, JONAS, jr., came with the first company of settlers

from Wethersfield. His name is on the second and third lists of the colonists. He received, in the first distribution of land, seven acres.

Wood, Edmund, came with the first company of settlers from Wethersfield. His name is on each of the first three lists of the colonists. He received in the first distribution of land, seven acres. He went to Hempstead L. I., in 1644, having come from Springfield to Wethersfield, and thence to Stamford.

Wood, Jeremiah, came with the first company of settlers from Wethersfield. His name is on each of the first three lists of the new colony. He received in the first allotment of land, six acres. He went to Hempstead, L. I., and was accepted a freeman from that town in the Connecticut colony in 1664.

Yates, Francis, is on Chapin's list of the residents of Wethersfield, between 1634 and '73. He went to Stamford, where he staid until 1644, when he removed with Mr. Denton to Hempstead, L. I. He made his will in Westchester, N. Y., 1682, and it names five children: Mary, John, Dinah, Jonathan, and Dorothy.

CHAPTER IV.

THE SETTLERS AND THEIR FAMILIES.—1642-66.

This chapter reports the earliest appearance of those settlers who came to the town, or who came into active life, between 1643 and 1660. Possibly some of these names should have appeared in the earliest list, yet the present condition of our records did not furnish the needed proof. It will be noticed that some of the family names on this list are the same as those on the earlier list, and belong, it may be in most instances to the same family. To make the record reliable, I have therefore deemed it best to avoid presuming on relationship, which the records, as preserved, did not clearly state.

AMBLER, RICHARD, was here very soon after the settlement, at which time he was in Boston, whither he had gone from Watertown. How early he was here the records do not show. In 1663, he is said, on the court record, to be about 55 years of age. His wife Elizabeth, is on the records, as dying in 1685. By his wife, Sarah, before coming to Stamford he had born, Sarah, Dec. 4, 1639; Abraham, Sept. 27, 1641, who died soon; and Abraham, Sept. 22, 1642, who came with his father to Stamford. He probably removed with this son to Bedford, as both names are among the purchasers of that town from the Indians in 1685. Possibly he may, on coming to Stamford, have located himself within the limits of that town as the most of it was included in Stamford. He lived until 1699.

AMBREY, ROBERT, had a son Robert born here in 1652, and his death is recorded in 1656, his children, as appears from the will of George Belding, of Westchester, were John, Samuel, Joseph, Moses and Mary. To each of these children of goodwife Ambrey, Mr. Belden made bequests, bearing date June 10, 1657.

ANDREWS, or ANDREAS AARON, bought land here in 1657, with Garret Rivis. He is called a Dutchman. Is he the ancestor of the Andreas family? The name Andrews and Andrus occurs often, and also interchangeably. Jeremiah Andrews is said to be of Bedford, after 1687.

AUSTIN, JOHN, was one of the eleven Greenwich men who, in 1656, acknowledge allegiance to the New Haven jurisdiction, to constitute part of the Stamford colony. The name is usually spelled Astin and Asten, on the records. A son of his, Samuel, died here in 1657, the year, also, of his own death. His inventory, taken by Richard Law and Angell Husted, Sept 5, 1657, was presented in court in Stamford, by his widow "Katherine Astine," May 13, 1658. It amounted to £78 8s. 04d. Several of this name are reported on the land records during the first century of the town.

BAYLY, ELIAS, was Mr. Denton's attorney for the settlement of his accounts here, in 1650. In 1651 he buys land of John Coe, with a house, and sells it to John Wood in 1657, when he was living in Newtown, L. I.

BASSET, ROBERT, was here early. In 1651 he is witness to a deed given by Robert Rugg to Richard Webb. He was a landholder, as appears from the land records. The will of his wife, dated May 17, 1656, makes bequests to her son Robert, the house and homelot at New Haven; to the eldest four of her children, John Emery, John Webb, Sarah and Elizabeth Basset, her personal estate; the bedding and linen and clothes, to be equally divided between goodwife Emery and goodwife Webb. The care of her daughter Elizabeth she entrusted to Robert Basset.

BISHOP, JOHN, Rev., came, as is elsewhere shown, in 1644.

In 1650, Robert Lockwood of Fairfield, deeded to him the house and lot which he had purchased of Elias Bayley, Rev. Mr. Denton's attorney. His will, made Nov. 16, 1694, names his wife Rebecca, and children, Steven, Joseph, Ebenezer, Benjamin and Whiting. He married, for his second wife, Joanna, widow of Rev. Peter Prudden of Milford, and daughter of Capt. Thomas Willett. What we know of him will be found in our record of the first Ecclesiastical society of the town. His descendants have been among the most respectable citizens of the town down to the present time.

Brown, Francis, was here early. Savage tells us that he had been a servant of Henry Wolcott, of Windsor, and bought out the rest of his time in 1649, and was a small trader in 1651; and that he bought and sold lands in Farmington in 1656. He seems to have been a pertinacious stickler for the largest liberty to the individual. In 1662 he headed a petition to the general court at New Haven, respecting the franchise of all the citizens, respecting equalizing the rates of the several colonies then under the jurisdiction of New Haven, and respecting the Colony School. The court, rather curtly, gave him to understand that "whatever liberties or privileges our laws do allow them, that they should have." He then desires a special court in Stamford for the settlement of these questions. In 1663, he is sworn a constable for the town of Stamford in the general court of Connecticut, and in 1665, '7, and '9 he represented the town in the General Assembly. He married, here, Martha, widow of John Chapman, and had one son Joseph, to whom he gave land in 1683. In 1686 he is reported in a gift of land to his son Joseph, as now of Rye.

Peter Brown lost his wife Elizabeth here, Sept. 21, 1657; and a child Ebenezer Aug. 21, 1658. His will was presented in the court, Aug. 19, 1658, and his inventory in Nov. of the same year, and testified to, upon oath, by widow Brown and Thomas Brown, Feb. 10, 1658. He had come from New Haven, where he had a daughter baptised Mercy, April 6, 1645, and Elizabeth

Aug. 1, 1647. He married here, July 27, 1658, Unity, widow of Clement Buxton, and died Aug. 22, of the same year. His widow married Mar. 9, 1659, Nicholas Knapp.

THOMAS BROWN owned land here in 1658. In 1669, then in Rye, he sells his house, and land in Stamford to John Pettit. He was born in 1638, as appears from his testimony in court at New Haven in 1660.

BUXTON, CLEMENT, died here in 1657. He owned land here, as appears from the boundaries of other lands on record still earlier. The inventory of his estate was taken Sept. 3, 1657, and apprized by Richard Law and John Holly. It was given in upon oath of the widow Unica Buxton, May 13, 1668. Clement Buxton, 2d, gave bonds here, April 19, 1686, of twenty pounds, in an action against Daniel Scofield. This name is still represented among the citizens of the town.

CHAPMAN, JOHN, owned land here in 1640. The inventory of his estate was presented to the magistrates' court in May 1667, and had been taken Jan. 30 or June 13, 1655, and prized by Richard Law and Francis Bell. According to the town records it was attested by oath of the wife of Francis Brown Oct. 30, 166—. The legatees are his widow, and his daughters Mary and Elizabeth. In 1656 Martha Chapman sells to George Slawson, a parcel of land lying in Northfield, on the east side of Mill River.

COLGRAVE, THOMAS, had lived here before Oct. 10, 1650, as the following record shows: "Thomas Morehouse affirmeth upon oath that he heard Thomas Colgrave say, in his house, that if he did not come back to Stamford, that he would give Elias Bailey all he had in Stamford; and particularly he named his part in the 'bark.'"

CLAYSON, (CLASON) STEVEN, married here 11, 11, 1654. Elizabeth Periment, (?), and had children recorded to him. Jonathan, his son, died in 1685, leaving son Stephen. and daughter Sarah, as the settlement of this estate, June, 22, 1685, shows. This Stephen in his will, dated Mar. 15, 1699—1700 gave his estate to his son Samuel, his wife while she remained his widow and no longer—sons Stephen and David, daughter Elizabeth, wife of Francis Dan, grand-son Stephen, son of Jonathan, and his sister Sarah.

CORKRYE, THOMAS, does not appear to have been a very reputable member of the new colony. He was living here in 1648, was complained of for being drunk and committing sundry other offenses against the good order of the town, was whipped, according to the usages of the age, and then fined for the Marshal's fees. Perhaps it is a fortunate thing that his name does not afterwards occur among the records of the town.

DEAN, SAMUEL, was early here, having lands assigned to him in 1650. His son John was born here in 1659, and Joseph in 1661. His death is recorded in 1703. His descendants have been numerous and have given name to one part of the town, where several of them still reside.

DIBBLE, JOHN, died 1646, and his widow married, the next year, William Graves, of Stamford. The two sons, Samuel and Zachariah Dibble, probably came with their father. Zachariah married, May, 10, 1666, Sarah Waterbury, and had a son Zachary, born in 1667. His wife obtained a divorce in 1672, and afterwards married Nicholas Webster.

DISBROW, PETER, married Sarah Chapman, here, about 1650. The name in various forms, appears subsequently on the records, though none of the descendants are now known to be left here.

ELLIOT, JOHN, was here early though his name is variously spelled on the records. He was a landholder in 1650. He lost his wife Margret, in 1658; and no later record of the name appears.

ELLISON, JOHN. This name occurs early on the records of the town, and is reported on the list of those who accompanied Mr. Denton to Hempstead, L. I., in 1644.

Fordham, Robert, according to Thompson's History of Long Island, was one of the settlers at Stamford. He went with Mr. Denton and his colony to Hempstead.

Garnsey, Joseph, came, probably, from New Haven, about 1647, and married here, May 11, 1659, Rose, widow of John Waterbury. He had a son Joseph born here in 1662. He died Nov. 11, 1688.

Gifford, William, was before the court here in 1647 or before. The sentence of the court against him was that he be whipped at the court's discretion, and banished.

Green, John, lost his wife, Mary, here, in 1657. He was declared freeman of the Connecticut Colony in 1662, and represented the town in 1669. Joseph Green mortgaged lands here in 1651, to Thomas Morehouse; and William Green appears on the records as landholder in 1650. His land was next to Daniel Scofield.

Hardy, Richard, was here in 1650, and gave name to the low grounds just west of our harbor, which are still known as "Hardy's Hole." He married, probably, Ann Husted, whose daughter Mary, was born April 30, 1659. He is probably the one who in 1639 was living in Concord. In 1683, he gave his son Samuel a house and land. In his will, on record at Fairfield, he makes bequests to his daughters Mrs. Elizabeth Pearson, Hannah Austin, Susanna Sherman, Sarah Close, Ruth Mead, and Mary and Abigail. He was a man of some distinction, representing the town three times in the State General Court. He was declared freeman of the Connecticut Colony in 1662. Robert Hardy was a landholder here in 1650.

Hill, William, was here in 1650, as is evident from the court record.

Holmes, Francis, was a resident here 1648, as appears from the testimony against Robert Penoyer. His will, on record at Fairfield, dated Sept. 6, 1671, makes mention of his wife Ann, and his children Stephen, John, Richard, and Ann, wife of Samuel Dean. Stephen Holmes has lands assigned him, by the town, 1667. Richard Holmes witnesses here, June 17, 1658, the will of Henry Akerly. John Holmes is on the land records often before 1660. This name has always been among the most respectable of the town.

HUNT, THOMAS, was here early in 1650, as the land records show. The Hunt Genealogy says he came from England, and was a High Churchman. He went from Stamford to Rye, by 1652, and was a representative in 1664. He is represented in the family genealogy as one of the most valuable men in the colony. His title was Goodman.

JACKSON, HENRY, had lands here in 1649, as appears from the boundary of Robert Rugg's land. In 1657 he is brought from Fairfield to testify for John Waterbury. Robert Jackson is said by Thompson, in his History of Long Island, to have been one of the settlers of Stamford. He went with Mr. Denton to Hempstead, in 1644. In 1656 he was one of the settlers at Jamaica.

JESSUP, EDWARD, had lands here in 1649. This is probably the one to whom was given the patent of West Farms, Westchester county, in 1666. The other patentee was John Richardson. His will, (see Bolton's Westchester), is dated August 16, 1666, in which he mentions his daughter Elizabeth Hunt, Hannah Jessup, Edward Jessup, grandchild Mary Hunt, and his wife Elizabeth. In notes on the Jessop family, in the tenth volume of the Genealogical Register, we find this record: "Edward Jessop, of Stamford, 1641; Sascoe Neck, Fairfield Co., Conn., 1653; Newtown, L. I., 1653–62; representative for Westchester, 1662–6; proprietor at West Farms, 1666, and died at Westchester, N. Y., 1666." We still have this name among us, as appears from our list of voters.

JONES, CORNELIUS, was evidently here in 1657. He married the widow of Thomas Hait, or Hyat, as is evident from the receipts which three of Thomas Hoyt's children give him. On the 17th Dec., 1657, there is a record made of the age of his children, probably by a former wife. There are six of them, aged respectively, eleven, ten, eight, six, and three years, but the margin on which the names are written is gone. His will, found at Fairfield, is dated June 2, 1690, and mentions his son Joseph and his grand-child Ruth "Hyat," explaining also why he does not make bequests to his daughter, Mary Hyat.

Joseph Jones, son of the above, died here before 1690. The inventory of his estate, of that date, attested by Elisha Holly and Daniel Scofield, gives the names and ages of his children, as follows: Mary, 13; Hannah, 11; Joseph, 9; Samuel 6; and Cornelius, 3. It also gives Rebecca as the name of his wife. In the distribution of the estate of Joseph and Cornelius Jones deceased, 1703-4; Joseph Jones, jun.; Samuel Jones, jun.; Cornelius Jones, jun.; Cornelius Seely, husband to Mary Jones, "dafter" to Joseph Jones; David Miller, husband to Hannah, "dafter" to Joseph Jones, are named as the heirs. The estate thus distributed is said to be "their father's and grand-father's names, Cornelius and Joseph Jones." Cornelius, jun., when of age is to pay a debt due to Daniel Scofield and John Ambler.

Karman, John, as Thompson in his history of Long Island tells us, was one of the Stamford settlers. He went with Mr. Denton's colony to Hempstead, L. I., where his son was the first child born in the colony.

Knapp, Nicholas, had land here in 1649, as appears from the land records. His wife, Eleanor, died August 16, 1658. Savage thinks he may have come in the fleet with Winthrop and Saltonstall in 1630. His children were Jonathan, born Dec. 27, 1631; Timothy, Dec. 14, 1632; Joshua, Jan. 5, 1635; Caleb Jan. 20 1637. Sarah, Jan. 5, 1639; Ruth, Jan. 6, 1641; and Hannah, March 6, 1643. After coming to Stamford he had probably Moses and Lydia. After the death of his wife, Eleanor, he married, March 9, 1659, Unity, widow of Peter Brown, who had also been the widow of Clement Buxton. He died in April 1670, and his will, now in the probate records of Fairfield, dated the 15th of that month, names the children in the following order: Moses, Timothy, Caleb, Sarah Disbrow, Hannah, Lidea, Ruth, and Sarah and Unica Buxton, daughters of Clement.

Knapp, Caleb, son probably of the above, had a son, Caleb, born in 1661. His will, bearing date, 10, 3, 1674, names his children: Caleb, John, Moses, Samuel, Sarah, and Hannah.

Knapp, Joshua, son of Nicholas, was married here in 1657 to Hannah Close. He had one child recorded here—Hannah, born March 26, 1660. He lived later in Greenwich, having had then seven children, Joshua, Joseph, Ruth, Timothy, Benjamin, Caleb, and Jonathan. His inventory bears date Oct. 27, 1684.

Lareson, John, is complained against for selling wine in 1648, without license from the court. In 1651, Obadiah Seely discharges John Lareson of all debts due himself "from the beginning of the world to this day." A James Lareson appears on the land records in 1650.

Lockwood, Edmumd, in 1650, Oct. 14th, sold all his right and title in Stamford to Ann Akerley. How long he had been here at that date does not appear. He was probably a son of Edmund, of Cambridge. His children were John, Daniel, Edmund, Mary, and Abigail. Under date of March 24, 1698–9, the town grants the children of Edmund Lockwood, deceased, liberty to take up as much land for their father's estate in the second "lotment" at Runkinheag, as he had in the first division there, "his lotment in the first division being not to be found." He died here in Jan. 31, 1692, as appears from inventory of his estate, now on record. Book 1st, page 119, amounting to £305. This name has been numerous and prominent here to the present day. It now stands next to the Scofield name in numbers.

Lockwood, Jonathan, was here in 1659, as appears from his

testimony in court, at Fairfield, Feb. 24th of that year. He is reported as then 24 or 25 years of age. This corresponds with the presumption that he was son of Robert Lockwood, of Fairfield, and that he is the son born in Watertown, Sept. 10, 1634. His children were Jonathan, Robert, Gershom, Joseph, and John. He sold his estate here in 1665, and was afterwards a prominent citizen of Greenwich, representing that town in the state legislation for four years.

Lockwood, Joseph, went in 1644 to Poundridge, where he had sons, Joseph, James, Soloman, Israel, Reuben, and Nathaniel. His wife was Hannah, daughter of Soloman Close. His oldest son Joseph, had two sons—Major Ebenezer, of Poundridge, who lived until 1821, and was the father of the Hon. Ezra and Horatio Lockwood; and Joseph had also sons, among whose descendants are the Hon. Albert, of Sing Sing, N. Y., and Gen. Munson Lockwood, of White Plains.

Lyon, Thomas, was here as landholder in 1650, as appears from land records of Daniel Scofield.

Martin, John, buys land of John Bishop here May 1, 1650, in the East Field, seven acres of upland, lying between said Bishop and Richard Ambler.

Mills, Richard, was here in 1654. In 1657 he pledged his house and home lot and a parcel of land in Northfield to pay Jeremy Jagger a debt. On page 32 of record book No. 1, "Richard Mills, of Stamford, in New Haven jurisdiction," sold to Joseph Alsupe (Alsop), of New Haven, for the use of Mrs. Margaret Skief, of Boston, his "housings and homelot and all accomodations thereunto belonging." This sale was March 16, 1662; and Joseph Alsop transferred the same property to John Miller. June 21, 1687, the town vote Mr. Mills, ship carpenter, four acres of land on east side of Noroton River above the path, "so that he improve it for his own use." In 1691 John Mills, shipright, sells his pink called the Blossom, built in Stamford, with burthen of "seventy odd tons." In 1693–4, Jonathan and John Selleck, brothers, enter a caution, or cavitt (caveat), against all the lands and housings of John Mills, sen. In a sale of land, Jan. 18, 1695, executed by John Mills, Mary Mills, and John Mills, sign the deed; and in another land record John Mills' sons are named John, William, and Robert. "Ye Antient widow mary mills dyed ye 19th day of November, 1732."

MEAD, JOSEPH, of Stamford, sells his house and land to John and Daniel Weed. From his testimony given in court at New Haven in 1660, it appears that he was born in 1630. He went to Greenwich, which town he represented in the Connecticut Legislature, from 1669 to '71.

Mead, Jonathan, sells land in 1650, and in '59 he sells land to Henry Smith.

MITCHELL, DAVID, son of Mathew, had lands here in 1650. He had come hither with his father, and removed not many years after to Stratford. He had four sons—Matthew, who settled in Southbury; John, who lived in Woodbury; Nathan in Litchfield; and Abraham in Southbury. Cothren's History of Southbury has a catalogue of the descendants of the first two of these sons. The Rev. Justis Mitchell, who was settled in New Canaan, was a descendant of this David, of the fifth generation—the steps in the descent being John, of Woodbury, Lieut. John, Captain Asahel, and Rev. Justus. He married Martha, daughter of Rev. Josiah Sherman, of Woodbridge, sister of the Hon. Roger M. Sherman, and had a gifted family—among whom were Minot, the eminent lawyer of White Plains, and Chancy R., the gifted and brilliant orator; also a lawyer, settled at Delhi, N. Y., where he died in the very opening of his business career.

MORRIS, THOMAS, had land here in 1650, as appears from the boundaries of William Potter's land.

NEWMAN, DANIEL, made freeman 1670 (son probably of Willian), died here August 7, 1695. The inventory of his estate is on page 141, book 1st. His widow Sarah, August 31, 1695, makes over to her brothers, Thomas Newman, David Waterbury, Increase and John Holly, all her right in the estate of her husband Daniel Newman.

NEWMAN, THOMAS, probably son of William, had land here, as appears from the boundaries of other lands, recorded in 1649. His will, dated June 2, 1659, at Easttown, New Netherlands, gives his estate to his son William at Stamford, who is made his sole executor. It also requires him to provide for his wife Mary; to give Catherine Carles, alias Archer, the wife of John Archer, twenty shillings; and unto each of his (Archer's) surviving children five pounds. The will was witnessed by Richard and Samuel Mills, and was probably made in Stamford.

OLINESON, HENRY, had land here in 1649, as the record of Thomas Morehouse's land shows.

OLLIVER, WILLIAM, was here in 1658, having June 17th of that year witnessed Henry Ackerly's will, and had property as appears from testimony given by goodwife Slawson, Isaac Finch, John Holmes, and Richard Law, respecting a heifer which had been swamped.

PENOYER, ROBERT, or PENOIR, as the name is spelled frequently, was here early. In 1648 he is complained against for drinking wine and becoming noisy and turbulent, and abusing the watchman. He had a son Thomas, born here in 1658. He had several parcels of land assigned him soon after the settlement of the town. Savage says he came in the Hopewell, 1635, aged twenty-one, and that he was sentenced to be whipped in 1639.

PETET, JOHN, was here early and had children recorded to him before 1650. His inventory, dated 5, 4, 1676, made by Richard Law and Francis Bell, mentions his widow Sarah, and his two sons, names not given, and his daughters, Sarah, Mary, and Bethia. Richard Law was appointed guardian of his children in a court of magistrates, the governor being present, 14, 4, 1662.

Pettit, Debrow, died here in 1657. This name is afterwards spelled Petit.

Potter, William's, name occurs frequently on the early records. His home lot is on record, 1650. In 1652 he sells his house lot to Thomas Lyon, and purchases a parcel of land from John Finch. In 1661 he sells land to Jacob Pearson. His will, dated March 9, 1684–5, gives to the church in Stamford five pounds, "to be improved for the use of the Lord's table." The silver cups now in the service of the table of the First Congregational Church are still witnesses to this bequests. He also made bequests to the three sons of Mr. Bishop, the minister, Joseph, Ebenezer, and Benjamin; and to the children of his son-in-law, John Mead, viz.: John, Joseph, Ebenezer, Jonathan, Benjamin, Nathaniel, Samuel, Hannah, Abigail, Elizabeth, and David. In 1656 he appeals to the general court at New Haven, to excuse him from training in consequence of his weakness. The court do so, but notify him that if he recover his strength he must resume the service again. In 1684, in his testimony before Jonathan Bell, he says he is 75 years old.

Rivis, Garret, bought land here in 1657. He is called in the records a Dutchman. He purchased of Peter Ferris, and also of John Rockwell, and seems to have been in partnership with Aron Andreson, or Andreas.

Rugg, Robert, in 1651, sold to Richard Webb, his housing and home lot. The sale is witnessed by Thomas Lyon and Robert Basset. The inventory of his estate is on record and was prized by Francis Bell and Richard Law. The general court records make the date of it Jan. 29, 1655. This is probably the one of whom the record of the Connecticut Court of June 5, 1646, makes this unenviable entry: "Robert Rugge stands bownd in 40 *l.*," and that he "keepe good behavior and appeare the next court."

Scofield, Richard, owned land here in 1659, as appears from the recorded lands which Daniel Scofield sold to John Mead. His inventory was recorded by his widow, then the wife of Robert Penoyer, May 6, 1671. His daughter Elizabeth was born here in 1653, and his son Jeremy in 1658. There was also a Daniel Scofield here at the same date, with a family. This family has become more numerous than any other in town, and the present representations of it are among our best citizens.

Seeley, Obadiah, was early a resident here, as several entries in the records show. In 1651 he acknowledged payment of a debt due him from John Lareson. He died in 1667, and his inventory taken 24, 12, 1665, by William Newman and Robert Usher, mentions his widow Mary and his sons Obadiah, Cornelius, and Jonas. His widow Mary, had been the widow also of John Miller, of Stamford. He was probably a son of Robert Seeley, of Watertown, who settled afterwards in Wethersfield, and became quite famous as a Lieutenant in the Pequot war; and still later of the New Haven force under Sedgwick and Leverett against the New Netherlands. This name has been well represented in all its generations in the town.

Sherwood, Thomas, sells land to John Holly in 1648. His will, dated July 21, 1655, was probated Oct. 25, 1655, and mentions his wife Mary; his sons Steven, Mathew, and Isaac; and daughters Margaret, Ruth, and Abigail, the children of his first wife; and probably those of his second wife, Thomas, Joanna or Jane, daughter Thompson, Mary, Sarah, Hannah, Rose, and Rebecca.

Stevens, Thomas, died here in 1658. He had been a landholder as early as 1649, as appears from the land records. His will and inventory of estate are on record, dated Nov. 30, 1658. His property was bequeathed to his wife, for the children; but if she should marry, she was to have her third and the rest to be divided; the oldest son, if deserving and of godly carriage to have a double portion, if not to share equally with the rest.

In 1670,the county court made Obadiah, his son, Administrator, giving him the home and house lot, and requiring him to pay the legacies. His children were—Obadiah, Thomas, Benjamin, Joseph, and Ephraim, of whom, Dec. 20, 1686, Obadiah, Benjamin, and Joseph, give bonds for the settlement of their mother.

STEWARD, JAMES, probably a son of Alexander of Watertown. That he was a resident of Stamford in 1649 is evident from an action in court of that date, in which he was defendant, and Robert Hustice and Jeffrey Ferris, plaintiffs. It was shown that he had engaged to keep the town oxen; "to keep them from coming home, and out of the Indian's corne;" and that he neglected his duty so that the oxen injured the corn, to the extent of twelve and a half bushels of corn and two and a half bushels of peas. The court ordered him to pay the corn and peas, and "to beare the charge of the court." He was a landholder in 1650.

STOKEY, GEORGE, bought Henry Jackson's house and lot in 1650, and was still a resident in Stamford in 1660, as appears from testimony of Cornelius Jones in court of that year. His will was probated in court, at New Haven, in 1663, made in 1660, and witnessed upon oath by Daniel Scofield and John Holly, before Richard Law, at Stamford, Feb. 25, 1660. The name is spelled Stuckey on the town records. Elizabeth Stuckey, the wife, probably, of the above, died here in 1656. In his will he makes bequests to his daughter-in-law Mary Close, then not of lawful age; because she hath been obedient to her mother, to his wife Ann, and his daughter Elizabeth, who was also under age. He appoints as overseers for the daughters, his well beloved neighbors and friends Francis Bell, Robert Bates, Richard Mills, and George Slawson.

SYMINGS, HUMPHREY, was here in 1648, a creditor of Peter Brown, from whom he received his house and homelot.

TAINTER, CHARLES, witnessed here a deed in 1650. I have seen no other evidence of his presence here.

TAYLOR, GREGORY, died here Sept. 24, 1657, and goodwife Taylor, probably his wife, the month before him. In 1655 he made application to the general court at New Haven, to be freed from watching and training, in consequence of his bodily weakness. He had come from Watertown, where he was constable in 1642. He had two children by his wife Achsa; but they probably died young, as, after his wife's death, Aug. 18, 1667, his property is given by the court to John Waterbury and his wife. The inventory of his estate amounted to £48 14s. 6d., taken Oct. 1, 1657, and prized by Richard Law and Francis Bell. They testified in court, at Stamford, June 14, 1662, "that these goods within written, were presented to them and acknowledged by John Waterbury and his wife, to be the estate which the said Taylor, deceased, had in possession, and left at ye time of his death, but ye sd. Waterbury would not acknowledge that this was all, nor would his wife attest it upon oath to be a true inventory of the whole estate. Alsoe the said apprizers doe testify yt the apprizement is just according to ye best of their skill."

THEALE, NICHOLAS, was here in 1650, as appears from land records. He was in Watertown, in 1638. He was a landholder, and died here Aug. 19, 1658. His will, witnessed by Nicholas Knapp and Joseph Theale, makes bequests to his son Joseph; his daughter Elizabeth, who married, Oct. 27, 1769, William Ratcliff; and his wife. The inventory of his estate, taken Nov. 29, 1658, was proved in court Dec. 16, 1658, by widow Thell. He must have been somewhat prominent. His name still remains attached to the bridge on Broad Street, over Mill river. Joseph Theale son of the above, made freeman in 1669, represented the town five years, between 1670 and 1677, and removed to Bedford, N. Y., in 1687.

UFFIT, THOMAS, had lived here before 1660. His widow and her three children in that year agree to use their portion of his estate, which was in their custody, to pay any debts against him in Stamford, provided Thomas Uffit, of Stamford, and his two brothers, should agree to it, and engage to pay any debts against him, out of Stamford; that is, any debts due from him before his marriage to the present widow Uffit, late widow Theale. The widow, however, hopes the brothers may allow her and her children something, in view of the many debts she assumes. The witnesses to this agreement are: Joseph Theale, William Ratcliff, John Archer, Thomas Uffit, John Uffit, Roger Ferril, and one whose name is unreadable. In a subsequent record, Thomas Uffit, Roger Ferril, and John Uffit, refuse to make any further allowance for debts to the widow.

Usher, Robert, had land here in 1650. He took the oath of allegiance at New Haven in 1644, and came to Stamford. He married May 12, 1659, Elizabeth, widow of Jeremy Jagger. He was a man of some note, as his appointment by the Connecticut government, as constable, and his appointment as representative will show. He died in 1669, leaving his estate to his two children, Robert and Elizabeth.

Waterbury, John, came here soon after the settlement, and had land recorded to him in 1650. He died in 1658. He had lands here as early as 1650, as appears from assignment of lands of that date. His inventory bears date in April 1659, amounting to £185 12s. His sons were John, Jonathan and David, and possibly still others. Those three make over to their father-in-law Joseph Garnsey, in 1674, a parcel of land then in possession of John Miller. His widow had married Joseph Garnsey, in May 1661, when she attested his will. This is one of the most numerous as well as respectable of the Stamford names, down to the present day.

John Waterbury, jr., married Mary ——, and died here, Nov., 28, 1688. His will was entered on the record, on the testimony of Jonathan Bell, Dec. 11, 1688. It had been witnessed by Jonathan Bell and Joseph Bishop. In this will he makes bequests to his wife, of his "now dwelling house and orchard,"

&c., for her use while she remains his widow, after which they were to return to his eldest son John, and to his sons John, David and Thomas; and to his daughter Mary. He also makes his loving brothers Jonathan and David, the overseers of the children till they should come of age.

WEBB, RICHARD, probably came to Stamford from Norwalk, about 1654. The "Mill" in Norwalk was that year abandoned as worthless, and we find Mr. Webb here, soon after, engaged in the Stamford "Mill." He was probably a son of Richard of Norwalk, though he is not mentioned in his father's will, of date 1655. Mr. Webb was a man of some estate and note, representing the town in the Connecticut general court as early as 1667. The will of Richard Webb, sen., of Stamford, is on record in Fairfield, having date 7, 1, 1675–6; and the death of Richard Webb is on our town records as occuring Mar. 15, 1675–6, eight days after the will. The inventory of his estate bears date Apr. 29, 1676. His legatees were: his wife Margery; Joseph, who took the mill in Stamford, but who was to run it jointly with the widow; Richard, who had the uplands at Wescott's; Joshua, who took lands in Newfield, and the tools, which were in Huntington, L. I.; Caleb and Samuel, whose legacy was to be in the care of their mother; and Sarah. In a deposition of Richard Webb, made Nov. 22, 1667, he is said to be "aged 44 years or there about." Joseph Webb died here in 1684, leaving children Joseph, Mary, Hannah, Sarah and Margery. His inventory, dated Mar. 8, 1684, makes his wife's name Hannah. This name is among the most numerous and reputable names on the Stamford list.

WEBSTER, NICHOLAS, was early here. He married Sarah, daughter of John Waterbury, who had been divorced from Zachariah Dibble. He died Aug. 12, 1687. His will, dated July 19, 1687, makes bequests to his wife Sarah, and his children John, David, and Rachel; and to Zachariah Dibble "if he settle here." He makes his brother Jonathan Waterbury trustee for his estate. David Webster appears later on the land records, and had children born here. A John Webster, 1696, buys a saw mill and land here; and Rachel Webster married Henry Atwood, Aug. 18, 1708.

CHAPTER V.

STAMFORD UNDER THE NEW HAVEN JURISDICTION.

We have now found who the men were to whom mainly was entrusted the settlement of Stamford. Let us follow them through their experimental process of organizing a government, until they are at length safely and permanently at rest, under the jurisdiction which to this day their descendants do not fail to honor.

From the tenor of their title to the soil, they were at first a part of the New Haven confederacy. Their allegiance had been pledged in their acceptance of the territory. Their partners in the confederacy were New Haven, Milford, Guilford, Branford, and Southold. New Haven, the oldest and largest of these new towns was the capital. Here a general court was held at least twice a year, to which were admitted from each settlement two classes of members, magistrates and deputies. The magistrate held what would now be called senatorial rank, and the deputies were mere representatives. To this extemporised legislature, called in the expressive language of the times, the general court of New Haven, Andrew Ward and Francis Bell were admitted members, Oct. 27, 1641. Their title made them the honorable members from Rippowam; and to them was entrusted the responsibility of legislating for the Rippowam colony. The only business done in the court at that first session in which Rippowam was represented, having reference to the Stamford colony, was the appointment of Thurston Rayner as constable at Rippowam. His office was a very different one, from that which is now discharged under that name. It was one of high dignity and of solemn responsibility. In the original commis sion given our townsman by the August court, we learn their impression of its solemn and responsible trust. We will preserve that commission as a permanent witness to the style of legislation which prevailed in that early day in the colony. It is in these terms: "to order such business as may fall in the town, according to God, for the next ensuing year, butt is nott to be established in his office till he has received his charge from this court and testified his acceptance to this court."

On the sixth of the next April, 1642, Mr. Mitchell and John Whitmore are accepted from Rippowam, as members of the New Haven Court, and "accepted the charge of freemen." At this session of the court Rippowam is by legal authority changed to "Stamforde." Whether this was done at the request of the deputies or not, does not appear from the record of the transaction.

During the spring session of the court of this year, Stamford engages their attention. The deputies had reported the suspicious appearance of the Indians residing in the vicinity, and called for the advice of the court. The following conclusion is found on their minutes:

"Whereas, the deputies of Stamford, complain that their plantation are at some difference with the Indians, and therefore require the help of advice from the court how to carry towards them; it is therefore ordered that the magistrates and deputies for this plantation shall advise with the aforesaid deputies of Stamforde what course may best conduce to their peace and safety."

In the October session of the court, "Goodman Warde" is chosen constable for Stamford, with powers similar to those of his predecessor.

In April, 1643, a formal letter from constable Ward gives official notice of the choice by the townsmen of John Underhill and Richard Gildersleeve as the deputies from Stamford. The same letter makes a plea for a magistrate to be appointed by the general court, with senatorial rank in the legislative body.

It also proposes the names of two approved citizens, who were nominated by the townsmen, as those who were suitable to be entrusted with this authority. These were Matthew Mitchell and Thurston Rayner. After carefully weighing the merits of these men, the court made choice of Rayner, and appointed him to the high office.

The first business which they introduced, pertaining to the colony which they represented, was the organization of a plantation court at Stamford. By a formal resolution this court was to be composed of Thurston Rayner for chief judge, and Capt. Underhill, Mr. Mitchell, Mr. Ward and Robert Coe, as his associates. To them were entrusted all judicial questions which should arise in the colony, excepting such as were reserved for the adjudication of the general court at New Haven. These exceptions were in all those civil cases in which the property in question exceeded "in valew twenty pounds," and every criminal cause "when the punishment by scripture light, exceeds stocking and whipping, and if the fine be pecuniary, when the fine exceeds five pounds." This court was held here from time to time as occasion called for it for several years. When business of special interest or difficulty came up for adjudication, the governor and one of his assistants came down from New Haven to sit with the court.

In addition to the organization of this court, provision was made for appointing two of the officers of a military company for Stamford. This ordinance is still more illustrative of the spirit of the times than the appointment of the constable. We will give it entire: "Ordered, that the trayned band may chuse or confirm inferior officers, sergeant and corporal, or both, to exercise them in a military way, provided that such officers be both members of the church and presented to and approved by the magistrate and deputies from Stamford, the fundamental agreement for votes and elections being still preserved intyre and inviolable."

In this ordinance we have reference to the peculiarity of the

New Haven policy as differing from that of the Connecticut government. Church membership was the test of citizenship. No man could vote or be eligible to any civil or military office, who did not first qualify himself by a credible profession of religion. For twenty years, therefore, all the freemen and officers of the town were taken from the church.

That such a policy would give satisfaction in a community in which but a minority of the adult population were church members could not rationally have been expected. And the evidence that it was here an impracticable theory of government, is found in the fact that it did not long succeed. That it greatly retarded the growth of the Stamford colony will be made apparent as we proceed.

We have now reached a period of severe trial to the new colonists. The mere advice of the general court at New Haven, given in conformity with their decision of April 1641, did not relieve the dangers of the colony from Indian hostility. The Dutch had excited the intensest hatred of the surrounding Indians, and nothing but blood would henceforth appease it. The steps taken by the colonists to meet this peril, will be given in our chapter on Indian History. Those were days and nights of peril and of fear. Our colonists could never intermit their watch. Every day had its minute men, with arms at hand, all primed for sudden use. And for weeks, no day passed without a formal review of those capable of bearing arms. Not even the Sabbath was a relief to their fears or their military preparations. Their first sanctuary often witnessed, on the Lord's day, the gathering of musketed worshipers—at least four guns, well conditioned, being a legally appointed defense for that place of worship. The meeting house itself became the fortress of the town. A strong barricade around it, made it a safe refuge for the people, should a sudden irruption of the Indians render their dwellings insecure. The faithful sentinel, by day and by night, was to give no uncertain signal of approaching danger.

In the midst of these constant and pressing dangers, it was most fortunate for the colony that John Underhill was here. In October of this year, he makes an appeal to the New Haven court for help to check and destroy the Indians, who were threatening the very existence of the town. He had appealed in vain to the Dutch to raise for him a hundred men to prosecute the war. In the name of the Stamford settlers he now asks for a loan of twenty pounds. The loan was to be repaid out of the salary which Stamford had engaged to give him "yearly." So that it is evident that the handful of settlers at Stamford had been obliged to enter on this defensive war, at their own cost. The reception which this appeal met, is a marked tribute to the character of our military leader.

It appears that the Dutch had now become so much alarmed that they were anxious to secure the services of Underhill. To retain the captain within their own jurisdiction, the New Haven colonists vote the loan, giving as the reason for it, their wish "to prevent the success of larger offers for his remove."

The Stamford deputies of this year made, it would seem, a very earnest plea in court for a vigorous prosecution of the war. They set forth the imminent dangers hanging over their exposed town. Their wives and children were every hour in fear of the stealthy and relentless foe. The Indians of the vicinity greatly outnumbered them, and were now laying their plans for the sudden extermination of the last pale face who should stand in their way. Without some speedy and terrible blow inflicted upon them, they would inevitably overrun and destroy the entire settlement. And as a final appeal, they warn the court that if they fail of furnishing the means now called for, they should bear the responsibility of whatever harm should come to the exposed town.

Meantime the extreme peril of the Dutch settlement, to the West of Stamford, had led to the movements which will be mentioned in our Indian narrative, and comparative peace was soon assured the settlement.

The only incidents which appear on record, for some years after the peace are very few, and of but little importance. The attack upon Mrs. Phelps will be hereafter given. In the June session of the court in New Haven, Mr. Rayner calls for an efficient force to find and bring the offender to trial. The court ordered the search to no purpose. In August. of the same year, Wachebrough, a Potatuck Indian, succeeded in capturing Busheag, the fugitive assassin, and delivered him over to the Stamford authorities. The charge against him was made good, the testimony of the woman who had been so nearly killed by him being positive as to his indentity. His death was ordered. Decapitation was executed upon him, as he sat firmly erect, defiantly gazing into the eye of his unskillful executioner.

In 1643 an incident occurred in the town, which shows so clearly the manner in which justice was dispensed, that it will justify our notice. One of the planters, Richard Crab, had a servant, probably an Indian boy, who had been guilty of a public misdemeanor, such as was an offense to the community in those days when morals were strictly cared for. Mr. Rayner, the appointed magistrate, in the undoubted right of his sacred office, ordered the public chastisement of the boy.

Mr. Crab took offense at the exercise of such power, and claimed that the punishment was excessive and unjust. He claimed that he had already punished the boy at home, and that one punishment was sufficient. He went still further, and insisted that as the boy was his servant, and responsible to his administration, no authority existed which could rightly interfere in the case. This was, therefore, a case of rebellion against the legally constituted authorities. An appeal is made by Mr. Crab to the court. The case is heard. The court brought in their decision. It was designed to settle all similar questions which might subsequently arise. They fully justify the magistrate as having done only his duty in the case. The ground they took was that the "family correction," though sufficient for all the purposes of correction at home, being there a timely and suitable expression of righteous abhorrence of such an offense, and a sufficient warning to all who witnessed it against the commission of a similar crime; yet it could never answer the demands of public justice which had been outraged, or appease the public indignation which was justly aroused. As the community had been insulted and harmed, a public expiation should be made. The court, therefore, would sustain and honor the magistrate. And since the charges made by Mr. Crabb, if not rebuked, would serve to bring the authority of the public minister into contempt, and so undermine all authority, the court proceeded to make Mr. Crabb himself a public example. They order him bound over to appear at the next meeting of the court in Hew Haven.

At the appointed time, Mr. Crabb appeared and was fined five pounds sterling money, for his presumptuous upbraiding of a public minister for the performance of his public duty.

From the first there seems to have been a degree of restiveness among the settlers in regard to the limited franchise they enjoyed under the jurisdiction of the New Haven colony. As early as 1644, but a little more than three years after the settlement, this impatience, under such restrictions, was shown by the secession of quite a portion of the colony. Mr. Denton and those who agreed with him, decided to try their fortunes under the Dutch government on Long Island, and accordingly removed and located at Hempstead. This removal took away from Stamford the followiag list of the settlers: Richard Denton, father and son, Robert Coe, John Karman, Jeremy Wood, Richard Gildersleeve, Wm. Rayner, Benjamin Coe, John Ogden, Jonas Wood, John Fordham, Edmund Wood, Thomas Armitage, Simon Seiring, Henry Pierson, John Coe, Robert Jackson, Thomas Sherman, Francis Yates, and John Ellison.

And while this local rupture was taking place, and endangering the continued existence of the settlement, a sudden enemy appeared on the stage, adding to the confusion and danger. The Dutch, now for some years established in New Amsterdam, at Manhattan, thought their opportunity had come for extending their boundaries permanently to the Eastward, and sent out an expedition to demand the surrender of the settlement, at Stamford and Greenwich, to their authority. But the timely division of the settlers had left those disposed to be loyal to New Haven, free to assert their preference and maintain their choice. The Dutch found themselves powerless against such loyalty, and soon gave up their attempt. Twenty years later, when Sir George Downing, their English minister at the Hague, wished to recapitulate the provocations given by the Dutch to his government, we find him referring to this same invasion of the English territory in Connecticut. In his own impassioned style, he asks the Dutch council:

"Did not the Dutch about 20 years agone come to an English town called Stamford, where none but English lived, and summoned them to come under obedience and pay them contribution, and set up the Dutch arms there? Did they not send armed men to an English town called Greenwich?"

But no Dutch temptation or threat could seduce the English colonists at Stamford to forswear their allegiance to the New Haven, English jurisdiction, even though so many of them disliked the tenor of their franchise and the character of much of their legislation.

But even the large removal, from the young colony to which we have referred, did not put an end to the disaffection. So positive had this dislike of the New Haven administration become in 1653, that a formal protest seems to have been sent from Stamford, with complaints of their rates and other grievances. At the same time, the commission appointed by the New Haven general court, to settle the controversy between the town and one John Chapman, reported an alarming degree of disloyalty, if not of open and avowed treason. The commissioners, Mr. Goodyear and Newman, had been sent to quiet what was thought to be a slight disaffection, on the part of the principal actor, in opposition to the New Haven jurisdiction. But they found their authority stoutly denied. Mr. Chapman claimed the right of being heard in full court. Whereupon the commissioners "caused the town to be called together, and being met they found them, for the most part, full of discontent with the present government they are under, pleading that they might have their free votes in the choice of civil officers; making objections against their rates; and propounded to have their charges of watching and warding the summer past, with some other work made about their meeting house for their defense, borne by the jurisdiction; and that they might have twelve men sent them at the jurisdiction charge to lye there all winter for their defense."

The principal speakers for the town before the commissioners were Robert Basset and John Chapman. The commissioners debated the question, asserting the authority of the general court, but without allaying the mutinous disposition of the town. They then read the order of the parliament committee, requiring their submission to the government they were under, "which did somewhat allay their spirits for the present." On receiving this report from their commissioners, the general court ordered that the governor, if he see cause, shall issue a warrant "requiring John Chapman and Robert Basset to appear here at New Haven, at such time as the governor shall appoint, to answer such things as shall be laid to their charge."

In the following March, the marshall of the Connecticut colony with a posse, had been sent down to Fairfield to arrest Thomas Baxter, a sort of border desperado of that town, whose high handed measures had outraged the government and imperiled the peace of both the Connecticut and New Haven jurisdictions. On the way they call at New Haven, to get aid from the government there. Two men are here added to their number, with instructions for Richard Law, the constable at Stamford, to take men at Stamford and proceed to Greenwich if Baxter should have escaped from Fairfield, and "if Baxter's strength be not too great for them to seize him and bring him to New Haven." Thus commissioned the arresting party proceeded.

They found the offender and arrested him, when Robert Basset who seemed to have been a confederate with the offender, attempted by force to release him. They disarm him, and the marshall orders him to assist in guarding the prisoner. He seemed to consent to do so, but soon stole away. Soon, as if under his instigation, the party were attacked by a gang of the citizens, who made a desperate effort to liberate their prisoner. In the skirmish one of the Baxter party was killed and one of the arresting party wounded. Soon after, Basset again appeared, and began to expostulate with the marshall for arresting Baxter, when the marshall took him into custody. Arresting two other of Baxter's accomplices, the marshall takes them safely to New Haven. Baxter and the Fairfield accomplices are dismissed to their trial before the Connecticut court in Hartford; but Basset is arraigned before the court of his jurisdiction at New Haven.

In this trial it was made clear that Basset had been guilty of seditious conduct; he had expressed himself against the government of the jurisdiction; he had been active to raise and carry on an insurrection in both the colonies; he had, without any commission sought to raise volunteers against the Dutch; and had "been a ringleader in these ways of disturbance, and undermining the government of this jurisdiction; and all this, contrary to his oath of fidelity."

How much of a disturber, and how far an exciter of sedition Basset had been, appears in the testimony of both the Stamford deputies of this year, those eminently loyal men, sergeant Bell and goodman Law.

On the seventh of March, the day before the general court was to hold its session, Stamford held its town meeting, to choose its deputies. Not many less than three score substantial citizens constituted that body. How many of them were voters we do not know. That there were men present who deeply resented the civil disabilities which rested upon them, and who were ready for revolutionary proceedings to secure what they deemed, and what we have conceded to have been their rights, will appear from the spicy discussion which then took place.

Immediately after the meeting had been opened, Basset, the readiest speaker of the disaffected party, springs to the floor, and with great excitement demands to know what this meeting means. "To choose deputies for the general court at New Haven," answers the constitutional law officer of the town.

"We acknowledge no New Haven court, here," quickly retorted the unintimidated revolutionist.

"We took our title from the New Haven jurisdiction, and are here to make proof of our loyalty," was the ready answer.

"But we know no laws but England's, and shall heed no authority but hers," exclaimed a sharp keyed voice, which had been pitched in the tone of thoroughly radical excitement.

"My authority," coolly replied the law officer, "is from England."

"Give *us* then English law," shouted the heated and now clamorous partizans for reform. "Let *us* have *our* votes. There is no justice in your New Haven tyranny."

"But we cannot violate the fundamentals of the government to which we owe allegiance," solidly replies our right worthy deputy, Francis Bell. "Mr. Moderator, will you proceed to call the vote," continues, as if finally, the law-abiding minister of the government.

But not yet had the radical and revolutionary leader exhausted his resources against the hated power. Rising to his utmost height, wielding his most significant menaces in tone and looks and gestures, he bursts forth in an uncontrolled and uncontrollable torrent of passionate abuse.

"We have no English laws or rights; we have no votes; we have no liberties; we have no justice here; we are mere asses for fools to ride, and our backs are well nigh broken. You make laws when you please and what you please; you execute them as you please; you lay what rates you please, and give what reasons you please. We are bond-men and slaves, and there will be no better times for us till our task-masters are well out of the way."

Such were the testimonies brought against Basset in the New Haven court by the deputies from Stamford. In his defense, which consisted mainly of humble apologies, he implicated as his inciters and encouragers at Stamford—John Chapman, Jeremiah Jagger, Old Newman and William Newman.

The court remanded Basset to the care of the Marshall until the writings which had been left at Richard Webb's in Stamford, and which were thought to prove other and more treasonable offenses against him, should be produced. He was also to be put into irons.

At the next sitting of the court in two weeks, three of the above-named offenders appeared in court and acknowledged they had taken the oath of allegiance to the New Haven government. Chapman is first put on trial, the others having been removed from the court room. He is charged with aggravated guilt, because he had once been a deputy from Stamford in the general court. It is proved against him that he had engaged in soliciting aid to make war upon the Dutch without approbation; he had resisted the legal authority established at Stamford; he had gone with Basset to Norwalk to stir up sedition there, and would have continued on to disturb all the towns towards New Haven, had not the New Haven commissioners met them on the way to Fairfield; and that his real aim was to overthrow the churches and subvert the civil government of the jurisdiction.

Jagger was next put on trial. Similar charges are made against him as against Chapman. He had been even more bitter in his invectives against the magistrates and against the general government. He had spoken with great contempt of the commissioners sent from New Haven to check the turbulence of the Stamford radicals. He had rated the magistrates as so many Indians, and had threatened the rate gatherers that the votes should do them no good. On being allowed to plead, against the charges, he made a beginning but soon cooled down and confessed his folly and sin, and expressed his sorrow for them. "He sees now more in these things than ever he did before, and were they to do again, he should not do them, and hopes it will be a warning to him hereafter."

"William Newman is then called. He is informed by the court of the charges against his loyalty. He is told, also, that his father had been specially offensive to the town and to the court, but that they had excused his arrest from his great age. To all this Newman offers the excuse that he had done only as others in Stamford had done, in claiming and insisting on more liberty in votes. Yet he confesses his fault and testifies that his father also "wished him to inform the court that he is sorry for what he hath done, and hopes he shall act so no more."

The trial here ends, and the court proceeded to sentence the parties. Chapman and Jagger are solemnly admonished by the court of their grave offenses. By the law of the jurisdiction they had brought themselves "in question for their lives;" yet the court were inclined to a lenient treatment even of so serious an offense. They accordingly fine Jagger twenty pounds, putting him under a hundred pound bond to maintain his loyalty hereafter; and Chapman ten pounds, under a bond of fifty pounds for his future loyalty. Newman is to give his bond of twenty pounds, "to attend his oath of fidelity hereafter, and maintain the foundations laid for government here and the laws of this jurisdiction, to the utmost of his ability, avoiding all ways of disturbance in this kind which he hath formerly gone on in."

The court proceed to instruct the Stamford deputies that if others in their town give similar offenses, "they are to bind them to answer it at the next court of magistrates, in the latter end of May, and particularly, Tuckee, Theale, Webb and Finch who hath carried it ill as the court is informed."

It appears that Basset, in view of his sincere penitence, was allowed to return to Stamford, where he atoned for his past irregularities, by his straightforward loyalty. Two months later, in May 1664, he was called before the court again, and informed that he was expected to make some acknowledgment for his offenses and give some pledge for his future good conduct.

He makes a full and humble confession of his sin, and ascribes to God's timely interposition his deliverance from the toils of sedition into which he had been drawn. He sees the evil of his course and is ready to acknowledge that the government is all right, "and settled according to God." As to those "uncomfortable words in the town meeting which have tended much to disturb the peace of the place and much grieve the heart of God's people," he testified to his deep sorrow for them, and expresses the earnest wish that he may do so no more. The court express to him their confidence in his reformation, and remit his offense, but require from him a bond of a hundred pounds, that his future course shall be one of unwavering loyalty.

At the May session of the general court, in 1655, the Stamford deputies enter their complaint against the people of Greenwich for sundry irregularities, and ask for protection. The grievances were such as could not be tolerated. The greedy Greenwichers had made use of the Stamford commons for pasturing their cattle; they were disorderly in their daily walk; they allowed both the English and Indians in drunkenness, and so brought on much mischief; they protected disorderly and vagrant children and servants who ran away from their proper guardians; and they had converted their town into a notorious Gretna Green for all sorts of clandestine and illegal marriages. To avoid these irregularities in future, the deputies ask that the men at Greenwich be required to unite under this jurisdiction.

On hearing the complaint the court drew up a formal order for the immediate submission of the Greenwichers to their authority, and forward it by the Stamford deputies. To this a reply is prepared and forwarded the next year to the court.

This reply provoked the court. They get the governor to answer it in the name of the court. They stoutly assert their claim to Greenwich, and commission the two Stamford deputies, Law and Bell, to go over to Greenwich, deliver the letter, and "demand in the name of the court the number of their males from sixteen to sixty years of age, to be delivered with the other males of the jurisdiction to the commissioners the next year at Plymouth."

If the Greenwichers denied their authority or delayed to furnish the names, they were to be warned to attend the next meeting of the court of magistrates at New Haven. If they should fail of appearing in court, "Richard Crabb and some other of the more stubborn and disorderly ones were to be seized at Stamford or thereabout and sent to New Haven to answer for their contempt of authority."

The court of Magistrates came off in June, but none of the men who had been summoned from Greenwich appeared. The Stamford deputies report them as positively refusing to submit. The court decide to wait a month longer, as the people of Greenwich had appealed to England, to see if a new patent should not reach them from England, then a summary seizure must be made of the contumacious and rebellious subjects and the supremacy of the New Haven government vindicated.

No further notice seems to have been taken of the Greenwich men until June 1657. At the general court then assembled in New Haven, the deputies of Stamford, Richard Law, John Waterbury, and George Slawson presented the following paper from the men at Greenwich:

"At Greenwich ye 16th of October, 1656.

Wee the inhabitants of Greenwich whose names are under written doe from this day forward freely yield ourselves, place and estate, to the government of Newhaven, subjecting ourselves to the order and dispose of that general court, both in respect of relation and government, promising to yield due subjection unto the lawfull authoritie and wholesome lawes of the jurisdiction aforesaid, to witt of Newhaven, &c.

Angell Husted,	Peter Ferris,
Lawranc Turner,	Joseph Ferris,
John Austin,	Jonathan Reanolds,
Richard Crab,	Hanc Peterson,
Thomas Steedwell,	Henry Nicholson,
Henry Accorley,	Jan, a Duchman,
	comonly called Varllier."

The court accept the submission and order that they "fall in with Stamford and be accepted a part thereof."

From this date, until both Greenwich and Stamford were received under the jurisdiction of Connecticut colony in 1664, Greenwich seems to have had no town organization distinct from Stamford. The Stamford deputies in the general court spoke for Greenwich. The constable of Stamford had jurisdiction also in Greenwich. And the townsmen appointed for Stamford, served also for "town occasions" of Greenwich. We find, therefore, such orders as the following on the records of the general court:

"The Court orders that those who are in public trust for Stamford shall require of the inhabitants of Greenwich a list of their ratable estate, and send it to the treasurer at New Haven." Nor did there seem to be any serious jealousy on the part of the Greenwich people at this exercise of supervision from the Stamford authorities. Indeed, the most of the English at Greenwich had probably come originally with the Stamford colony, and in their exposure to the Indian and the Dutchman, had in some sort, relied upon their close union with Stamford for their safety and defense.

The boundaries, indeed, between the two settlements appears not to have been determined. Several times in the records of those days, a person mentioned, is spoken of as living about Stamford and Greenwich. One such record occurs immediately after the above submission of Greenwich; and as it reveals the continued exposure of those days to savage incursions, we will insert it:

"Abraham Frost, who at present lives about Stamford or Greenwich, presented a petition to the court, desiring some relief from them because he is very poor, having lost all by the Indians about a year and a half ago, his wife and children taken captives, but after brought to this jurisdiction, where they have lived since in a poor and mean way. The court considered the case, and ordered that ten bushels of Indian corn, or the value thereof in other corn, be paid him from Stamford, which to be allowed them in their rates."

We have already seen that the limitation of the franchise to church members, by the New Haven Government, was the occasion of much dissatisfaction among the Stamford colonists. There were also other prohibitions in the fundamental laws of the colony which we shall see were not to be borne. In the chapter on "Ecclesiastical Provisions," every man was forbidden to use any discourteous language toward the minister, or regarding his preaching, and every person was to attend meeting on the Lord's days, at least, and on days of public fasting or thanksgiving. No person was allowed to broach or maintain any dangerous error or heresy. No sinful or servile work, no unlawful sport or recreation was to be allowed on the Sabbath.

Besides these strict fundamental laws, in 1657 a special order had been passed to guard the faith of these puritan churches, and to meet an evil which was beginning to show itself:

"It is ordered that no Quaker, ranter or other heretic of that nature, be suffered to come into, nor abide in this jurisdiction, and that if any rise up among ourselves that they be speedily suppressed and secured, for the better prevention of such dangerous errors;" and the next year in May a lengthy act is passed to secure the churches against harm from "the cursed sect of heretics lately risen up in the world which are commonly called quakers."

While this latter enactment was under discussion before the general court, the heresy which it would punish was being secretly spread through the jurisdiction. It found its way into Stamford. Zealous disciples of the new faith sought to propagate their creed, and found some who were ready to entertain and embrace them. Members of the church became tainted with the subtle heresy, and still more who owed the church a spite, were glad to find in the fiery apostles of this anti-church creed the heartiest sympathy and support.

Nor did the zealous disciples of the new faith cease with merely publishing the new gospel. They were hotter still with zeal to mend the old. They went mad for reform. They renounced the old ministry and meetings and worship; and at once assailed and wished to supplant the civil government which sustained them. So officious were they that the church felt called upon, in self defense, to enter an earnest protest; and the central government were obliged either to vacate or justify their authority.

Daniel Scofield, then marshal for Stamford and vicinity, authorized by the governor's writ, took a posse of his neighbors and started for the western side of the town, now Greenwich, to arrest one Thomas Marshall, who for some time had been insulting and outraging the majesty of the government. They found him at the house of Richard Crabb, who was also lying under charge of serious miscarriages.

The arrest was made, but not without an attempt at interference by Mr. Crabb, and a torrent of abuse from his enraged wife. Both of these sympathizers with the vagrant heretic were put under arrest, and bound over to the next court of magistrates, to be held in New Haven in May 1658. At the appointed time Mr. Crabb and his accusers appeared in court. The witnesses against him were the party who had assisted in the arrest of Marshsll, and also Mr. Bishop, pastor of the church in Stamford. The court inform him that he must now answer for his several miscarriages; for his many clamorous and reproachful speeches against the ministry, government and officers; for neglecting the meetings of the Sabbath by himself and his wife, for whose offenses, as they were justified by himself, he must be responsible.

William Oliver, one of the arresting party, testified that when they came to Mr. Crabb's to arrest Marshall and seize the Quaker books which were supposed to be in Mr. Crabb's possession, Madam Crabb retreated to another room and closed the door against them. Nor would she yield until the door had been forced open by violence.

Then followed an exciting scene. The plucky woman who would not open the door of her castle, now could not shut her mouth; nor could the utmost expostulations of her more placable husband, united with the utmost array of governmental authority before her do it. Neither the one nor the other, nor both united, could intimidate the zealous defender of her personal rights. We may never recover the entire speech which that audience were required to hear. It had not been written, and there was no time for the stenographer to be called. It had no formal exordium, fashioned after the calm rules of rhetoric; there were probably but few of those well rounded periods which give so much dignity to discourse; and the peroration was doubtless as abrupt and pithy as the rest.

The door being opened, the way was clear for her, and she used it, apparently, without help or hindrance, and we may be assured that she had no listless or sleepy auditors to the very end.

"Is this your fasting and praying?" breaks forth the impassioned woman, as she fastens her searching glance upon the marshal and his attendants. "Do ye thus rob us and break into our houses? How can you Stamford men expect the blessing of God? Will He bear with your mean hypocrisy? You have taken away our lands, without right. You have basely wronged us, and let me tell you what I see without your hireling priests' help; the vengeance of God Almighty will burst upon you. And when it comes, your priest can't help you. He is as Baal's priest, and is no better than the rest of you. Ye are all the enemies of God and God's saints, and their blood shall be on your souls forever."

Fastening her sharp eye on goodman Bell, the same who from the first had been a pillar in the Stamford church, and who had now come over with the marshal, hoping by his fraternal intercession to win back the estranged and now perverse hearts of his erring brother and sister, she continued her bitter invective. "Thou arch traitor and hypocrite, thou villainous liar, God's wrath is on you and shall burn hotter and hotter on your godless children. Out on you! poor priest-ridden fool!"

Springing next upon John Waterbury, who had also accompanied the marshal to aid in the dispensation of justice, she administers to him a similar castigation. Then she tries the force of her cutting reproaches and sharp retorts upon the marshal, for selling himself to do the dirty work of the God-forsaken government at New Haven, and of the over-reaching and heaven-defying, and priest-cursed crew in Stamford. Then she assailed George Slawson, that exemplary member of the church, a peace-maker, and one whom all delighted to honor, and poured upon him her heaviest abuse. He had hoped to quiet her irritability, and in his most winning way had most gently expostulated with her, reminding her of the former days in which she had walked joyfully and hopefully with God's people in Stamford, and in which she had counted the communion of saints there, the most precious of all her earthly blessings. He ventured to express the hope that they might again welcome her to their fellowship in the old church, and that she might again listen there to the same gospel in which she had once testified her great interest. This was carrying his persuasion too far. It seemed to kindle her intensest ire. She was now for once, put to it for words rapid enough, or hot enough to express her rage. Every possibility of indignant resentment in her soul was taxed to its utmost. Scorn and rage and defiance seemed struggling together in her utterance for the mastery over each other, and they seem to have ended the attempt at her reconciliation. It was a settler to that well-meant parley in which her womanly temper rejoiced in securing the last word. "Never, never, shall I or mine trouble your Stamford meeting more. I shall die first. My soul shall never be cast away to the devil so easily as that;" and with uplifted hands, she invoked on their heads the most sudden and the direst vengeance which heaven could inflict. When she had exhausted herself in these rapid maledictions, she called for drink to revive her strength; and the ministers of the law could do no more than go through the ceremony of binding her, with her husband, over to the court.

On the narration of the case before the court as just stated, the governor, Francis Newman, informed Mr. Crabb that these were notorious doings, not to be allowed. Mr. Crabb, for his wife it appears had not obeyed the summons to attend the court, attempted an apology. He could not manage his wife. He did not justify her evil way, but he would have the court understand her case. She was a well-bred English woman, a zealous professor of religion from her childhood, "but when she is suddenly surprised she hath not power to restrain her passion."

To all this the worshipful governor made answer; "that what he had said did greatly aggravate her miscarryings, for if she have been a great professsour it was certain she had been an ill practiser, in which you have countenanced her and borne her up, which may be accounted yours, as having falne into evills of the like nature yourself, revileling Mr. Bishopp as a priest of Baal and ye members as liars, and yt Mr. Bishopp preached for filthy lucre."

Mr. Crabb vainly attempted to explain away or deny what abundant testimonies corroborated. Mr. Bishop, the pastor of the church had been so sorely tried, that he "could not continue at Stamford, unless some course be taken to remove and reform such grievances." Mr. Bell felt that an end of all government had come, if the ministers of justice were to be so opposed and insulted with impunity. The "citizens of Stamford wished the court to preserve the peace among them, maintain the ordinances of religion and government, and encourage their minister. To all which Mr. Crabb made no further plea. The court sentenced him to pay a fine of 30 pounds, and give bonds to the amount of 100 pounds for his good behaviour, and that he make public acknowledgements at Stamford, to the satisfaction of Francis Bell and others whom he had abused. The remainder of the sentence is missing, and so we shall probably never know what disposition the court made of the sharp-tongued Madam Crabb who was really the chief offender in the case.

No other case of conflict with the Quakers, which was deemed worthy a public prosecution, seems to have occurred in Stamford or its vicinity. There was disturbance by them in other parts of the jurisdiction, especially in their settlement at Southold on Long Island; but the majesty of the law was maintained and the churches defended.

That there were still occasions of disturbance at Stamford needing the strong arm of the law for their repression or control, the following special ordinance of the general court will attest. This provision for a permanent annual court, instead of the occasional courts which from the second year had been provided for, may also indicate the increasing importance of Stamford in the jurisdiction.

"At the general court in New Haven, May 30, 1660, upon weighty grounds presented, the court desired the governor and deputy governor, Francis Newman and William Leete, to go to Stamford, there to keep court. Richard Laws and Francis Bell were chosen to assist in the said court; which court hath power committed to them equal to any plantation court, assisted by two magistrates. It was further ordered, while there is need, that two magistrates shall be yearly sent to Stamford to keep court, at the charge of the jurisdiction, the charge of entertainment at Stamford to be excepted, which is to be borne by themselves."

We now come to the beginning of the struggle between the two jurisdictions of Connecticut and New Haven, for the supremacy over the territory thus far held by the New Haven jurisdiction.

The next notice we find of Stamford in the colony records is of date, Oct. 9, 1662. The new charter of Connecticut had been received, and was decided to cover the territory of Stamford and even of Westchester, now in New York. The Connecticut court, therefore, call upon the Westchester colony "to demean themselves in all things as may declare and manifest their readiness to subject to his Royal will and pleasure herein." But their minute regarding Stamford is: "This court doth heartily declare their acceptance of ye plantations of Stamford and Greenwich under this government upon the same terms and provisions as are directed and declared to ye inhabitants of Guilford; and that each of these plantations have a constable chosen and sworne." Robert Usher is ordered to be sworn as constable for Stamford for one year, or until a new is chosen.

The same session of the general court—the prospective State legislature—declare the following Stamford men to be "freemen of this colony," viz.: John Green, Richard Hardey, Joseph Mead, Richard Webb, Joseph Theed, (Theal), and Peter Pheries, (Ferris). These are probably all of those capable of citzenship in the Connecticut colony, who were thus early ready to secede from the New Haven jurisdiction. And indeed it would seem, that as late as the spring session of 1669, only two more of the townsmen, Richard Law and Jonathan Sellick had accepted citizenship in the new jurisdiction.

At the same session of the court, Stamford, Greenwich and Westchester are to "have liberty of ye court at Fairfield, to issue controversies that may arise among them for future."

We now find Stamford claimed as a colony of the Connecticut jurisdiction, and the general court proceed to enroll such freemen from the new town as offer themselves for that purpose; and Mr. Gould is authorised to give them the oath of freemen at the next court in Fairfield.

At the May session of the court for 1663, we find this record which indicates the division still existing in Stamford respecting the transfer of their allegiance from New Haven to Connecticut.

"This court orders that Rob. Usher and John Meggs shall continue in the place and office of a constable over those that have submitted to this government in there respective plantations, until the court see cause to alter otherwise; and all those that have submitted are to attend the former order made in October court last."

The order referred to here is undoubtedly that which prescribed their duties as citizens of the new jurisdiction. They were to be admitted on the same terms as Guilford had been, as thus indicated:

"And this court doth advise the said persons to carry peaceably and religiously in their places towards the rest of ye inhabitants, that yet have not submitted in like manner. And also, to pay their just dues unto ye Minister of their Towne; and also all publique charges due to this day."

But the transfer of jurisdiction had not yet been approved by the leading men of Stamford. They still acknowledged the authority of New Haven, and in May 1663, by vote decided to send their deputies, as before, to New Haven. Francis Bell and Richard Law were chosen, and Mr. Bell took his seat and was sworn in and deputed by the court to give the oath to Mr. Law. And again in October, they send Mr. Law and George Slawson to represent them in the New Haven court. At this session of the court not a little bitterness was shown towards the Connecticut colony, for encouraging those at Guildford and Stamford who were disposed to object to the New Haven administration; and they were inclined not to treat further with the offending government unless it would first return these revolted or seduced subjects to their former loyalty. A committee were appointed by the New Haven assembly to state their grievances and demand redress. In a lengthy document they make their statement and their plea. The following passage from the statement shows the part Stamford was taking in the struggle, and how important her decision was felt to be.

"Before your general assembly in October last, 1663, our committee sent a letter unto the said assembly, whereby they did request that our members by you unjustly sent from us should be by you restored unto us, according to our frequent desires and according to Mr. Winthrop's letter and promise to authority in England, and according to justice, and according to the conclusion of the commissioners in their last session in Boston, whereunto you returned a real negative answer, contrary to all the promises, by making one Brown your constable at Stamford, who hath been sundry ways injurious to us and hath scandalously acted in the highest degree of contempt, not only against the authority of this jurisdiction, but also of the king himself, pulling down with contumelies the declaration which was sent thither by the court of magistrates for this colony, in the king's name, and commanded to be set up, in a public place, that it might be read and obeyed by all his majesties subjects, inhabiting our town of Stamford."

But the majority of the Stamford people were evidently inclined to transfer their allegiance to the Connecticut jurisdiction; and, as is not unusually the case, the politicians of the old school, who had been the ministers and law officers of the old authorlty, were at length also brought to see the need, if not the desirableness of accepting the destiny. At this point, also, the greater question at issue between the New Haven and Connecticut colony must be settled. The charter made no divided jurisdiction. From the Narragansett river on the East, and the sea on the South, across the continent towards the west, and up to the Massachusetts grant on the north, "all firme lands, Soyles, Grounds, HAVENS, Ports, Rivers, Waters, Fishings, Mynes, Mynerals, Precious Stones, Quarries, and all and singular other commodities, Jurisdictions, Royalties, Privileges, Francheses, Preheminences, and hereditaments whatsoever" within the said tract, were made over to his "Worshipful John Winthrop, Governor; John Mason, Deputy Governor; and their twelve assistants and their successors, forever." There could be no question as to whether New Haven was embraced in this charter or not. Accordingly, a committee was appointed Aug. 19, 1663, consisting of the Deputy Governor, Mr. Wyllis, Mr.

Daniel Clark and John Allyn or any three of them, "to treat with our honored friends of New Haven, Milford, Branford, and Guildford, about settling their union with this colony of Connecticut." They were instructed, if unable to effect a union, to declare to them "that this assembly cannot well recent their proceeding in civil government, as a district jurisdiction; and this assembly doth desire and cannot but expect that the inhabitants of New Haven, Milford, Branford, Guildford and Stamford, do yield subjection to the government now established." Again, in Oct. 1664, the court appointed Mr. Sherman and the Secretary to go to New Haven, and the other hesitating towns, and "by order from this court, in his majestie's name, to require all the inhabitants of New Haven, Milford, Branford, Guilford and Stamford, to submit to the government of this colony and take their answer." They were, also, to declare all the freeman of those towns, who were qualified according to law, and who would take the freeman's oath, to be freemen of the Connecticut colony.

Mr. Law, of Stamford, who had already sent in his submission to the Connecticut jurisdiction, was appointed with "magistraticall powers," to assist in the government of the plantation. The appointment of Mr. Law, who had been the leader of the New Haven party in the town, was a stroke of good policy on the part of the general court. They had now won over the last formidable opponent to their claims, and with his surrender dates the last formal attempt or purpose, so far as records show, to sustain the falling dynasty which, since 1638, had essayed its scriptural sway over a people, that with all their theoretic and practical godliness, had nevertheless proved themselves too worldly, if not too wicked for the test.

It now only remained for the general assembly to proceed formally and with authority to "require all householders inhabiting this colony to take the oath of allegiance, and that the administration of justice be in his Majestie's name."

They agreed to "bury in perpetual oblivion" all the former

acts of the New Haven Jurisdiction, which concerned this colony. And it only remained for the New Haven colony to accept the place assigned them by the new charter. In December 1664, they make a conditional submission, and in the following January, finally, and in good faith, accept the charter, and acknowledge thenceforth the supremacy of the Connecticut government.

CHAPTER VI.

INDIAN TREATIES AND HISTORY.

Let us now return after our details of the settlement here by the English, to see what we can learn about the aborigines whom they came to supplant. Our introduction to them shall be through such original records as are still within our reach.

The following papers, six in number, show us the terms on which the Indians alienated their lands. The necessity for so many successive "agreements" or "grants" will appear from the terms of the grants themselves. The first document is a simple acknowledgment, over their own signatures, of the four original proprietors of the soil, that they had disposed of it, for an equivalent, to Capt. Turner; and it is probably the only proof preserved of the original grant by which the settlers came into possession of the territory. We shall give these papers, excepting the sixth, as they are recorded.

(No. 1.)

ACKNOWLEDGMENT OF SALE JULY 1, 1640.

Bought of Ponus, sagamore of Toquams, and of Wascussue, sagamore of Shippan, by mee, Nathaniel Turner, of Quenepiocke, all the grounds that belongs to both the above said sagamores, except a piece of ground* which the above said sagamore of Toquams reserved for his and the rest of said Indians to plant on—all of which grounds being expressed by meadows, upland, grass, with the rivers and trees; and in consideration hereof, I,

* This exception was probably that beautiful headland now owned mainly by Capt. B. L. Waite and the Scofield Brothers, Alfred and Benjamin. This tract, in 1672, was given to the Rev. Eliphalet Jones, then just called to assist the Rev. Mr. Bishop. The terms of the gitt are: "Mr. Jones shall have that peice of land at Wescus whicn was improved by the Engins in case it be cleared from all English and Engins and this land to be Mr. Jones' proper right in lue of that piece of land granted to him on the west side of the Southfield."

RESIDENCE OF BENJAMIN L. WAITE, SOUND VIEW, STAMFORD.

the said Nathaniel Turner, amm to give and bring, or send, to the above said sagamores, within the space of one month, twelve coats, twelve howes, twelve hatchets, twelve glasses, twelve knives, four kettles, four fathom of white wampum : all of which lands bothe we, the said sagamores, do promise faithfully to perform, both for ourselves, heirs, executors, or assigns, and hereunto we have sett our marks in the presence of many of the said Indians, they fully consenting thereto.

Witness, { WILLIAM WILKES,
JAMES ———,

PONUS his mark

OWENOKE, Sagamore Ponus' son

WESCUSSEE his mark

———

pd in part payment 12 glasses
12 knives
04 coats

(No. 2.)

DEED OF THE EASTERN PART OF THE TOWN, 1645.

These presents testify that I, Piamikin, Sagamore of Roatan and owner of all the land lieing between Fivemile river and Pinebrook so called by the English, for diverse reasons and considerations have given and granted unto Andrew Ward and Richard Law of Stamford for the use and property of sayd town, from me and myne to them and theirs forever, all the above sayd lands lying between the sd Fivemile river and Pinebrook, quietly to possess and enjoye in a full and free manner with all the privileges thereto belonging or apertaining, as witness my hand in Stamford this twenty-fourth day of March, anno one thousand six hundred forty and five.

PIAMIKIN, his mark

Witness
JEREMY JAGGER
GEORGE SLASON

WASASARY his mark

PEMGATON his mark

MAMAIEMA his mark

TOQUATUS his mark

(No. 3.)

WARD AND LAW'S REPORT OF DEED OF 1645.

At a general court held at New Haven for ye jurisdiction June 9, 1654—Several writings recorded concerning lands in question betwixt Stamford and Norwalk, which upon the desire of Stamford is ordered to be recorded—this may certify that Piamikee, Sagamore did upon ye twenty-fourth of March in ye year 1645 make a deed of gift of all ye land from that which is comonly called ye Pine brook by ye English and that which is called Five mile river or Rowayton, where their planting land doth come very near unto ye said land, was by a deed of gift made over unto Andrew Ward and Richard Law; which they did receive for ye town of Stamford and at the same time did give unto the said Sagamore one coat in ye presence of George Slason and after yt three more with some quantity of tobaca, and ye said Sagamore did confirm ye same by setting his hand to a writing then made, ye said Sagamore upon ye gift did except against setting houses because ye English hoggs would be ready to spoil their corn, and yt ye cattle in case they come over ye said Five mile river, to which it was granted, yt to inhabit we did not intend, and our cattle we intended they should have a keeper, and in case any hurts was done they should have satisfaction, yt this land as aforesaid was by the said Piamikee in ye presence of other four or five Indians resigned for ever to ye English, in witness whereof we have set to our hands, Stamford, first month 4, 1654.

ANDREW WARD, RICHARD LAW.

(No. 4.)

DEED RENEWED BY PONUS AND ONAX, 1655.

Our agreement made with Ponus, Sagamore of Toquamske and with Onax his eldest son: Altho' there was an agreement made before with the said Indians and Capt. Turner and the purchase paid for, yet the things not being clear, and being very unsatisfied, we came to another agreement with Onax and Ponus for their land from the town plot of Stamford north about 16 miles and there we marked a white oak tree with S. T. and going toward the Mill River side we marked another white oak tree with S. T. and from that tree west we were to run four miles, and from the first marked tree to run four miles eastward, and from this east and west line we are to have further to the north for our cattle to feed, full two miles further, the full breadth—only the said Indians reserve for themselves liberty of their planting ground: and the above said Indians, Ponus and Onax, with all other Indians that be concerned in it have surrendered all the said land to the town of Stamford, as their proper right, forever, and the aforesaid Indians have set their hands as witnessing the truth hereof) and for and in consideration hereof, the said town of Stamford is to give the said Indians 4 coats, which the Indians did accept of for full satisfaction for the aforesaid lands, altho' it was paid before, hereby Ponus' posterity is cut off from making any claim or having any right to any part of the aforesaid land, and do hereby surrender and make over, for us or any of ours forever, unto the Englishmen of the town of Stamford, and their posterity forever, the land as it is butted and bounded the bounds above mentioned. The said Ponus and Onax his son having this day received of Richard Law 4 coats acknowledging themselves fully satisfied for the aforesaid land.—Witness the said Indians the day and date hereof, Stamford, August 15, 1655.

Witnesses
WM NEWMAN
RICHARD LAWS

PONUS. ———.
ONAX. ———.

(No. 5.)

AGREEMENT OF 1667.

An agreement made this 7th of January Anno 1667 between the inhabitants of the town of Stamford, the one party, and Taphance son of Ponus and Powahay son of Onax, son of Ponus, the other party, for a full and final esew of all questions about all and any rights of lands formerly belonging unto Ponus Sagamore of Toquams and any of his race or lineage surviving, and for a more full confirmation of the sales of lands, meadows, rights, privileges formerly made by the foresaid Ponus and Onax unto the inhabitants of the town of Stamford, the contents of this agreement as followeth. That, whereas Ponus Sagamore of Toquams, and Wescus, Sagamore of Shippan, sold unto Capt. Nath'l Turner of Quennipiocke, all their lands belonging to either of the forementioned Ponus and Wescus—the said sale expressing all uplands, meadows, grass, with the rivers and trees belonging to the foresaid Sagamores, except a piece of ground which the foresaid Sagamore of Toquams reserved to plant on—the said sale specified by a deed under their hands; dated the 1st of July anno 1640. Also the payment according to the agreement was made to satisfaction of the foresaid Ponus and Wescus—these forementioned in the deed are sold and alienated from the foresaid Ponus and Wescus and their heirs, executors, administrators and assigns unto the foresaid Capt. Nath'l Turner, and his heirs, executors, administrators and assigns forever—moreover, after this former agreement in the year Anno 1655, the Inhabitants of Stamford and Ponus Sagamore, and Onax, Sagamore came to an agreement, for the convenient settlement of their planting ground at Shehauge, as also how far the bounds of the inhabitants of Stamford should go, which joint agreement was to extend sixteen miles north from the sea side at Stamford; and two miles short of that the said parties marked two trees with S T; the aforesaid Ponus and Onax agreeing and granted the inhabitants of Stamford that their bounds should run from the aforesaid marked trees four miles east, and from the foresaid marked trees four miles west; their whole breadth to be eight miles and for full satisfaction of the foresaid Ponus and Onax for all and every part of tho lands with the Demensions thereof forementioned and the Indian's planting Land excepted, four coats was paid and accepted by the said Indians viz: Ponas and Onax, upon which receipt the said Ponus and Onax gave a full surrender of all the land forementioned from them and their heirs, executors, administrators, and assigns, and in the behalf of all the Indians unto the English Inhabitants of Stamford and their heirs, executors, and administrators, and assigns for ever, quietly to possess and enjoy in free and full manner. Unto this agreement the Indians forementioned viz: Ponus and Onax subscribed their mark for full confirmation, witnessed by Richard Law and William Newman. Now these presents witnesseth, that we Taphance, son of Ponus and Powahay son of Onax as abovementioned, do hereby acknowledge the several grants and sales of lands and the several agreements thereabouts as above specified with the payment for satisfaction given for the same, and do hereby for us and ours fully confirm the said grants and sales with the dimensions thereof as above specified—furthermore we the foresaid Taphance and Powahay do hereby both for us and our heirs, executors administrators and assigns, grant and surrender up unto the inhabitants of the town of Stamford their heirs, executors administrators and assigns forever all our land or lands formerly reserved to us for planting at Shehauge and Hoquetch with all other lands of any sort and privileges of any kind to us and our predecessors formerly belonging; the said lands and privileges lying between Tatomock near Greenwich on the west and the land formerly granted by Piamikin to the men of Stamford on the east with the forementioned dimensions of length and breadth; Quietly to possess and enjoy without future molestation by us and ours—In consideration hereof the inhabitants of Stamford do both for themselves and theirs give and grant unto the foresaid Taphance and Powahay and their male issue and posterity twenty acres planting ground in convenient place or places—with these conditions following agreed unto—first, that the said Indians fence their ground with a sufficient fence—secondly, that they shall not at any time take in other Indians or Indian to reside with them—thirdly—only Taphance with his wife and children ;and Penahay and Paharron and an old woman called Nowattonnamanssqua are allowed—thirdly that neither Taphance nor Penahay, nor any of theirs shall at any time sell, or any way directly or indirectly make over or transfer the said twenty acres of land or any part thereof to any; but if the said Taphance and they shall desert and leave the said land, or if in case the said Taphance and Penahay their male issue and posterity shall cease and extinguish, then the forementioned 20 acres of land shall fall to the inhabitants of Stamford, emediately without any further consideration, as their proper right; fourthly, the foresaid

Taphance and Penehay both for themselves and theirs do hereby bind and engage themselves unto a *dew* and orderly subjection to all town orders of Stamford and the laws of the jurisdiction that are or shall be made from time to time and for the true performance of the foresaid covenants and agreements respectively the parties abovementioned do hereby bind themselves and theirs firmly. In witness of truth they have hereto set their hands the day and date above written.

Signed and delivered in presence of		In behalf of Stamford.
Richard Beach	TAPHANCE ——	Richard Law
John Embrey	PENAHAY ——	Francis Bell
Samuel Mills		George Slason
		Jonathan Selleck
		John Holly

[No. 6.]

CONFIRMATION OF GRANTS, ABOUT 1700.

Still later, about the year 1700, as its locality in the records would indicate, we find still another agreement with the Indians. Catoona and Coee confirm all the previous grants of territory to the English, "westward as far as Bedford." They acknowledge the receipt of "considerable and valuable sums of money. They make special mention of deeds or grants made to the English, by Taphassee, Ponus, Penehays, old Onax, young Onax, a deed to Capt. Turner, and also a deed by Hawatonaman, which our records have not preserved. The following witnesses attest the acknowledgment:

John Eye alias John Caukee		Catona
Pohornes	Awaricus	Capt. Manin
Renohoctam	Mockea	Wequacumak
Ramhorne	Papakuma	Aquamana
Smingo	Simorn	Pupiamak
Amtaugh		

The preceding papers constitute nearly all the recorded witness that we have to the number and character of the original proprietors of the soil. They report to us the names of some thirty of the most honored of the Indians here. But they teach us very little respecting these signers themselves, and still less respecting the tribes they represent. They only go to show that when the white race were in need of these old Indian realms the red race had been made ready to alienate them. They suggest that the great leaders whose prowess had won for them Sachem dominion and honors had all passed away. What names, illustrious for gifts of Indian eloquence or for deeds of Indian daring, may once have ruled here; of how extensive and populous empire this may have been the seat; how long the old races may have here held sway; or whence they had come to these wild shores; all are questions which no records can ever answer. And then the number of the Indians who occupied the territory settled as Stamford will probably never be known. It could not have been very large. Petty chiefs and mere fragments of what might once have been small tribes of their race, were all that the historian can find to reward his most diligent search.

Yet it must not be inferred that the Stamford colony escaped the hazards, or were altogether strangers to the startling incidents of Indian neighborhood. There was enough of the savage left to suggest what savage life was, when it had entire sway over the country. There was enough of Indian cunning and power left to make the pale face constantly wary and fearful. It would have been no easy task to subdue here the wildness of the forest and its beasts of prey; it was doubly difficult and hazardous to live in constant exposure to the stealthy movements of suspicious and suspected savages.

The settlement of Stamford succeeded the complete overthrow of the most spirited and formidable tribe within the limits of Connecticut; and the utter dismemberment of the Pequods had struck surviving tribes and clans with a wholesome terror of the white man's power.

The eastern part of the State had been pretty effectually delivered from all danger from the savages. The Mohegans now left, with Uncas their chief, were henceforth, as the most politic course, to count themselves as the white man's friends; and in that part of the State it would be a contest between hostile tribes of the natives rather than between the aborigines and the immigrant colonies. In the western part of the State were many tribes, the most of which were inferior in numbers and either faint or reckless in spirit, and they were more likely to burn with revenges against their formidable enemies towards the West, the fierce Mohawks, than against the more harmless pale faces, who were quietly locating themselves here and there upon the hunting grounds of their race.

Still the red man could not be expected to see himself steadily alienating the ancestral possessions of his race, steadily wasting away before the increasing colonies of a people whom he thoroughly despised, without some struggling against so humiliating a destiny. Accordingly, the period of colonial settlements throughout New England, was also a period of constant collision between the immigrant and the aboriginal races. The very year in which our pioneers were taking possession of Rippowam, was marked by one of those combinations of Indian strategy, whose aim was the forcible expulsion from Connecticut soil of the last pale face to be found.

The plot disclosed by a neighboring Sachem to Mr. Ludlow, of Uncowa, (Fairfield), and by a Long Island Indian, to Mr. Eaton, of New Haven, and by still another native on the Connecticut, warned the few colonies in time to avert the threatened doom. While a portion of the Stamford settlers are on their way to their new home, the General Court of Connecticut find themselves called upon to issue the following orders:

"It is Ordered, that there shall be a letter writ fro the Courte to the Bay to further the prsecution of the Indeans, to pr'uent their mischevus plotte in their late Combination."

"It is Ordered that there shall be a gard of 40 men to com compleate in their Arms to the meeting every Sabbath and lecture day, in every Towne within these liberties vppon the River."

The combination referred to in these orders was the last formidable attempt of the great Miantonomo of the Narragansetts; Sequassen, the patriot Sachem of the Connecticut River; and the jealous and revengeful Sequin, to save their name and possessions from the sudden extinction which they foresaw.

In the same year, so imminent had the danger become, that the Court interdicted all traffic with the Indians except by permission of two magistrates; no smith was to work for an

Indian; two wardsmen were to be appointed in every town within their jurisdiction to give notice of any sudden danger that may come upon the plantations; a competent number of men should remain in every town daily for its defense; and "90 coats should be provided within ten days, basted with cotton wool and made defensive against Indian arrowes."

It was in the midst of such alarms that Stamford was settled; and we may be assured that it required no little nerve to attempt, and no ordinary prudence and courage to effect the settlement.

In the territory itself were traces of at least four distinct clans. On the west side of the purchase, with his seat not far from where the line now separates the town from Greenwich, was the bold and warlike Mayano, with his vindictive band of warriors, already experienced in the conflict, both with savage and civilized foes. Whence they had come, or how many they might count, we shall never know; we shall soon see that they or our sturdy pioneers must ere long maintain the possession by the stout heart and arm.

Further to the East, with his princely residence overlooking both the bays which inclose our finest headland, was Wascussue, Lord of Shipan. Not as spirited as Mayano, he seemed to linger with a handful of his tribe, in a sort of princely repose upon the fair field which his more youthful arm had won, unwilling to leave the charming heritage which in his sadness he saw now for the first time seriously invaded.

Still farther towards the rising sun and beyond the lovely Noroton bay, was the empire of Piamikin, whose deed of alienation makes him Sagamore of Roatan, and whose jealous eye guarded the hunting and fishing grounds, as after him our Stamford colony did, out to the waters of the babbling Rowalton, (Five Mile River.)

On the north of these sea-washed realms, lay the more extended realms of Ponus. From his ancestors he had received the wooded hills and brook-washed vales that stretch far away to the north until they are lost in the forests which even the red men did not claim—a wild border ground between the eastern and the western tribes; and he hoped to hand them all over to his idol, Powahay, the bright faced son of his first-born Onax. But the old patriarch of his wasting tribe, saw his warriors fade and perish as if touched with the power of his own decay, and he yielded gracefully to the stern necessity. He lived to sign with his own hand the deed which forever alienated from himself and heirs, "all the uplands, meadows and grass, with the rivers and trees," that had once been his rejoicing and his pride.

These four clans, under these leaders, with perhaps a few fugitives from other scattered tribes, temporarily living here in their isolated independency, constituted the only aborigines within the limits of Stamford, with whom the new colony had to contend. Occasionally other tribes would sweep across the town and leave in their track of terror some witness to their ferocity. Single Indians would now and then steal in upon the unsuspecting settlers and startle them with some threatened or accomplished revenge.

While the second company of the colony were locating themselves, a tragedy was enacted, a little to the west of the town, which for a while threatened the very existence of the new community. Some of the Dutch traders had stripped an Indian who had been tempted by them to drink too much, of a valuable dress of beaver skins. On recovering from his drunken fit, the insulted red man revenged himself by killing two Dutchmen, and fled to feast his memory with the great revenge among a distant tribe. He could not be found. The Dutch governor at New Amsterdam, Kieft, sought an opportunity to punish the Indians for the revengeful deed. The next winter the Mohawks fell upon two of the Hudson river tribes, and after killing their warriors, scattered the remnant in utter destitution to find food and shelter from the piercing cold among the Dutch on the South. The time for a civilized revenge had now come; and at the instigation of Kieft, with the sanction of his counselors, more than a hundred of those helpless fugitives from their savage foe, were sent from their quiet sleep on earth to the spirit world of their race, by a blow from the Dutch soldiers, so sudden that they could not even beg for life.

Then Indian blood was stirred. Savage vengeance awoke. With almost electric despatch, Indian warrior pledged to Indian warrior, and clan to clan, the direst vengeance on their foe. "More than fifteen hundred warriors," according to De Forest, rallied from the confederacy of eleven clans, to constitute this avenging army. "A fierce war blazed wherever a Dutch settlement was to be found; on Long Island and on Manhattan, along the Connecticut aud along the Hudson." From Manhattan to Stamford the coast was desolated, Dutch and English alike, atoning to the inexorable spirit of Indian revenge, for the needless injuries that had been heaped upon the Indian's race.

The white race were in the ascendant. Their arms were more than a match for the red man's muscle; their science triumphed over his cunning; and the desperate Indian had only the fiendish pleasure of dealing in his death struggles, now and then, an avenging blow.

Within hearing distance of the Stamford settlement* were three Dutch settlers who had excited the wrath of the restless and brave Mayano. He nobly met them, armed as they were, with his bow and arrows and brought two of them to the ground. The third only saved himself by a well-directed blow which laid the fearless savage at his feet; and the daring of the fallen Sachem had made the extermination of his tribe a necessity to the safety of the whites. A company of soldiers were immediately dispatched to capture them. At Greenwich they were directed by Capt. Patrick to the rendezvous of the maddened Indians, but on reaching it not a soul could be found. Proceeding on into the Stamford settlement they find Patrick with his own former comrade in arms, our Captain John Underhill. They immediate suspect him of having given the Indians notice of their approach. They taunt him with the treachery.

*Between Greenwich and Stamford.—O'Callaghan.

He who had led his trusty men so successfully against the bravest of the New England savages, could not brook such insolence from Dutchmen, even though in arms. He contemptuously spat in the face of their leader and turned to walk away. A pistol ball brought him to the ground in death, and the Dutchmen returned to the pursuit of their savage foe.

Underhill, who had been no friend to the Dutch settlers, now sympathized with their mortal hatred of the Indian enemy. He had already signalized his bravery in the Pequod war. His was already a name of terror to Indians far and near; and to his presence our Stamford colony had doubtless owed their comparative exemption thus far from savage invasions. It was no time for him to rest inactive when his friends and neighbors were exposed every hour to some sudden and relentless massacre. He offered his services to the Dutch governor, and was at once sent into the field. The troublesome Indians about Stamford were the first to feel his power. With one hundred and thirty men he started from New Amsterdam, on a cold and cloudy morning in the February of 1644. They were able to land at Greenwich Point, that evening, in a furious storm. With the early dawn of the next morning the resolute Captain was again on the march. All day did the sturdy Dutch soldiers, under their valiant leader, plod their toilsome way through the snow, until, at eight in the evening, they had reached the vicinity of the hostile camp. Soon the clouds gave way, and a clear, bright moon, flashing from the snowy crystals, lighted their way to their horrid work. By a little after ten they filed round the Southern spur of a ridge, stretching toward the Northwest, and the village, a tripple range of wigwams, lay reposing before them, awaiting their attack. With marvelous celerity, the captain circles the doomed village with his trusty men. Now spring upon them, as hounds unleashed upon their prey, the stalwart forms of more than a hundred warriors, all prepared for their death grapple with the foe. But neither their sudden rush, nor their wild war-cry, could intimidate their assailants. Coolly they are received, a tenth of them captured, and the rest impetuously hurled back. For a whole hour the unrelenting struggle went on. A hundred and thirty men wrestled in mortal strife with more than five hundred of the enemy, and when the doomed Indians were at length driven back within their lines of defense, one hundred and eighty of their fallen comrades were already still and stiffening in the blood stained snow. Nor would they yet raise the flag of truce, or cry for quarter. Each undaunted spirit, left beneath such shelter as his own or his neighbor's wigwam could give, continued the fight. This was the opportunity for which Underhill was prepared. He called for fire. Torches lighted the wigwams. Indian men, women, and children, issuing from their burning homes, were driven back to perish in the flames. Before the morning dawned, more than five hundred, who, the night before, had gone to their usual rest, were now sleeping their last sleep with the unconscious dead.

By noon, of the next day, the victors had already reached Stamford, on their way home, having in this signal chastisement of the Indians of this neighborhood, secured the perpetual peace of the English settlements. From this time there would be no gathering of clans and tribes against the now victorious white race. Occasional depredations and stealthy and assassin stabs, now and then, from some treacherous or revengeful red man, would be the only further harm the colonists in this vicinity would have to fear.

Not long was it before an illustration was given of the savage revenge which burned among the neighboring Indians. Just to the north of the village, a family by the name of Phelps had just located themselves. The husband had left the house one morning, in the fall of 1644, leaving his wife, with an infant child at home. An Indian, who had already made himself somewhat notorious for his hatred of the English, had seen the husband leave, and knew the defenseless condition of his family. He gloried in such an opportunity for vengeance. Entering the house, he took up a hatchet lying upon the floor, and when the mother bent herself, as a sheltering angel over her defenseless babe, he savagely buried it in her brain. After plundering the house he left.

Again the settlers were aroused. They felt that there was no safety for them. They rallied in large numbers to search for the Indian. They sent messengers to New Haven and Hartford for assistance; and were determined to avenge the deed so signally as to hinder the repetition of it among them. Meanwhile, Mrs. Phelps, who survived the blow which the Indian thought to be fatal, rallied so far as to enable her to describe the assassin. He was at once recognized. His tribe were at length prevailed on to give him up. He was taken to New Haven for trial, and sentenced to death by decapitation. Now, Busheag, the convicted savage, showed the fearlessness and more than stoic endurance of his Indian heart. He showed no sign of concern for himself, none of sorrow for his deed. He asked no pardon, he simulated no regret. He promised no suppression of his hate or his vengeance. He looked his executioner sternly in the face, as he unflinchingly received the repeated blows which severed his head from his body.

The execution of Busheag, following so soon the signal overthrow of the Indians to the west of the town, rendered the surviving Indians more cautious and peaceful. They made a formal treaty of peace with the English, and pledged a due observance of every usage of good neighborhood. They who could not endure the humiliation stole away, some of them to live for a while among the Ridgefield Indians, to the north, and others penetrated still further into the unbroken wilderness of the west.

During this period the utmost caution was used among the settlers, to avoid exciting or provoking the Indians. No man was allowed to furnish intoxicating liquors to them, under heavy penalty. And in 1648, at the Stamford court, it was also ordered "yt non shall ether sell or give any of our English doggs unto ye Indians at ye displeasure of ye courte."

Yet no forbearance or caution on the part of the intruders upon these Indian domains, could long secure their immunity from Indian revenge. The Indian felt that he and his race were losing ground; and it is not to be wondered at, that his hitherto unbroken spirit should rouse his utmost endeavors to regain it.

In the autumn of 1649, a new tragedy was enacted in Stamford. John Whitmore, one of the most respectable of the settlers, who had already won a good name here, left his house one morning to look for his cattle in the common grounds to the west of the village. He never returned. The utmost excitement prevailed throughout the settlement. The most diligent search brought no clue to the discovery of the body. Messengers were sent in every direction. Help was summoned from New Haven and Hartford, but the search and help were of no avail.

The perplexity and apprehension occasioned by this mysterious disappearance were very extensive. The general court at Hartford made it an occasion of serious deliberation. They felt that none of the colonists, in any of the Connecticut settlements, would be secure, if such surprises were to be possible. They enter on their record this minute, as expressive of their convictions of what was due themselves in the perilous crisis:

"This courte, taking into serious consideration what may bee done according to God in way of revenge of the blood of John Whitmore, late of Stamford, and well weighing all circumstances, together with the carriages of the Indians (bordering therevppon,) in and about the premises: doe declare themselves that they doe judge it lawfull and according to God to make war vppon them. This courte desires Mr. Deputy, Mr. Ludlow and Mr. Taylecoat to ride to-morrow to New Haven and conferr with Mr. Eaton and the rest of the magistrates there about sending out against the Indians, and to make returne of their apprehensions with what convenient speed they may."

Meanwhile the search for the body of Mr. Whitmore was going on. By a providential arrangement, Uncas, the great Mohegan, who for years had now been the politic friend of the whites, was now, with a band of his clear-sighted warriors, in this vicinity. So unusual was such a visitation, as to leave the impression that his main object in the expedition was to aid the Stamford men in their search. To this he might easily have been induced by the Connecticut colony; and to this he set himself earnestly and successfully to work.

As, nominally at least, sachem over the tribe whose limits had once embraced all this territory, he spoke with some show of authority. Assembling the neighboring Indians, he demanded of them the body of the murdered man. Taphance, the son of Ponus, and Rehoron his subject, both of whom had been suspected as being either the principals in the murderous deed, or chief instigators to it, now feeling the pressure of Indian resolution and fearing the consequences of further endeavors to mask themselves in the presence of these sharp-eyed and now suspecting detectives, led the way into the woods directly to the mangled remains.

It would seem that this would have been sufficient to justify the prompt arrest of these two suspected guides. It is true they denied having any hand in the murder. They had previously charged it upon Toquattoes, an Indian who had come down from among or near the maddened Mohawks, with a deep revenge in his soul, to be appeased by the scalp of some white man. Meeting Whitmore alone and without defense, he had satisfied his vengeance against the race by his sudden death, and escaped beyond their knowledge and pursuit. But from the day of the murder, whenever questioned by the neighbors, these two neighboring and now suspected Indians, had shown the deepest concern and fear; and now, while leading the way to the remains, which had already lain three months concealed, they are seized with a terror which makes them pale with fear, if not with conscious guilt. And yet the authorities allowed them to escape. They concealed themselves so effectually as to elude the officers of justice for several years.

At length, in October, 1662, Taphance is brought before the

Court of Magistrates, held in New Haven, on a warrant issued by the governor. The trial is detailed at length in the New Haven Colonial Records, transcribed and published by Charles J. Hoadley, pages 458—463. The court decided that there was strong grounds of suspicion against Taphance. His own acknowledgment, his trembling, his stealing away after promising help in searching for the murderer, his suspicious looks and actions before Uncas, were in evidence against him. The testimony of Mr. Whitmore's wife and children as to his fawning manner on the very day of Mr. Whitmore's murder, was also in proof. The testimony of Mr. Law and John Mead, who were together when he came to Mr. Law's the second morning after the murder, and the testimony of Richard Ambler and Goodman Jessop, who also saw and heard Taphance at Mr. Law's, was in proof. These agreeing testimonies influenced the court to decide, "that in ye whole there stands a blot vpon him of suspicion; that there was sufficient grounds for his aprehending and comitting to durance, and all that he hath said at this time canot clear him of a stain of suspicion; but as being guilty of ye murder, directly or accessory, he did pronounce him not guilty in point of death; but yet must declare him to stand bound to pay all charges that hath been about him and leave him guilty of suspicion; and that he stands bound as his duty to doe his best endeavour to obtain ye murderer, and now to remain in durance vntill ye next session of ye court, about a fortnight hence, except he can give some assurance of his payinge the charge before, which charge was concluded to be ten pound."

Taphance accepted the judgment of the court and promised to do his best towards securing the murderer. He pleaded his poverty and asked to have his chains removed, pledging himself not to run away under forfeiture of his life. Upon which he was set at liberty, after providing to appear at the next court.

No further mention of the case appears on record. The spirited contest between the New Haven and Connecticut jurisdictions had now commenced, and probably directed the attention of the court from all less important matters; and when, in 1665, the Connecticut had asserted its authority over the New Haven colony, there was probably no need of further prosecuting the now harmless Indians. Yet, as the following record shows, the contest had imposed upon the infant colony a burden they were still to bear. And that they did not shrink from acknowledging the claims of those who defended them against the wily savage our records abundantly attest. The following is a sample of this testimony:

"In December, 1667, the town granted Jonathan Silleck a piece of land on the west side of the landing place, beginning at Hardy's Hole, as a reward for his meritorious services while engaged against the common enemy."

Evidently the neighboring Indians never again became so formidable as to disturb the quiet or arouse seriously the fears of the town. Throughout the century our citizens were occasionally called upon to aid in punishing Indians elsewhere, and that they did good service when thus engaged we find occasional proofs in our records.

Once more, indeed, our townsmen were somewhat apprehensive of danger from a foray of savages. Philip, of the Pokanokets, the brave son of brave old Massasoit, had witnessed with increasing sorrow the inroads which the English were making into the cherished hunting grounds of his dwindling race. He could not endure it, thus to bear the doom which was settling upon him. He rebelled against his fate. He resolved to regain his alienated grounds, and bring to the dust the pale-faced invader of his ancestral rights. He maddened every Indian heart within his reach to an Indian's revenge; and the English settlers, from the Kennebeck to the Hudson, began to see and feel the avenging desolations of a remorseless Indian war. Driven from his peninsular home, the outraged chieftain, swift as the winds, yet noiseless as the flight of swallows in the air, moves from wigwam to wigwam, and from tribe to tribe, drawing even the hitherto peaceful Narragansett into the current of his remorseless revenge, embittering the concealed but now inexorable hate of the Nipmuc, the Hadley and Springfield, and all the Connecticut river Indians, and even those still further west; until, within six weeks, he had pledged almost the last stout heart and arm of Indian warrior over all the territory he had traversed, to one final, terrible blow against the invaders of his domain. He had done all that Indian cunning, and eloquence, and hate could do, and he and his awaited the issue of the struggle. Their great, grand war-dance, ending in their wild war-cry, left them no alternative, but the utter extermination of themselves or their foe. June 24, 1675, had now come. The war torch was lighted at Swansey; and no less than twenty-four of its peaceful citizens poured forth their life-blood, only to whet to keener relish the thirst of the savage murderers. Suddenly, town after town was surprised; and to the horror of their burning was everywhere added that of an indiscriminating and unsparing massacre. Brookfield, Deerfield, Hadley, Northfield, Springfield, Lancaster, Medfield, Weymouth, Groton, Marlborough, Warwick and Providence were successively attacked.

It was during the progress of these desolations of savage warfare that our townsmen became again alarmed. No immediate attack was threatened, but neither had the slightest signal foretokened the fate of either of the above named towns; and still, at a moment when they least expected it, the fire and the tomahawk were doing among them their terrible work and their doom was written in letters of blood. And why may it not be so here was the anxious inquiry of our unguarded townsmen.

That a practical answer was made to such an inquiry is shown in the following record:

"In March 1672, Francis Bell, Francis Brown, and John Green were appointed a committee to treat with the 'Engins,' and understand what they have to say to the town, and to make return of what they have to say to the town, that the said Indians may receive an answer from the town."

What report this committee made is not to be found on record. That it did not allay the fears which had been excited, the following records of a later date wlll show. The first of these is found in a letter, dated Stamford, Dec. 29, 1673, and directed to the General Court at Boston. It was intended as an earnest plea for help:

"Wherefore, in expectation of the armies coming against this open declared enemy we have been hitherto silent, but by the long retard and no intelligence upon any prosecution upon that account we are afraid (it) is laid aside, whereby we shall be much endangered if not ruined, if your honors do not by some speedy means relieve us, for we are frontiers and most likely assaulted in the first place."

The above plea for help seems to have been made jointly by Stamford, Greenwich and Rye. Again, on the tenth of October, 1675, governor Andros sends word to the governor at Hartford that five or six thousand Indians are in league and ready to fall upon Greenwich, Hartford and other places still further east at the next full moon.

On the nineteenth of the same month he sends word that it is rumored that the Stamford Indians are in arms; and he commends the colonists in the state for putting themselves "in a fitting posture for all events." What this means we may learn from our records, which show that in March 1675 '6, Mr. Bell, sen., John Green, Peter Ferris, John Bates and Daniel Weed were chosen to attend to the work of fortification, according to the order of the council; and another vote requires that the stockading of the town shall be fully finished.

Under date of Sept. 22, 1676, we find the following vote: "The town agrees that all those soldiers that went out upon service, out of Stamford, against the common enemy, shall have land of the town; namely, all that did service." In carrying this vote into effect, the town then voted the following persons these lands: to Serg. Daniel Wescott, one and a half acre home lot on the north side of Joseph Webb's lot. and that swamp by the flood gate; to Thomas Lawrence an acre and a half house lot on the south side of Joseph Webb's, to be laid out, having due respect to the highway; to Samuel Hoyt, Increase Holly, David Waterbury, Obadiah Seely, John Waterbury, Thomas Newman, Joseph Fish, Obadiah Stevens, Benjamin Stevens, John Jagger, Moses Knapp, Daniel Ferris, Jonathan Seeley, Joseph Jones and William Penoyer, severally, house lots for their services.

At the end of the list is this record: "the town doth give unto John Green two house lots for his sons, next to Abraham Ambler's front, which homelots were given as they were soldiers."

In Dec. 1677, the town votes to Capt. Jonathan Sellick, "as was upon service against the common enemy, all that piece of land lying upon the west side of the landing place, beginning at the mouth of the brook commonly called Hardy's Hole, in length to the Southfield fence."

The only other local record which refers to these local struggles with the Indians are those in which, occasionally, a citizen asks for an appropriation for his services. The last of these claims was preferred in 1692, when Joshua Hait asks for a piece of land on account of his going out, a soldier, against the common inimy;" and two acres in the ox pasture were given him "as a gratuity for his good service in the late war." At the same time a piece of land is "layed out" to Simon Chapman, probably for the same reason.

Already our townsmen had felt themselves relieved of further danger so that they might safely order a final disarmament as the following record shows.

"18 Dec. 1695, per vote outcry the town doth sell the fort wood about ye meeting house to Stephen Clason for seventeen shillings and ninepence." "The town by outcry doth sell ye fort gates ye wheels of ye great guns and all ye wood belonging to ye guns it is now sold to Nathanall Cross and Jonathan Holly for five shillings and sixpence."

And who shall say that such was not a worthy disposal of the last witnesses to the struggles which the pioneers of the town encountered, with the race that had now almost entirely disappeared.

CHAPTER VII.

ECCLESIASTICAL, 1640–1746.

That the founders of this ancient town were men of religious principle, and that at the commencement of their settlement here they had an ecclesiastical organization, needs no labored proof. Their leader was a minister of religion. The church was the sacred body they were here to preserve, and the society was only the appointed means for her preservation. Whether fewer or more of the settlers here were of the select and honored company of the saints, all felt themselves to be the authorized defenders, and all were practically the cheerful supporters of the church. Had not the most of them left their homes in the fatherland from the love they bore the church? Had they not already attested by their patient and heroic suffering their devotion to the church? And was not their very mission hither an attempt to establish the church, where in purity and simple faith she might train her children by her simple and holy rituals for the service of her divine Lord?

We may never know how many of the first settlers were actually members of the church when they came here. That the most of them were afterwards united with it is more than probable. The first church of Stamford had already been organized in Wethersfield. Of the seven men who constituted the Wethersfield church, we have seen that four came to Stamford. These were the Rev. Richard Denton, who became the pastor of the church when transferred to Stamford, Jonas Weed, Robert Coe and Andrew Ward. It is probable that others of the Wethersfield party, immediately on the separation, attached themselves to the new body. How many of them may have done so, or how soon, no existing records probably will ever reveal.

But, whether larger or smaller, the church was the center and soul of the new society here formed; so much so, that of all the organizations formed, that only which had for its specific aim the care and maintenance of the temporalities of the church, came to claim for itself the title of "The Society." And so, in the view of those days, the very term society seemed to mean that visible company whose most characteristic object is the preservation and welfare of the militant church. To this organization every voting man among our Stamford settlers belonged. For its support every freeholder contributed, and this, at first, not from compulsion, but rather as a matter of course. The social necessity for it was as valid and potent as any legislative enactment could be. In Stamford, as in other of the early Connecticut towns, the church edifice was one of the first to be built. Though the local records of that transaction are now gone probably beyond recovery, we do not need to attest the fact. We may see the form of that rude meeting house, not many rods from where the present Congregational Church now stands, almost as distinctly as though it were standing there still. Square built and low; its posts scarcely a dozen feet in length; its four roofs meeting over the centre at a hight not much less than thirty feet; one generous door on the front opening into an area which was undivided by partition, and unseated save with rude benches around the three sides looking toward the minister's stand; unadorned by art of sculpture or of painting, and never relieved of summer sun by blinds, or of keenest winter's cold by furnace or stove.

Eyes that did not fear the light and stoutly beating hearts that could not well be chilled, were to be provided for in that primitive place for worship; yet neither the movable curtain, suspended as the movement of the sun might require, nor the tin hand-stove with its solid coals taken right from the great hearth-stone at home, was deemed needless or intrusive. No bell rang out its Sabbath call from that untowered house, but when occasion called for it, the beat of drum never failed to line the only paths that met at its door; and so, more promptly than now, the gathered congregation were awaiting the solemn and reverent invocation with which the minister was wont to open the important service of the day.

There was sanctity in those rude materials of that pioneer house. Hallowed place was that, where the man of God stood his two hours each Sabbath morning, and two hours more each Sabbath afternoon to feed those hardy pioneers with the bread of life. Solid thoughts were those which could minister to such hearers amid such surroundings. Nor has more acceptable worship been paid to Him who dwelleth in temples not made with hands, in any of the costlier sanctuaries whose graceful spires and polished altars and cushioned seats have since that day borne witness to the spiritual glory and power of that first house of the Lord in Stamford.

One, only incident detracted from the pleasant and grateful memories of that house. Tradition has it, and in this case the witness is so respectable as to justify the record of it on these pages, that when the assembled pioneers in our settlement had reached the point in the raising of the building, of fastening together the heavy timbers over its center, a lad, the son of one of the principal citizens, was sent up to insert the key pin. He bravely mounted to the perilous hight and his nerve failed. "Which of the holes shall I put the pin in, father;" asked the lad, with wavering tones. "O, my God!" exclaims the agonized father, "my child is dead."

Turning suddenly over and falling headlong, that little boy had sealed with his instant death, his deep interest in that house for his parents' worship, almost before the father could give that passionate expression to his agonized heart.

Nor was that rude and uninviting meeting house allowed to

be neglected. Every settler here was expected to report himself and his family each Lord's day. And on no account could the people consent to have its door closed when that holy day, the Puritan's only holiday, called them to worship. If the minister was sick, had they not men of "gifts in prayer," who could "orderly lead them" in every act of reverent and acceptable worship? Should the minister leave them, need they abandon their "altar of hope?" We shall see. Scarcely three years had passed over the colony before some disagreement between the minister and the people led to his removal. And what can this isolated people do? There were no ministers as now within calling distance in readiness to fill such openings. Coming together, after much deliberation and prayer, the people selected two of their most trustworthy number, Lieut. Francis Bell and George Slauson, furnished them with food for the way, and sent them on foot to Boston to see if they could not find one John Bishop, whose name had been reported to them, or some minister whom they could persuade to come back with them, that so this people might not be scattered and "suffered to sin against the ordinances of God."

They providentially find Mr. Bishop, then a young man, on whom was the seal of consecration and of promise, and with much persuasion, they prevailed on him to accept this pressing call from the Lord. Taking his staff and his well-used Bible in his hand, he starts with the two brethren for the field of his labors; and the meeting house thenceforth, as long as it stands, bears weekly witness to his faithful and acceptable labors.

Twenty eight years did that house magnify its office. The fathers of the town had most of them gone from its instruction to their final rest. One generation of children had been nurtured by its ministries up to a mature and vigorous manhood. One generation of adults had been made strong and patient to endure the service and fulfill the high responsibilities of their manly years. And so, after its noble work was done, that sanctuary of the fathers gave way to another.

But the rest and prosperity of the church during these twenty-eight years was not uninterrupted. Their minister found his work seriously hindered by the many trials incident to pioneer life. It was with the people a season of extreme physical activity. Their physical wants were all to be supplied—their homes were to be built—their lands must be cleared. Roads must be cut through hitherto pathless woods; and all those conveniences which, ordinarily, one generation finds prepared for them by the preceding, these fathers of Stamford had to gather about their new homes by the most unwearied industry.

Besides, the privations and discomforts incident to such a life are not helpful to a true social or spiritual culture. They try the tempers and often seriously compromise the manners of those who experience them. And their influence is still more disastrous upon the condition and character of that generation of children that are molded by them. The very rudeness and savagery of a wilderness home would reach the spirit and rule to some extent, at least, the manners of any community exposed to them. There is philosophy, as well as fact, in the sharply defined thesis of Dr. Bushnell, that barbarism is the first danger of colonization. Even when the leaders of such a community are men of culture and refinement, the very hazards and chances and excitements of the life itself will draw into it the restless and adventurous and unprincipled.

It would be very remarkable, if among so many men as settled at Stamford, there should be none who were impulsive, wayward and insubordinate. In the local government, committed to the settlers, it would be very strange if there were not diversity of views, both as to the ends to be secured, and the methods of securing them. It would be strange if religion itself, which pledges eventually the peace and millenium of the world should not prove in such a community a source of alienations and of earnest conflict; and especially when, as in this case, its professors alone were to hold all the responsible and coveted offices in the people's gift.

Besides, in the case of our Stamford settlers, there were special reasons inducing disturbance. Their previous discipline had been amid the conflict of an exciting strife. They were, themselves, protestants, and among protestants, they had achieved divisions. What more could be expected from them than that sharp divisions should arise, and that heated and obstinate maintenance of perpetual views and opinions would end in new animosity and feuds? When the leading men who composed the new community had already rendered themselves obnoxious to the civil power in the colony from which they had come, as several of them had, who could hope that they would carry everything along in quiet, in the colony they were to form?

That there were immoral and dangerous men among the settlers, is manifest from repeated records. That great trials came upon the church, testing the patience and faith of the minister and his brethren, is also apparent. The first great division of this body in 1644, already recorded in a preceding chapter, though mainly a political movement, is in proof. The contest with the Quaker element is still another proof. And after these temporary settlements,still other troubles introduced themselves, to such extent as to threaten more serious disaster to the usefulness and existence of the church.

At the May session of the general court in New Haven in 1659, report is brought that Mr. Bishop at Stamford finds so much discouragement that he thinks of leaving his post. The court refer to Mr. Bell, then one of the deputies from Stamford for his account of the matter. He acknowledged the existence of evils, but thinks the pastor should be sustained and encouraged. After giving the report due attention, the court declared that if no reformation should be reported from Stamford, they would send down a commission to examine the case, ascertain the cause of the complaints, and remove whatever may "hinder the work of God" under Mr. Bishop's care, adding this quaint reason for their decision: "for if the ministry and ordinances fall, what will the people do?"

The same case appears again in the October court of magistrates. Mr. Bishop, in the presence of two of the brethren of the church, made a formal statement of the "uncomfortable unsettled state of the affairs of the church and town." The court advised and ordered: that on returning home, they should seek, within twenty days, some effectual course of making a satisfactory settlement of their difficulties among themselves. They were then to forward to court a certified record of such a settlement. If they could not effect the settlement, within that time, two of the magistrates and two of the elders, (pastors), should be sent down before winter, if the weather should prove suitable; if not, then early in the spring, to help towards the settlement.

In May, 1660, at the request of Mr. Bishop, the general court desired Rev. Mr. Davenport, of New Haven, and Pierson, of Guilford, to go to Stamford "to afford their counsel and help for the well settling of their church affairs." These elders were to have "a man to attend upon them at the jurisdiction charge, excepting expenses at Stamford, which were to be paid by the Stamford people. I have found no record of the meeting held in Stamford by the court then appointed, but that they did not heal all the difficulties existing between the pastor and the people, is evident from another petition from Mr. Bishop and others, sent to the general court at their session in May 1662. The court authorized the governor, William Leete, and magistrates Fenn, of Milford, and Crane, of Branford, to repair to Stamford, with the authority of any plantation court, extraordinarily assisted, to settle any matters in controversy there. And by such methods the disturbing elements at work in the church and community were apparently overruled or expelled, and further and more serious evils averted.

Meanwhile, from the increase of population, the old meeting house had become too strait for their accommodation, and doubtless, also, was felt to be too rude for their improved condition. If the Lord's people were now beginning to dwell in their ceiled houses, it was every way fitting that they should honor the place of their worship. No one, probably, had yet thought of such a result as a division of the territory into two or more parishes; and there was no serious thought of any other denominational service to divide the people. And so the necessity, besides that of repairing, of enlarging, also, the Lord's house, began to press upon them. The steps taken towards this measure, will show how inseparable the civil and ecclesiastical matters of the colony were.

The first public vote on record is that of March 1669, at a town meeting, orderly warned, when it was voted that there shall be a new meeting house built. Voted, also, "that this new meeting house, before mentioned, shall be a stone meeting house."

And so, not the congregational church for its sectarian uses merely, but all the dwellers in the town, with a unanimity which on no other subject will they ever again attain, agree to enlarge and improve the House of the Lord. There must be room in it for all who shall dwell within its reach. From the Reeds, near "the stadle by the oke tree," on the margin of the Rowalton, to the Crabbs, who live on the outskirts of the parish, near where the Mianus seeks its cove, all the dwellers on hill top and in vale, must be provided with at least one place of resort. Did they not all of them need the instructions of the sanctuary? Had not the whole community with one voice, and with a hearty godspeed, sent those venerable fathers, Bell and Slawson, on foot, through the wilderness, out to the Massachusetts colony, to procure a man who should be to them and their children a religions teacher and spiritual guide? And how could he ever accomplish the work to which they had called him without a larger and better house for worship?

Accordingly, in October of the same year with the above votes, a committee was appointed by the town, (Mr. Law, Goodman Holly, Goodman Webb, Goodman Ambler, and Joshua Hoyt,) and invested with full power from the inhabitants of the town "to make a bargain with a workman, and so to agree with him as to suit men's convenience in point of pay, and if they cannot get a house built with stone they have liberty to get it done with timber, and to endeavor to get it done with as much speed as they can with convenience."

On Feb. 18, 1670, of this year, the town decided to rescind the former votes, and resolved to repair the old meeting house "forthwith for the safety of the town." This decision seems not to have been satisfactory to the town, any more than the former one. At any rate, if repairs were made, they must have proved their own insufficiency; for again, on the 25th of the same month, a vote is passed to build a new meeting house. On the 26th of the next month, Mr. Law, Left. Bell, goodmen Holly, Ambler and Newman have "full power committed to them to procure a stone new meeting house, and to fully finish agreement with the workman that hath been treated with; and to have an oversight of the work, and to choose overseers and to call men and teams forth to get stones and other necessary things." The house was to be "for the worship of God, according to the word of God," and was to be thirty feet square.

In September, provision is made to assess the cost of the meeting house equitably on the town; the vote respecting the form of the house is reconsidered, and instead of thirty feet square it is changed to forty-five feet in length and thirty-five in breadth, "with a house roof, abating two feet in the hight of the wall, from the first figure, viz: twelve feet hight."

In the following January, 1671, they vote that the "ould meeting house shall be taken down forthwith by a committee called forth by Joshua Hait."

In April, finding it impossible to come to any agreement in the town, they resolve to leave the determination of the form or figure of the church to the solemn decision of God in the casting of lots. They only decided that if the lot should require the house to be square, it should be thirty-eight feet square and the posts twelve feet; and that there shonld be a funnel on the top, of such hight and size as the committee should direct. Then follows this record as a part of the doings of that town meeting; "The solemn ordinance being as above had, the lot carried it for a square meeting house as above."

Under such auspices the new house was erected. It was entrusted to the sole management of the committee appointed in April of the preceding year. In case they needed advice of the town, provision was made for them to call a legal meeting "about an hour by sun in the evening," and whatever the major part of the voters who should gather within a half hour of the summons should decide upon, if not in conflict with the previous vote of the town, should be deemed valid.

The way was now clear for a new house, and without needless delay, it was doubtless completed. It must have been a great improvement upon the old one, in size at least, if not in architectural proportions. It must have constituted the most noticeable work of art in the town. There could have been nothing else here comparable to this pyramidal block, with its triple stories ascending, as if to furnish a trinity of steps heavenward. For more than half a century it was the only house of worship in the town. In it, six ministers, John Bishop, Eliphalet Jones, John Davenport, Ebenezer Wright, Noah Welles, D. D., and John S. Avery, none of them unworthy the sacred trust, made proof of their fitness for their work. About two generations of the entire town, and four of the congregation of the first church of Christ in Stamford, here received their spiritual training, and from its training went to their final account.

It must have been in this meeting house that the first bell in Stamford was hung. There is no record, I think, of this transaction now existing, but tradition is very distinct as to an accident which occurred at the hanging of the bell. It hung over the center of the house and had to be raised up through the building. Just as it had reached the frame which was to support it, the rope which held it gave way and the bell fell to the floor, killing instantly Mr. John Holmes, the great-great grandfather of John Holmes, Esq., of New Hope district, recently deceased. This meeting house was subject to a regulation, peculiar to that age, which would hardly be endured by the descendants of those who required it. We find the regulation, which in the language of that day was called the "orderly seating of the meeting house," provided for in the following enactment:

"The town order that the inhabitants shall be seated in the meeting house by the following rules, viz: dignity, agge and estate in this present list of estate; and a committee shall be chosen to attend it forthwith; the committee, Capt. Jonathan Selleck, Lieut. Fra. Bell, Lieut. Jona'th Bell, Joseph Theale and Joseph Garnsy, who have full power to seat the inhabitants as above."

By special note, 25th, 2mo., 1673, "Mr. Law, lef. Senor. Bell and William Newman, are chosen committy to seat the women in the meeting house." I think this is the only time when the ladies were so signally honored. Certainly, I find no other similar records.

But the new meeting house required other changes. The pastor, Mr. Bishop, either from temporary failure of his health, or from the excessive burdens of his extensive parish, reaching as it did from Norwalk out to the borders of New York, found it necessary to secure a helper in his work. A Mr. Eliphalet Jones seems at this time to have been in Greenwich, engaged probably as a sort of evangelist, and his labors were within the jurisdiction of the Stamford church. He was, also, very acceptable to the Stamford people. Fearing, doubtless, that his acceptable services among the Greenwich settlers would eventually lead to a new parish, and unwilling to have such a diversion, the TOWN pass a vote, May 3, 1672, to give Mr. Jones an invitation to be a minister of the gospel in this place, "if he remove from Greenwich."

In November of this year he is "accommodated with a piece of land in his own right," provided he settle here in the work of the ministry. At the same time Mr. Law, Mr. Holly and

Jonathan Selleck, are chosen to treat with the Greenwich men "about their compliance with Stamford for the upholding of the ministry in this place." Mr. Jones evidently accepted the proposal from Stamford, and the next year a house is provided for him at the town charge. A vote is also passed that "the town doth agree to give one hundred pounds yearly unto the ministry in this place as long as there be two ministers in the place." Mr. Jones remained here probably until 1676, as at that time the town by vote return to the former ministerial rate, voting only the sum, sixty pounds, which Mr. Bishop was to have.

No other attempt seems to have been made to employ an assistant to Mr. Bishop during his life. No change of much importance took place in the parish. The Greenwich men were required to pay their rates for the support of the gospel here, and there was no serious resistance on their part to the necessity.

One of the votes of this period is so characteristic that we will record it. Its date is Dec. 2, 1680:

"The town doth grant unto the ministry in this place sixty pounds for the present year; one-third part in wheat, one-third part in porke, and one-third part in Indian corn; winter wheat 5s. per bush., summer wheat 4s. 6d., and porke at 3½d. per pound, all good and merchantable, and Indian corn 2s. 6d. per bushel."

Under such pay it would seem that the church and society continued to prosper. The congregation increased and again it became necessary to re-arrange the seating of the house or build a larger one. The former course was adopted, and in November 1689, the seats of the house were by vote of the society turned round and the pulpit set at the north side of the house.

At this period the town meeting house had another office to subserve. It was evidently the theory of that early day that the house of the Lord intended the temporal as well as the spiritual welfare and safety of the people. Our citizens drew from it the weapons and motives of the carnal as well as spiritual warfare, as the following record of June 7, 1681 will testify:

"Pr vote, a convenient place should be made in the meeting house for receiving the town ammonision. Left. Jonathan Bell is chosen to take care of the ammonision."

In November, 1692, it appears that the ministers of the county had proposed to the Stamford men to join with the Greenwich men in "carrying on the works of God there;" but by vote the town declared that they cannot see cause to concur with their motion. And so for a while the matter was dropped.

A single congregation at the center was all that the town felt needful, excepting occasionally when extra religious services were held at private residences in other parts of the extended parish. One pastor continued to keep watch over this large flock, and nothing appears to show that his ministrations and care were not acceptable to the people.

But the newly seated meeting house soon became too straitened, as the first had been, and the congregation needed more room. The first step towards this result seems to have been taken May 13, 1691, when the town voted "to alter the seats so as to make them seat more persons." The only restriction put upon the action of the committee was to leave the pulpit where it had stood before, and to make no breach in the wall. This change was probably made, and the congregation was duly reseated by the usual committee.

And now, the good bishop, who so long had kept spiritual watch over this widely scattered people began to feel the infirmities of age pressing upon him. At the town meeting held Sept. 12, 1692, he expresses an earnest desire that they would find some one to relieve him. It is equally due to Mr. Bishop and to the history of the times to record the action of that meeting. It will be borne in mind that it was the action not of a mere ecclesiastical society, nor of a church, but of the town of Stamford.

"The town desire in compliance with his motion, being also sensible of their own necessity, do therefore think it their duty, first, to settle a maintenance upon Mr. Bishop, that may be to him yearly paid, during his life time, in case we have a supply of another minister."

They then vote the annuity of forty pounds, to be paid in rate and specie, that is in such products as had been customary before.

"Furthermore, in pursuance of this work, for a supply of another minister it is the desire and mind of the town to endeavor by advice and endeavor necessary otherwise, to procure an able, faithful, orthodox minister, in judgment to comply with and act, so far at least, according to the synod in New England, in the year 1662."

They next vote fifty pounds to be paid annually to another minister during Mr. Bishop's life; and appoint Captain Selleck and Lieutenant Bell to advise with the ministers of the county respecting a suitable man for settlement here.

The only other votes recorded which testify to the continued acceptability of Mr. Bishop here, are occasional gifts of land to him in his own right. In December, 1667, they vote to free his estate from the annual minister's rate or tax. In 1681 they donate to him by vote the fortification wood about the meeting house, and during the same year make his salary seventy pounds.

They then add as a guide to their committee, "that the minister who shall be brought into the town shall be called to office in convenient time; and such ministers as shall come, shall promise to the church and town to take office charge upon him."

In November, 1692, the town by vote manifest their desire to have Mr. John Davenport, of New Haven, for their minister; and appoint Abraham Ambler, Daniel Weed and Joseph Turney to treat with him and report to the town. In December of the same year they again express their confidence in him as the man for the place, and are glad that he does not discourage their hopes. They commission their committee to engage him to come among them for trial and promise to furnish him with "suitable maintenance and satisfaction."

On the 16th March, 1692-3, the town "at a full meeting, being duly warned, and also more fully by warrant from authority added, * * * do now further order and appoint a

17

committee to manage this affair, to treat with Mr. Davenport in order to a settlement in this place as a minister of the Gospel amongst us; * * and they have power to agree with him and provide for his comfortable settlement in respect of house and lands, and what else is needful for his encouragement the committee have full power to do according to their best discretion and the town's ability; and that the matter be forthwith attended."

The committee were: Capt. Sellcck, Left. Bell, Mr. Ambler, Mr. Jonat. Selleck, Serj. Samuel Hait, Daniel Weed, Serj. David Waterbury, Jonas Weed, sen., and Mr. John Selleck.

In April they also vote, "the town doth ingage to finish the pasinedge house, fence in the lott, digg a well, plant an orchard and give it to Mr. John Davenport when he is a settled minister in Stamford."

In July, 1693, the town vote to Mr. Davenport, when he shall be a settled minister, one hundred pounds a year. They vote further to give him "ten pounds a year during Mr. Bishop's life," that is to say, ten pounds to be added to the sixty pounds if Mr. Davenport doth settle in a family before Mr. Bishop's death. They then vote to send for Mr. Davenport, whenever and however will best suit him. The last vote of this date is characteristic.

"The town by vote doth give and grant to Mr. John Davenport, when he is settled here in a family, his firewood, which is to be done in a general way and not by rate upon the town, and to be done when the townsmen do order a day or two in the year for it; further it is to be understood that it is to be done by the people of the town, all male persons from sixteen years and upwards."

On the 18th of December following, they vote to Mr. Davenport "forty pounds for the time he has been here in Stamford and until the next March." They vote also to Mr. Bishop fifty pounds for the year. They renew their desire that Mr. Davenport be called to take office, and this desire was answered by his settlement by ordination here in the following year.

In conformity to the vote of July 17, 1693, respecting fire-wood, we find the following vote of Oct. 23, 1696, in which "the town do now further order that every inhabitant of this town shall cut and carry to Mr. Davenport for his use a good ox-load of good wood to be done by the last of November annually, upon the penalty of the forfeiture of four shillings to be paid to the town by the person neglecting his duty herein." Mr. Ambler was appointed to take account of the wood and report to the town. These votes were repeated almost annually during Mr. Davenport's ministry.

That this duty was not always promptly discharged the subsequent record shows. Under date of Mar. 25. 1696, we find this record: "per vote, John Slason, senior, and Increase Holly are impowered to appoint a day and to call forth those men yt are behind to attend ye work of getting and bringing wood to Mr. Davenport, and to doe it as soon as may be."

And that the town were jealous lest their minister should be wronged, we find proof on the records, of the same date, in this vote: "the town impower Daniel Scofield, sen., and Jonas Weed, jun., to order those men that are behind in the fence of Mr. Davenport's pasture, to make up the posts, and if they shall neglect to do it up, then to hire men to set it up and to strain for the pay according to law."

In the year 1698, an incident occurred here illustrating so clearly the religious and ecclesiastical character of the times, and also the position and character of Mr. Davenport as a minister in the county, that we will let the record speak for itself. For the record I am indebted to the kindness of Rev. Joseph Anderson, one of Mr. Davenport's successors in the pastorate. It was found in a manuscript volume detailing the journeys of Roger Gill and Thomas Story between Rhode Island and Carolina in 1698. They were members of the proscribed sect of Quakers, and were bent on propagating their religious tenets,

After describing their journey from Philadelphia to Westchester, in the State of New York, the journal continues as follows:

"Ye next day we sat forward, ye land way, for new Ingland—2 friends to bear us Compn'y. Came yt Evneing to a tovn Caled Stamford in Conacktecok Colony—it being a prity larg bvt a very dark tovn; not a frind living in all yt provenc, as we had hard of, nather wovld they sofer the testymony of trvth to be declared amonght them, nor had it ever bin declared—they being Riged prespetrions or independents, I know not whither, but one thing I am shure of, they had one father. so we went to an Inn. I asked ye woman of ye hows if yt shee wovld be willing to sufer a meting to be in her hovs. She said yes, she wovld not deny no sivel Company from coming to her hovs. now I felt a Grat power and wight of darkness, so yt I Could not be Clear in my spearet to peas thorow ye town of Stamford, and thar for I sent those frinds yt war with us to go and invite ye peopel to com to our inn, for we ware of those peopel Caled qoekers, and we had somthing to say to them. and whilst our frinds went to invite the peopel, we went to aqvint ye Jvstes of ye town of our intencons, and to open ovr minds to him, for he was a independent, and seemed to be somwhot moderated before we parted with him—who answered us thvs, I will not spek mvch to you, for we heve a low yt no qvaker shal prach; so I will not tolerate yov. then he aded ye word. bvt. imploying as much as he wovld wink at ye meeting. So we appoynted a meeting to be next day at ye 9 ovr. So when ye tim Came, saveral of ye peopel cam acording to ye time: a Constabel Cam with them, with a warant to Comand us to go ovt of ye town, being filed with surallvs words and bed names, Comanding ye peopel to depert, and Comending ye women of ye hovs not to sufer us to prech in her hovs. so thomas stod vp to shov ye vnresnapelnes of ye werant, and with all disered a Copy, but it Covld not be granted. then when thomas had spak a few words to yt pvrpvs, I was moved to stand vp and to spek to ye peopel. then Came ye Constable, Comanded me in ye governer's name to to be silent, and pvshed me ovt of ye hovs by my arm. but ye pover of ye Lord yt wos vpon me wovld not be silesent by him. so when he had haled me ovt of ye hovs, ye sperit and pover of ye Lord Cam vpon me, and I lift vp my vovs in ye streets, cryed ovt. wo. wo. wo. vnto all ye inhabetenc of ye tovn of Stamfort, who hold a profeshon of Christ ovt of ye Life of Christ. this Chry, with some other words to ye same pvrpos so alarmed ye peopel yt ye hovl body of ye tovn hard; and meny of them being gathered together, I had time to easey my speret a monght them. then after I was easey, we Retvrned to ovr inn, when saverall of their dispvtants Came to disspote, who wos very fvrvs at first, pvt war so handeled by thomas vpon saveral poynts, bvt espesaly vpon Election and repprobation, yt svm Confesed svm trvths and departed very calm—ye Lords trvth yt day wos over them. So being both Clear of ye town, we Cam yt night to farefeeld. Lodged at philiph Lewies."

"Ye next day ther wos a Lectver held at faerfeld, by 7 preests, and to it wos gathered abvndanc of peopel: and finding a Consarn to Com vpon my sperit to visit yt people at their lectver—for I wos mvch boved vnder ye Consern—tovld thomas, who wos wiling to go with mee. So up to their meeting wee went, but went not in vntil ye singing of their song was over: then in we went, and vp towards ye pvlpit I want, thomas fovlling of me. I looked stidfastly vp to ye pvlpit, wher wer 5 preests sitting; and to sat below. then ye ovld preest took his text ovt of ye profet Isaiah. lv.

first, second. ye words wer Com, bye wine and milk, without money and without priser, fovlloing with these three heads—first, wherefore spend ye yovr mony for yt which is not bred, and your labor for yt which satisfieth not? harken diligently vnto me, and eat ye yt which is good, and let yovr sovl delight itself in fatnes: Secondly, incline yovr ear and come vnto me, hear and yovr sovl shall Live: thirdly, Christ sends ovt his sarvents by his Sperit, with a free invitation to ye peope [l], but ye make excuses. So wee stood still to here him make ovt his sarment: and poore man, to give him his dew, he mad it with no small labor, as wel as no Litel terer; for he drove it on like Pharoah Charats whilees very heavily. so when he had mad an end, I being moved of ye Lord stood vpon a form wher I might both be seen and hard both of preests and peopel. then I spake as follveth to ye peopel: freinds, yov heve all seen this day yt I heve hard yovr minester with peacheno, neither heve I interopted him nor mad any disturbance: therefore I disire ye same Christian Liberty of you: for I heve somthing from the Lord to deliver a mounght yov. then were ye peopel very still. so then I began with thos words yt ye preest took for his text. but befor I had spoken them, down Came ye preests ovt of ye pvlpet, Like disstracted men. one Cried ovt, wher ye povers of ye Church? wher are ye magistrates? what, is ther no Constabels here to take him away? another of them Interrapting me sad, Sur, yov are not called to be a minister to this peopel. whereupon I asked him by whot he was fited, prepered and called to ye worke of ye ministry. he sad, by ye voice of ye peopel. then I spek with a loud vice to ye peopel, bad them take notes yt their minister sad yt he wos fited, prepered and Called to ye work of ye ministre by their voyces. wherevpon the preest wovld heve denied it, saying, yov cat[c]h me. then ovld preest yt prechod the sarmant Caught me by my hand, saying, dear sor Come dovn. who strooking my hand aded, dear sor, I prey come down, ye peopel are well satisfied. bvt abovt this a Constabel Came to me and wovld heve pvled me down bacward. then up steps one of the hearers, as thomas told me, and pvlled him from me. So by this time the first preest, whos name is John devenport had mvstered vp one Jvstes & to Constabels, who by vilence pvled me dovn, halling ovt of ye meeting. I spak thes words to the peopel. O peopel, fear and dread ye Lord God, and mind ye Light of Christ in yovr Consencenes yt will show yov yovr state & will let yov see what sperit yovr ministers are of. So when I wos ovt of their meeting I demended my liberty. but they sad no. then ye Jvstes Comending ye peopel to depert, some of them did, bvt others wovld not. allso he Comended ye Constabels to take me into a back lane wher my voyce should not be hard: for I speke to ye peopel as he haled me a longe and several fovled us into ye lane . . then thomas desered to know by what Low ye proseeded against vs. they sad they had a Low yt no quakers shovld prech a movnght them. then I demanded to see their warant. they sad they had none. So I comended my liberty, as they wovld answer it, Caled to ye peopel 'to know their nams, who wer very Redy to tell vs their names. then they leet me goo. so vp to ye meeting hovs green I went, where wer sevrall hondreds standing. then a peesebel & a Good time I had amonght. ye Lords pover Came over them. saverall were soled, some tendered. So when I had Clered my sperit amovnght them, Greet pees I witnesed whith ye Lord.

"So when I was Clere, thomas felt somthing vpon his mind, to speek to ye preests. so we tovld ye peopel of it, asking into what hovs they wer gon they into ye percons. so we fovlloed them; & I do beleve an hondred of ye heds of ye seven perishes fowlloed us. So Coming to ye hovs we went in. ye preests wer in a Larg room, seeing vs met vs, taking vs by ye hand invited kindly to dine wh them, tovld vs we shovld be as welcome as any of them yt wer ther yt day. bvt we refvesing, they sad, why wovld wee not? why should ther be any diference in society alltho ther might be some in princebles. then I sad, had wee met with a Christian sperit amonght yov, we might have dined with yov: but inasmuch as we did not mett with a sperit of humanity, how covld we heve any society? & as we had not interopted them in their worship nother wovld we; so we wovld withdraw to ovr inn, tel ther diner wos ended, and Come up to them ageyn. So wee came to them; ye peopel stil remened abovt ye hovs, went unto ye hovs with vs. So then after a few bantering words we receved from preest devenport, thomas fell into a dispute with devenport abovt babtisem, which hald more than on over: and had not thomas binn interupted by ye rest of ye prests, devenport had confesed babtisem as they held it, to be a Rellik of popery. whervpon, I being much greeved to see ther unfar delings with us—for I had mad an agreement with them yt ther shovld be no interoption between them on either side, before all ye peopel—then I spake to ye peopel, saying, let ye evidence of gods sperit in all yovr harts bear witness between vs & them this day. moreover I sad we wer here to vindicate ye thruth agenst all vnthrvth, ading with a lovd vovice befor them all sad, senc they had bin so vnfar, if yt they wovld call vp ye Congregation together, wee wovld tary to days in town, & wovld prove yt babtisem as yt hald it not to be [neither?] instituted by Christ nor eny of his abostels, nor practised. bvt not one man mad one word of an answer, all being silent. so after a litel pawes, they sad they had a select meting; therefor they disiered vs to withdrow—their time was spent. So then, after a few words wee parted with them, ye peopel wer Loveing to vs and one Justes of ye peece folloed vs, & sad, frinds, yov hsve incovnted with a body of divinity to-day. So we took hors & a way we Came yt night to Stratford: & had greet peece with ye Lord."

No noticeable changes occur in the next few years. Mr. Davenport seems to have won the esteem and confidence of the people, and to have stood high among his brethren in the county. The congregation increased to the full capacity of the house and at length beyond the possibility of being seated.

Resort is now had to "galeries," for which provision was made in Mar. 1700. When the galleries were done a committee were to reseat the people. But the old meeting house was not to be made roomy enough for the growing congregation. A vote is passed, July 8, 1702, to build a new meeting house next fall, fifty feet square, of customary hight, where the pound stands. Major Selleck, Capt. Selleck, Dea. Hait, Left. Waterbury, Daniel Scofield, sen., Sergt. Webb, Sergt. Knap, Mr. Stephen Bishop and Ensign Holly, are made the building committee, with instructions to get the shingles at home and have them of cedar.

In May, 1703, they vote to raise the meeting house as soon as conveniently it may be; and as late as Nov. 14, 1705, we find this vote: that when the floor is laid and fitted to meet in, the pulpit and seats shall be removed to the new, for the present. But a far different use was to be assigned to the old floor of that hallowed house. The town had just voted to repair their mill-dam; and as mill-dam and churches were equally the care of the town, the good economy is practiced of voting to use the "pauke flore" of the old meeting house, on the dam.

It would seem that this third house of worship had no bell as provision was made in 1707 for beating the drum in the "ferrate" (turret) of the new meeting house for one year, and to begin the first of March next.

The "orderly" seating of the congregation in this meeting house was still deemed of so much importance that the following provision was made for it, in full town meeting, July 4, 1710.

"The town by vote do agree for the more orderly seating of the meeting house that these rules be observed in the seating thereof: first, that it be done in proportion to the whole of its charge by which the house was built, and finished, as may appear by those lists of Eastates by which the several rates or levyes were raised for the defraying the charge of the same; also that a christian due regard be had unto, and suitable respect given unto civil authority, age and military commission office, commissioned by the court."

To do this delicate work the same town meeting duly appointed Major Jonathan Selleck, Deacon Samuel Hoyt, Mr. Daniel Scofield, sen., Mr. Elisha Holly and Mr. Joseph Bishop. In another vote the meeting provided that "the major part of the committee agreeing," shall have power to order the seating, and they are to do it as soon as convenient.

There is no record of the seating, as above directed, but very frequently at this period the town voted as a special honor the use of the first seats to those of the citizens whose dignity would bear such promotion.

There is this special provision made in 1722, that "the town do grant that the pew at the east end of the gallery shall be for the proper use and benefit of Mr. Davenport's family, forever, he bearing the charge and cost thereupon."

In 1757, the society vote that "Jonathan Waterbury, lieut. Weed and capt. Weed are ordered to set in the fore pew in the meeting house; and Caleb Smith and Joseph Webb in the second pew, and capt. Peirre Fitch, in the fore seat."

But in the growth of the town, all of the citizens still maintaining their connection with this congregation, this house, as its predecessor had done, soon became too small, so that in 1723 it was necessary to build extra galleries. At this time Capt. Samuel Hayt, and Capt. Jonathan Hayt were "to take their place to set in the second pue;" and Samuel Weed in the fore seat.

At this date also appears the curious provision which was made to accommodate those who had come from a great distance to meeting. The town gave James Slason permission "to set up a house for ye advantage of his having a place to go to on Sabbath days, at ye west end of Mr. Blachly's shop."

"The town grants to James June and all that live at Larence's farm to set up a house upon the town's land on the west side of Ebenezer Weed's lot to "a Commodate for their conveniency of coming to meeting on the Sabbath day."

It is the tradition that a part of the house, recently removed from the northwest corner of Main and Atlantic Streets, occupied by the Jarvis family, was originally built as a "Sabbath day house," for the comfort of families coming from a distant part of the parish.

It would seem from the records that at this period an unsteady currency was the occasion of much trouble between the pastor and the people. This seems to have been the occasion of the only variance between Mr. Davenport and the parish. It was to come to some mutual understanding respecting the obligations of the parish, that, in 1725 Mr. Davenport requested of the town their understanding of the contract regarding his pay in money—whether they were not to pay money "fully to answer two thirds of one hundred and thirty pounds, according to the known reckoning of our place." "Answered by the town: that upon the payment of the town to Mr. Davenport, eighty-six pounds thirteen shillings and four pence money, doth fully answer the town's obligation to Mr. Davenport of a hundred and thirty pounds pay."

Again, in Feb. 1728–9, by vote, Mr. Davenport was "introduced" into the town meeting and allowed to state his understanding of the contract above referred to. Dea. John Hoyt, Jona. Maltby and Jona. Bates were chosen to "Discors" with him, relating to his "Sallory." They proposed arbitration to settle the difference, which was negatived. They propose an addition to the above sum, which was also negatived, whereupon Mr. Davenport submits in writing his statement and demand. On this, the meeting adjourned to the 14th instant. At this meeting they vote the additional sum, forty-three pounds six shillings and eight pence, to be paid in current bills of credit or in provision at price current.

Capt. Jona. Hoyt, Samuel Blachly, Samuel Weed, Benjamin Weed, and Jonathan Pettit entered a protest against the negative vote of the previous meeting.

Feb 18, 1731, fifteen days after the death of Mr. Davenport, a special town meeting was called. Capt. Bishop was chosen moderator and deacon Hoyt was to assist him. The town had been plunged into universal grief by the late sore bereavement. Scarcely any calamity of that day could compare with it. So thought, at least, the fathers of the town as they came together. They felt their need of Divine comfort and guidance. Their first vote, and every vote, showed that their only hope was in the faithful God, whose ambassador they had so recently lost. These were thoughtful and appropriate words, in which, by vote, they express this conviction: "By vote the town AGREE that there shall be a day of humiliation kept, and to call in such ministers to assist in the work as shall be thought needful."

They appoint the first Wednesday in the following month as the day, and appoint Capt. Bishop, Dea. John Hoyt, and Capt. Jonathan Hoyt a committee to make the needed preparations. They also impower this committee to advise with the elders respecting a minister, and also to invite in a minister to be accepted by the town.

They adjourn to the first Tuesday of April. At this meeting they vote to give Mr. Sherman "something further of tryall in order to settlement." There were ninety-four votes and twenty-one blanks, making at that meeting one hundred and fifteen voters on the question of settling a minister. One more meeting was held by the town in May, and the committee was increased by adding Capt. Samuel Hoyt and Jonas Weed. This enlarged committee were authorized to hire a minister "for a day or more as there shall be occasion."

And now occurs a change in the administration of civil and ecclesiastical affairs. They are separated in 1731. The former are managed in what are henceforth called society meetings, and the latter in town meetings. The same book, however, contains, down to 1759, the records of both meetings. The same moderator presides, and the same scribe officiates at both. The same page will show, in two separate records, what was done in the town, and what was done in the society meetings. In 1760 a new book was procured, and from this time the records of the society are kept separately from those of the town. Joseph Bishop, who, since 1738, had been clerk both of the town and society, is continued still for one year as clerk of the society, when his office was given to Abraham Davenport, who was sworn in to the faithful performance of its duties.

The first of the meetings of the society proper was held July 28, 1731. It had been orderly warned according to law. Deacon Hoyt was its moderator and Samuel Weed its clerk. It was called on the minutes a "Sosiatys" meeting.

"Mr. Right" was, by an "almost unanimous" vote, invited to become the minister of the town. In September, at an adjourned meeting the vote was unanimous in favor of Mr. Right. They engage to buy him a homelot and build him a "credable Decent Dwelling house," and pay him a salary of 150 pounds. This meeting adjourned to the annual town meeting in December. Mr. Ebenezer Wright accepted the call thus made to him. In the December meeting arrangements were made for his settlement. They set apart the third of the following May as a day for humiliation and prayer, and the seventh, for the ordination of Mr. Wright, now pastor elect.

The society now takes upon itself, also, the care of the schools. This year the record shows there were five schools in the town: the center school, the one over the Noroton, the one west of Mill river, the Simsbury, and the Newfield schools. At the society's meeting, in December 1733, Mr. Wright being now fairly installed, a new "seating" of the people was ordered. The committee, in discharging this trust, were to consider the former charge of building the house, and the charge of making the galleries, and also the age and dignity of persons, and still further, the present list of estates, and others foregoing.

Those persons that pay the minister at Five Mile river were discharged from paying Mr. Wright, for three months, if they bring sufficient proof that they pay as much there. In 1734 the society grants to the people at the Five mile river, and at Woodpecker Ridge their proportion of the minister's rate for three months in the winter, provided they hire a minister to preach for them. The next year they extend the time at the Five Mile meeting for four months.

In 1735 the society saw " cause to seat Mr. Abraham Davenport and Mr. James Davenport in the foremost pew, on the west side of the meeting house."

At this meeting they also provide for repairing the house. At their meeting in May 1736, on a proposition to give the people at the east end of the town the right to organize a society, they voted promptly in the negative; and Capt. Jonathan Hoyt and Mr. Jonathan Maltby were appointed their agents to appear at the general assembly and show why the separation should not be made. In 1736, the society grant the people east of Stony Brook their minister's rate for four months; and the people of Newfield, as low as Josiah Hoyt's south; and also the people of "Shitten" plains, as far as Joseph Hunt's. In 1838, Capt. Jonathan Maltby was "ordered to set in the fore pew and his wife to set answerably thereto." It was also "per vote agreed that the committee that formerly seated the meeting house should at their discrision advance sum elderly parsons in the seting in the meeting house." This, I think, is the last instance in which the town or society are reported as seating the meeting house.

Again the Stamford first church are called to part with their minister. Mr. Wright, who had served them with great acceptance, was removed by death in May 1745, and the society appointed the 18th of June as a day of fasting and prayer. Again the ministers of the county are called in to advise in the selection of a new candidate.

By September a candidate had been so far "tryed" by them that a society meeting was called to consider his claims. The form of the vote will illustrate the gravity of the question before them. With Col. Jonathan Hoyt in the Chair, it was "put to vote, whether the society were so well satisfied in what they have already experienced as to Mr. Noah Well's ministerial qualifications so as to proceed further to the settlement of him forthwith." "Voted in the affirmative one hundred and four votes, and in the negative twenty-three votes, and many more sent their desires in the affirmative."

Whereupon the meeting instruct their committee to "discourse" with Mr. Welles regarding his wishes on the subject, and report at a meeting to be held in four days. The report being favorable to the settlement, arrangements are made to consumate it.

The following vote shows the care taken for securing to the minister his full pay.

"Whereas this society at their meeting on Sept. 22, 1746 did agree to give Mr. Noah Welles seventy-five pounds silver money at eight shillings per ounce, for his yearly salary, or the equivalent in the old or new tenor currency; and lest there should a difficulty arise to know what should be the equivalent above, the society do now agree, per vote, that their committee for the time being shall have full power yearly to agree with him, what the equivalent shall be; and if they can't agree, then the committee are hereby impowered to leave the matter to some indifferent men, whom they and Mr. Welles shall chose in the 'naibourwood,' which agreement and judgment as above shall decide the controversy."

But by this time the process of dividing the territory into separate parishes had commenced; and already there were many indications that these parishes themselves could not long continue to worship together under the old denominational standard.

For nearly a century one parish and one creed had sufficed. The few who could not heartily subscribe to either condition of the infant settlement, seemed to yield, with some sort of grace, to the manifest propriety of a quiet submission to the only "standing order" known, and await the coming time for an open assertion of their cherished theories, either in the doctrine or in the government of the church. The necessity for the twofold division which so soon resulted in so many separate parishes and distinct churches, could not by any expedients have been long postponed.

Practically, already, the dwellers on the outskirts of the town had been gradually dropping out from attendance on the public worship of the people, held only at the center of the town; and for years occasional services in the more distant neighborhoods had endeavored to supply their want. Practically, also, the germs of new ecclesiastical organizations were beginning to show themselves; and under the liberal indulgence granted by the easy civil administrations of the day, nothing could hinder their rapid growth.

It will be the object of the following chapter to exhibit the progress of this disintegration and its results. We shall first indicate the territorial division into three distinct parishes and the fragments of three others, and, in a following chapter, examine the denominational organizations, which, in the process of time arose on the ground which, from the settlement of the town had been held, and not unsuccessfully improved, by the one puritan church of the congregational order.

CHAPTER VIII.

SEPARATE PARISH ORGANIZATIONS.

At the settlement of the town, and for many years after, the entire territory embraced in the grant received from the Indians, about eight miles wide east and west and sixteen long north and south, constituted but one civil ecclesiastical jurisdiction. This was under the control of the town. By the town the church of Christ was supplied with a place or places for worship, and to the town every citizen was responsible for attendance upon the worship for which provision had been made, and for meeting his share of its expenses. In the progress of settlements in the vicinity where the dwellers on the outside of the town could be more conveniently accommodated elsewhere than at any place within this tract, special permission was given to them to embrace such opportunity, and a special vote released them from the legal support required here. These special votes are very numerous all along the early history of the town for more than a hundred years; and this method was resorted to to obviate the necessity of permanently cutting off any portion of the jurisdiction. Of course, as the population increased, and the central congregation became so full that the absence of large numbers would scarcely be missed, it became an easier thing for the most distant families to get away. It would seem that there was no need of an apology or a very earnest plea, for Thomas Potts and Noah Parketon, who must have lived about eleven miles north of the village, and their neighbors living still further north, to obtain permission to attend meeting at Poundridge, as late as 1771. And yet, such permission was sought and granted for several successive years. But no strength of ecclesiastical bond could hold in perpetual unity the broad tract with its increasing population; and we shall find it resolving itself into at least six territorial jurisdictions.

OLD SOCIETY OF GREENWICH.

The first step towards alienating any portion of the old ecclesiastical territory of Stamford, seems to have been taken on the southwest corner of the parish. Down to about 1678 no regular and permanent society had been organized at Greenwich. That the people of Greenwich were regarded as belonging to the Stamford parish is abundantly shown by our early records. As late as March 2, 1774–5, in town meeting, it was voted, "the town do iudge it meet that Grinwich while they have the benefit of the ministry among us, yt thay allso should pay to ye ministry." Indeed, the General Court or Legislature of Connecticut had decided ten years before this, that the only condition upon which Greenwich could become a township, "intire of itself," was that they "procure and maintain an orthodox minister; and in the meantime, and until yt be effected, they are to attend ye ministry at Stamford, and to contribute proportionably with Stamford to ye maintenance of ye ministry there."

There is now, probably, no record of the surrender of the present territory of Greenwich by this ecclesiastical society, but as the line of separation between the two towns was run by the Committee in 1681, and confirmed by the Patent in 1685, it is probable that the town limits were made also the limits of the two thenceforward separate societies. This line has probably not been materially changed since.

BEDFORD PARISH.

The first step towards setting off any of the northern part of the town was taken in January, 1720–1.

This portion of the town had been bought with the rest of the tract in 1660 and reconfirmed in 1655, and again in 1680.

The Indians who signed the last surrender, December 23, 1680, were Katonah, Stockawac, Segotah, Jovis, Tohonacogyah, Yannayo and Kackennond; and the persons recognized as the occupants or holders of the tract, then called the Hop Grounds, were: Richard and Abraham Ambler, Daniel Weed, John Wescot, Jona. Petit, John Cross, John Miller, Nicholas Webster, Richard Ayres, Wm. Clark, James Seeley, Joseph Stephens, Dan Jones, Benj. Stephens, Thos. Tomoyou and Joseph Cheoles. The surrender was signed in presence of Joshua Knap and David Waterbury. Yet this entire tract was still subject to the ecclesiastical jurisdiction of Stamford. At the Court of Election in Hartford, May 11, 1682, the Court "grant the liberty of a plantation to the people of the Hop Ground, to be called Bedford; and appoint Joseph Theal to be for the present the chief military officer of the train band of Bedford, and Abraham Ambler is empowered to grant warrants to several officers and witnesses, and to join persons in marriage."

James White, Michael Warin, John Ingersol and John Right, living towards the northern end of Long Ridge, in January, 1720–1, were released from paying towards the ministry in Stamford for the year ensuing, they observing the following conditions, viz: "that they shall duly attend on the public worship at Bedford, and shall bear their part in proportion with the people of Bedford in the maintenance of the ministry there, they bringing a certificate from the town of Bedford of their so doing."

In 1722 the inhabitants of Chesnut Ridge, viz: Geo. Dibble, Timothy Concklin and Thomas Corey, were also allowed to pay their minister's rate in Bedford, "if they bring Rev. Mr. Tennant's certificate that they have paid to him, to next town meeting."

STANWICH SOCIETY.

This society is made up of parts of the Greenwich and Stamford societies The first local meeting whose records I have found was that of February 5, 1730, when forty-eight men from these two societies met and voted to call for the organization of a new society. In May, 1731, they petition the legislature for an act of incorporation, which petition was summarily dismissed. Immediately, twenty-seven of the petitioners from Greenwich and nineteen from Stamford notify the two towns that they shall renew their petitions and persist in their organization. Accordingly in October of the same year, fifty-three send in their second petition to the Assembly, which from some informality in the proceedings was withdrawn, when the petitioners gave their legal notice to the two towns of their purpose to prosecute their plea.

In May, 1732, they forward their petition the third time to the Legislature, stating that they have already raised their meeting house, a suitable building forty feet long and thirty wide, and that the "most of the stuff" for it is provided.

Twenty Stamford families notified the Stamford society of their action; and a remonstrance against it, signed by twenty-four members of the Stamford society, was forthwith forwarded by interested and influential men to defeat the project before the legislature. An agent from the society in Horseneck was also sent to the assembly to oppose the plea of the petitioners. An earnest protest was urged by both the societies on the ground that the division would weaken them, and endanger their very existence. Besides these counter appeals, another remonstrance was sent forward from the dwellers in the vicinity of Round Hill, a little to the west of the proposed society, on the ground that if the new society should be organized it would interfere with the one they were contemplating, and which was much more needed.

But after listening to the petitioners and the remonstrants, the legislature in their October session, 1733, passed the act incorporating the Stanwich society. As a part of the new society was still within the limits of Stamford, in their town meeting of Dec. 14th, among other town officers, John Newman and Ebenezer Smith were appointed tything men for the new parish of Stanwich. These appointments were annually made until the society at Stanwich became permanently independent of the parent societies.

NEW CANAAN.

This parish was made up of parts of Norwalk and Stamford. The first notice of it as a distinct parish on the Stamford records is of date Dec. 8, 1730, when "John Bouton and others ask liberty of moving out of town to join with a part of Norwalk in order to be a society." The town voted in the negative. Yet the opposition could not have been very strenuous, because we find under date of Dec. 14, 1731, Ebenezer Seely and Nathaniel Bouton are, in town meeting, appointed tything men for the new society. The next year, John Bouton and Ebenezer Seely are chosen to the same office, and their field of service is called "Cannan Parrish."

There could not have been as much opposition to the organization of this parish as there had been to that of Stanwich. Our records have a vote passed Dec. 27, 1733, which shows good will towards the New Canaan enterprize, which is also expressive of the town's regard for the ordinances and institutions of religion.

"The town agree that there shall be a committee chosen to agree with those men that have land lying where it may be thought needful for a highway for the conveniency of 'Canaan parish to go to meeting,' and to lay it out where they think it may be most convenient."

Of the twenty-four members constituting this church when it was founded, eleven were from Stamford, and two of these—John Bouton and Thomas Talmadge—were its first deacons. The names of the Stamford members were: Deacon John Bouton and his wife Mercy, deacon Thomas Talmadge and his wife Susanna, John Davenport, John Finch, Eliphalet Seeley and Sarah his wife, John Bouton, jun., and Mary his wife, and Jerusha, the wife of David Stevens.

The society was incorporated in 1731, but the town continued to belong to Norwalk and Stamford until 1801.

The first meeting of the New Canaan society was held July 1, 1731, when John Bouton was made moderator, and John Betts, sen., clerk. The committee appointed were, Samuel Seymour, Zerubabel Hoyt, and David Stevens.

In 1732 the list of the Stamford portion of the New Canaan settlers, as reported on the society records of New Canaan, is as follows:

Bouton John,	36.00.0	Hoyt Job,	36.02.0
Bouton Nath'l,	61.11.9	Hoyt Joshua,	26.00.0
Bouton Daniel,	22.01.0	Slason Eliphalet	41.02.0
Bouton Eleaser,	41.10.0	Seeley Eliphalet,	32.09.0
Bouton John, jr.,	27.04.0	Seeley Ebenezer,	38.00.8
Davenport John,	68.08.0	Talmadge Thos.,	71.02.9
Finch John,	55.08.0	Stevens David,	54.05.0
Green Nath'l,	49.12.0	Waterbury David,	44.00.6
Hoyt James,	39.00.0		

MIDDLESEX (DARIEN.)

How early separate religious services were held in this part of the town no existing records show. Probably for years before Dr. Mather was settled here in 1744, there had been preaching, with more or less regularity.

At a society meeting, held in the first society of Stamford, Dec. 20, 1733, by vote "the society agree that those particular persons that pay to the minister at Five Mile river, shall be discharged from paying their proportion of Mr. Wright's rate, during the term of three months, provided they bring sufficient proof to the society's committee that they pay as much to the minister there, as their proportion to Mr. Wright for the time above said."

In 1734, forty-six planters on the west side of Norwalk river petition for a new society. The next notice taken of this project, as far as records show, was simultaneously in Stamford and at the May session of the legislature, in 1736. Sixty-nine petitions, representing eighty families, and a list of £5,880, made a formal request to be incorporated as an ecclesiastical society by themselves. The petition was negatived, only to be renewed in October of the same year, by fifty-six men. The urgency of the petitioners led to the appointment of a special committee to examine their claims. In May 1737 the committee report favorably, assigning as proper boundaries of the society the Five Mile river on the east, and the Noroton on the west. In October of this year the act of incorporation was passed. It is curious to note upon what frail boundaries they relied. The moment they leave the rivers, which they might presume to be permanent, they fix upon the most perishable objects, in the most indeterminate of localities, to answer as permanent bounds for the society. On the west side of the parish, to separate it from the older society of Stamford, they define, as the westernmost limits of Middlesex, "an old chimney about two and a half miles east of the Stamford meeting house," and "so to run a strait line midway between Stephen Bishop's house and David Dibble's house," and thence to where the Noroton crosses the Canaan line. But this separation was not to be a peaceable one. Though no blood seems to have been shed in the struggle, there were many earnest and clamorous appeals and remonstrances between the parishes themselves and between the parishes and the legislature; so that the peaceful settlement of the Middlesex seceders was not accomplished before the summer of 1741, about a dozen years after the need of such a society was felt and its incorporation demanded.

Eleven somewhat lengthy documents, now on file in the state library at Hartford, testify to the great interest shown in both the old and the new parishes in the proposed division.

These papers indicate the most obstinate determination on the part of the first society not to allow any further alienation of any part of their ecclesiastical jurisdiction. Assuming a sort of indefeasible right to the territory, the society, by a unanimous vote of all excepting the seceding portion, declared that they would "not grant to the people at the east end of the town the liberty of a society apart." They also appointed Captain Jonathan Hoyt and Mr. Jonathan Maltby as special agents to the legislature to report the reasons of the TOWN against forming the new society. But the seceders at length prevailed.

The names of the petitioners to the "Five Mile river peticion," dated the second Thursday of October, 1736, the original petition being now before me—are: Thos. Reed, Edmond Waring, Jona. Cristy, Jona. Bates, Robert Mills, John Reed, Joshua Scofield, Isaac Bishop, Jona. Bell, Josh. Morehouse, John Bates, Jona. Petit, David Selleck, Nath'l Bates, Ed. Waring, jun., Jos. Pengban, Thos. Reed, jun., John Petit, Joseph Whiting, John Reed, jun., James Slason, jun., David Bates, Elias Reed, John Raymond, Nath'l Selleck, David Scofield, Sam. Richards, Jos. Waterbury, Jonas Weed, Deliverance Slason, Chas. Weed, Theop. Bishop, John Andrus, Nath'l How, John Dean, David Waterbury, Eb. Bishop, Zach. Dibble, Thomas Bishop, Sam. Bryan, Nathan Sturgis, Benj. Dibble, David Slason, David Dibble, Nathan Selleck, Nathan Waring, Sam. Brinswade, Eb. Green, John Bolt, Jacob Waring, John Waring, Dan. Reed, Abr. Raymond, Comfort Raymond, Isaac Wood, and Sam. Reed.

The first record of a society's meeting in Middlesex bears date June 15, 1789. Ensign Nathan Bell was its moderator and Joshua Morehouse was appointed society's clerk. The meeting was held at the house of John Bates. At an adjourned meeting held June 21st, Thos. Reed, Jona. Bates, Daniel Reed, Isaac Bishop, Jonathan Selleck, Samuel Reed and ensign Jonathan Bell were appointed a committee to "caryon" the building of the "metting hous." They were instructed to make the house fifty fect long, thirty feet wide and twenty feet post.

They then voted a tax to meet the expenses of the building, and to pay Mr. Buckingham "for His preaching the time agreed." Jonathan Weed was appointed collector. The society records from this date to that of the organization of the church show that the following ministers labored here either simply as supplies or as candidates: Rev. Mr. Birdseye, Gideon Mills, Ebenezer Mills, David Judson, Mr. Ells and Mather. At a meeting held Dec. 11, 1741, the society voted, by a large majority, forty-two to four, to settle Mr. Judson. But to give every man in the society an opportunity to vote, Mr. Morehouse, the clerk, was ordered to carry a paper with the vote "about and read the same to those persons that belong to said society, which were not at said meeting, that they might have opportunity to subscribe to the same."

At their meeting Sept 1, 1742, while Mr. Mather was still preaching as a candidate for settlement, we find this vote: "Ye Society by major vote granted to ye Rev. Mr. Right (Wright), to preach in any part of Middlesex parish on any needful occasion as often as he shall see fit."

A record of the doings of this society in 1747 respecting the seating of the meeting house explains more fully the process of this custom than any record now existing of any other parish in town, and is worth preserving as a curiosity of the times. Besides, it indicates some of the principal men of that day, in this part of the town.

By the first vote the society decided to seat the meeting by a committee.

2. pr vote ye society a lowed ye first pue to be ye hiest in Dignity.
3. pr vote the 2 pew to be 2 hiest in Dignity.
4. pr vote, the fore seat alowed to be the 3 hiest in Dignity.
5. pr vote, the front pew, by ye great Dorr to be ye 4th hiest in Dignity.
6. pr vote, the corner pew at the norwest to be ye 5th hiest.
7. pr vote, to be ye 6th hiest.
8. the west pew nex ye norwest to be ye 7th hiest.
9th per vote 10th per vote 11th per vote 12th per vote 13 per vote Capt. John Raiment, Capt. Jona. Bates, Left. Jona. Bell. sr., Saml Bishop, and Daniel Reed chosen a comety and a pointed to seat ye meeting hous as the society shall by their vote direct.
14. pr vote Mr. David Tuttle, Mr. Thos Reed, Cpn. John Raiment, Mr. Edmun Wearing, Mr. Jona. Bates, Mr. Nathan Selleck, Mr. Jeams Slason and Mr. Jona. Bell all to set in ye fore pew.

15 and Decon Bishop also by ye vote of ye society to set in his seat be fore ye pulpit.
16. pr vote, the Society Impowered the comety to seat ye remainder of ye hous a cordin to their own discretion.

The above record is of date Aug. 9, 1747, and the next meeting of the society was held "genewary ye 28th, 1747–8." A record of this meeting is also so characteristic of the times as to justify insertion.

"Voted yt Mr. Jona Bell or any other man a greed upon to sing or tune ye salm in his absence in times of publickt worship may tune it in ye old way or new which suits you best. vote yt Elijah Jones shall tune ye salms in times of worship in Mr. Bell's absence. Vote yt Left. Jona. Selleck shall Reed the salms in Mr. Bell's absence."

We have now cut off from what was the parish of Stamford under the first three pastors here, from the west side portions of the First society in Greenwich and of the Stanwich society; to the north we have transferred a section to the Bedford parish and to the east a portion of the New Canaan and the most of the Darien societies. There remains, therefore, only the central portion of the old parish left, extending over two miles east of the meeting house in the village and about a mile and a half west, and stretching from the waters of the Sound ten or eleven miles towards the north. Only one other sub-division of this territory into ecclesiastical societies remains to be noticed.

NORTH STAMFORD SOCIETY.

For several years before the incorporation of this society, religious meetings had been held in this part of the town. As early as Dec. 9, 1742.

First Society meeting, grant to the people of Woodpecker's Ridge and such as formerly used to joyn with them or may still joyn with them in those limits, an abatement of their part of the ministerial rate for the year ensuing during the time of three months, if they employ a regular and orthodox person to preach among them, in case said people in an orderly and regular manner attend all the stepts of the law for the obtaining and improving a person to preach in such a capacity.

Vote this meeting is adjourned to 23 day instant at one of the clock at this place; viz: the house of Joseph Judson.

Met and adjourned to first Mond. Feb. next, same place.

Dec. 27, 1743. Woodpecker Ridge shall have the liberty to introduce the Rev. Mr. Writ to preach unto them; if the said Mr. Writ shall be willing, for this four months next coming, viz: one Sabbath in a month.

Dec. 22, 1762. The inhabitants of the Society living at Woodpecker Ridge and Scofield Town and Thomas Potts, John Dean and Reuben Weed shall be excused from paying their society's rates this year for the time they shall hire a preacher, provided it shall not exceed four months.

In 1763 vote to pay to the inhabitants living as above, and those beyond Woodpecker Ridge, their proportion of one hundred pounds, for the time they shall hire preaching, if not for more than four months.

Similar votes were passed annually by the first society until 1773, when it was voted that "twelve pounds, lawful money raised in the first society on the list of this year, be given to the people of Woodpecker Ridge," and Benjamin Weed and Hezekiah Weed were appointed to receive and disburse it. The next five years a similar vote was passed, increasing the appropriation until it reached eighteen pounds.

In 1779, after maintaining separate worship for nearly forty years, the people living at and near Woodpecker Ridge sent a formal petition to be set off as an independent society. Now commenced one of the most heated contests which the town has ever witnessed. The petitioners were earnest and revolutionary in spirit, determined to regulate their own society affairs; and the remonstrants, the entire southern portion of the town, were as earnest in opposing them. Both parties besieged the legislature, and the Supreme Court of the State hesitated. Both were well represented, and such was the vigor of the contestants and so nearly balanced their opposing pleas, that they prevailed to postpone for another year the final action of the legislature. The next season, May 1780, a committee consisting o- Lemuel Sanford, Clap Raymond and Mathew Mead, was constituted by the legislature to run a line for the southern boundary of the proposed society, if on a local examination they were satisfied there was any need for the new organiza tion. The committee decided in favor of the division and located the line of separation. They presented their report at the next session of the legislature, and the plea they make is based on this justification: "There is a number of considerable farmers in the place, where they have already built them a meeting house, and it will admit of considerable improvements, and many more inhabitants."

Against so conclusive reasoning, no plea of the remonstrants could find weight. Their fears of the "utter weakening" of the parent society, their dislike of the committee's line, which so encroached upon the territory they needed, and the utmost eloquence of their champion, the weighty colonel Charles Webb, were alike ineffectual, and the last excision from the first ecclesiastical society was at length sanctioned by the state legislature in their spring session 1781.

Simultaneously with the above territorial division of the town ecclesiastically, another process of excision was going on. By this process, portions of the territory were cut off and assigned to new towns as they were organized. Greenwich seems first to have been relinquished.

The town limits to the north extended some four miles further than now, and in 1731 the present line was run, leaving the territory north of it in Poundridge, Bedford and North Castle. In 1860 the northeast part of the town was set off as a part of the town of New Canaan. In 1830, all that part of the town lying east the Noroton river was incorporated as Darien. These successive excisions from the territory leave for the present township a territory of about three miles in width at the southern end, about four and a half miles width at the northern end, and about ten miles in length from north to south.

The accompanying map gives the original territory covered by the purchase made by Capt. Turner for the Wethersfield men, and indicates the portions cut off for the new towns as they were organized.

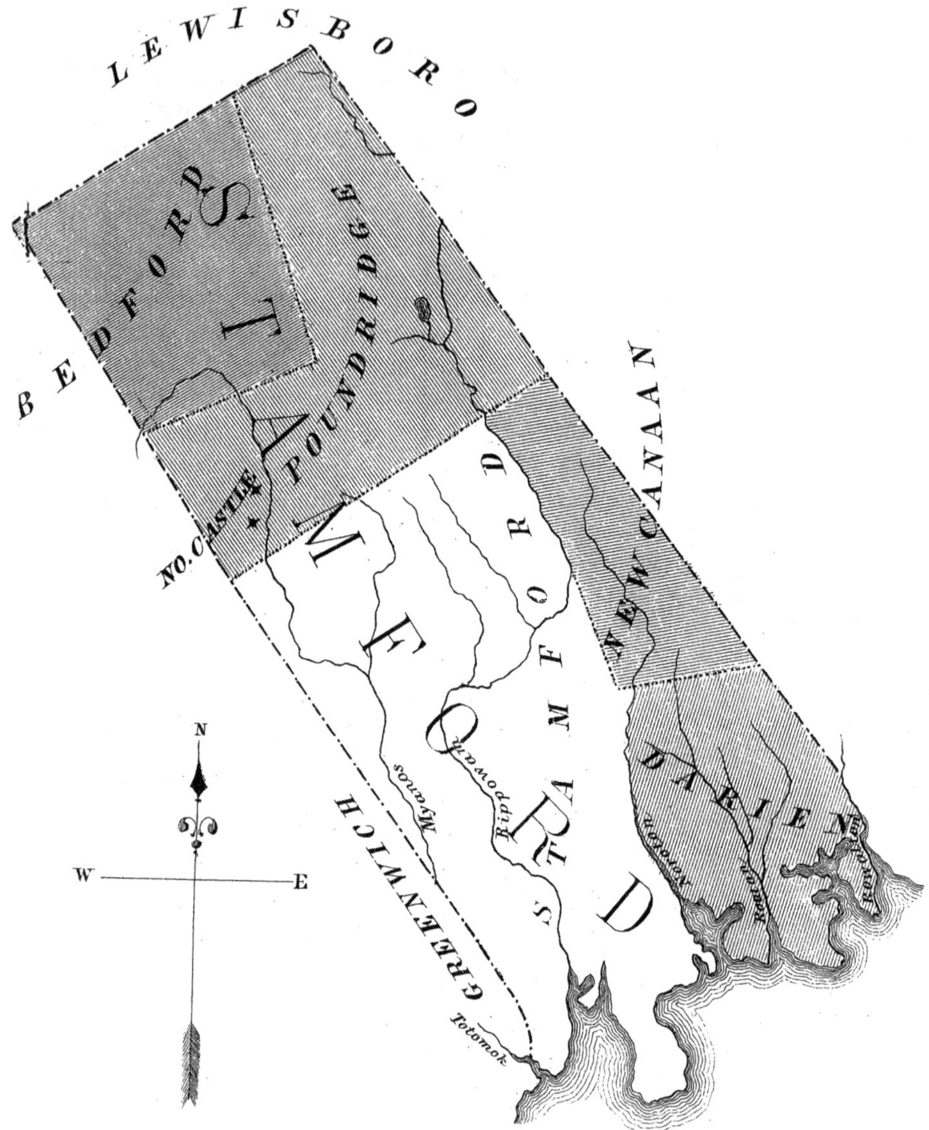

THE STAMFORD OF 1685.

CHAPTER IX.

BIRTHS, MARRIAGES AND DEATHS TO 1700.

In this chapter we shall give an alphabetical list of births marriages and deaths, found on the town records, down to the year 1700. It was the intention of the author to continue this list through the first hundred years of the town, but neither time nor the expense would allow it. It is believed that before the year 1700, no record of this class has escaped the author's notice. Though but a small part of the entire number which must have been registered, with our two chapters of the settlers they will probably indicate nearly all of the different family names found in town, down to the beginning of the eighteenth century.

Akerly, Henry, died June 17, 1650.

Ambler, Elizabeth, wife of Richard, d. March 27, 1685.

Ambler, ——— and Hannah Gold, married Jan. 12, 1692.

Ambler, Ambram and Mary Bates m. Dec. 25, 1662. Their children were: Mary, b. Jan. 15, 1663—Abram, Jan. 5, '65—John Feb. 1, '67—Joshua, Sept. 8, '70—and Sarah, Oct. 6, '72.

Ambler, John, son of John, b. Feb. 15, 1695—Stephen June, 22, '98—and Martha, March 17, 1700.

Ambler, Abraham, son of Abraham, b. Sept 6, 1693.

Ambrey Robert, d. July 21, 1656—Moses, son of Robert, b. Dec. 16, 1652.

Andrus, Jeremiah and Hannah Ambler, widow, m. Sept. 8, 1997. Their children were: John, b. Jan. 31, 1700—Ann, Aug. 3, '02—and Jeremiah, Dec. 5, '05.

Astin, John, d. 6, 24, 1657—and Samuel, his son, 21, 7, '57.

Banks, John and Abigail Lyon, m. April 3, 1672.

Bates, John and Elizabeth Lockwood m. Jan. 18, 1693-4. Their children were, John, b. Nov. 6, 1694—Nathaniel, Oct. 4, '97—Elizabeth, Dec. 10, '99—and David, May 23, 1702. Elizabeth, wife of John Bates, d. May 23, 1702. He m. Sarah Smith Dec. 28, 1702, and had Nehemiah, b. March 29, 1704—and Hannah, May 5, 1705.

Bates, Thomas, of Rye, and Mary Butcher, m. Feb. 21, 1669.

Bates, Robert and Margaret Cross m. June 26, ——.

Bates, Robert, d. Jan. 11, 1675, in the night.

Bell, Francis, d. Jan. 8. 1689—Rebecca, his wife, d. May 17, 1684. Their children were: Jonathan, b. Sept. 1640—Rebecca, Aug. 1643—and Mare, the last of May, 1646. (Old family bible now in possession of Abraham Bell, of Hope Street.)

Bell, Jonathan and Mercy Crane, m. 22, 8, 1662. Their children were: Jonathan, b. Feb. 14, 1663—Hannah, 29, 8, '65—and Rebecca, Dec. 6, '67, and died Sept. 24. 1689. Mercy, wife of Jonathan Bell, d. Oct. 26, 1671. He then m. Susanna, daughter of Rev. Abraham Pierson of Branford, Oct. 31, 1672, and had Abigail, b. 23, 12, '73, and d. 5, 4, '74—Abraham, June 22, '75—Mercy, Nov. 5, '78—John, Jan. 16 '81—a daughter, b, and d. Aug. 3, '83—James, Dec. 11, '84—Susannah, Dec. 25, '86—and Mary, Sept. 29, '89.

Bell, Left. Jona. d. Mar 11, 1698.

Bell, Left. Jonathan and Grace Kitchell m. March 22, 1693. Their son Jonathan was born Jan. 15, 1693-4. Grace died in February.

Bertley, Henry, d. Sept. 17, 1656.

Bishop, Abraham and Stephen, sons of Stephen, b. Oct 28, 1684—Theophilus, Feb, 1, '87—Isaac, Oct. 30, '89—Rebecca, April 9, '92—and Ab igail July 15, '96.

Bishop, Mary, daughter of Mr., d. 25, 5, 1658.

Bishop, Benjamin and Susanna Pierson m. 24, 6, 1696. Their chlidren were Abigail, Oct. 3, 1697—Susana, July 2, '99—Benjamin Nov. 28, 1701—James, April 3, '04—Ruth, June 13, '06—and David, June 26, '08.

Bishop, Joseph and Elizabeth Knowles m. Nov. 3, 1691. Their children were: Joseph, b. Oct, 16, 1692—Alexander, April 15, '94—Charles, May 5, '95—Andrew, Oct 3, '96—Hannah, July 8, '98—Nathan, Oct. 29, '99—Elizabeth, Jan. 3, 1700—Sarah, Dec. 27, 1701—and Rebecca, Aug. 17, 1703.

Blachley, Samuel and Abigail Finch, m. April 6, 1699. Their children were: Samuel, b. March 8, 1699-1700—Sarah, Nov. 7, 1702—and Abigail, Sept. 23, 1705.

Boull (Buel) John and Elizabeth Clements, m. 23, 9, 1694.

Brown, Joseph, had a son, b. Dec. 24, 1686—a second son March 11, '89, Hannah, Sept. 21, '92—Nathaniel, June 16, 96—Nathan, Oct. 29, '97—Jonathan, May 14, 1701—David, March 22, 1703-4—and Mary, October 2, 1705.

Brown, Elizabeth wife of Peter, d. 21, 7, 1657.

Brown, Ebenezer, child of Peter, d. 21, 6, '58.

Brown, Peter, d. 22, 6, '58.

Brown, Eleanor, wife of Peter, d. 21, 6, '58.

Brown, Peter and Unica Buxton, m. 25, 5, '58.

Brown, Francis and Martha Chapman, m. 17, 10, '57.

Butler, John and Mary Clements, m. 23, 9, 1694.

Burr, Daniel and Abigail Prigter, m. Feb. —, 166-.

Buxton, Clement, died Apr. 6, 1657.

Buxton, ——, died Aug. 21, 1657.

Buxton, Clement, had Clement, b. Aug. 16, 1683—Moses, Aug. 21, '86—and Mercy, Nov. 5, '92. Clement Buxton, jr., married in Danbury April 4, 1711, to Elizabeth Ferris.

Buxton Samuel, ye son of Clement and of Judith Buxton, was born in Stamford, and was 14 years old on ye 15 day of July, Anno Domo. 1713.

Buxton, Eunice, dau. of do., was 35 years old, Nov. 3, 1713.

Buxton, Sarah and Abigail, do., were 24 years old Aug. 14, 1713.

Buxton, Elizabeth, do., was 17 years old June 7, 1713.

Cloyson (Clason), Stephen and Elizabeth Periment m. 11, 11, 1654. Their children were: Jona., b. 11, 12; 1655—Stephen, 17, 12, '57—Rebecca, Mar. 1, '59-60—and a son May, 18, '62.

Cloyson, Jonathan and Sarah Roberts, m. 16, 10, 1680—and Stephen, b. 2, 10, 1681—Jonathan, d. 10, 4, '85, and Sarah his wife, 30, 6, '84.

Cloyson. Mary, dau. of David, b. Aug. 17, 1689—Deborah, Nov. 2, '95—Hephzibah, Nov. 4, '98.

Clawson, —— and Mary Homes, m. Dec. 1, 1692.

Clason, Samuel and Hannah Dunham, m. Dec. 7, 1693.

Copp, John and Mary, widow of late Ephraim Phelps, m. March 16, 1698.

Cressy, John and Abigail Knap, m. Dec. 1, 1692. Their children were: Sarah, b. April 25, 1693—Abigail, March 8, '95—John, Feb. 2, '96—Deborah, Feb. 14, '98—Nathaniel, Sept. 16, 1700—Moses, Feb. 14, 1701-2—and Mary, Feb. 15, '04-5.

Cressy, John, son to William, b. May 15, 1695.

Crissy, Mary, d. 25, 5, 1658.

Cross, Nathaniel and Abigail had Hannah, b. Feb. 23, 1687—and Abigail, April 8, '94, and d. Sept. 5, 1710.

Cross, Nathaniel and Hannah Knapp, m. Nov. 6, 1696, and had Deborah, Feb. 17, 1701-2—and Nathaniel, April 13, '03,

Dann, Francis and Elizabeth Clason, m. Nov. 19, 1685, and had Elizabeth, b. August 27, '86.

Davenport, Rev. John and Mrs. Martha Sellick, widow of John Sellick, m. April 18, 1695, and had Abigail, b. July 14, '96—John, Jan. 21, '98—Martha, Feb. 10, 1700—Sarah, July 17, '02—Theodora, Nov. 2, '03, d. Feb. 15, '12—Deodate, Oct. 23, '06—Elizabeth, August '08—Abraham, in '15—and James, in '16.

Dean, John, son of Samuel, b. Dec. 10, 1659—and Joseph, April 6, '61.

Dean, Samuel, d. Dec. 27, 1703.

Dibble John, d. Sept. 1646.

Dibble Nathaniel and Sarah Waterbury, m. 10 3, 1666.

Dibble, Zacharia, and Sarah Waterbury, m. May 10, '66, and had Zachariah, b. Dec. 19, '67.

Dibble, Zachariah and Sarah Clements, m. August 13, 1698, and had Zachariah, b. July 16, 1699—John, Oct. 22, 1701—Daniel, Feb. 19, '03-4—Ebenezer, July 18, '06—and Reuben, Oct. 2, '08.

Disbrow, John and Sarah Knap, m. 6, 2, 1657.

Disbrow, Peter and Sarah Knap, m. April 6, 16—.

Elliot, Mary wife of John, d. 17, 6, 1658.

Ferris, Joseph and Ruth Knap, m. 20, 9, 1657, and had Peter, b. 8, 9, 1660.

Ferris, Jeffrey, d. 31, 5, 1658.

Ferris, Susannah, wife to Jeffry, died at "Grinwich," Dec. 23, 1660.

Ferris, Elizabeth, daughter of Peter, b. 28, 11, 1659, d. 5, 2, '60.

Ferris, Joseph, son of Peter, b. 20, 6, '57—a son, 20, 6, 59—Mary, May 2, '62—and Elizabeth, Jan. 2, '64.

Ferris, Martha, dau. of Isaac, b. June, 19, 1672.

Ferris, Joseph, son of Joseph, b. March 31, 1688—Mary, Dec. 12, '90—Nathan, Oct. 22, '94—Samuel, Sept. 5, '96—Elizabeth, March 19, '98-9—Abigail, April 13, 1701 —Hannah, June 20, 1704—and Deborah, August 27, 1706.

Finch, John. d. Sept. 5, 1657.

Finch, Joseph and Elizabeth Austin, m. Nov. 23, 16—.

Finch, Isaac and Elizabeth Basset, m. — 8, 1658, and had John, b. 20, 9, '59— ——, April 12, '62—Abraham, July 5, '65, before day—Elizabeth, Nov. 14, '69—Martha, June 19, '72—Rebecca March 17, '82-3—Sarah, 23, 11, '86—Jacob, Oct. 9, '91, and died 15, 2, 1702—and Benjamin, Jun e 29 1695.

Finch, Samuel and Sarah, had Mary, b. March 2, 1692-3—Susannah, March 3, '93-4—Sarah, Sept. 25, '95—Abigail, July 15, '97—Hannah, March 23, 1700-1—and Martha, July 23, 1703.

Finch Israel and Sarah Gold, m. Dec. 1, 1692.

Finch, Ann, d. Nov. 9, 1703.

Finch, Samuel, sr., d. April 23, 1698.

Garnsy, Joseph and Rose Waterbury, m. 11, 3, 1659, and had Joseph, b. June 30, 1662.

Garnsey, Joseph and Mary Lockwood, m. march 2, 1692-3, and had Mary, b. Sept 8, 1693—Joseph, April 23, '95—John, May 23, '97—Rose, April 11, '99—Jonathan, Nov. 14, 1701—Hannah, Jan. 27, '02—and Debro, Sept. 10, '04.

Graves, Sarah, d. Sept 13, 1656.

Graves, Benony, son of William d. April 12, 1657.

Green, Mary, wife of John, d. 14, 9, 1657.

Greer, John and Martha Finch, m. —, 7, 1658.

Green, Benjamin and Susan, had a daughter, b. April 19, 1684—a second daughter, July 8, '86—Lucretia, July 20, '90—and Benjamin, Nov. 5, '93—Susan, wife of Benjamin, d. Nov. 5, 1694. Benjamin and Hester Clemence, m. March 26, 1696, and had Hester, b. Dec. 19, 1696—Debro, April 25, 1701—and Joanna, March 14, 1702-3.

Green, Joseph, had Mary, May 30, 1681—Elizabeth, August 5, '83—Waightstill, Nov. 26, '85—Joseph, Jan. 23, '87—and John, Sept. 22, '91.

Hardy, Mary, daughter of Richard, b. 30, 2, 1659.

Hardy, Samuel and Rebecca Hobby, m. Nov. 18, 1686, and had Rebecca b. Sept. 28, 1687.

Hardy, Samuel and Rebecca Furbust, m. May 12, 1693, a second wife, They had Samuel, b. Aug. 8. 1701.

Holly, Elisha, son of John, b. 6, 1, 1659— ——son of John, b. March 1, 1662-3.

Holly, John, Mr., d. May 25, 1681, in 63d year of his age.

Holly, Increase and Elizabeth Newman, m. April 2, 1679, and had John, b. Feb. 29, '79—Jonathan, Feb. 23, '84—Joseph, March 24, '86-7—and Nathan, Sept. 26, '92.

Holly, Jonathan and ——, had Jonathan, b. Aug. 16, 1687—Sarah, Dec. 4, '90—Charles, Aug. 21, '94—David, Jan. 16, '95-6—Bethia, Feb. 4, '97-8, d. Jan. 20, '98-9—Jabez, Nov. 20, 99—John and Increase, Sept 2, 1703—John, dying Sept. 20—and Deborah, b. March 11, 1705-6.

Holly, John and Hannah Newman, m. April 2, 1679, and had Daniel, b. 9, 3, 1680, and died 4, 6, '80—and Abigail, July 6, '82.

Holly, John and Mary Cressy, m. March 10, 1697, and had Abigail, b. Dec. 15, 97—Ebenezer, March 31, '98-9—and Noah, Jan 3, 1700-1.

Holly, Jonathan and Sarah Finch, m. Dec. 2, 1686.

Holly, John and ——, had John, b. April 14, 1685—Nathaniel, Feb. 9, '86-7—Josias, Feb. 27, '89-90—Hannah, Nov. 20, '94—Elizabeth, March 4, '97-8—and Sarah, Sept. 30, 1701.

Holly, Samuel, son of Samuel, b. Jan. 31, 1686-7.

Holly, Elisha and Martha Holmes, m. Dec. 2, 1686, and had Elisha, b. Nov. 10, 1687—Elizabeth, March, 2, 90—Martha, Dec. 28, '91—Elizabeth, Jan. 28. '93-4—Elnathan, March 20, '96—Israel, Jan. 16, '97-8—Abigail, June 8, 1700—John, Nov. 20, 1702, and died Dec. 8,1702—and Mary and Sarah, b. May 5, 1705, Mary, dying May 8, 1705.

Holly, Samuel and Mary Close, m. June 25, 1668, and had John, b. April 20, 1670—Samuel, May 10, '72—Hannah, Aug. 15, '76, d. April 10, 1700—Joseph, b. April 2, '78—Mary, 26, 2. '80—and Benjamin, Oct. 4, '84.

Holly, Samuel, d. in ye 68th year of his age, May 13, 1709.

Homes, John and Rachel Waterbury, m. 12, 3, 1659, and had Mary, b.

Sept. 25, 1662,—Stephen, Jan. 14, '64—Rachel, Dec. 7, '69—and John, Oct. 18, '70.

Homes, John and Marcy Bell, m. Jan. 15, 1701-2, and had Jonathan, b. May 21, '03, and because of his father's death, re-named John.

Homes, Stephen and Mary Hubby, m. Nov. 18, 1686.

Hyat, Thomas, d. Sept. 9, 1656.

Hoyt, Simon, d. 1, 7, 1657.

Hoyt, Mary, daughter of Joshua and Mary, b. Dec. 22, 1664—Rebecca, Sept. 21, '67—Joshua, Oct. 4, '71—Sarah, April 17, '74—Samuel, July 3, '78—Hannah, Sept. 1, '81—Moses, Oct. 7, '83—and Abigail, Aug. 20, '85. Joshua, the father, d. Nov. 9, '90, as recorded will attests.

Hoyt, Benjamin and Hannah Wood, m. Jan. 5, 1670, and had Benjamin b. Dec. 9, '71—Mary, Sept. 20, '73—Hana, June 3, '76—Simon, March 14, '77.

Hoyte,, Samuel and Hannah Holly, m. Nov. 16, 167—and had Samuel, b. July 27, '73—John, Jan. 9, '75—Hannah, Nov, 23, '79-'80—Jonathan, June 11, '83, and died six weeks old—Joseph, June 12, '86—Ebenezer, Nov. 29, '87, and "dyed"—Nathan, Mar. 24, '91—and Nathaniel, April 1, '94, and died July 27, 171—.

Hoyt, Joshua and Mary Picket, m. March 16, 1698, and had Jerusha, b. Dec. 8, '98—and Joshua, June 7, 1700.

Hait, Benjamin, jr. and Elizabeth Jagger, m. June 10, 1697, and had Deborah, b. Aug. 9, '98—Benjamin, Aug. 24, 1700—David, Jan. 23, '02—Abraham, June 16, '04—Samuel, who died Aug. 29, '06—Elizabeth, b. Sept. 26, '10, and died July 31, '12—Ebenezer, b. Oct. '12—Hannah, Dec. 8, '16, and Jonas, May 8, '20.

Hoit, Samuel and Susanna Slason, m. Oct. 24, 1700.

Hoyt, Mr. Samuel, Sr. and Mrs. Mary Gold, m. Sept. 20, 1714.

Hait, Dea. Samuel, d. April 7, 1720.

Hait, Rebecca, wife of Dea. Samuel, d. Dec. 8, 1713.

Hughs, Robert and Elizabeth Buxton, m. Jan. 6, 1655.

Jackson, John had a daughter b. July 21, 1662.

Jagger, Elizabeth, daughter of Jeremy, b. Sept. 18, and d. Dec. 17, 1657.

Jagger, Jeremy, d. 14, 6, 1658.

Jagger, Jonathan and Rebecca Homes, m. Aug. 22, 1700.

Jones, Cornelius and Elizabeth Hyat, m. 6, 8, 1657.

The age of the children of Cornelius Jones, entered this 17th Dec. 1657. eleven year old ye 20th of Aug. last ;——ten year old next Feb. ;—— nelius eight year old ye beginning of Nov. last ;——six year old, May next ; and ——three year old last Jan.

Jones, Mary, daughter of Joseph, b. Jan. 4, 1677 ; Hannah, March 16, '79–'80—Joseph, Dec. 20, '82—Samuel, March 1, '84–85—and Cornelius, March 1, '87–'8.

June, Peter, had Sarah, b. Jan. 30, 1680—Peter, Nov. 22, '83—James, June 29, '87—Thomas, July 23, '90—Mercy, Sept. 11, '92—and Mary, July 30, '99.

Knap, Joshua and Hannah Close, m. June 9, 1657, and had Hannah, b. March 26, '60—Joseph, in '64—Ruth, in '66—Timothy, in '68—Benjamin, in '73—Caleb, in '77—and Jonathan, in '79.

Knap, Elinor, wife of Nicholas, d. 16, 6, 1658.

Knap, Nicholas and Unica Brown, widow of Peter, m. 9, 1, 1659.

Knap, Caleb, son of Caleb, b. Nov. 24, 1661—and John, July 25, '64.

Knap, John and Hannah Ferris, m. June 10, 1692, and had Samuel, b. Aug. 27, '95—John, Aug. 14, '97—Hannah, March 10, '98–'9—a son, b. Aug. 15, '01—Charles, March 9, 1703—and Deborah, June 28, 1705.

Knap. Moses and Elizabeth Crissy, m. —— 168—, and had Elizabeth, b. Sept. 7, '90.

Knapp, Caleb and Hannah Clements, m. 23, 9, 1694—Caleb, b. Sept. 30, '95—William, Dec. 15, '97—Sarah, Jan. 18, '99—Abigail, Jan. 9, 1701–2—Joshua, April 10, 1704—Joseph, Dec. 10, '06—Hanna, April 10, '10—Jonathan, Jan. 12, '12–'13. The next two children of this family were born in Norwalk.

Lawrence, Thomas, d. Aug. 16, '91.

Leeds, John and Mary, had Jonathan, b. Oct. 12, 1693—John, March 8, '94—Sarah, Feb. 8, '96—Samuel, Feb. 21, '97—Ebenezer, Jan. 17, 1700—and Mary, Oct. 23, 1702.

Lounsbury, Henry, son of Richard and Elizabeth, b. Aug. 15, 1684.

Lockwood, Eliphalet and Mary, daughter of John Gold, m. Oct. 11, 1699.

Lockwood, Edmun, d. Jan. 31, 1692.

Lockwood, Joseph and Elizabeth Ayres, m. May 19, 1698, and had Joseph, b. May 15, 1699—Hannah, March 24, '01—John, Sept. 18, '03—and Nathaniel, April 1, '06.

Mead, Benjamin and Sarah Waterbury, m. May 10, 1700.

Mead, wife of William, d. Sept. 19, 1657.

Merwin, Miles and Sarah Scofield, m. Nov. 30, —.

Merwin, Joseph, son of John, b. May 2, 1657.

Mills, —— son of Richard, died Dec. 25, 1660.

"Jno. Mills of Stamford, and Mary Fountain daughter unto Aron Fountain, who was born unto him by his wife Mary whose maiden name was Mary Beebe, who was ye daughter of Mr. Samuel Beebe of new london, ware married in Fairfield, by major Peter Burr, Assistant, October ye 2th, 1702."

Miller, Sarah, daughter of John, b. Nov. 10, 1662.

Newman, Hannah, daughter of William, b. 29, 10, 1657—Mary, d. 18, 10, '59—and Jonathan, b. April 21, '61.

Oliver, —— born 20, 6, 1657.

Oliver, —— son to William, b. 19, 9, 1659—a second son, April 14, '62.

Penoyer, Thomas and Lidde Knap, m. May 22, 1685. and had Abigail b. 13, 8, '86—Mary, Nov. 22, '88—Mellicent, April 13, 91—Mercy, Sept. 28, '93—Samuel, April 3, '96—and John, May 26, 98.

Penoyer, Thomas, son of Robert, b. March 29, 1658—Mary, Nov. 25, '60—Martha, Sept. 26, '64—and Abrigail, 13. 8, '66.

Pettet, Debrow, d. 7, 9, 1657.

Pettet, John's wife d. 27, 7, 1657.

Pettet, —— and Sarah Scofield, m. 13, 6, 1665.

Pettet, David, son of John, b. July 20, 1654, and d. 2, 8, '57—Jonathan, b. Feb. 23—, Sarah, 27, 6, 1666—John, b. 26, 8, '68—a son, 20, 6, 72—and Mercy, b. 5, 9, '74.

Pettet. Jonathan, son of Jonathan, b. latter end of Oct. 1693—John, March 8, '94-5—Sarah, Feb. 8, '96-7—Samuel, Feb. 21, '98-9—and Ebenezer, Jan. 17, 1700-1.

Pond, Abigail, daughter of Nathaniel and Elizabeth, b. April 18, 1698—Elizabeth, Nov. 22, '99—Josiah, Jan, 13, 1701—Hannah, Feb. 13, 1702-3—and Naomi, March 22, 1704-5.

Potter, John and Sarah Sellick, m. August 30, 1698.

Ratliffe, William and Elizabeth Thele, m. 29, 8, 1659' and had Mary, b, Oct. 27, 1662.

Reynolds, Saragh, d. August 21, 1657.

Reynolds, Jonathan, had Rebecca, b. 1656—Jonathan, '60—John, '62—Sarah, '65—Elizabeth, '67—and Joseph, about 69. The father, Jonathan, d in 1673.

Rich, Henry, and Martha Penoir, m. 21, 10, 1680.

Rock, Hittabel, died Sept. 14, 1656.

Rockwell, child of John, died 31, 5, 1658.

Roberts, Thomas and Sarah Elliot, m. 27, 11, 1658, and had Sarah, b. Sept, 4, 1561, and a child, April, 1, '83.

Scofield, Richard, had Elizabeth, b. Nov. 27, 1653, and Jerimy, 10, 1, '58.

Scofield, Mercy. daughter of Daniel, b. the latter end of Nov. 0 9, 1657.

Scofield, John and Hannah Mead, m. Juiy 10, 1677—and had Samuel, b. July 10, '78—John, Jan. 15, '79—80—Ebenezer, Jan. 26, '85—Nathanial, Dec. 10, '88—Mercy, Oct. 30, '90—Mary, Aug. 4, '94—and Susanna, March 2, 97-8.

Scofield, John, died March 27, 1698-9.

Scofield, Richard and Ruth Brundish, m. Sept. 14, 1689, and had Jeremiah, b. April 1, '91—Joshua, Nov. 5, '93—James, April 1, '96—Jonathan, Oct. 9, '98—Hannah, Nov. 14, 1700—Debro, Feb. 14, 1702-3.

Scofield, Daniel and Hannah Hoyt, m. April 17, 1701, and had Nathan, b. April 14, 1702.

Seeley, Obadiah, d. August 25, 1657—Habakuk, d. 13, 6, 1658.

Seeley, Martha, daughter of Jonas, b. Sept. 20, 1690—Jonas, July 22, '92 Susanna, June 12, '94—Ebenezer, Jan. 18, 96-7—Nathaniel, August 23 '99—and Elizabeth, August 20, 1701.

Seeley, John, son of Obadiah, b. August 25, 1693—Nathaniel, June 19, '95—Mercy, Jan. 30, '98—and Obadiah, August 7. 1701.

Seeley, Sarah, daughter of Jonas, born Feb. 1694-5.

Sellick, Jonathan. and Abigail Law, m. May 11, 1665.

Sillick, Jonathen, son of Jonathan, b. July 11, 1664—David, Jan. 27, '65

Selleck, John and Sarah Law, m. Oct. 28, 1669, and had Sarah, b. August 22, 1670—David, Dec. 27, '72—Nathaniel, April 7, '78—John, June 7, '81.

Selleck, Mr. John, had Susanna, b. Feb. 2, 1683, and Johanna, b. May 31, '86.

Selleck, Jonathan Jr., and Abigail Gold, m. Jan. 5, 1685—and had Abi gail, b. April 3, 1685—Nathan, Sept. 12. '86—and Theophila, Feb. 11, 94-5.

Selleck, Nathaniel and Sarah Lockwood, m. Jan. 25, 1699—and had Daniel b. Dec. 23, 1700.

Selleck, Capt. Jonathan, d. June 11, 1710.

Selleck, Maj. Jonathan, d. Jan. 10, 1712-13.

Shepard, Mary, widow, d. August 15, 1683.

Simkins, Jonathan, d. 7, 8, 1657.

Skelding, Thomas and Rebecca Slason, m. June 11, 1701.

Slason, Sarah, daughter of John, jr., b. Jan. 20, 1693—John, Oct. 4, '95 —Martha, Sept. 17, '99—and Elizabeth, April 18, 1703.

Slason, Jonathan and Mary Waterbury, m. Feb. 4, 1699-1700—and had Abigail, b. March 8, 1700—Mary, Jan. 20, 1704.

Slason, John, son of John, b. Sept. 9, 1664—Sarah, Jan. 20, '67—Jonathan, July 25, '70—Elizabeth, Jan. '30, '72—Mary, April 21, '80—Thomas, 3, 12, '81—and Hannah, March 12, 85—6.

Smith, Samuel, son of Henry, died 16, 8, 1658—Mary, 3, 10, '58—and a daughter, August 9, '61. Ann, wife of Henry, died second week in June, 1685.

Smith, Elizabeth, wife to John, d. Oct. 6, 1703—and his youngest daughter, Oct. 10, 1703.

Smith, Hannah, daughter to John, d. Oct. 27, 1703.

Stevens, Thomas, died, 19, 6, 1658.

Stevens, Obadiah and Rebecca Rose, m. Dec. 18, 1678—and had Thomas, b. Sept. 6, 1679—Ephraim, Jan. 28, '80—Rose, Oct. 14, '83—Rebecca, 12, 2, '86—Elisha, April 23, '88—Daniel, Nov. 30, '90—Nathan, Dec. 1, '94 and Deliverance, a son, August 1, 1697.

Stevens, Joseph and Sarah Buxton, m. June 24, 1680—and had Joseph b. May 21, '81—Unica, Dec. 5, '83—Sarah, Jan. 27, '86—and Mary, Jan, 30, '91—Stevens, Obadiah, d. Dec. 24, 1702.

Stukey, George, and Ann Quimby, m. 28, 9, 1657.

Stukey, Elizabeth, d. Sep. 4, 1656.

Stukey, George, d. Nov. 28, 1660.

Taylor, Gregory, d. 24, 7, 1657.

Taylor, Goodwife, d. 18, 6, 1657.

Theal, Nicholas, died 19, 6, 1658.

Uffert, Elizabeth, widow, d. Dec. 27, 1660.

Usher, Robert and Elizabeth Jagger, m. 12, 3, 1659, and had Elizabeth b. Feb. 25, 1659-60.

Waterbury, John, d. 31, 5, 1658.

Waterbury, Sarah, daughter of Jonathan, b. August, 15, 1677—Unice, Oct. 7, '79—Rose, Jan. 21, '81—Rachel, Aug. 26, '84—Jonathan, Feb. 9, '85—Abigail, July 1, '88—and Joseph, Jan. 26, '91.

Waterbury, Jonathan, d. Jan. 14, 1702.

Waterbury, Mary, daughter of John, b. March 20, 1679—John, Oct. 30, '82—David, Jan. 24, '84—and Thomas, May 12, '87.

Waterbury, John, son of David, b. Jan. 25, 1681-2—Elizabeth, Jan. 19, '83-4—and Sarah, Jan. 10, 84-5.

Waterbury, David and Sarah Weed, 2d. wife, m. August 11, 1698—and had Ruth, b. Jan. 3, 1699—and David, Nov. 9, 1701.

Waterbury. ——, son to Jonas, b. Sept. 12, 1694.

Webb, Richard, d. Jan. 1, 1656.

Webb, Joshua, son of Richard, b. —— — ——; and —— Nell, March 30, 1662.

Webb, Richard, died, March 15, 1675,-6.

Webb, child of Richard, died, Jan. 1, 1656.

Webb, Joseph and Hannah Scofield, m. Jan. 8, 1672, and had Joseph, b. Jan. 5, 1674—Mary, April 14, '77—Hannah, March '79—Sarah, Oct. 16, '81—and Margery, Oct. 4, '83.

Webb, Waitstill, child of Samuel, b. Jan. 6, 1690-1—Samuel, Nov. 6, '92 Mercy, April 11, '93—Charles, March 12, '96-7—Mary, Jan. 7, '98—9—and Nathaniel, Nov. 6, 1700.

Webb, Joseph, and Mary Hait, m. Feb. 23, 1698—and had Joseph, b. Jan. 26, 1700-1—Ebenezer, b. March 7, 1704, and died, April 16, 1704—Benjamin, August 24, 1705.

Weed, Jonas, child, d. July 15, 1656.

Weed, Jonas, son of John, b. Feb. 5, 1667—Daniel, Feb. 11, '69—Joseph, d. Jan. 7, '90, aged 12 years—Isaac, April 20, '91, aged 9 years—Mary, April 21, '91, aged 7 years, and Hanna, March 22, '91, aged 4 years.

Weed, Jonas and Bethia Holly, m. Nov. 16, 167—.

Weed, Jonas, son of Jonas, (Shoemaker), b. July 26, 1678—Benjamin April 5, '81—Jonathan, April 15, '84—Abigail, April 5, '95—John, Nov. 19, '98—Miles, Feb. 24, 1700-1—Sarah, March 10, '02-'03—and Nathan, May 20, 1705.

Weed, Jonas, (Shoomaker), d. Nov. 18, at eavening, 1706.

Weed, Daniel and Mary Webb, m. Sept. 23, 1697.

Weed, Daniel, had Abraham, d. 18 years old, Aug. 18, 1698—Sarah, 23 years old, Nov. 18, '98—Daniel, 13 years old, March 19, '98—Ebenezer, 6 years old, Oct. 22, '98—Nathaniel, 2 years old, Oct. 22, '98—Joseph, b. Aug. 18, '98—David, Aug. 19, 1700—Joanna, Nov. 8, '02—and Daniel, May 14, '05

Weed, Samuel and Abigail Scofield, m. April 17, 1701.

Weed, Joseph and Rebecca Higginbotham, m. Dec. 10, 1701.

Weed, Jonas, at Noroton Corners, and Sarah Waterbury, m. Jan. 20, 1703-4, and had Jonas, b. at Noroton Corners, Dec. 24, 1704.

Weed, Jonas, Sr. d, Nov. 19, 1704.

Wiat, Nathaniel, son of Nathaniel, b. July 18, 1697.

Youngs, John and Ruth Eliat, (Elliot), m. Jan. 30, 1690, and had Elizabeth, b. April 22, '94, and d. April 15, 1706—Ruth, b. May 21, '96—Mary, Aug. 30, 1700—John, May 5. 1703—Abigail, March 13, '05-6—Thomas, Feb. 21, '07-8—Elizabeth, May 30, '10—Samuel, Sept. 30, '12—and Sarah, June 18, '15.

CHAPTER X.

STAMFORD IN 1700.

This year finds in Connecticut twenty-seven towns incorporated, of which Stamford ranks the thirteenth on the grand list. The population of the town is probably somewhere between five and six hundred. The territory is about seven and a half miles in width and not far from eleven in length.

Sixty years have now passed since its settlement; and they have been years which must have left many and well defined traces of their course.

Already Eastfield, Southfield, Northfield and Newfield, embracing a large part of the territory south of what is now the North Stamford Parish, had been "layed out" to the proprietors or their children, or were yet used as common grounds for "winter corn" or summer pasture. Enough had been learned of the several parts of this domain to have already established in common use names long since outworn or forgotten.

Runkinheag and Short Rocks, Hardy's Hole and Slason's Wolf Pit, Elbow Plain and Rump Swamp, Great Fresh Meadow and Jagger's Den, Clabord Hill and Hollow Tree Ridge, are names of less significance in these modern times than when they expressed localities closely connected with the most important interests of the young colony. A well built fence running across its neck, and which twenty years ago had taxed the common time of the whole people, had secured the whole of our beautiful headland, Shipan, as the yearly corn ground of the proprietors; while another fence running across eastward from below the landing place to the north of where our new cemetery now lies, cut off the early Rocky Neck as their nearest pasture ground.

Across this territory ran an irregular road, near the course of the present principal street through the town. From this, cart paths radiated at different points, out to the several fields which had then been laid out, embracing the most of the southern part of the tract, while almost all the northern portion of it was still a forest,with openings for here and there a pioneer home on the two northward routes leading from the present center of Darien and Stamford over Woodpecker Ridge into the new settlement at Bedford across the Dutch lines.

Of the state of these roads at this period, even the best of them, that which formed the chief landward route between New Haven and New York, we find a very reliable description in the private journal of Madam Knight. She had started on horseback from Boston, Oct. 2, 1704, to visit New York. Dec. 6th she left New Haven attended by a kinsman of hers, Thomas Trowbridge of that city, also on horseback. They made the journey together, and started on their return Dec. 15th. The journal thus mentions the route across Stamford. As she left Rye she says: "here we took leave of York government and descending the mountainous passage that almost broke my heart in ascending, before we came to Stamford, a well compact town, but miserable meeting house which we passed, and through many great difficulties, as bridges which were exceeding high, and very tottering, and of vast length, steep and rocky hills and precipices (bugbears to a fearful female traveler). About nine at night we came to Norwalk, having crept over a timber of a broken bridge about thirty feet long and perhaps fifty to the water." On the journey to New York she says that between Norwalk and Rye they proceeded "walking and leading their horses neer a mile together, up a prodigious high hill." This is the hill of which she speaks on the return. Of the condition of the other roads traversing the town we have no account.

Already were visible the germs of at least two other centers on this tract, at Middlesex and at Woodpecker Hollow. But as yet no effort had been made to establish church or permanent school privileges elsewhere in all this stretch of territory, than at the very center of the town plot. Here, close by where the first rude church had been built, stands the third edifice, now in its sixth year of good service rendered the town, yet already undergoing such changes in its interior as the increasing population demands. This very year the order is given to transfer the pulpit to the north end, and turn the seats to face it, and to throw galleries around the hitherto unused walls to accommodate those for whom there are now no seats.

The fathers of the town were nearly all gone, and the third generation were now coming forward to the responsibilities and honors of social and civil life. We will see who are still here and in what positions, as far as the records of that day will show.

The chief man of this now somewhat organized town, Rev. John Davenport, has for some six years held his throne in the hearts of the people who had voluntarily placed him there; and there seems to be no abatement of their loyalty or their love. They still, with great unanimity, vote his annuity of the usual "specia," and a most bountiful supply of wood. Early November of this year gathers them together in formal town meeting, and the first and most important business of the day is to see that all the temporal wants of their faithful pastor are supplied. See how fully those citizens of the year of grace, 1700, provide for one of their pastor's wants. The whole town are assembled. Samuel Hoyt, the same who was to sit with Mr. Davenport, ere long, in the famous Saybrook Convention to aid in framing the famous Saybrook Platform, was doubtless their Moderator. The drum has ceased its summons, and the ready pastor has invoked on his people the presence and blessing of God. He retires and the second man of all this people, moderator Hoyt, calls for such business, as now the providence of God orders them to "attend."

The first response, introduces as of first importance the claims of the good pastor, who was in charge of the spiritual interests of the whole town.

Nineteen closely written lines, in the hand writing of the the honored recorder of the town, Samuel Holly, Sen., report to us all that was done in that November meeting; but fifteen of them are devoted to recording the care which the people took of him whose sacred office they had been trained to honor, and whose personal character they had learned to respect and love.

They now vote Mr. Davenport, his annuity of wood. Lest any part of it should be lacking, the amount was provided for in the town rate; yet each inhabitant dwelling between Norwalk and Greenwich was allowed "reasonable time and warning" for carting his proportion of the wood, which, from a previous record we learn must be deposited in the minister's yard before the end of November. They, then, vote the price which each person must pay who fails to carry his proportion of the supply,—eight shillings for each load—and order that none of the wood carried shall be cut over "six foot" long. And lest these orders should fail of practical execution, the following vote secures the desired result.

"By voate ye town doe appoint Daniel Scofield and Elisha Holly to apportion to each man what wood he shall carry to Mr. Davenport, and to order ye time when it shall be carried; and do Impower ye sd Scofield and Holly to hire all such men's proportion of sd wood as shall neglect or refuse doing their sd proportions, after Reasonable warning and time allowed for ye performing of ye sd worke, and shall pay all such as are hired, town Rate not exceeding eight shillings ye coard, and for their incouragement to ye sd persons improued In ye worke they shall have allowed them so much as their proportion is in ye town Rate; yt is of wood."

I have introduced this item of town business in its full proportions, as most distinctly revealing the leading aim and spirit of the town, a hundred and sixty-eight years ago and to indicate the manner in which they sought to realize it. Religion and its support was this aim, and for this the town government was framed and pledged.

Let us now name the men who are here, and their recorded positions.

At the first town meeting held this year, March 5, 1700, the following offices are filled:

For "viewers," that is, for those who were to inspect the fields and see that that they were closed so as to "turn creturs" by the fifteenth of March, but who were obliged to officiate the twentieth day of the month, we have the names of John Slason, sen., and Isaac Finch, sen., for the Northfield; Joseph Garnsy and Daniel Cloisen for the Southfield; and John Slason, jr., and John Crissy for the Eastfield.

For "pounders," that is, for those authorized to impound lawless cattle, there were: Thomas Slason and Samuel Finch for Northfield; Daniel Lockwood, for the Southfield; John Green and John Bishop, for Eastfield; and Clement Buxton for Rockyneck.

For "suruaires," (surveyors,) were: Richard Scofield and Nathaniel Cross for Southfield and westward; Benjamin Hoit, sen., and Dan. Scofield, for Northfield and "Norward; Steven Bishop and Steven Homes for Eastfield and eastward and Rockyneck.

Mr. Samuel Hait and Elisha Holly are added to the committee for laying out Runkinheag or Short Rocks.

Mr. Jonathan Selleck, jr.. Mr. David Waterbury and Elisha Holly, are appointed to prosecute all "found defective upon the account of lands." Benjamin Green and Nathaniel Cross are to "vewe" the land west of Joseph Garnsy's lot and report.

Zacri Dibble is allowed ten acres from the sequestered lands,

Elisha Holly is to have six and Jonathan Crissy ten. David Waterbury and Elisha Holly are to report a place on Stonybrook for Mr. Bates to set a fulling mill, as he wishes leave to do.

At the town meeting held August 23, 1700, Peter Ferris, jr,, and Jonathan Bates are appointed to make out the town list, and Samuel Holly, sen. "is to fit it for ye corte." No other vote of this meeting is recorded.

At the town meeting held November 8 of this year, in addition to the votes respecting Mr. Davenport already reported, John Holly, "Increasis son," has donated to him "a corner of land within the Eastfield gate next his lot, not preyising the highway," and Stephen Bishop, Jonathan Waterbury are to vewe ye sd land and stake it out to him.

Daniel Scofield. sen. and Elisha Holly are chosen auditors. At the meeting held December 27th of this year, Benjamin Hoyt, sen. and John Ambler are chosen collectors to gather Mr. Davenport's rate.

John Slason, sen. and Joseph Ferris, constables.

Daniel Scofield, sen. Jonas Weed, sen. Richard Scofield, Elisha Holly and Samuel Holly, sen., are made townsmen.

Left. Waterbury and Daniel Scofield, sen.. "Sheep masters to take care of ye flock."

Joseph Turney and Increase Holly to lay out the land granted by the town to "Zacry Debble," and Jonathan Cross and Elisha Holly. The above are all the names which occur on the business records of the town for the year 1700. Others who were living on this tract at the time, will appear from the assignment of land by lot, December 26, 1699. There were sixty-nine lots, and they were drawn by seventy-five persons in the following order.

Stephen Clawson	Ensign Bates	William Clemance
John Arnold	Nathaniel Cross	Joseph Garnsy
John Crissy	George Slason	John Pettit
John Holly, sen.	Lieut. Bell	Daniel Scofield
Jonas Seeley	Peter June	Increase Holly

Abram Finch	Stephen Holmes	Abraham Ambler
" ye prSonage	Francis Dan	Jeremy Jagger
Mr. Mills	Jonathan Waterbury	Joseph Brown
Elawzer Slas on	Samuel Hoyt	Joseph Hoyt
Isaac Finch	Thomas Lawrence	Jonas Weed
Mr. Bishop	Benjamin Green	Elisha Holly
John Holmes	John Scofield	Thomas Newman
John Slason	Joseph Green	Moses Knapp
Jonathan Holly	Clement Buxton	Daniel Weed
Joseph Turney	Samuel Webb	Jonathan Jagger,
Capt. Selleck	Peter Ferris	Widow Webster
Mr. Lawes	John Miller	Seely, deceased
Richard Scofield	John Wescott	Samuel Holly
Joseph Thell	David Waterbury	Obadiah, Stevens
John Smith	Samuel Finch	Benjamin Hoyt
Ed. and Jo. Lockwood	John Waterbury	John Finch
Thomas Penoyer	John Austin	Cornelius Jones
John Weed	John Finch, jun.	John Goold
Caleb Knapp	Joseph Stevens	
Samuel Hardy	Samuel Dean	

In addition still to these names we have others in the following list of estates made out in January, 1701. This list will also be in proof of the relative pecuniary standing of the citizens at this date. The list is said to be that "belonging to ye proper inhabitance in Stamford." It is alphabetically arranged on the original record, and may be found in Book of Records A, page 376.

	£ s. d.		£ s. d.
Ambler, John,	92 10 0	Holly, Samuel, sen,	52 00 0
Andrews, Jeremiah,	96 18 0	Holly, John, ser.	71 10 0
Austen, John,	34 04 0	Holly, John,	63 00 0
Bates, John, sen.	135 00 0	Holly, Elixabeth,	61 16 3
Bates, John, jun.	90 00 0	Holly, Jonathan,	58 10 0
Bell, Mrs.	105 00 0	Holly, John, jun.,	30 00 0
Bell, Jonathan,	55 05 6	Holly, Samuel, jun.,	20 00 0
Bishop, Stephen,	143 10 0	Holly, Joseph,	25 00 0
Bishop, Joseph,	55 12 0	Holly, John,un ,	20 10 0
Bishop, Ebenezer,	33 00 0	Jagger, Jonathan,	39 05 0
Bishop, Benjamin,	38 10 0	June, Peter,	75 15 0
Brown, Joseph,	78 10 0	Jones, Orp, (orphan?)	04 00 1

Buxton, Clement,	112 00 6
Blachley, Samuel,	37 07 3
Crissy, John,	40 16 0
Crissy Jonathan,	18 00 0
Cross, Nathaniel,	54 00 0
Closon, Daniel,	64 05 6
Closon, Samuel,	55 12 0
Chapman Simon,	26 00 6
Clemance, William,	27 12 0
Clark, Joseph,	21 00 0
Dan, Francis.	27 00 0
Dibble, Zechary,	26 05 3
Dean, Samuel,	14 13 0
Dean, John,	30 00 6
Dean, Mathew,	18 00 0
Ferris, Peter,	118 12 0
Ferris, Joseph,	72 02 0
Ferris, Peter, jun.	39 00 0
Finch, Isaac, sen.	27 10 0
Finch, Abraham, sen.	37 02 0
Finch, John,	22 00 0
Finch, Samuel,	46 02 6
Finch, Joseph,	42 02 6
Finch, Abraham, jun.	35 00 0
Finch, Isaac, jun.	22 00 0
Garnsey, Joseph,	46 10 0
Green, John,	28 17 6
Green, Benjamin,	55 09 0
Green, Joseph,	81 01 0
Gold, John,	88 02 6
Hardy, Samuel,	47 00 0
Higgingbothum, Mr.	30 00 0
Holmes, Stephen,	83 05 0
Holmes, Samuel,	18 00 0
Holmes, John,	31 00 0
Hayt, Samuel, sen.	94 10 0
Hayt, Samuel, jun.	24 02 6
Hayt, John,	19 00 0
Hayt, Benjamin, sen.	112 00 0
Hayt, Benjamin, jun.	52 05 6
Hayt, Joshua,	31 12 6
Hayt, Samuel, (smith)	36 12 6
Knap, Moses,	45 05 0
Knap, John,	111 05 0
Knap, Caleb,	34 17 6
Lockwood, Joseph,	40 07 6
Lockwood, Daniel,	38 02 6
Lockwood, Edmund,	28 10 0
Mills, William,	21 00 0
Mills, John,	18 00 0
Newman, Thomas,	83 00 0
Pettit, John,	56 07 9
Penoyer, Thomas,	72 05 0
Pond, Nathaniel,	36 00 0
Slason, John, sen.	101 05 0
Slason, John, jun.,	57 15 0
Slason, Jonathan,	33 00 0
Slason, James,	43 02
Slason, Stephen,	18 00
Seeley, Obadiah,	26 00 0
Seeley, Jonas, jun..	18 00 0
Scofield, Daniel, sen.,	115 05 0
Scofield, Daniel, jun.,	55 10 0
Scofield, Widow,	66 05 0
Scofield, John,	27 03 0
Scofield, Richard,	56 02 6
Smith, John,	107 02 6
Smith, Daniel,	148 0 0
Stevens, Obadiah,	79 07 6
Stevens, Thomas,	18 00 6
Stevens, Joseph,	46 17 0
Stone, John,	22 00 0
Selleck, Major,	91 15 0
Selleck, Widow,	106 05 0
Selleck, Captain,	123 10 6
Selleck, Nathaniel,	57 0 8 0
Seeley, Jonas, sen.,	116 170
Trahern, Edward,	41 10 0 0
Turney, Joseph,	63 05 0
Waterbury, Daniel,	136 10 9
Waterbury, Jona.	100 00 0
Weed, Jonas, sen.,	154 10 0
Weed, Widow,	96 10 0
Weed, Daniel,	26 07 0

Weed, Samuel,	22 15 0	Webster, Daniel,	30 0 0
Weed, Joseph,	55 06 3	Wood, Mr.	119 10 0
Webb, Samuel,	56 10 0	Youngs, John,	46 10 0
Webb, Joseph,	61 08 9	Davenport, Mr. John,	100 00 0
Webster, John,	41 00 0		

Entered this 28th of Jan. 1701-2, by Sam'l Holly, recorder.

The following choice morceau, found in the New York colonial records of this date, will enable us to estimate the influence of Stamford, in what has since become the metropolis of the continent. It bears date, New York, November 28, 1700, and was written by the "Earl of Bellomont," to the English Lords of Trade, his masters. It will give us a pretty clear idea of the Yankee enterprise of at least one of the Stamford boys of that day. The record will also, reveal the natural results of the nearness of Stamford to the great metropolis of the country, indicating thus early in its history how strongly our business men are tempted towards the city.

"Theres a town called Stamford, in Conn. Colony, on the border of this province, where one Major Selleck lives, who has a ware house close to the sea, that runs between the mainland and Nassau, (Long Island). That man does us great mischief with his ware house, for he receives abundance of goods from our vessels, and the merchants afterwards take their opportunity of running them into this town. Major Selleck received at least £10,000 worth of treasure and East India goods, brought by one Clarke of this town from Kid's sloop, and lodged with Selleck."

CHAPTER XI.

NEW FAMILY NAMES BETWEEN 1660 AND 1775.

This chapter proposes to record the introduction of new families between 1660, to which date our fifth chapter brings down the list, and the opening of our revolutionary war. We shall, as in the former chapters on the settlers, give such account of these new families as we have been able to secure. A few other names may appear in the text, but of persons probably transiently here. We regret a want of space which compels quite an abridgment from our original draft of this chapter on the pioneer names of these new families.

ARNOLD, Joseph, 1685, by vote of the town is allowed to set up a shop on the town lot, towards the northwest corner.

In 1688, with such help as he could command, he was found engaged in rigging up a brigantine under suspicious circumstances. They could not or would not report the object or destination of the craft. This, too, was at the time when the English government were continually finding fault with the New England colonies for allowing piratical expeditions to be fitted out in their harbors. The fathers of the town, against whom no suspicion of disloyalty or even remissness in civil duty could be raised, at once issued their injunction upon the proceeding. The mere fact that the cause for rigging up the brigantine was unknown, was the ground of the injunction.

He is called mariner, on leaving home, Mar. 20, 1688–9. The record states that "being designed on a voyage to sea, by God's grace," he appoints his brother John and his loving friend

Peter Chocke his attorneys. Several families of this name must have been here during the first half of the last century.

Ayers, Richard, sen. gives son Philip land, Dec. 19, 1705; and his house and use of land to son "Harence." Mary his wife died, Jan. 19, 1715-6. Richard, jr. said to be of Stamford, buys land, April 5, 1703, of Richard Scofield. He, or another of the same name, married, Abigail ———, Dec. 18. 1712, and had a son John born in '14. The widow of Richard Ayres, married John Mott; and in '35, John and Abigail Mott quit claim to their sons John and Ebenezer Ayres and their daughter Mary Ayres, all their interest in the estate of their honored father Richard Ayres.

Baker, Samuel 1775, buys of Wm. Budd Lucas, on Bald Hill. The name disappears for three quarters of a century, to re-appear in Luke Baker. whose family now live on South St.

Banks, John, 1730. This family have continued in the north west part of the old township until the present day.

Beachgood, John and Hannah, had children born here; Mary, Nov. 18, 1721; Martha, March 6, '25; Peter, March 17 '26-7; Hannah, Sept. 8, '31.

Beldin, John, 1691, is a partner with Jonathan Selleck in the purchase of the Pink Blossom, built in Stamford, by John Mills. This family was quite numerous and evidently had both means and influence about the middle of the last century.

Bellamy, Matthew, teacher, buys land of Robert Usher in 1688, when he is said to be of Stamford. In 1670 he was hired to teach school; and the town give him a house lot, binding him to build on it within two years. The name soon disappeared from the roll of citizens.

Blachley, Samuel, blacksmith, Aug. 15, 1695, buys land of Abraham Finch, and next year appears on the list of town officials. In 1708 he is on the school committee. In 1714, he was voted the liberty of Mill river, above Northfield for a mill, if he will build on it within three years. In 1723 he had a shop near the meeting house; and by 1730, he had made such progress in position as to be allowed the honored prefix, Mr. to his name. By his first wife, Abigail Finch, he had Samuel, Sarah, and Abigail; and by the second whose name was Sarah, a Mary, b. Aug. 24, 1710. His death occurred Oct. 14, '56.

Blackley, Joseph, 1736–7, married Abigail Hoyt. Children, Sarah, b. Sept. 20, '37, and Joseph, June 24, '39. The wife Abigail died, June 27, 1739.

This name is spelled Blatchely, Blachly, Blackesly, and in several other ways, making it difficult often to decide what family is indicated. The name appears often on the land records of the town.

Blackman, Josiah, married here, Aug. 5, 1714, Sarah Brown. Children, one who died Feb. 25, '14–15; Josiah, born in 16; Sarah, b. Oct. 15, 1718; Joseph, b. Nov. 5, 1719; Elizabeth, d. April 11, 1730; Josiah, jr., d. Mar. 14, 1738–9. His name is several times on the list of town officials and his death is recorded, June 17, 1747. His wife died, Aug. 16, '45.

Blanchard, William and Abigail, had children; Jacob, b. Feb. 28, 1744–5; Abigail, b. Sept. 7, 1746; William, b. Jan. 8, 1749–50, and a second Jacob, b. Feb. 5, 1752. He is among the officials of the town as early as 1751.

Boardman, Israel, was here in 1724, when his "ear mark" was entered to him. An Israel Boardman, married here March 13, 1745–6, Mary Blackman. Children, one that was b. and d. same day, and Mary, b. Feb. 1, 1753.

Booloch, Richard, then 66 years old, owned a farm here in 1677, which had been given by John Budd to his son-in-law, John Ogden.

Bostwick, Ephraim, purchased Dec. 3, 1745, of Peter Quintard of Norwalk, and Hannah Quintard and Nathaniel Hubbard of Stamford, the land of Isaac Quintard deceased.

From similarity of names in their families he was doubtless a grandson of that Arthur Bostwick whom Savage brings with his son John from the county of Chester, Eng. to Stratford. He was probably a cousin of the Rev. Ephraim Bostwick who was recorded here, as married to Mrs. Abigail Allen, March 1, 1738–9, and who was settled as pastor over the First Church in Greenwich, from 1730 to 1746. To this Rev. Ephraim, there were born and recorded here, Zachariah, b. Nov. 39, 1737; Ephriam, Oct. 25, 1741; Mary, Aug. 4, 1743; Abigail, Aug. 16, 1745; Ebenezer, March 14, 1749; William, April 19, 1751, and Samuel, July 29, 1753. Ephraim Bostwick seems to have been active and prominent in the school society.

BORDEN, Nathaniel is on the list of the town officers in 1737.

BOUTON, Richard, had died here June 27, 1665, when his will was probated. His wife Ruth had the use of his property, and at her death, if there should be any left, it was to go to his son John's son John.

John, 1722, is on the official list of the town, and Nathaniel is admitted an inhabitant the next year by vote of the town. John, jr., and Mary Pettit, m. Feb. 18, 1731–2. Children, Mary, b. Dec. 24, '32; Gold, b. Jan. 24, '33–4. This name has been quite numerous and furnished a good number of respectable citizens.

BRIGGS, Daniel in 1707 had lands here. He had married, Nov. 24, 1704, Elizabeth Newman at Rye, and his daughter Sarah is recorded as seven years old, March 29, '12–13. They had a daughter Mary, b. Jan. 24, '16–17. The name has continued until the present time though never very numerous.

BROOKER, Samuel, 1748, is on the official list of the town and for several years must have been quite active and prominent.

BRYAN, Samuel and Augustin had families here during the first half of the last century.

CHESTER, Richard, tailor, in 1708–9 buys dwelling house here of Joseph Lockwood.

CHICHESTER, Daniel, 1722, married Abigail Bishop and had children.; Abraham, b. '25; Abigail, b. '27; Susannah, b. '33; and Daniel, b. '35.

CLEMENTS, William, 1671, seems to have succeeded Mr. Rider as teacher. In 1677 he is given a house lot if he and his "do forever maintain all the town fence lying by the two Northfield gates, and for secHrity the above land shall be bound forever." Clements, Widow Elizabeth, died here in 1727–8.

CLUGGSTON, John, 1721, takes his cattle mark. He and Elizabeth had children, Elizabeth, John, Ann, Deborah, Samuel, Mary, Abigail. He had been twice married.

CLOCK, John, was admitted an inhabitant by vote in 1725. He married Deborah Scofield, and had a daughter Catherine born, Jan. 6, 1725, and a son Albert, May 9, '29. This name is still in the eastern part of the old township.

COREY, Thomas, 1720, when the following children are recorded to him and his wife Elizabeth; Jane, six years old, Feb. 17th; Mary, four years old, Oct. 6th, and Thomas, one year old, Feb. 10th.

CONKLIN, Cary, 1728, in north part of the town, has liberty to pay ministers rate in Bedford.

CRAWFORD, James and Abigail had children; John James, b. June 10, 1763, and d. April 21, '66; Joanna, b. Nov. 24, '65, and John, July 2, '67.

CRISSY, William, Jan. 16, 1666, testifies in the Stamford court. His son John was born in 1665; and probably it was his daughter Mary who died in 1658. In 1672, in a deed of land sold to Nicholas Webster, he is styled planter. This name has been both numerous and respectable.

CROSS, Nathaniel, 1673, was voted a home lot. In 1687, he buys of Ebenezer Mead of Greenwich, land in Stamford. In

1693, John Cross of Windsor, sells his house and home lot in Stamford to his brother Nathaniel of Stamford.

Curtiss, Cornelius, Oct. 3, 1712, married Deborah Green. Timothy, in '47 was one of the school committee and prominent among the town officials afterward.

Dan, Francis, the first of this name in town, bought land of Isaac Finch, March 17, 1684–5. By his wife, Elizabeth, he had children, "born in Stamford;" Abigail, b. March 30, 1699; Rebecca, Aug. 25, 1706; Jonathan, Nov. 9, '09. This family settled in the north part of the town and gave name to a part of it.

Daniel, (Daniels) Richard, married Bethiah Hoyt, March 1, 1750, and had a son Abraham, b. Sept. 24, '52.

Davis, John, 1709, is admitted by vote an inhabitant of the town.

Davenport, Rev. John, the ancestor of this family came here as our Chapter of Ecclesiastical history shows in 1693; and his family from that date have been prominent in the history of the town. See Biog. Sketches; and for an account of the descendants of Mr. Davenport, the first of the family here. uee also the Davenport Family, by A. B. Davenport, Esq., of Brooklyn, N. Y.

Delavan, Cornelius, was probably the first of this name here. He had property here in 1713, and his wife Deborah had son Timothy, b. July 29th, of the same year; and in '46 appears among the officials of the town. John Delevan must have been here about as early, as he had a son Cornelius born here in '15. The family settled in the northeast part of the town where the name is still respectably represented.

Demill, Peter, of French parentage, was here in business in 1703. He was evidently a man of means and of business energy. He lived on the ground now occupied by the Congregational Church. He died here in '22, when he was styled captain. Peter, son, probably of the above, had son Peter, b.

May 23, 1731, and son Abraham, Dec. 21, 1735. He and Anthony Demill a brother, probably, in 1727, were granted the privilege of building a grist mill at the mouth of Mill river, twenty rods below where "Harriss's old mill" was. For several years the name was quite prominent in the records of the town; and is still well represented among the business men of New York.

De FOREST, Anthony and Martha had son Reuben, b. Dec. 1755.

DIXON, John, married Ruth Hait of Norwalk, and had son John born here, Nov. 25, 1761. He married for his second wife, Rachel Sherwood of Stamford, and they had a son Hugh, b. Oct. 29, '70. The name is still found on our roll of citizens.

DREW, Dr. John, married here Feb. 4, 1714, Elizabeth Green. Mercy Drew, a daughter, probably of Dr. Drew, married here Jan, 8, '35-6, Jonathan Weed. (See list of physicians.)

DUFREES, John and Mary, and Stephen and Sarah had children here between 1760 and '75. They were land owners here during the revolutionary war and occupied a part of "Bauld" Hill, Canaan parish.

EMERY, John, 1668, sells house and land to Richard Law.

FANCHER, John, and Emice Bouton, m. Nov. 19, 1736, '34, fireman, '47, buys land of John Jacklin, and in '50 is on the official list of the town. Hanna, m. Joseph Garnsey, June 6, '28.

FOUNTAIN, Mary, dau. of Aaron and Mary, m. John Mills, of Stamford, Oct. 2, 1702.

Fountain, Sam. and Martha Scofield, m. Nov. 23. '74 Moses; b. June 3, '76; Sam. b. June 4, '78.

Fountain Eneas and Elizabeth Smith, m. July1779; Joseph, b. Jan. 3, '80.

GAGER, Jeremiah, 1666, in the Court Records is said to be 25 years of age; and John, has lands assigned him in 1667.

GALE, Joseph, a town officer in 1758. By wife Rebecca, he had children born between '32 and '44.

GAYLOR, Jeremiah, the first of this name on the town records, had land assigned him in 1668. The name is still well represented in our list of town officials, and in families of other names.

GOLD, John, is on the list of freemen in 1734, and sells land here in 1681. John, his son, probably married here, April 3, 1707 Hannah Higginbothum. John sen. died in '02. This name is found often on the land records of the town for about fifty years.

GORUM, George, the first of this family in Stamford, was licenced to sail from New London to Barbadoes, with his sloop Hennah, in 1727.

He soon after this came to Stamford and settled on the spot now owned by Capt. Isaac Weed, in Darien. He afterwards went down to the landing, near the mouth of Goodwin's river, where his descendants still remain.

In 1743, Capt. George Gorham, appears among the town officials. He had married, in New Rochelle, July 20, '26, Hannah Banks ; the service being performed by "a Church of England Minister." Their children, recorded, were: Hannah, '28 ; Puella, '30 ; Abigail, '31 ; Phebe, '35 ; Daniel, '37 ; Jonathan, '40 ; Sarah, '42 ; George, '44 ; Joseph, '45 ; and Deborah, '48.

GRAY, Daniel and Prudence Waterbury, married here, Nov. 15, 1765, and had daughter, Mary, b. May 18, '67. Joshua and Elizabeth Dibble, married, May 20, '66, and had daughter Abigail, b. Feb. 9, '69. The name disappears from the records soon after the close of the war.

HARRIS, Robert and Elizabeth, were here about 1710, and had several children.

RICKOX, Benjamin, was here in business in 1715. He married, Feb. 3, '13–4, Sarah Selleck, and had two children recorded to them, Abigail and Bethel.

HIGGINBOTTOM, Richard, 1696, buys land of Daniel Wescot. According to Savage, he had gone from New Haven to Elizabethtown, whence he removed to Stamford. He was a tailor and had married Elizabeth, daughter of Thomas Munson, and had a daughter, Rebecca, b. Oct. 12, 1682. He married, Dec. 11, 7107, Youne Waterbury. At her death, in 1710, She is called Eunice. By vote of the town, Richard Higginbothom, is accepted an inhabitant Jan. 31. 1708–9.

Hobby, John, 1663, had land bounded by William Hubbard's of Greenwich, and is, probably, the ancestor of the families of this name in town. The names spelled Huby, Hoby, Hubbe, Hubey. Hubbey, and Hobbey.

How, John, 1710, married Comfort Finch; Isaac and Elizabeth, had a son David, b. in 1720; Ebinezer, in '23, and James, '25. In '32, Isaac How was chosen ensign of the 1st company or trainband of Stamford.

Hubbard, William, "formerly of Greenwich," bought lan here in 1697, and again in 1704–5, he buys another parcel, west of Mill river, on "Pepperwood Ridge." The name is spelled Hubert, and Hubbart. He was probably a grandson of George and Mary Hubburd, who came from England in 1635 or '36, and settled at Wethersfield. This George removed to Milford, and had a large family; John, George, Daniel, William, Mary, Sarah, Abigail, Hannah and Elizabeth.

Hull, Josiah and Hanna, has son Samuel, b. March 2, 1740–1, the father being dead.

Hutton, Samuel, 1744, buys land of Joseph Judson & Joseph Brown. He was a man of some prominence in the town for a number of years. In '48 he paid forty shillings fine for refusing to serve on the grand jury. By his wife Rebecca, he had a daughter, Rebecca, and a son, Samuel, Feb. 20, '57.

Ingersol, John, 1721, is the first of this name on record here, and Simon, who appears twelve years later, when he married Hannah Palmer. This family has since then een well represented in all the generations.

Jarvis, Samuel, bought dwelling house, homelot, barn and

shop, Jan. 11, 1744–5 of Nathaniel Finch. To Samuel and Martha Jarvis are recorded the following children: Monson, b. Oct. '42; Samuel, July 4, '45; Polly, Feb. 21, '46–7; Sarah, Nov. 28, '50 John, Oct. 11, '52; William, Sept. 11. '56; Hannah, Sept. 27, '58, and Lavina, Oct. 5. '61. This family for several years was quite numerous and has always been in all its branches highly respectable. (See list of loyalists.)

JEFFREY, John, admitted an inhabitant in 1727. The children of John and Sarah recorded here, are John, Samuel, and Mary.

JOINTER, Isaac, admitted an inhabitant by vote, 1713.

JUDSON, John and Charity Smith, married, Mar. 17, 1768, and had children; James, Mary, John, and Sarah. In '73 he buys land of Wm. Wheaton.

KING, William, 1728, is allowed a lot, four rods north and south, and two rods east and west, below Long Bridge, west side of Mill river for a tannery.

KETCHUM, John, of Huntington, and Hannah Bishop, m. June 11, 1728; and had, Hannah, Sarah, Joseph, Jonas, Zophar, Rebecca, and Ruth. This family is still represented here.

KIMBALL, Henry, 1690, blacksmith, late of Boston, binds himself to pay Moses Knap, jun. blacksmith, forty-three pounds.

LAWRENCE, Thomas, sells land in the rear of his house lot to John Thompson, in 1667–8, and was made freeman in 1670. He was one of the wealthy men of the town, as the list of 1687 shows. "Lawrence's farm" was a noted locality in that day. He died in 1691, as his inventory testifies.

LEEDS. How early this family came to Stamford or whence they came, no records probably show. Our catalogue of the births before 1700, gives us the family of John and Mary, recorded here; and their children are: Jonathan, b. Oct. 12, 1693; John, b. March 8, '94; Sarah, Feb. 8, '96; Samuel, Feb. 21, '97; Ebenezer, Jan. 12, 1700, and Mary, Oct. 23, 1702.

An interesting letter from H. H. Leeds, Esq., of New York city, to his kinsman, J. W. Leeds of Stamford, indicates the locality of the family in England.

Two brothers, John and William Leeds, once owned mainly the territory on which the present city of Leeds is built, and from them the city takes its name. One of the descendants of William, was that Doctor Leeds, of Clare Hall, Cambridge, who purchased the manor of Craxton, near the middle of the 16th century. Three of his descendants came to America about 1650, one of them settling in Stamford, one in New London, and the other in New Jersey. The first record, I think, in Stamford, in which that name occurs is found under date of Sept. 30, 1692. It states that Mr. John Leeds made complaint before Jonathan Bell, commissioner, against a Mr. Johanes Courtland, merchant of New York, "for want of the iron work for carrying on of the vessel which he the said Leades is in building, for the said Courtland". Cary Leeds buys land here of John Waterbury, in 1708.

A Cary and Martha Leeds, were living here early in the last century, having children; John, b. Dec. 13, 1714; Gideon, b. May 4, '16; Israel, b. Sept. 29, '19; and Cary, b. to his widowed mother, Sept. 4, '30, the father Cary having d. June 7, '30. This Cary, m. Sept. 6, '57, Mary Giles, and was the grandfather of the present John W. Leeds, president of Stamford Bank.

LLOYD—The first mention of JOHN LLOYD, the ancestor of this family in Stamford on our town records, bears date Dec. 17, 1747. He makes a plea to the town for permission to cart a "parcel of small stones out of his orchard on to the "slough-hey" plaçe in the road between the town and the common landing place, by Peter Demills especially "in the flat land all along the front of my orchard"; and that he might be credited with this expense on the town-tax account. The record of this family is so exact, on the register of births, that I will copy it. The family did not remain long in town, yet he must have been a prominent man during our revolutionary period to have been appointed to offices which he held.

"HENRY was born in Stamford, in Connecticut, unto John and Sarah Lloyd, on Friday ye 22nd day of July, 1743, at ten minutes after eleven a clock in ye day, and was christened by ye Rev. Mr. Richard Caner of Norwalk, ye 5th day of August, 1743.

JOHN, was born Feb. 22, 1744, nine minutes after six o'clock, evening, and christened by Rev. Mr. Samuel Seabury of Hamstead, Nov. 31, 1744; Rebecca, born in Stamford on Fryday, Jan. 2nd, 1746-7, at four o'clock in ye morning, and was baptized by ye Rev. Mr. Ebenezer Dibble, June ye 29th, 1746.

Abigail, on Wednesday, Feb. ye 13, 1750, at four o'clock in the morning, and was baptized by Rev. Mr. Ebenezer Dibble, March ye 3, 1750.

Sarah, born Monday July ye 2nd, 1763, at 40 minutes after one of the clock in ye morning, and was baptized by the Rev. Mr. Ebenezer Dibble, July 29th, 1753."

LEWIS, John and Martha Finch, married here April 23, 1729, and had a daughter Sarah recorded to them, Aug. 11, '39, and a son James, March 27, '41-2. Jonathan and Millecent Weed, married, March 20, '74, and had son James, born July 15, '75.

LINES, David and Mary Cheson, married, Jan. 14, 1747-8, and had Mary, born April 9, '49; Polly, January 21, '52; Esther, Jan. 12, '55, and Nancy, Feb. 28, '57.

LONGWELL, John and Susannah, had a David born, Feb. 3, 1736-7, and a John in '46.

LODER. Several of this name were living here after, about 1710, the name first occurring in 1685.

LOUNSBURY, Richard, the first of this name recorded, was here in 1684. He and his wife Elizabeth, had son Henry born in that year. Michael Lounsbury in 1702, bought land on "Pepper Ridge, near Taunton." He married Sarah Lockwood. This name has been quite numerous in the north part of the town.

MARSHALL, John, has land assigned him by the town in 1667; and in 1687, he buys land of Richard Scofield. Nehemiah Marshall and Patience Webb, were married April 4, 1743, and had two children, Bethiah and Nehemiah, recorded to them.

MALTBY, Jonathan and Sarah, had son Jonathan, born June 29, 1720. He was one of the prominent men of the town for a number of years. He attained colonel's rank in military life, and held various civil offices in the gift of his townsmen.

MATHEWS, Thomas, shepherd, appears as an inhabitant on the land record in 1690, and on leaving town on an expedition for Albany and "Canadey," mortgaged his real estate as security for his debts. The land had been laid out to him in 1687.

MIDDLEBROOKS, Nathaniel and Elizabeth Hoyt, married 1749, and their child Mary was born March 16, '53, at which date the father was one of the town school committee. In '59, Nathan Middlebrook is named on the town committee.

MOTT, John, 1735, had married widow Abigail Ayers, and with her gives quit claims to her children for their father Richard's estate.

NICHOLS, Robert and Elizabeth had recorded to them, Ruth, Mary, Robert, Sarah, Abraham, Noah, David and Reuel. Thomas Nichols was here on official list of the town in 1763, and Robert in '74. The family name is still well represented here.

NORTON, Hugh and Mercy ——— had a son James born in May, 1729, and a son William who died, Aug. 16, '31. The death of the father is recorded, May 12, '38, and that of the mother, May 11, '34–5.

OSBORN, Abner and Marcy Pettit, married here, May 13, 1752, and had Samuel, Ebenezer, Benjamin, Mary and David.

PALMER, Samuel and Hannah Cross, married Mar. 31, 1715, and had daughter Hannah. This family name is still honored not only on our citizens' list, but in one of our finest hills.

PARDEE, John, married Sarah Webb, and Joshua married Elizabeth Webb, and both of them had families here soon after the middle of the last century.

PARKETON, James and Mary, had children here; Mary, James, Denne and John. In 1752, he is allowed £20, "old tenor money" for keeping his mother-in-law Abigail Whiteing, (Whiting.)

PELTON, Robert, 1744. PERRY, John, '09.

PARDY, Joseph, admitted inhabitant, 1718.

PHILIPS, George 1688, is admitted an inhabitant "if he comes here to settle with his family."

PLATT, Stephen, admitted inhabitant, from Huntington, in 1757.

POND, Nathaniel, 1696, "blacksmith, late of Branford," buys land east of Noroton river of Jonathan Selleck, and in 1698, he also buys and sells land on Stony Brook. He was by vote admitted an inhabitant, Jan. 31, 1708–9. He had a large family.

POTTS, Thomas and Hannah Garnsy, were married, Jan. 1, 1735–6, and had children here.

POWERS, Andrew, buys land in 1775, of Peter Weed in Canaan parish.

PURDY, Joseph and Elizabeth Ferris, m. Dec. 25, 1723, had Mary, Joseph, and Elizabeth.

PROVORCE, (Provost,) Samuel and Sarah Bishop, m. Jan. 5, 1765, and had nine children. A brother of this Samuel came to Stamford about the same time and had also a family.

QUINTARD, Isaac. This pioneer of the Stamford family of this name, as his grave stone in the north east corner of the Episcopal burying ground testifies, was "born in Bristol, in Old England," and died "February ye last day 1738, aged 42 yrs." How early the family came to Stamford no record shows. Our records have the marriage of Isaac Quintard and Hannah Knapp in 1716, from which, it is probable that the pioneer, then a young man of twenty years, had found his way out of New York and been ensnared by one of our Knapp maidens. Five children are recorded here, the first born April 1721; the second born May, 1722; Hannah, b. June 28, '24; Isaac, b. Dec. 29, '27; and Peter, born in '30. The first appearance of the name on our records which I have found, is in a record of sale of land from Robert Embree to "Isaac Quintard of New York City, merchant," dated Oct. 1, 1708. The land was

RESIDENCE OF E. A. QUINTARD, STAMFORD.

bounded by the home lot of Bates, north; by the home lots of Sam. Hait and Sam. Scofield, deceased, east; by the common, west and south.

Peter, son of Isaac, married in 1761, Elizabeth De Mill, and had five children, of whom Isaac the second child, married Hannah Palmer, March 20, 1786, and had six children, of whom, Isaac, the third son now occupies the house which his father was occupying at the opening of this century.

Reed, John, the progenitor of this family in Stamford, according to the family history, was born in Cornwall, England, and in his sixteenth year entered Cromwell's army, and on the restoration of Charles II. came to America. He is supposed to have stopped first in Providence, R. I.—thence he went to Rye, N. Y.—thence to Norwalk, where we find a John Reed in 1666 or '67 John Reed, jr. of Norwalk, son of the John above, in '91, buys land of Stephen Clason, of Stamford. In 1709, he buys of Cornelius Jones, and '13, of Jonathan Bates. The land was lying on the Five-mile river, near his father's homestead. This family has been quite numerous.

Rich, Henry, purchases of Caleb Webb land 1681, and of Samuel Webb his home lot on the west side of Mill river, in the "Ox pasture so called." In '80, on publishing his intention of marriage with Martha Penoyer, a minor, her guardian objected. They, however, drew up articles of agreement between themselves and the parties to be married, on signing which "with witnesses, legally, then ye overseers do so for consent yt ye partys may proceed in marriage; ye 20th of December, 1680." Both "Hennery" and Martha, sign the bond with their marks. In '85, this Henry Rich mortgages his land and house lot on Horseneck, to secure Thomas Penoyer of Stamford, having sold his real estate in Stamford in '84.

Roberts Zachariah, by special vote is admitted an inhabitant, Jan. 31, 1708-9. He was said to be of Bedford, when he first purchased land here in '01.

Richards, Samuel and Esther Hadyn, married, Nov. 24,

1768, and had Sarah, b. '70; Esther. '71; Lewis, '73; Noyse, 1777.

SKELDING, Thomas, 1701. married Rebecca Austin and their son, Thomas, was b. in '03

ST. JOHN, David, blacksmith, 1758, is allowed by vote of the town to settle at Woodpecker Ridge.

James, and Hanna Hait, m. Sept. 19, 1753, and had a large family.

SELLECK.—This family, natives of Wales, as the tradition is, were in Boston as early as 1643. Two of the sons of David and Susanna Selleck of Boston,—Jonathan, born, May 20, '41, the very year of our settlement, and John, b. April 21, '43; came to Stamford about the year '60. Jonathan had house and land recorded to him in '63.

Jonathan, married Abigail, daughter of Richard Law, and had his first child, Jonathan, born here, July, 11, 1664. He had two other sons, David, b. Jan. 21, '66, and John, who graduated at Harvard, in '90. These sons all died, so Savage tells, us before the father's death, which is recorded as taking place, Jan. 10. 1712–13. This Jonathan was a prominent man, and at his death he bequeathed his Latin, Greek and Hebrew books to the Rev. Mr. Davenport.

JOHN, the other pioneer of this name, made freeman, 1669; married Sarah Law, a sister of his brother Jonathan's wife and had children, Sarah, b. August 22, 1669; David, b. Dec. 27, 1672; Nathaniel, b. April 7, '78; John, b. June 7, '81; Susanna, b. Feb. 2, '83, and Joanna, b. May 31, '86. This John was a wealthy ship-owner and captain. Under date, Feb. 25, '68–9, the town granted Mr. John Selleck a piece of waste land by the landing place to set a dwelling-house, or ware-house. He was taken prisoner on a voyage to England, in May, '89, by the French, and never returned to Stamford. His estate was settled here in 1700, and was very large. A branch of this family went just after our revolutionary war to Oyster Bay, on Long Island, where, down to the present day there are found worthy representatives of the name. Abigail, wife of Maj. Selleck, d. Dec. 20, '11.

STONE, John, in 1701, sells to Zach. Roberts, sen. of Bedford, the land and house he bought of Samuel Dean. He was one of the townsmen for a number of years.

STUART, Charles, was here in 1763.

STUDWELL, Joseph, was here in 1667. Thomas was here in March, '67–8, and binds himself to pay for, or return a catalogue of goods, among which were hatters tools. As security, he mortgaged three acres of meadow in the East field.

STURGES, Christopher, admitted inhabitant by vote in town meeting, 1718, and had a son, Jabez, b. here, '21. For several years after '23, he is enrolled among the town officials. His wife, Mary, d. Feb. 17, '46–7.

STURDIVANT, Wm. In 1682, Nicholas Webster, receives from the townsmen a piece of land in the rear of his lot, which had been layed out to this Wm. Sturdivant.

TALMADGE, Thomas, was here in 1709, and by vote admitted an inhabitant. He married Mary Weed, and had a daughter Hannah. He had married again in '21, when his son James was born.

THOMPSON, John, "gunsmith and resident in Stamford," sells house and lands to Jonathan Selleck, May 7, 1667. He was here, also, in '69 and in '70—sold land to Richard Webb.

TRYHERN, (Tryon) Edward, appears on the land record as early as 1684. One of his daughters married John Webster. Sarah, his wife, died here, Sept. 2, 1702, and his death occurred May 14, '74; down to which date his name is found quite frequently in the records.

THORP, Charles, was living here in 1738, when his son Edward was born.

TODD, John, jr. was an inhabitant in 1774.

TURNEY, Joseph, had lands laid out to him in 1686 on the

other, (east) side of Noroton river. He was a man of some means. The family has never been numerous here.

Walsh, James and Rebecca, had children; Hannah, b. at Croswise, Jan. 17, 1736; Catherine, at Stamford, Aug. 12, '38; Mary. Feb. 8, 1701–2; James, Aug. 28, '44; Jane, Oct. 17, '46; Lydia, Daniel and Abraham, Feb. 7, '49–50. The name is spelled both Walsh and Welsh.

Waring, Michael, came from Queen's Village, L. I. in 1717 in company with James White and Thomas Brush. They purchased on Longridge. The family for two or three generations must have been quite numerous. In the first deed the names is Waron.

Waters, John, married here in 1753, Oliver Delavan, and had a large family in the north part of the town.

Wardwell, (Wardell) William, is the first of this family on our records. He was a son of Usual and Grace Wardwell of Ipswich, Mass. and was born in Bristol, R. I. May 13, 1693. The name appears here, Dec. 7, 1726, with that of Margaret his wife. Their daughter, Hannah is in the record of births. In '35, in Society's meeting, four pounds and nineteen shillings were granted to him for work, which by committee's order, had been done to Mr. Wright's house. In '43 he is recorded as sealer of measures.

Wescott,—Spelled first Westgatt and variously afterward. Daniel was here pretty soon after 1660, and was propounded for freeman of the Conn. Colony, at the Hartford Court, in Oct. '69. He and his brother John had come probably from Fairfield, to which place they had come from Wethersfield. Both of them are reported frequently on the land records.

Wescott, John and Rose Holmes of Bedford, married April 9, 1702.

Wheeler, Justus and Elizabeth had a son Justus, born in 1731.

Whitney, Eliaseph is reported on the records in 1748.

WHITING, Joseph, is in business here, 1724, and same year had recorded the birth and death of a daughter, Sarah. His wife Abigail died in '33, and he married Hannah Beachgood, Jan. 25, '33–4.

WHITE, James came from Huntington, L. I. in 1717. In company with Michael Waring and Thomas Brush, he purchases of John Holly a tract of 246 acres, bounded by the New York State line on the north, by hills east of Great Meadow on the east, by Stony Brook on the north, and Miannus river on the west. He married Elizabeth Waring, Feb. 30, 1720, and had children, Timothy, Sarah, Jacob, Richard, Uriah and James. The family are still in possession of a part of the first purchase made by James, the pioneer, on Long Ridge.

WIATT, Nathaniel and Mary, had son Henry, born in 1726. He was among the town officials in 1737.

WHEATON, Benjamin and his wife Ruth had son Samuel, born here in 1750–1. How long the family had been here does not appear. The marriage of Jemima Wheaton to Reuben Holly is recorded in 1748–9. Samuel Wheaton and Mary Skelding were married in 1776, and had here, Mary, Samuel S., John S. and Eliza Ann. The Wheatons of New England, are said to be descended from an immigrant from Swansea, Wales, who settled in Rehoboth, Mass.

WILLSON, John, Dr. 1765, began the practice of medicine here, and was the father of a family of physicians. That his father's family were living here previous to his birth, our records do not show; though his descendants suppose that they were.

WILMOT, Zophar and Sarah Webb, married Dec. 29, 1760, and had children; John, b. July 9, 1762; Enos, April 18, 1766: and James, Nov. 17, 1769.

WILMOT, Joseph and Hannah, had a son Isaac, b. Nov. 20, 1775.

WILLIAMSON, John, married Mercy Hoyt, Sept. 17, 1746, and had children, Joanna, b. May 5, 1748; and Mary, Sept. 8, 1750.

WOOLSEY, Gilbert, buys land here of Thomas Morehouse, in 1672. The name reappears again in Ebenezer and Margaret his wife who had children here; Anna. in 1717; Thomas, in 21; and Mehetable, in '23. In '25,, he is said to be of Fairfield, when he buys land on Ox Ridge, of David Waterbury. In '28, he is said to be of Stamford, and sells land to Abraham Wooster, of Ripton Parish, Stratford. In '30, he is allowed by the society to pay his church rates elsewhere. He died in Jan. '65. There must have been quite a family of this name here down to about 1800.

CHAPTER XII.

THE PERIOD OF THE FRENCH AND INDIAN WARS.

The second quarter of the eighteenth century was marked in this country by the varying struggle between the English and French for supremacy, on the border ground of the colonial settlements. With a more persuasive policy, the French had made friends of the Indians more readily than the English, and as early as 1737, attempted to use the advantage thus gained by erecting a fort at Crown Point—then claimed as within English territory. From this time until 1763, there was no settled peace between the two parties, and the conflict which ensued called for large forces from all of the English settlements. How many of the three thousand soldiers, called into the service from Connecticut were from Stamford, we have no records to show. That the people of the town were not indifferent witnesses to the struggle is evident from occasional records still preserved. Of these we shall give the fullest account which can now be made up from reliable authorities.

Two men appear now on the stage here, who were to become, before our revolutionary period should close, the two most eminent representatives of the town, the one in civil and the other in military service. Abraham Davenport, now entering upon the prime of his manhood, was one of that band of large minded citizens of the State, who attempted the permanent occupancy of the Susquehanna grant. This movement was originally made in the interest of the English against the Indians—a colony which should be so mature and so thoroughly protected, as to furnish a sort of bulwark against any future invasions from hostile Indian tribes. And upon the success of such a colony would largely depend the future conduct of the Indians, as they should be tempted by Spanish or French appeals to them for aid against the English.

David Waterbury, another son of Stamford, was now brought forward into military life, and we find him before the close of these French hostilities doing acceptable service with his regiment, having already attained a major's rank. We must always regret the loss of the personal journals and letters, which these and others who were with them in the conflicts of these years of strife, must have written. From our town records, however, we shall find enough to hint, at least, the temper and mettle of the people, though a full catalogue, even, of those who served in these wars from Stamford it will be impossible now to make.

The following records still found in our book, No. I, of births, marriages and deaths, show how faithful the good clerk, Joseph Bishop was to make honorable mention of the soldiers' sacrifice. His own son is the first victim of the war whose fall he has to record.

"Joseph Bishop, a Sholger, son of Joseph Bishop of Stamford, died with sickness at Lake George, Nov. 25, at night in the year 1755."

"Stephen Ambler, a soldier in the expedition at Lake George in 1754, son to Sergeant Stephen Ambler, died on his return at Sharon, Oct. 19, 1756."

"Ezra Hait, of Stamford a sholger, dyed at Albyny Dec. 28, 1755."

"Joseph Ferris, a Shoulger from Stamford in ye expedition towards Crown point in ye year 1756, in his return from the expedition dyed with sickness at Newfilford, on December ye 18, 1756."

Peter Scofield, Reuben Scofield, and Abijah Weed, were also active in the military service of these years: and, also, among the revolutionary soldiers of the war of independence. Benjamin Webb, grandfather of Benjamin S. Webb, was at the taking of Quebec by the English under Wolfe in 1759 ; and Charles Webb, who became so prominent an actor in the revolutionary period began here, also, his military career.

The following record shows that Stamford was not yet utterly wanting in allegiance to the government of her sovereign, and also indicates three of the principal, perhaps the three most prominent citizens of the town.

At a town meeting held in 1757, the town voted, that if the "Lord of London" shall send regulars into this town, the town will bear the charge of accommodating them with what shall be necessary for them." A tax of one penny on a pound is voted and Samuel Broker is appointed collector to gather it in by the first day of March next and hand it over to the committee, Col. Jona. Hoyt, Mr. Abraham Davenport and Ensign Holly, if the regulars come, and if not, he is excused from collecting the rate.

In December 1758, we find the following record. "Col. Hoyt, Mr. Abraham Davenport, and Ensign Holly are appointed a committee, to supply his majesty's regular forces now quartered in this town, with fire wood for their guard room and hospital and what bedding they shall think proper to provide them with, to be paid for out of the town treasury." We find, also, that the Governor and company of the Colony of Connecticut, at their meeting in New Haven, on the second Thursday of October, 1758, ordered the colony treasurer to pay the town of Stamford 369£, 13 shillings and fourpence half penny to reimburse the town for cost of keeping "a part of Colonel Fraser's Highland battalion the last winter." The following certificate from the committee is also on record.

These may certify your Honors, that the Highland soldiers ordered to be quartered in the town of Stamford, arrived at said town, Nov. 30, 1757, and were quartered there until March, 30, '58. The number of soldiers, officers included was 250. There were also belonging to them, seventeen women and nine children. They were at the cost of the town provided with house-room, bedding, firewood, candles, &c., &c. Their officers insisted upon their being kept within a small compass, which exposed us to much more trouble and cost than otherwise would have been necessary.

Stamford, April 28, 1758.

JONA. HOYT,
ABR. DAVENPORT,
JNO. HOLLY, } Committee, to take care of the Highlanders.

In addition to the names already reported as prominent citizens of the town at this period, we find those of Jonathan Dibble and Charles Webb, in the Legislature. In military commission, the town had David Waterbury, a captain in the 9th regiment, Conn. Militia, and in 1658, major in the 3rd regiment; Col. David Wooster, who in the revolutionary war became a general; and Joseph Hoyt, 1st lieutenant, who became one of the most gallant of our revolutionary colonels.

The rolls of military papers preserved in the State Library in Hartford, gives us also the following names of Stamford men in the service during these wars.

In 1754, Charles Knap, ensign, was discharged and Joseph Husted chosen in his place. In Nov. of this year, Joseph Wood was chosen lieutenant of Capt. White's company.

In 1755, co. 5th of 4th regiment, was officered by Samuel Hanford, capt.; Joseph Hoyt, lieut. and Isaiah Starr, 2d lieut. to go against Crown Point.

March 10, 1757, Col. Jonathan Hait, notifies Capt. David Waterbury that his ensign, John Waterbury, had asked for discharge from having fallen from his horse and broken his leg. Samuel Hutton was chosen in his place.

Jonathan Maltby was captain of Co. 2; and on his resignation, Ebenezer Weed was chosen capt. Ezra Smith, lieut., and Charles Knap, ensign.

In the east part of the town the company called out in 1747, had for its officers, Jonathan Bates, capt.; Jonathan Selleck, lieutenant, and Thomas Hanford and Nathan Reed, ensigns.

These wars did not of course expose our township to any hostile invasion from the French forces, and so Stamford, felt no other interest in them than that of a loyal colony of His Majesty's royal government. But the service which the town here rendered, was not without its value, in fitting her sons for the great struggle, whose seeds were everywhere being sown.

The Earl of Loudoun, whose forces we find quartered here, must have left among our observing citizens the feeling that it would not be always safest for the colonies to be at the mercy of so much haughtiness. His sway must have at times seemed too imperious to be borne; and the inference would be, that the government which would commission and sustain such ministers of their authority, could not be long endured. Already the Bostonians had muttered, not indistinctly, their discontent. "If the English cannot protect us from the French and Indians, let us have the management of our affairs and we shall at least know what we can do"—was the under current of feeling which was beginning to unite the English colonies, for their own defense and control. That our townsmen shared largely in this feeling we shall soon see.

The following are the only other names I have been able to recover of the citizens of the town engaged in these wars:—

Jonathan, Sylvanus and Deliverance Slason, sons of Deliverance and Hannah (Hoyt) Slason, of whom Jonathan was in the navy of the war. Neither of the sons ever returned.

Ebenezer and Walter Weed sons of John Weed, were also in the service, of whom Ebenezer died while on shipboard.

Nothing else of material interest to our history occurred during these years, save what will be detailed in our religious and ecclesiastical record in a future chapter. There was a moderate growth in population and wealth in the town; and doubtless a smoothing off of the early roughness of the ruder period. New roads were opened, new and better bridges spanned our streams, school-houses multiplied as the population scattered over the territory, a better culture was increasing the agricultural productions of the soil, and preparation was going on for still more marked improvements in the future history of the town. Of the capabilities of the town in means, and men, and patriotism, the following chapters will furuish us the best proofs.

CHAPTER XIII.

REVOLUTIONARY WAR.

At the commencement of the revolutionary war, Connecticut numbered but sixty-seven towns, and Stamford ranked in population the sixteenth. Her grand list was £34,078 8 shillings, which evidenced a still higher rank in means than in population. The year 1775 found her represented in the State Assembly by David Waterbury and Charles Webb, both of whom had seen service in the old French war, and were therefore competent to advise in the present emergencies of the state; and by an unusual stroke of good fortune, she was also honored in the senate of the state, by the first name among her civilians, the Hon. Abraham Davenport, who also had been active and influential during the long struggles of the French and Indian wars. The long expected crisis had now come. Everything indicated war. Yet though there were many reasons why our townsmen would be likely to shrink from an earnest contest with the mother country, they were not altogether unprepared for it. They had both the men and the means to begin and prosecute the struggle.

At the head of our ministers, of which the town then counted only five, was that patriot and scholar, Dr. Noah Welles, who, since his sermon preached Dec. 19, 1765, to arouse the people over the great outrage attempted against them by the Stamp Act, had missed no opportunity of encouraging his townsmen to a manly resistance against all such oppression; and who, though called to lay down his useful life even at the beginning of the struggle, yet lived long enough to preach his annual thanksgiving sermon, Nov. 16, 1775. In that sermon, a manuscript copy of which is in my possession, he moved his people to a grateful commemoration of the goodness of their father's God as shown them in "frustrating the plans of our enemies," especially in their attempts to secure the aid of the Canadians, and Indians and negroes; in so signally preserving the lives of our exposed people; in granting the remarkable success attending our military enterprizes at Lexington, Charleston, and more lately to the north, in which though "engaged with the best British troops" he assures them we were "yet never worsted;" and in inspiring the remarkable union and harmony through the colonies in the present struggle for liberty."

Nor behind him, in his fervent patriotism, was that faithful co-adjutor, Rev. Dr. Moses Mather, then the patriot minister of the Middlesex, (Darien) Church, and so soon to test his patriotism, amid the insulting jeers of the ruthless soldiery who were to drag him from his own consecrated sanctuary, and still more triumphantly, amid the cruel hardships and threatened horrors of the execrable Provost prison to which he was doomed.

At the head of our civilians stood the honorable Abraham Davenport, a man of college education, long familiar with the public service in civil life, well grounded in such legal learning as enabled him, with no misgivings, to rely upon the essential justice of the revolutionary cause, endowed, more than most men, with an instinctive reverence for what was right and an inflexible purpose to insist upon it, and what was of scarcely less value to him for the part he was called to act, the inheritor of a large estate, and the father of an educated and now influential family who thoroughly sympathized with him in his espousal of the patriot cause.

Side by side with him, ready to the utmost of their means to sustain any measures which might promise to aid them in asserting the rights of the colonies against the unjust demands of the crown, stood the substantial citizens of the town—the Hoyts, and Hollys, and Lockwoods, and Knapps, and Scofields, and Smiths, and Seelys, and Warings, and Waterburys, and Webbs, and Weeds.

Nor were we without military men for the emergency. There were the Waterburys then known as senior and junior, the former long a colonel in the continental service who had earned some reputation for good judgment and military ability in the field, and the latter soon to earn by his personal fitness for it, the rank of general of brigade; and also the two Webbs, father and son, the one now a colonel, to test and prove his claim still more fully in several well fought battles of the pending strife, and the other to pay the forfeit of his active and not unmeritorious service with his own imprisonment and death. Then there was the spirited Joseph Hoyt, the leader of our minute men, who only needed to hear that patriot blood had been shed at Lexington, to fly to our exposed metropolis for its defense, and who was so soon to become the fighting colonel of our fighting seventh; and then our captains and lieutenants and ensigns, and, still more needed and helpful than they, our long list of resolute privates, honoring the name of all our principal Stamford families and cheerfully girding themselves for manliest defense of their homes. Thus with one brigadier, two or more colonels, a half dozen captains, a full dozen lieutenants, with a number of commissaries and agents of the military power, sustained by a gallant band of the rank and file of the army for independence, Stamford, in spite of the special temptations to the opposite course, maintained her honor in that great struggle which made these British colonies forever free from the dictation and greed of an unscrupulous foreign power.

An incident occurred in March, 1774, which might seem to forebode indecision and weakness among the patriots of the town. A special town meeting had been called to appoint delegates to the convention to be held, March 27th in Middletown. After the meeting was opened by the appointment of Colonel Abraham Davenport, moderator; it was voted that the town will appoint a committee to meet at Middletown on the last

Wednesday in March, instant, there to consult proper measures to be pursued to evade the evils which the town apprehend they are in danger of concerning Susquehannah."

After this vote, which for aught that appears was unanimous, Capt. Fyler Dibble and Dr. John Wilson were appointed the committee. The meeting adjourned to meet again on the 11th of the following month to hear the report of the committee. At the appointed time the adjourned meeting was held. The town make an appropriation to cover the expenses of the committee and vote, that the petition recommended by the Middletown Convention, should be signed by the town clerk, Samuel Jarvis, in the name of the town, and forwarded to the Assembly at its next Session.

This petition was a lengthy argument framed in the interests of the Pennsylvanians against the claims of Connecticut to the territory then held by her citizens and subject to her authority. The convention authorizing it, was made up of delegates from only twenty-three of the sixty-three towns belonging to the state; and their action received but little sympathy from the mass of the people. Their petition was couched in terms indicating an excessive loyalty to the English government and a readiness to abide by almost any decision of the crown. Mr. Ingersoll of Pennsylvania, was later an avowed tory. Captain Dibble and Mr. Jarvis of Stamford also enrolled themselves among those loyal still to the king; and it would seem that the Stamford people, in mass, were by this action committed to the side of the crown against the revolution, whose beginnings were already felt and seen.

But a few months will show how erroneous such a conclusion would be. We shall find ample record to show, that during that long struggle, the great majority of our townsmen were heartily and self-sacrificingly for the war. Before the opening of hostilities on the eventful 19th of April, 1775, our citizens had expressed themselves unequivocally for the patriot cause. The insolence of the crown, exhibited in the arbitrary and tyrannical acts which disgraced the records of the English parliament from the time Grenville, in 1763, accepted Jenkinson's Stamp Act as the legal process for collecting revenue in America, down to that most odious coercion act which closed the port of Boston, had most effectually schooled the great mass of American citizens to an earnest and impassioned resistance to any further demands of the English government. Henceforth, not even the former concessions to the crown would be allowed; and the people of the several colo nies, needed only a few months of mutual interchange of opinions and purpose to be fully prepared for their irrevocable declaration of independence. To prepare the way for that declaration, the voice of Stamford was not wanting. The Boston Port Bill had been passed and great suffering was the result. Our patriot citizens felt that the insult and injury done to Boston was also intended for themselves and all who had ventured to question the right of the British parliament to issue and enforce such demands; and they would not meanly shrink from an open espousal of the cause which had already brought down the vengeance of the crown upon their suffering brethren. Accordingly they met on the 7th of October, 1774, in the town house, which proving too small for the patriot band, they immediately adjourned to the meeting house, when the following minute was promptly passed.

"The inhabitants of this town sensibly affected with the distress to which the town of Boston and province of Massachusetts Bay are subjected by several unconstitutional acts of the British parliament; * * * * hoping to convince the people of this continent that notwithstanding our long silence we are by no means unwilling to join with our sister towns to assert our just rights and oppose every design of a corrupt ministry to enslave America, do declare that we acknowledge our subjection to the crown of Great Britain and all the constitutional powers thereto belonging as established in the illustrious house of Hanover; that it is our earnest desire that the same peaceable connexion should subsist between us and the mother country as had subsisted for a long time before the late unconstitutional measures adopted by the parliament of Great Britain; and we hope that some plan will be found out by the general congress to effect the reconciliation we wish for; yet we are determined by every lawful way to join with our sister colenies resolutely to defend our just rights: * * * that we are pleased that a congress of deputies from the colony is now met at Philadelphia, and relying upon the wisdom of that body we declare that we are ready to adopt such reasonable measures as shall by them be judged for the general good of the inhabitants of America."

This action testifies to the heartiness with which our townsmen entered upon the great struggle against the encroachments of the mother country. Before the opening of the war the people had been prepared for it. And when the news of the first battle at Lexington and Concord reached the town it was found ready with a prompt response. New York, then rapidly advancing in importance, was thought to be in especial danger from an invasion of the enemy. Joseph Hoyt of Stamford, who had now for about twenty years been in military life enlisted immediately a company of thirty men and started for the city. As no immediate danger was apprehended to the city the company returned to Stamford and reported only eight days service.

The bill of service thus rendered, would in these days be deemed a model for economy. I append it in full.

Whole pay for men's time,	£20 8 4
Cash expended by Capt. Hoyt on the march,	3 12 0
Cash expended by Lieut. Webb,	0 17 0
Cash expended by Lieut. Ezra Lockwood,	0 6 9
A sloop with part of the company and 12 men belonging to Greenwich, under Capt. Hoyt, from New York to Stamford,	£2 11 9
Capt. Hoyt's horse hire,	0 12 6
	£28 8 4

The Ezra Lockwood here reported as lieutenant, is enrolled on the company list as a private. All of the names are found in our alphabetical list.

But not thus easily were our townsmen to meet their obligations to the patriot cause. On returning Captain Hoyt commenced raising another company, for the continental service wherever needed. By the sixth of July, he had organized a company of seventy-five men who were reported ready for duty. The names would indicate that nearly all of them were Stamford men. This second company continued in the service until December 24, 1775, and the entire cost of the service rendered by them was reported as one thousand one hundred and thirty-nine and a half pounds sterling.

A third company was raised here early in the Spring of 1776. In one of the pay-rolls of this company it is called the "Company of Col. David Waterbury, in the regiment of forces of the United colonies under command of Colonel David Waterbury." On the list David Waterbury is enrolled as colonel and captain, and Sylvanus Brown as captain and lieutenant. The number of days service is appended to the names, and this will indicate the company in the alphabetical list at the end of this chapter.

In the summer of 1776, we were also represented in the service by a part, at least, of another company under Captain Webb, who were stationed in New York city. How many other companies or parts of companies were raised in Stamford, we have no means of knowiug. Our catalogue of revolutionary men at the end of this chapter, will doubtless fail to report many who honored Stamford in the war. Every record, it is believed, which our town and State can now furnish has been carefully examined to complete it; and every local record has been sought for the purpose of reporting fully all engagements and skirmishes and every form of military movement here, during the struggle. But Stamford was not destined to become the theater of any general engagement between the opposing armies. A few excursions of small detachmeuts of the British troops, and more frequent sallies from their loyal holds on the Island, or from their tolerated tory homes in the town, of the still trusty subjects of the crown, constituted all the warlike enterprises whieh disturbed the quiet of the town. No British army, it is believed, ever crossed the entire breadth of the territory, and probably, never more than a single brigade of the patriotic troops at a time, were quartered here. Once, at least, after the memorable repulse of the revolutionists at Horseneck, and that still more memorable feat of the daring Putnam, in his fearless flight to Stamford for aid, the British did probably insult the extreme borders of our soil; but the gallant general had so far outstripped them. as to have rallied our townsmen in sufficient numbers with the aid of the garrison in our fort, to meet them and turn their invasion into a precipitous retreat. Once, also, probably, was the eastern margin of our patriot town desecrated with the stealthy tread of British armed men; but their safety demanded a hurried return to the transports which had landed them, and so the town was spared the ravage they had designed.

The following letter from our most distinguished townsman, is authentic respecting the standing of two other of our citizens, and shows how our people managed their foreign commerce during the war:

Stamford, Dec. 8, 1775.

RESPECTED SIR,—Mr. Selleck and Mr. Bates, two of my neighbors own a vessel of about fifty tons, with which they are desirous to make a voyage to the West Indies, to carry cattle and provisions and bring back military stores, if a permit can be obtained of your Honor, for the performanee. I suppose that is expected that Mr. Bates will go Master, if the vessel is permitted to go. I believe he may be depended on ; and I do not know a man better calculated for the business. The vessel is said to be a prime sailor.

We have but a few pounds of powder in our town stock, and I believe it will be universally agreeable to the inhabitants of the town, thet a permit should be granted. At the desire of Mr. Bates, I write this. He informme that Mr. Selleck will apply to your Honor for the permit, and will give bond, if required, for the faithful conduct of the master. Mr. Selleck is a man of considerable interest, and his bond will be quite sufficient.

I am with the greatest esteem and respect, your Honor's most obedient and humble servant,

ABRAM DAVENPORT,

HON. GOV. TRUMBULL.

But the most extensive invasion of the town by the British and their loyal abettors here, occurred Sunday, July 22, 1781. The leaders in that sacriligious foray were from among the tories of the eastern part of the town, and their depredations and captures were confined to their own neighbors and friends. During the night preceding they had crossed the Sound from Lloyd's neck in seven boats, and stealthily secreted themselves, about forty in number, in a swamp a few rods south of the meeting house, waiting the gathering of the congregation for their usual worship Providentially several of the leading patriots were not at church in the morning, and the attack was delayed. In the afternoon the unsuspecting citizens had taken their seats as usual. The services had commenced. Dr., then Mr. Mather, was in the pulpit which he had now occupied for nearly forty years, and it was undoubtedly his earnest patriotism which had led to this attack. Its object was to capture that fearless preacher of treason, and the leaders of his people whom he had so effectually seduced from their loyalty. Suddenly the house was surrounded and the summons to surrender was issued, in the well known voice of their neighbor, Captain Frost. Small chance had been left for the congregation to escape. Yet, a single old lady, thoroughly patriotic and as thoroughly plucky, marched through their encircling line. Four youths who had noticed the incipient move of the tory invaders, had also made proof of their agility and were out of reach of the sentinel's shot. One other lad, a son of the officiating minister, ventured also an attempt at escape. Seizing his hat he started for the door where he encountered a leveled gun, and the insulting exclamation, "there, I've got you now"! "Not yet," he quietly said, as he struck down the gun and leaped from the door. Nor was the sentinel quiek enough to cut short his flight, though the shot which was meant to do it, left its scar, life-long, on his heel. And now commenced in earnest the work of tory revenge. With derisive jeers, the venerable pastor was called down from the pulpit to lead his congregation in a very different service.

The men and older youths of the congregation were drawn up two and two in marching order, and tied arm to arm. The pastor was ordered to the front, alone, to lead the march. All was now ready for the start. The valuable articles of jewelry, found on both the men and women had been appropriated by the excellent captain. Every horse needed for the invading band had been taken, and the women and children consigned to the care of the rear-guard, until the captors with their prisoners and spoil should be well under way. The orders are given, and, driven by their former neighbors and the venial soldiery of the British power, some forty-eight of our townsmen were hurried away to the boats awaiting them at the shore. They were thence taken over to Lloyd's Neck. Here they found, not congenial friends, but many of their life-long neighbors and kindred, whom the revolution had alienated and made their open and bitterest enemies. But they were soon disposed of. Twenty-four of the number were released to return home on parol. The remainder, twenty-six in number, were ordered on board a brig and confined below deck. They were taken to the Provost prison to New York city, where they endured every conceivable indignity. Here they were kept until the 27th of the following December, when those of them who survived the horrors of that confinement, nineteen in all, were exchanged.

We have in Dr. Dwight's travels, the following account of the sufferings to which Mr. Mather was subjected during this imprisonment.

"This venerable man was marched with his parishioners to the shore, and thence conveyed to Lloyd's Neck. From that place he was soon marched to New York and confined in the Provost prison. His food was stinted and wretched to a degree not easily imaginable. His lodgings corresponded with his food. His company, to a considerable extent was made up of a mere rabble, and their conversation, from which he could not retreat, composed of profaneness and ribaldry. Here, also, he was insulted daily by the Provost marshal, whose name was Cunningham,—a wretch remembered in this country, only with detestation. This wretch, among other kinds of abuse, took a particular satisfaction in announcing from time to time to Dr. Mather, that on that day, the morrow or some time, at a little distance, he was to be executed. But Dr. Mather was not without his friends, however, who know nothing of him, except his character. A lady of distinction, having learned his circumstances, and having obtained the necessary permission, sent to him clothes and food, and comforts with a liberal hand."

I hoped to be able to make out a complete list of the men who were carried away in this expedition of the British and tories. No contemporaneous records, within my reach, have enabled be to do so.

But if there were no great engagements between large armies within this territory, it must not be inferred that the town was unaffected by the war. Every neighborhood in the town, and almost every year of the war, witnessed events of greater or less importance, which contributed according to their measure, towards the great result. In many ways the loyalty of our people was testified, and they who were never in arms, were called at times, to show a soldier's courage. They who seemed to do least in furtherance of the cause, made often the most costly sacrifices of affection and treasure to its success.

The little, every day contributions, which really constitute the most unequivocal testimonies to a people's spirit and power, are not of a character to seek or win publicity. No diary of the times reports them. No actor publishes them. They come unheralded and pass by unchronicled. Nevertheless they are neither unknown nor forgotten. Their influence is felt, and that influence determines the people's destiny.

Let us gather some of these floating waifs of our revolutionary period. They come down to us with the authority of chance-saved letters perhaps, preserved, no one knows how, in spite of our proverbial waste of all this most precious material for human history. They have been tossed about and along on mere tradition, it may be, yet so credibly preserved, as to warrant our fullest confidence, or they were intrusted to the faithful guardianship of some memento of transmitted love, voiceless indeed, yet with a language that can never be misunderstood.

What a story of family affection and family exposure the following narrative tells. During the war the family of Capt. John Holly was living in the house now owned by Samuel Leeds, Esq., on Clark's hill. Among their most precious treasures was a quarto bible, an elegant edition for those times, printed in London in 1763. This bible had been given to Miss Holly, afterwards Mrs. David Waterbury, at the early age of five years for the ease and correctness with which she read one of the chapters in Chronicles, filled with scripture names. When the family, for their earliest patriotism were exposed to stealthy depredations both from British and tory vengeance, the bible was carefully buried in the back yard with other family treasures. There it remained through the war. When it was exhumed, it was found in good condition excepting the heavy clasps upon it, which had been rusted off. That old bible still remains a precious relict in the possession of Mrs. Abigail H. Seely, a daughter of Mrs. Waterbury, and its story shows what trials belonged to the period of our revolutionary war.

And now let us see how the war entered our families in another way, taking off their sons to the field, or to garrison exposed points, wherever needed. The following stray letter is one of thousands written during the war from the town, but this has survived the fate of the most of the rest. It was written on a half sheet of coarse foolscap, now, of course, brown with age; and directed in a large fair hand "to Silas, Thaddeus and Bates Hayt, in Capt. Webb's company, in Main street, near the chapel, New York. Per. favor of Henry Marshall." The entire letter, for which I am indebted to Mr. John Holmes of New Hope, recently deceased, is as follows:

STAMFORD, Aug. 20, 1776.

DEAR CHILDREN,

We recived Bates' Letter of Aug. 19th, and greatly rejoice to hear of your welfare. We gladly improve the present opportunity of writing to inform you that we are all well; and that we send a pail of butter, two pounds of which belongs to Bates, one pound to Henry Wix and the remainder to Silas and Thaddeus. We should have been glad to send you potatoes if to be had. We send you some sauce, which you must distribute. Henry Wix has some by himself. After wishing you the Divine protection, we remain your affectionate parents,

ABR'M HAIT.
HANNAH HAIT.

P. S.—"Mr. Merceir has applied to me for your horse, bridle and saddle; and if you are willing to part with him you will inform me thereof. I shall be willing to make you a present of my horse, a new saddle and bridle and a watch in lieu thereof."

What a revelation of neighborhood estrangement and its cure is found in this morceau of our family history.

The Jarvis family were excellent and prominent people here, but their affections were with their king, rather than with his rebellious subjects. When therefore it seemed necessary that this family should be sent over the line, Capt. Samuel Lock.

wood of Greenwich was appointed to execute the order. This he did with the ready zeal of a revolutionary patriot; and of course his officiousness alienated the two families. No loyal Jarvis could thenceforth endure one of the notoriously rebellious Lockwood tribe. But the years roll on and work strange cures, as well as aggravate maladies not to be healed. A grandson of the inexorable captain was won to a surrender by the maidenly graces of a grand-daughter of the courtly royalist, and so far at least the old feud was healed, as the family of our worthy citizen judge Ferris will attest.

Take also this illustration of the restoration of confidence and affection on the return of peace.

Captain Slason and deacon Joseph Mather, while on guard one night in the eastern part of the town, recognized two of their former neighbors, now tories, landing with a boat load of contraband goods, with which to drive a profitable trade with the knowing ones in that neighborhood. The captain and deacon at once take possession of the men and their boat. Going eagerly to the work of landing the choice goods which in the process became their prize, they incautiously left their muskets on the shore. Naturally enough, Smith, one of the tories, seized the captain's gun and called upon his comrade to take the deacon's; and so, they could make themselves more than even with their captors. But the stalwart captain was not so to be trifled with. Springing from the boat, he dashes down with a single blow the exulting tory, and remains master of the field. The end remains to be told. After the war was over, the tory Smith remaining here, by due course of nature came to his end. The doughty captain, who had so signally humbled him, spent his last years as the happy husband of the reconciled and happy widow.

What a touching picture of tragedy, unnatural, the following fact exhibits. Zachariah Hoyt and several of his neighbors were on guard near the mouth of Goodwives river; and as nothing betokened the presence of British or tory foe, they were enjoying a pleasant hour of merry chat and sport. Suddenly a volley from loyal muskets, mortally wounded two of their number, when the rest hurriedly escaped. And now the concealed tory band came forward, to see whom of their old friends and neighbors they had made to bite the dust. One of them, as if momentarily grieved for the shot he had fired, could only ask, in soothing terms: "Cousin Zach, is this you?" And a mournful "Yes" was the only answer of the dying man.

Among the memorabilia of our revolutionary period should be recalled the athletic frame and reckless and successful daring of "Uncle Thad." Thaddeus Hoyt, who had lived a few rods south west from the place where Alfred Hoyt, Esq., now lives, was one of our most earnest whigs. His active patriotism had aroused the hatred of every tory in the neighborhood, and exposed him to incessant annoyance and hazard from their raids upon his property or their attacks upon his person. So much exposed was he in his house by night, that he often retired in the evening with his gun and blanket to a neighboring clump of cedars which afforded him safer shelter. His cattle were all marked for seizure and one by one they were stealthily carried off. Having pretty good evidence that one of his tory neighbors, Samuel Lockwood, was a leader in these depredations, he determined upon confronting him, on one of his predatory incursions. The opportunity soon came. The neighbor had selected just such cattle as would best answer his purpose and was hurrying off to the British lines with his prize. Suddenly, "uncle Thad" arrests his progress. The tory thus unexpectedly caught, quickly levels his gun and snaps. The musket, loyal to the king, failed her duty to his subject. Not to be thus defeated, "uncle Thad" strikes down the gun, grapples with the tory, himself, and holds him in his unrelenting grasp. Nor does he release his hold before, thoroughly subdued, he begs for quarter and pledges a future abandonment of his tory practices.

And the prowess of our townsmen was witnessed on the water, also, as well as on the land. The following will best illustrate our marine heroism during the war. I will let this story stand, as my predecessor in this field of research, Rev. J. W. Alvord, tells it.

"A frigate and sloop-of-war, belonging to the enemy, were lying in Oyster Bay, opposite this village, and the whaleboats from this place, commanded by Captain Jones, determined on taking the sloop. On a foggy morning they rowed silently around her, and coming nearer and nearer, they were at length discovered and instantly hailed—"Who's there?" "A friend." "A friend to whom?" "I'll let you know," said Jones, "the rebels have been rowing round the bay all night and you've known nothing about it. I'll report you to the Admiral for neglecting your watch." By this time the men in the boats were climbing up the sides of the British vessel, while Jones, who was as rough as the ocean on which he had been brought up, kept storming away at the captain for his negligence. The British officer trembled from head to foot, thinking that he had run foul of some violent old tory, who would certainly report him to his commander. He assured Jones that he had kept the strictest watch—begged him to look at the order of his vessel—the training of his guns, and the priming of his muskets. A number of these muskets were by this time in the hands of the assailing party, when instantly Jones' foot stamped heavily upon the deck, and in the next moment the sloop was theirs! She carried fifteen or twenty guns, and was fully equipped for service. Another vessel was about this time captured by these whaleboats as she lay in the narrows below. They attacked her in open day—one, as they approached, had its rudder carried away by a cannon shot, and swinging under the stern of the English vessel, the men entered her cabin windows, just as the crew were driven below, by the men in the other boats, who had obtained possession of her deck. After a short and desperate fight with broadswords and bayonets, in the cabin, the crew surrendered, and the vessel was brought to Stamford."

Among our enterprising townsmen who did good service in harassing and weakening the enemy was one of our numerous Smiths of that day. It has come down to us, well authenticated, that a British officer who had been landing the loyalty of the leading tories of the town, wound up his eulogy with this comforting reflection: "and in fact we could get along well enough with you Stamford Yankees if it wasn't for that old red haired Smith."

Take this incident, illustrative of the exposure of the revolutionists to another sort of treatment when the tories gained some temporary advantage. The house of deacon Joseph Mather was visited one night by a band of these prowling loyalists. They had heard that the deacon's house was used as a safe depository of the valuables of his neighbors. Finding Mrs. Mather at home, they drove her, at the point of the bayonet to the place where her silver had been buried. They take the collection, and then drive her back to the house and compel her to cook them a warm supper. On leaving they take the deacon with them down to the shore, to prevent him from giving an alarm.

The following are two illustrations of the dreadful wreck which a period of war sometimes makes. Among those who were engaged, July 22, 1781, in capturing the congregation in Middlesex, was Rowland Slason, an incorrigible tory. He resided but a short distance from the church, and those on whom he then laid violent hands, were his life-long neighbors and friends. After the war he was allowed to remain in possession of his home and property, but he could never more have rational enjoyment from either. He had sunk under a heavy cloud, which no earthly sun was ever to pierce. His mental faculties had given way, and he at length roved aimlessly about, a pitiable maniac.

Not less painful was the effect of the war upon the mind and the life of Stephen Weed. His first experience of British and tory treatment had been a lesson he could not forget. The sanctuary to which he had gone with his parents, was no defense against their ruthless violence. They had stealthily surrounded that hallowed place, and seized and carried off his friends and neighbors and even his venerated pastor. Nothing but his own agility, had saved him from the cruel doom of his friends. He was one of the five who escaped from the congregation. But the lesson had taught him that he had nothing more to hope from the forbearance or mercy of the enemy, and he at once enlisted in the service of his country. He cheerfully offered himself to whatever peril the sacrifice might involve. In the march and on the field, by day and by night, in heat and in cold, he stood at his post and did nobly what a good soldier should do. To the end of the war, he lost no opportunity of making proof of his courage and his patriotism. But the incessancy and severity of his duties aggravated by his confinement in the execrable Provost prison of New York, were more than he could sustain. He gradually broke down and at length sunk into a state of mental derangement, from which there was to be no recovery. Yet in his insanity, he remained a soldier still. His talk was of the battalion. His walk was a soldier's march. His work was that of the field, in front of or near a threatning foe. He lived in constant expectation of the invasion of a foreign enemy. He had a clear presentiment of the time and manner of the approach. He long and steadily insisted that the invading march was to be up the Noroton valley, and unless its progress could be resisted, the whole country to the north would be mercilessly laid waste. The line of march was to be just to the west of his own residence, and he could never leave his own home and country to be thus laid waste, without exhausting all his means for their defense.

Nor was he long in planning his defense. Choosing a felicitous position commanding the intervale below, he commenced the work of fortifying. He built a stone fort enclosing a subterranean retreat which might answer for a magazine, and surrounded the whole with a ditch. One only entrance admitted friend or foe to this work. After having thus completed the fort, day after day, for nine weary years, he stood sentinel or paced his appointed beat, with his watchful eye ever ready on his trusty lock, or scanning the opening vale to the south for the first glimpse of the coming foe. Here he was proud to receive the notice of strangers as they visited his fort to witness his military drill. He never tired of telling over his old campaigns and seemed to have an accurate remembrance of what had transpired during his service in the war of his country. But he would allow no change to be made in the works on which he must rely for defense. One little addition only to his own arrangements was permitted. A huge black snake was one day found coiled up in the sun on his grand promenade in front of his works, and the idea seized him that this was to be his relief sentinel. He therefore only took note when his relief was posted, and would neither tempt the faithful sentry to leave his post nor allow any one else to disturb him. Day after day did the faithful and apparently sympathizing sentinel take his post and relieve for a while the old man, until one day he located himself on another part of the ground than that to which he had been assigned. Immediately, in the exercise of his military authority the uncompromising old disciplinarian summarily dispatched him for being thus found off his guard.

But the years wore away, and the old soldier was called to lay down his arms. Nothing but physical exhaustion could cheat him out of the service in which he gloried, and he died as he had lived, under the shadow of that great war cloud which death alone could shake off from his burdened spirit.

We have now learned from the main drift of the incidents we have collected, that Stamford was exposed all through the war, to the petty annoyance of small bands of tories. The "cowboys," her own sons, or at least under their guidance, were everywhere on the alert to seize upon all unprotected cattle and grain with which to maintain their credit with the king and his army. They were not loyal enough to take sides openly with the king's soldiers, and either their fears or their hopes hindered them from espousing heartily the cause of their neighbors. And the social position of this class was such as to render their opposition all the more hurtful to the patriot cause. They were not the poorest and least influential of the community, who thus held back and so effectively opposed the struggle for our independence. Many of the most talented and wealthy were in their ranks. The arguments by which they sought to justify their course, were those to which the loyal and conservative of every age resort. At the first, the great body of the people, and to the last, a large minority could not think of breaking away from their allegiance to the crown. By every means in their power therefore excepting an absolute resort to the ranks of the king's forces, they sought to hinder and harass the king's rebellious subjects.

Incidental or purposed collision between these tories and the avowed revolutionists were very numerous. Sometimes serious damage to property, and even loss of life was the result. The following chapter will best set forth this feature of those days which "tried men's souls."

CHAPTER XIV.

CHRONOLOGICAL RECORD OF REVOLUTIONARY ACTS IN STAMFORD DURING THE WAR.

This chapter will report many facts which could not well be introduced into the preceding chapter, and yet of sufficient local importance to justify preservation in our history. In many instances the day of the month is not given in the record from which our extracts are made.

1774.

This year finds the town represented in the general assembly—David Waterbury and Thomas Young for the Spring Session, and Charles Webb and David Waterbury in the Fall.

Oct. 7.—At a meeting warned to consider the claims of the Bostonians then suffering from the action of the port bill, John Lloyd, Samuel Hutton, Capt. Samuel Youngs, Capt. David Hoyt and Charles Weed were appointed "a committee to receive subscriptions for the supply of the poor in the town of Boston."

The following is the clerks' attestation which follows the record.

"The above is a true copy of record, it being a very full meeting—almost an unanimous vote." S. Jarvis, Town Clerk.

1775.

Abraham Davenport, assistant; and Col. David Waterbury and Col. Charles Webb, representatives for the Spring Session, and Benjamin Weed and Thomas Young, for the Fall Session of the general assembly.

June 6.—Col. Charles Webb reports his mission of 22 days to Crown Point and Ticonderoga, and gives his note with six others for 500 pounds to raise funds to pay expense of the expedition.

June 15.—Col. Waterbury reports his command at Stamford ready for orders.

June.—Capt. Joseph Hoyt, with Chas. Webb, jr., for his lieutenant, and Samuel Whiting, ensign, Sam. Hutton, Benj. Weed, Sam'l Wheaton and Sam'l Webb, sergts. and 24 privates, march to New York for the defense of the city. Hinman's "war of the Rev." gives him only 23 men.

June 19.—New York calls for Wooster's and Waterbury's troops in Stamford, to march within five miles of the city. They marched.

July.—Charles Webb, appointed colonel of seventh regiment.

Sept. 19.—Committee of safety for the town, appointed agreeably to recommendation of the continental congress, Col. Davenport, Esq., Benj. Weed, Esq., Amos Weed, Charles Weed, Israel Weed, Nathan Lounsbury, Thaddeus Bell, Stephen Bishop, Deodate Davenport, Charles Smith and James Young. Witness: Sam. Jarvis, clerk.

Oct.—Daniel Gray is authorized to transport a sloop load of rye and corn to Machias and Falmouth, under 500£ bond.

Dec. 11.—Committee of safety re-appointed; Ab. Davenport, Esq., David Waterbury, jr., Esq., David Webb, Jona. Waring, jr., Lieut. Sam'l Hutton, Benj. Weed, Esq., John Hoyt, jr., Charles Weed, Abraham Weed, Nathan Lounsbury, Samuel Richards, Capt. Amos Weed, Chas. Smith, Isaac Lockwood, Jas. Young, Deodate Davenport, Jona. Bates, Hezekiah Davenport, Abraham Bates, Jos. Webb, jr., and Thaddeus Bell.

1776.

Abraham Davenport, assistant; and Benjamin Weed and Col. D. Waterbury, representatives at Spring Session, and Benjamin Weed and John Davenport at the Fall.

Jan. 22.—Gen. Lee in Stamford with 1200 continental troops.

Feb.—Jos. Hull and Philip Redfield who were here in Ward's regiment, were detailed as privateers in Captain Selleck's sloop to serve for six weeks.

March 1.—Captain Ebenezer Slason, made major; Henry Slason, captain; Ebenezer Scofield, 1st lieutenant; Daniel Waterbury, 2nd lieutenant, and David Purdy, ensign.

April 3.—Trial of Munson Jarvis and David Picket.

Joshua Stone, a spy, captured here, and imprisoned, and fined 20£.

June.—David Waterbury, jr., appointed brigadier general; Sylvanus Brown, captain; Joseph Webb, 1st lieutenant; Thaddeus Weed, 2nd lieut, and Gideon Waterbury, ensign.

June 22.—Gen. Lee at Stamford, with 1200 men, hoping to take them into New York. The committee of safety of New York are afraid and stop the force this side. Gen. Waterbury goes to the lines to see what can be done, while Lee, disabled with the gout, remains at Stamford.

Oct.—Captain Niles of the famous "Spy", to cruise between Nantucket and Stamford.

Sept. 16.—Corp. Chas. Steward, from Stamford, is confined in Halifax.

Nov. 8.—Robert Parke, stationed here to recruit for the army.

Nov. 14.—Disaffected citizens sent to Lebanon, Ct., as dangerous to the state.

Nov. 20.—A party of loyalists from a British tender landed, and shot and carried off two fat cattle.

1777.

Abraham Davenport, assistant; John Davenport and John Hoyt, jr., representatives in Spring Session, and Capt. Sylvanus Knapp and Capt. Isaac Lockwood in the Fall.

Feb. 14.—Benj. Betts taken from his bed and carried to Long Island and forced into the British service. He subsequently escaped, and being suspected of toryism, was arrested, imprisoned and fined, and requested to give bonds for future loyalty.

Feb. 24.—Samuel Crissy and Nathan Munday come home, and on signing a declaration of allegiance are permitted to remain.

Feb. 28.—Wm. Fitch, a tory convict, is allowed to return to Stamford and back to Canterbury in 20 days.

March.—Doolittle & Co., to forward to Stamford, 600 lbs. powder, 30 six-pound shot, and 30 three pound-shot. In May the Gov. orders the New Haven mill to send the same amount of powder. In June, the Salisbury furnace, to send 100 round shot to suit the Stamford cannon.

Saturday before May 23.—A number of British ships, vessels and flat bottomed boats appeared off the harbor.

Gen. Wooster is here with several regiments. The stores of medicines then here under charge of Dr. Turner, were ordered to be sent to Danbury.

July 7.—Capt. Reuben Scofield and Capt. Edward Rogers, ordered to march their companies to Greenwich and Capt. Bradley to march to Stamford.

Sept. 3.—A bushel of salt ordered to be sent to Stamford for the army.

Oct. 11.—"To the general assembly of the State of Connecticut now sitting at Hartford, by adjournment, the memorial of us the subscribers, select men of the town of Stamford—showeth, that the said town is overcharged in the number of soldiers as their quota filling up the Continental army, at least ten men, upon computation of the number of whites in said town according to the return of the number in the year 1774—that since that time more than 100 men have gone off to the enemy from sd town besides the number killed in battle and who have died in captivity and by sickness brought into the town from the army and otherwise which have greatly diminished their numbers and rendered it extremely difficult if not impracticable to supply their quota as now stated—and the more as they are a frontier town."

AB. DAVENP.	Senator
ISAAC LOCKWOOD,	and
SYLVANUS KNAPP,	Representatives

Nov. 14.—Gen. Ass. voted that the Committee of inspection of Lebanon, be and they are here by directed and, authorized to take care and custody of the prisoners sent here under guard from Stamford, as being persons dangerous to the state, and to dispose of and govern them in the best manner they can as their prudence shall direct, until further orders from the Gen. Ass. or the Governor and his Com. as aforesaid.

Dec. 1—Committee to care for families whose husbands had gone into the continental service; Jas. Young, Jona. Waring, jr., Chas. Knapp, Chas. Weed, Amos Weed, Thaddeus Bell, Jona. Bates and Thos. June.

At the same time, Jos. Ambler, Ab. Weed, Thad. Hoyt, and Samuel Richards, were appointed to supply the commissary with such clothing, &c., as the law required.

1778.

Abraham Davenport, assistant; Maj. John Davenport and Col. Chas. Webb representatives in Spring and Capt. Daniel Bouton and Capt. Isaac Lockwood in the Fall.

The year opens under the defense of an encamped artillery company, consisting of 24 men, to hold the post until June 1779.

Jan. 12.—Articles of Confederation read and assented to, and corresponding instructions forwarded to Capts. Lockwood and Knapp, representatives in grand assembly.

Feb. 6.—An artillery company under Lieutenant John Bear stationed here.

Twenty-four men levied on Stamford for coast defense.

March 20.—Vote that all the fines due from delinquents who

refused when drafted last winter to join the troops at the Sawpitts under Capt Jesse Bell or any other officer commanding any of Stamford drafted men, to be, by said officers, equally distributed among those non commissioned officers and soldiers who joined and faithfully did their duty at the Sawpitts last winter.

March.—Ebenezer Holly, taken in arms against the U. S. is imprisoned in Hartford jail.

John Morehouse, who had enlisted into the service in Silliman's brigade at 16 years of age was enticed out of Stamford, taken to New York and put on the sloop of the notorious renegade, Stephen Hoyt. He escapes into Rhode Island and reported himself to Gen. Washington.

Joshua Stone, who had been imprisoned in New York by the British, escaped to Stamford, is arrested by our committee of safety, imprisoned and fined 20£. He is released on enlisting for three years and paying 30£.

1779.

Abraham Davenport, assistant; Col. Chas. Webb and Capt. Daniel Bouton representatives in both sessions.

Mar. 26.—Gen. Putnam rides into the village from his perilous feat at Horseneck to rally help to drive back the British.

May.—Samuel Webb exchanged.

June 17.—Noah Welles taken prisoner at Horseneck and sent to New York.

Aug. 3.—Rev. Dr. Mather and four sons captured at the parsonage and carried off to New York by eight tories, of whom five were the doctor's parishioners.

Sept. 5.—Major Tallmadge with 130 light dragoons, crosses from Shipan point over to Loyd's Neck and at ten in the evening, attacked 500 tory refugees then entrenched, and before morning had returned, he landed again in Stamford with nearly the entire garrison, without losing a man.

Oct.—Capt. Jona. Waring with 50 or 60 men and Captain

Sam'l Lockwood of Greenwich, plunder the Greenwich tories of 20,000£, as appears from an appeal for restitution from John Mackay.

Dec.—Town grant liberty for a hospital under Dr. Coggswell, at Capt. Reuben Scofield's and elsewhere.

1780.

Jan.—Two Matross companies are reported at Stamford, numbering 26 and 67 men.

Of the 530 men to be raised in the county this year, Stamford was to furnish 57.

April 14.—Col. Chas. Webb, petitions the assembly to secure an exchange for his son Charles, then a captive in the Sugar House, New York, both of his feet having been frozen. He was exchanged for Wm. Addington, then in Hartford jail.

June 26.—Lieut Reuben Weed, Capt. Sam'l Hoyt, Lieut. Sam'l Hutton, Capt. Isaac Lockwood, Mr. John Bell, captain Chas. Smith, Mr. Tim. Reed, Mr. Silas Davenport, Capt. Reuben Scofield and Lieut. Jona. Whiting, are appointed to procure each a recruit for three years or during the war, for the continental army. Voted, a tax of threepence a pound to pay these recruits. Voted that David Bates and Enos Fountain be reimbursed for "two great coats and one pair of overhauls" which had been stolen from the goods which Thaddeus Hoyt was transporting for the army in 1778.

Nov. 13.—Lieut. Seth Weed and Mr. Silas Davenport appointed to procure the provisions needed from Stamford for the continental army and state troops.

Nov. 27.—Charles Webb, Joshua Ambler, Isaac Lockwood, Charles Smith, Gershom Scofield, Reuben Scofield and Jesse Bell, appointed to hire fifteen able bodied, effective recruits, as soon as may be done.

Nov. 30.—British land at "Rhoton" Islands, and march to Middlesex, capturing 35 cattle and five horses. This irruption leads to the appointment of a committee.

1781.

For this year, Major John Davenport reports in the service from Stamford as follows: In Capt. Chas. Smith's company, 5; in Capt. Fitch's, 7; in Isaac Lockwood's, 53; in Lieut. Jona. Whiting's artillery, 16; in captain Nathaniel Slason's, 15; in Ebenezer Jones' (naval), 30. Whole number killed 12; drowned, 6; taken prisoners, 60, seven of whom are dead and seven wounded.

The state gives credit to Stamford for 147 men in the service.

Jan. 8.—A tax is laid of one penny on a pound, to be be paid in flour, wheat at 24 shillings a bushel, rye at 16 shillings and Indian meal at four shillings.

March 1.—Smith Weed's account for provision for David Waterbury's command, embracing 182,623 1-2 rations, 120,173 lbs. of wheat flour and 39,005 lbs. rye flour.

April 1.—Samuel Webb appointed brigade major, and served to March 1, 1782.

May 18.—Select men Charles Weed and David Waterbury, complain that great numbers of the good subjects of the state in Stamford, have been plundered and driven into the woods and disabled from paying taxes. They ask a commission with power to recruit or abate the tax assessed upon them. The exemption asked was granted.

May 30.—Capt. Daniel Bouton and company march to Campo Bay, Norwalk, to repel the enemy. He is shot in the shoulder and lost his left arm. In the following January he petitions the legislature for pecuniary help and is allowed 65 pounds. This case is endorsed and the plea is urged by several citizens.

July 3.—A tax voted of "four pence on a pound to be collected in silver or gold."

July 22.—The church in Darien surrounded while the congregation were at worship and forty-eight of the worshipers driven off as prisoners. Eli Reed escapes with a slight wound in the leg. Mrs. Sally Dibble was wounded in her plucky defense of the horse on which she had rode to church.

Aug. 24.—D. Waterbury, in camp near Stamford renders his commissary account.

Aug. 30.—Lemuel Sanford, Eli Mygatt und Timothy Keeler, a committee appointed by the general assembly to make out a list of dangerous persons, report sixteen names from Stamford, as persons "inimical to the liberties and independence of the United States."

Sept. 26.—Gideon Lounsbury, whose name was on the list above, was acquitted of the charge.

1782.

Jan.—300 men are stationed here to relieve those whose term of service would end in February, to remain in garrison until May.

Number of town guards as reported by Major John Davenport, 124, and in the boat service, under Ebenezer Jones, 27.

March.—His certificate of this date also testifies that Capt. S. Knapp had transported 31 loads of public provisions from the landing to the town, "said to be a mile and a quarter," and eight loads from the town to the garrison being 3 1-2 miles.

Feb. 25.—Vote 120 non-commissioned officers and soldiers for the defense of the town, to be commanded by Capt. Jesse Bell, Lieut. Nath'l How, Lieut. Jesse Hoyt and ensign Jos. Mather. They were to serve until Jan. 1, 1783.

Feb.—Voted, that select men be desired to appoint some suitable person to manage the field pieces, and to fill all vacancies in offices, on refusal of any to serve

Voted, a tax of six pence on the pound.

June 24.—The town discharge Jesse Bell and the officers and soldiers from keeping town guard.

Voted to class themselves and go on duty by rotation for the defense of the town.

Oct.—Lieut. Col. Canfield in command at Stamford.

1783.

May 3.—The Stanwich people pray for an abatement of their

taxes, in view of their many and serious losses. Not granted.

May 24.—Silas Davenport reports his commissary expenses for 1781 and '82, and draws on the state treasury for pay. The funds were voted.

Dec. 8.—Sam'l Hutton, moderator. Voted, that the select men be directed, and they are hereby directed forthwith to warn out of this town all those persons who have heretofore put and screened themselves under the power and protection of the king of Great Britain, together with all other unwholesome inhabitants, and to see that they are kept out as the law directs.

1784.

Jan. 1.—William Brown, in a document stating that he had served the government as a soldier six years and two months, reports the loss of his pocket-book in July last, on the road to New Canaan, containing thirteen goverment notes, all his earning for his military service. He asks to have the loss made up to him which was granted.

May 4.—Capt. Dan'l Bouton, endorsed by twenty substantial citizens, reports to the assembly his disabled condition. The legislature in consideration of his condition and services, abate his taxes and vote him an annuity of 20 pounds.

CHAPTER XV.

CATALOGUE OF SOLDIERS IN THE REVOLUTIONARY WAR.

The following list embraces the names of all those who have been found as engaged in the revolutionary war from the town of Stamford. The most of the names were found in contemporaneous records, manuscript or printed, and a very few have been added on the testimony of descendants whose account the author deemed trustworthy.

Andreas, Jeremiah, was a pensioner.

Austin, Charles S. served 141 days in 1776, as appears from the manuscript pay-roll of Col. David Waterbury's company of that year.

Barnes, —— a soldier from Stamford, during one of the raids into the northern part of the town, was shot but a short distance east from the store on High Ridge.

Betts, Stephen, in 1774, at the age of 18 years, enlisted into Colonel Charles Webb's regiment. He went to Boston immediately after the action at Lexington where he remained until Howe evacuated the city. He was in the Bunker hill fight. In 1776, he was in the battle of Trenton, and in 1777 in the battles of Princeton and White Marsh when he was commissioned captain. In 1778 he was in the engagement at Monmouth. In 1779 he had command of a company of regulars at Norwalk and was there when Tryon burned the village. In 1781 he was in Colonel Hamilton's battalion of light infantry. He was at the siege of Yorktown, and was among the first of our troops to enter the redoubts of the British; though he paid the penalty of his daring by a bayonet wound which he received in his side. He died in 1832. See Sentinel of Dec. 11, 1832. His widow died here in 1838, aged 94 years.

Baker, Seth, enlisted July 6, 1775.

Bates, Thaddeus, served 211 days in 1776.

Beers, Abijah, enlisted July 6, 1775.

Beers, Daniel, enlisted July 6, '75, and was fifer.

Bell, Francis, enlisted July 6, '75.

Bell, Isaac, Capt. led a company to the defense of Horseneck.

Bell, Abraham, was pensioned.

Bell, Jesse, was in the sea battalion in 1778. He reported perilous service from March 25, 1779 to Jan. '80, and asks indemnity against loss from depreciated currency.

Bell, Jonathan, served 220 days in 1776, and was pensioned He was born in 1755.

Bell, John, enlisted July 6, '75.

Bell, Stephen, served 133 days in '76, and was pensioned. He was 2nd lieutenant in Captain Joseph Hoyt's company.

Bell, Thaddeus, see Biog. sketch.

Bennet, Benj. enlisted July 6, '75.

Besse, John, enlisted July 6, '75.

Besse, Peleg, enlisted July 6, '75.

Betts, Stephen, a serg't in '75, and ensign in '76.

Birchard, John, enlisted July, 6, '75.

Bishop, Hezekiah, enlisted at sixteen and was pensioned. Died in 1839.

Bishop, Jonathan, in company for the defense of New York, 1775.

Bishop, Stephen, served in '75, and 197 days in '76, and then re-enlisted. He was a sergeant and was pensioned.

Bishop, Jacob, served 133 days in '76.

Blanchard, Jacob, a pensioner died here, March 19, 1831, aged 78.

Blatchley, Jesse, served 118 days in '76.

Bouton, Daniel, Capt. was in the engagement at Campo, May 30, 1781, when he was shot in the shoulder.

Briggs, Isaac, was pensioned.

Brown, Bazalell, 1st lieutenant in 1776, in Col. Waterbury's regiment.

" Isaac, in company for defense of New York in 1775, served 217 days in 1776.

" Nathan, enlisted July 6, '75.

" Roger, served 149 days in '76.

" Jonathan was a pensioner.

" Stephen, served 149 days in '76

" William, was in the service six years and two months.

" Sylvanus, Capt. served 227 days in '76, and was capt. of Co. 2, 8th regiment of the line.

Brothswell, Joseph, enlisted July 6, '75.

Buxton, John, enlisted July 6, '75.

Brown, John, was a prisoner.

Bush, Samuel. This name should not be allowed to drop out of our revolutionary roll of honor. He was a humble man it is true, and of African descent. But he united with the patriots of that day and entered the army. It was the boast of his subsequent life, that he had served under Washington. It was the proudest achievement which he used to tell of himself while connected with the army, that on one occasion he personally assisted Gen. Washington to cross a stream in the way of the army. At the expiration of his service the general drew up, and signed for him, his discharge from the service; and as he handed the paper to him said: "take this and keep it with care, it may some day be of use to you." And so it proved, for when afterwards pensions had been provided for, Samuel found this autograph of his general, all that was necessary to attest his service. After the war he married, here, in 1784, Hannah Middlefield by whom he had five children.

Clock, John, was a pensioner.

Clason, Nathaniel, was a pensioner.

Clason, Isaac, was with the garrison on Fort Hill, and was pensioned.

Clason, Samuel, was a pensioner.

Clason, Stephen.

Clerk, Mathew, served 195 days in '76.

Clock, Jonathan, served 192 days in '76 and re-enlisted.

Coggins, David, enlisted July 6, '75.

Coleman, Wm. served 194 days in '76.

Coley, Daniel, enlisted July 6, '75.

Couch, Thomas, served 154 days as quarter-master.

Curtiss, Timothy, junr., in company for defense of New York in '75 and served 220 days in '76.

Curtiss, Jeremy, was a pensioner.

Dan, Nathan, served 178 days in '76.

Dan, Squire, served 194 days in '76 and re-enlisted. He was pensioned. He died here, March 25, 1839.

Daskam, Wm. Capt. served under Lafayette and received his discharge from Washington, himself. He was pensioned.

Davenport, Hezekiah, Lieut. was shot at Ridgefield, April 27, '77, after the burning of Danbury.

Davenport, James, appointed commissary, May 30, '77. See Biog. sketch.

Davenport, John, a commissary with major's commission. See Biog. sketch.

Defreere, Reuben, was pensioned.

Davis, Abraham, served 217 days in '76.

Davis, David, served 59 days and had "deserted" appended to his name.

Dean, Ebenezer, was pensioned. He died here Aug. 14, 1847, aged 32.

Dean, Samuel, entered the army at thirteen and served until he was twenty. He died here July 30, 1845, aged 83. He was pensioned.

Dibble, John, was pensioned. He died in Darien, in April 1852, aged 93.

Dogherty, Andrew, served 220 days in '76.

Duncomb, Wm. enlisted July 6 '75.

Eldridge, Wm. served 180 days in '76.

Ferris, Peter, was in both the French and revolutionary war.

Ferris, Jonathan, served and was entitled to a pension, which he refused. His wife secured it after his death.

Ferris, Ransford A. was in the battle at Bunker Hill, and pensioned. He died here Jan. 2, 1824, aged 72. Had a ball in his right arm till he died.

Finney, Daniel, went to the defense of New York in '75, and served 210 days in '76.

Fitch, —— was captain here in 1781.

Forster, Thomas, enlisted July 6, '75.

Fulton, Thomas, " " " "

Finch, James, was pensioned. He brought from the field a belt from an English officer.

Garnsey, Samuel, served 192 days in '76, as sergt.

Gibbs, John, served 176 days in '76.

Gould, Talcot, enlisted July 6, '75.

Green, Asabel, served 217 days in '76.

Gregory, Elias, enlisted July 6, '75.

Griffet, Wm. enlisted July 6, '75.

Gregory, Benoni, served 212 days in '76.

Hanford, Theophilus, served 214 days in '76.

Hawley, Thomas, enlisted July 6, '75.

Hay, James, served 196 days in '76.

Heacock, Bethel, served 193 days in '76, and re-enlisted.

" Ebenezer, served 216 days in '76.

" Morris, served 216 days in '76.

Hedden, Zadoc, died in Stamford, April 29, 1840, aged 82 years, he having been a pensioner for service in the revolutionary war.

Hine, Jared, enlisted July 6, '75.

Hinman, Enoch, enlisted July 6, '75.

Hobby, Thomas, Capt. 3d co. 5th reg't, April, '75, and was appointed major.

Holly, Abraham, served thro' the war and was pensioned.

" Ebenezr, junr., served 220 days in '76.

" Isaac, enlisted July 6, '75.

" Nathan, was in the commissary department.

" Stephen, was a pensioner. He was once a prisoner in the Sugar House.

Holmes, John, was in the Danbury fight and brought back a gun now in his grandson John's possession.

How, Nathan, served 174 days in '76. He was pensioned.

How, Nathaniel, was lieutenant in 1782, and at the close of the war captain. At one time with twelve soldiers he had charge of sixty tories who had been arrested.

Hoyt, Bates, was in New York city, in Capt. Webb's company in 1776.

Hoyt, Ebenezer, born in 1763 was pensioned.

" Elijah, enlisted July 6, '75.

" Jesse, Lieut. served 176 days in '76, and continued in the service pensioned.

" Jonathan.

" John.

" Joseph, Lieut. Col. of the 8th Conn. reg't, regular army. He had been captain in 1775.

" Josiah, enlisted July 6, '75.

" Nathaniel, enlisted July 6, '75, and was sergeant.

" Neazer, born Nov. 8, 1751, served 49 days in 1776. Died here Feb. 15, 1811.

" Samuel, captain in 5 Conn. militia, thro' the war. He was pensioned.

" Samuel, enlisted July 6, '75, and served 158 days in '76 as ensign. He was afterwards a lieutenant. He died in Darien, Dec. 30, 1832, aged 80 years. He was pensioned

Hoyt, Sylvanus, died on returning home from his campaign, Sept. 8, '76, leaving a wife and four children.

" Warren, was in the war in '75, and pensioned.

" William, took the small pox while in the service and died of it, Nov. 15, '78, leaving two sons, William and Rufus, who went to Black Rock, Fairfield.

" Thaddeus, Capt. one of the most fearless and resolute of our patriots, as our history elsewhere shows. He was in Captain Webb's company in New York city, in August '76, as appears from a letter from his parents.

" Silas, brother of Bates and Thaddeus was with them in New York city in '76.

Hubbel, Salmon, enlisted July 6, '75.

Hurd, Williston, was in Capt. Chapman's company, 5th Conn.

Husted, Nathaniel, served 78 days in '76, as corporal.

" Thaddeus, went in '75, for the defense of New York.

Hutton, Samuel, sergeant in Capt. Hoyt's company in '75.

Jackson, Nathan P. enlisted July 6, '75, and was serg't.

" William, enlisted July 6, '75.

Jennings, Justus, enlisted July 6, '75.

Jervis, Jonathan, enlisted July 6, '75.

Johnson, William, served thro' the war and was pensioned.

Jones, Ebenezer, Capt. commanded a boat, used to annoy the enemy's shipping in the sound—a man of great daring and courage. In 1781 he had under his command 30 of the Stamford men.

Jones, Ephraim, was a pensioner.

June, Reuben, entered the service at 16, and was pensioned.

June, Silas, was taken prisoner by the British at White Plains. He was pensioned.

June, Thomas, was shot as he was returning from hoeing in the field and his two sons were taken prisoners,

June, Israel, was a pensioner.

Ingersol, Benjamin, died in the service.

Ingersol, Samuel.

Keeler, Isaac, enlisted July 6, '75, a corporal.

" Lockwood, " 6, "

" Thaddeus, " 6, " and was serg't.

Kellogg, Asahel, served 191 days in '76, and re-enlisted.

Kenney, John, enlisted July 6, '75.

Knapp, Bouton, served 135 days in '76.

" Hezekiah, born in 1750, was a pensioner.

" John, served 223 days in '76.

" Sylvanus, was captain of the town guards.

" Usual, was pensioned. He had been a prominent man and much in favor with Washington. He died at Newbury, N. Y., when special honor was done to his memory.

" Timothy, enlisted July 6, '75.

" William, born in 1756, was a pensioner. He served under Putnam and was with him at Greenwich at the time of his famous plunge on horseback down the steps. He died here Jan. 31, 1844.

" Jacob, was a pensioner.

Lee, Seth, enlisted July 6 '75.

Lindsay, James, enlisted July 6, '75.

Lines, Holly, served 220 days in '76.

Little, John, was a pensioner.

Lloyd, Clement, served 194 days and re-enlisted.

Loder, Jacob, was a pensioner.

Lockwood, David, served 220 days in '76, and was taken prisoner at New York. He was a pensioner.

Lockwood, Ezra, went to the defense of New York in '75.

" Isaac, was captain of the town guard in '81. He was pensioned. He died here, July 31, 1836.

" Noah.

" Reuben, enlisted July 6, '75, and was pensioned.

" Titus, enlisted July 6, '75, and after the murder of his brother by the cowboys, he was the inexrable avenger of every injured patriot.

Lockwood, Timothy, served 176 days in '76. His tragic end will be found among the incidents of the war.

" Charles, was pensioned.

" Samuel, 2nd Lieut. in '75, in Col. Waterbury's regiment.

Lounsbury, David, enlisted July 6, '75, account balanced in Vol. 5th, in the comptroller's office, when he received £20 14 shillings.

Lounsbury, Jacob, enlisted July 6, '75, and was a pensioner.

McCurtiss, Daniel, enlisted July 6, '75, a drummer.

Mason, John, served 12 days in '76 and deserted.

Mather, Samuel, was a pensioner.

Mather, Joseph, served 216 days in '76, and was ensign in '82. He was pensioned.

Mead, Peter, served 220 days in '76.

Mead, Theophilus, enlisted July, 6, '75, and was fifer.

Mead, Reuben, was a pensioner.

Meeker, Ebenezer, enlisted July 6, '75.

Mills, George, captain and active in the war.

Mills, John, served 215 days in '76, quartermaster 31 days, and adjutant 139 days.

Mills, John, junr., served 216 days in '76.

Nichols, John, was pensioned.

Nichols, Daniel, was in the regular service in '76 one year, in the army of the north. Afterwards thro' the war he was often engaged as scout to find and report the tories. He was pensioned. He died here, Feb. 18, 1834.

Nichols, Abel, enlisted July 6, '75.

Nichols, Joseph, was pensioned.

Northrup, Camaliel, enlisted July 6, '75 and was a lieutenant.

Nichols, James, was pensioned.

Newman, Rufus, was pensioned.

Odell, John, enlisted July 6, '75.

Olmstead, Roger, enlisted July 6, '75.

Olmstead, David, enlisted July 6, '75, a corporal.

Pangburn, Richard served 196 days in '76, and re-enlisted.
Parrot, David enlisted July 6, '75.
Parsons, Ja's enlisted July 6, '75, and was marked as deserter.
Patchin, Elijah enlisted July 6, '75.
Patchin, Israel enlisted July 6, '75 and was corporal.
Peat, James served 153 days in '76.
Peck, Ephriam served 149 days in '76.
Powers, Andrew served 212 days in 76, and was serg't.
Provost, Thomas was pensioned.
Provost, Daniel was in the war. He died here Dec. 14, 1832, aged 79 years.
Provost, Samuel was a pensioner. He died here Nov. 30, 1843, aged 80 years.
Purdy, David was ensign in '76.
Quintard, Isaac was a pensioner.
Raymond, David was a pensioner. He was in the battle of White Plains.
Reed, Elias served 193 days in '76, and re-enlisted.
" Ketchel served 132 days in '76.
" Silas served 220 days in '76, as fifer.
Richards, Wm. was shot when on duty at Ringsend.
St. John, Abraham went in '75 for the defense of New York city.
" " Justin, enlisted July 6, '75.
Saunders, John M. served 218 days in '76.
Scofield, Abram served 175 days in '76.
" Benjamin went for the defense of New York city in 1775.
" Ebenezer was 1st Lieut. in the service.
" Elisha served 153 days in '76.
" Ezra enlisted July 6, '75, served seven years and was pensioned.
" Gershom, a lieutenant, died in 1824, aged 75. He preserved his powder-horn, on which while in the service he had carved, "Liberty, property and no tax in America."

Scofield, Gideon.

" Gilbert was drafted, but at his father's wish deserted.

" Hait, orderly serj't and was in many engagements. He was pensioned. He died here July 16, 1840, aged 84 years.

" Israel, 3rd, went in '75 for the defense of New York city.

" Jacob went in '75 for the defense of New York, and re-enlisted July 6, '75.

" Jared was a pensioner.

" Josiah 4th, went in '75 for the defense of New York, and re-enlisted July 6, '75. He was a serg't.

" Josiah W. was a pensioner.

" Joseph in '75 went for the defense of New York city, and re-enlisted July 6, '75.

" Peter enlisted into the revolutionary service July 6, '75. He died here April 28, 1830, aged 91 years.

" Pettit went in '75 for the defense of New York city.

" Reuben was serg't July 6, '75, and captain July 9, '77, in a battalion for the defense of the sea coast. He succeeded Jesse Bell who resigned. He served as captain several years, and received a captain's pension. He died here in 1835, aged 93 years.

" Thaddeus served 207 days in '76.

" Seth went in '75 for the defense of New York city.

" Enos was pensioned. He moved after the war to Bedford, N. Y.

" Sylvanus, a pensioner died here, Sept. 21, 1831, aged "about 80."

Scott, William enlisted July 6, '75.

Seeley, John was in the service three years. He died in 1832.

Selleck, Darling was at the battle of White Plains.

Selleck, David served 220 days in '76.

" Ebenezer served 187 days in '76. He went over to Oyster Bay after the war.

Selleck, Joseph was pensioned. He was a teamster.

" Simeon a commissary, served 32 days in '76, and succeeded in capturing the king's stores at Horseneck.

Share, Daniel served 193 days in '76, and re-enlisted.

Selleck, William.

Sherwood, Daniel enlisted July 5, '75.

Skelding, Thomas served in the commissary department.

Slason, Ebenezer was a major in '76.

" Henry was captain here in '76.

" Nathaniel was captain of the home guard in '81, and was pensioned.

Shelp, William was pensioned.

Smith, Austin, junr., reported 220 days service.

" Azariah, reported 77 days service in '76.

" Amos Capt.

" Charles Capt. of state guards between the lines in '81.

" " junr., was a pensioner.

" David 3d, was stationed at Greenwich. He was famous as a scout, hunting down the tories. He was a pensioner. He died May 26, 1840. His children were Joseph, Benjamin, Sally, Mary C., and Mrs. Lavina White.

" Daniel enlisted July 6, '75.

" Ezra, 3d, went to the defense of New York in '75, and reported 163 days service in '76.

" Ebenezer, captured by tories in the Farms district and put into the "Sugar House." He was a pensioner.

" Isaac, reported in '76, 220 days service.

" Isaac, served from '77, thro' the war. He was father of Chas. Edgar.

" Jabez, reported 154 days service in '76. Pensioned.

" Jabez, junr., went for defense of New York in '75, and reported 135 days service in '76.

" Job. enlisted July 6, 75.

Smith, Joseph, was ensign in '75.

" Joshua reported 148 days service in '76.

" Josiah, Lieut. was active thro' the war. Had one thumb struck off by a ball, and was badly cut in both arms and the face while warding off the strokes of a British officer. He died Nov. 29, 1830, aged 81 years. He was a consistent Christian patriot, a member of the North Baptist church of this town.

" Levi enlisted July 6, '75.

" Nathaniel reported 175 days service in '76.

" Peter reported 238 days service in '76. He was shot at the Noroton.

" William, Capt.

Sniffin, Reuben was in the battle of White Plains. He died here.

Stevens, Daniel.

" David was shot at Ridgefield. See incidents of the war.

" Ezra served 151 days in '76. After the war, was a justice and town lawyer. He lived in the north-east part of the town.

" Jacob was at the battle of White Plains.

" Obidiah, junr., went for the defense of New York in '75. He was an older brother of Mr. Peter Stevens, still living, 1864, on Hoyt street.

" Reuben, after the war moved into the State of New York. He was at the fight at Bunker Hill.

" Sylvanus served 191 days in '76, and re-enlisted.

" Thomas.

Stewart, Charles served 238 days in '76. He was corporal, and was captured and imprisoned in Halifax, N. S., Sept 16, '76.

Swords, Francis D. enlisted July 6, '75.

Thompson, William served 194 days in '76, and re-enlisted.

Todd, John.

Tryon, Samuel served 211 days in '76.

Wardwell, Isaac entered service at sixteen, near the end of the war.

" Jacob, b. Aug. 19, 1744, served thro' the war.

" William, b. Feb. 1760, before the war closed was enrolled in the army.

Waring, Benjamin served 196 days in '76.

" Joseph was pensioned.

" James was pensioned.

" John, Serj't served 151 days in '76.

" Jonathan was captain in '79.

" Simeon served 53 days in '76.

" Thaddeus was in the town guard and in a skirmish east of the Noroton.

Waters, Elisha joined Arnold to repel the British at Horseneck.

" John was imprisoned in New York.

Waterbury, Daniel was 2nd Lieut. in '76.

" David was in pursuit of the British retreating from Danbury. He saw Wooster shot and Arnold as he left his fallen horse, taking his pistols with him.

" David. See Biog. sketch.

" David 3rd.

" Enos, a commissary and pensioner. Died here about 18 years ago.

" Gideon, an ensign.

" John, ensign, served 178 days in '76.

" John 5th, a private.

" Joseph served 193 days in '76.

" Peter.

" Epenetus and David, both died in Canada during the war.

Waterbury, William, after the war, went to Saratoga, where he died July 20, 1846, aged 77.

Waterbury, William served 217 days in '76, was in Colonel Chandler's regiment three years and was pensioned. He was taken prisoner at fort Washington on the Hudson, and was seriously injured by the poisoned wine which his captors gave him. He served under Lafayette, and was in the batte of Monmouth. When Lafayette in 1825 passed thro' Stamford, he at once recognized his soldier and gave him a hearty salutation. He died in Stamford village June 22, 1830, in the 74th year of his age.

Webb, Benjamin who had been in the French war.

Webb, Charles Col. See Biog. sketch.

Webb, Charles, junr., was lieutenant in '75, served as adjutant 52 days in '76, and was still later in his father's regiment. He was a prisoner in New York. He was killed on a gun-boat in the Sound.

Webb, David was commissary in '76.

" Ebenezer died here Sept. 4, 1834, aged '70.

" Gilbert served 158 days in '76.

" Joseph junr., was 1st Lieut. and wounded.

" Hezekiah enlisted July 6, '75.

" Samuel was serj't in the company which went under Capt. Joseph Hoyt to defend New York city in '75. He served as clerk of Col. Waterbury's regiment, 196 days in '76, and re-enlisted. He was brigade major in '79, and was captured and exchanged.

" Nathaniel Capt.

Weed, Charles was a pensioner.

" James was a pensioner.

" Abishai was pensioned. He died here Jan. 31, 1840, aged 80 years.

" Abijah who been in the old French and Indian war, early entered the revolutionary service. He afterwards joined the British and went to Canada and died there.

Weed, Asahel.

" Benjamin went in '75 to defend New York city and served as serg't in that year 170 days. He was wounded in the Ridgefield skirmish by a ball which he carried the rest of his life. He was pensioned.

" Annanias went in '75, to the defense of New York city and served 222 days in '76. He was serj't and commissary and served thro' the war. He died here in 1820.

" Daniel was pensioned.

" Hezekiah was a pensioner.

" Elnathau served 212 days in '76.

" Ezra was captured and imprisoned in Canada.

" Gideon enlisted July 6, '75. He was the youngest member of Capt. How's company and during the absence of the captain he was appointed to take his place on the sudden appearance of a gang of tories. He drew up the company near the school house in Darien and was himself shot down as he stood between two of his brothers, Hezekiah and Jonas.

" Henry was pensioned.

" Jabez.

" Jared.

" Joel.

" John was a pensioner. He served under Lafayette.

" Jonas was wounded and carried a buckshot in his arm all his life. He was a pensioner.

" Jonathan was a pensioner. He died here Jan. 31, 1840, aged 80 years.

" Hezekiah 4th, went in '75 for the defense of New York city, and was wounded with a shot he carried all his life.

Weed, Seth Lieut. served 161 days in '76. He died Dec. 26, 1822.

" Silas went in '75 to defend New York city and served 220 days as corporal and 80 days as serg't in '76.

" Stephen was made insane by his exposures. See Biog. sketch.

White, Jacob was a pensioner.

Whiting, Jonathan, 2nd Lieut. in Col. Waterbury's regiment in '75.

Woolsey, Gilbert was a pensioner. He bears the name of the pioneer of the family who settled here.

Weeks, Henry died in 1824.

Wheaton, Samuel, sergeant in Capt. Hoyt's company in '75.

Young, Samuel, was in the service, he died July 8, 1827.

CHAPTER XVI.

THE LOYAL ELEMENT OF OUR REVOLUTIONARY PERIOD.

The Loyal element in that trying day was much more general and troublesome to the patriot cause, than our current history shows. In all of our towns it existed, and in a large number of them it was a serious hindrance to the effective prosecution of the war. In the immediate vicinity of the British lines, and elsewhere soon after British successes, it asserted itself with great distinctness; and at all times and in all parts of the land, it was sufficiently demonstrative to embarrass the patriot cause. It showed itself in many ways, and most unexpectedly. Stamford was of course not without this element. Indeed, it would not be strange if it existed here more offensively than in many other of our Connecticut towns. The British lines for several years were very near, at times even within hearing of the village. The Episcopal Church, which had already attained here a prominent position both in numbers and influence, and which as a matter of conscience had all along been accustomed to pray for "Our good King George the Third," were in their religious sentiments opposed to any such revolution as the war aimed to achieve.

Accordingly we find the very opening of the great struggle seriously checked, and the cause of Colonial independence constantly endangered by this secret or open opposition of those who could not or would not espouse it. They opposed enlistments into the army for independence. They concealed their neighbors who had been drafted or aided their escape from the service after they had been sworn into it. As a good illustration of this style of opposition to the war let the following instance answer. James Scofield's son Gilbert, a mere boy, had been drafted and sent with our recruits to New York. The father who was notoriously opposed to the war, mounted his horse and pursued. By adroit management he found his son and succeeded in releasing him and putting him beyond reach of those whose duty it was to find and arrest deserters. As this could not be done safely on the patriot side of the lines, the youth was transferred to the other side where for about two years he rendered such service as his years and ability would allow.

Witness also another fact in the very opening of the war for independence. I shall simply quote from the record of the general assembly, their action in March 1775.

"It having been represented to this assembly that Isaac Quintard of Stamford, in the County of Fairfield, Capt. of the 2nd military company, in the town of Stamford, in the 9th regt. in this colony, and Fyler Dibble of said Stamford, Capt, of the first military company of Stamford, in said regiment, at said Stamford, in January last, in contempt of the authority in this colony, did attempt and endeavor to prevent the introduction of certain barrels of gun powder into this colony for the government's use, agreeably to the orders and directions of legal authority, which conduct is inconsistent with the duty of their said office and of dangerous tendency; whereupon it is resolved by this assembly, that Gold Selleck Silliman and Jonathan Sturgiss, Esquires, be and they are hereby appointed Commissioners, and are fully authorized and empowered to notify said Quintard and Dibble to appear before them at such time and place as shall be by them appointed and to examine the witnesses relative to said conduct and examine into the truth of said representations and to report what they shall find to the general assembly at the session in May next."

No record of the arrest and trial of the captains has been found; but from the American Archives we learn that Fyler Dibble, Sept. 26, 1775, asks the forgiveness of the people for opposing the appointment of a committee of inspection, and promises to yield hearty obedience to the continental association. Captain Quintard, also, waived his further opposition and made a humble confession.

Yet these were by no means the only citizens who were opposed to the war, as abundant records of that day testify. The first Tuesday of June, 1775, must have been a day of no little excitement in this usually quiet town. The patriotism of the citizens had been outraged by the sale among them of that once innocent, but now proscribed article, tea.

Stamford must purge herself from the vile treason. She had not, like Ridgefield, refused to represent herself in the county convention which had in the preceding February sounded so clearly the tocsin for war, rather than a base submission to the taxation of the British Crown; nor had her select men like those of Newtown, contemptuously set up at vendue for a pint of flip, a copy of the patriotic address sent out by the general assembly, to indicate to all good citizens their future duty. But the occasion now offers for her citizens to make signal proof that their hearts and means are with all who will unite to sunder the ties which had held them as mere vassals of the English crown.

It appears, that though mainly ready for any personal sacrifice which the struggle might call for, there was one among them, whose greed out-weighed his patriotism. Sylvanus Whitney, more thrifty than patriotic, ventured to traffic in contraband goods. He thought he knew when it would be a money making thing to dispose of good tea for a good price, and he supplies himself. His friends or his traffic betray him. He is summoned to answer to his townsmen for his treasonable practice. Under the pressure of the moral or stringently physical force used on the occasion, Mr. Whitney submits himself and his, to their disposal, as follows:

"Whereas I, the subscriber, have been guilty of buying and selling Bohea tea, since the first of March last past, whereby I have been guilty of a breach of the association entered into by the continental congress; and sensible of my misconduct, do in this public manner, confess my crime and humbly request the favor of the public to overlook this my transgression, promising for the future to conduct myself as a true friend to my country; and in testimony of my sincerity, I do now deliver up the tea I have on hand unto the said committee of inspection to be by them committed to the flames."

"SYLVANUS WHITNEY."

On this confession and pledge the committee released the arrested culprit from further prosecution, but proceeded to arrange for the evening entertainment which had already been announced. We will report the festivity which followed in the words of the contemporaneous record, now preserved in the American Archives.

"About 8 o'clock, in the evening, a gallows was erected in the middle of the street, opposite the Webb tavern; a large concourse of people collected, and were joined by a number of soldiers quartered in the town. A grand procession soon began to move. In the first place, a large guard under arms, headed by two captains, who lead the van, while the unfortunate tea hung across a pole, sustained by two unarmed soldiers. Secondly, followed the Committee of Observation. Thirdly, spectators came to see the great sight. And after parading through part of the principal street, with drums beating and fifes playing a most doleful sound, they come to the gallows where the common hangman soon performed his office to the general satisfaction of the spectators. As it was thought dangerous to let said tea hang all night, for fear of an invasion from our tea lovers, a large bonfire was made under it, which soon reduced it to ashes; and after giving three loud huzzas, the people soon dispersed to their respective homes without any bad consequence attending. The owner of the aforesaid tea attended, during the execution, and behaved himself as well as could be expected on the occasion."

The next year, also, witnesses a trial in Stamford. Munson Jarvis and David Pickett are summoned before the committee of inspection, April 3, 1776. They had signed a seditious paper pledging themselves "to assist the king and his vile minions in their wicked, oppressive schemes to enslave the American colonies," and to discourage any military preparation to repel the invasion of the British forces and to dissuade persons from observing the orders, of the continental congress. They acknowledged their signatures to the paper, when they were pronounced guilty of a great crime.

Mr. Jarvis prepared a confession, professing himself sorry for what he had done and promised to obey every order of the continental congress, excepting as he was held back by a "religious tie of conscience."

Mr. Picket, also, makes confession and begs to have the past overlooked and he will henceforth "conduct himself agreeably to the good and wholesome laws and rules now in the colonies, which may be for the good of his country"

They were then asked what they meant by that "tie of conscience" which was to control their future course, and what were the laws "for the good of the country," which they were prepared to obey. In their reply, they protested that they could not join with the country in pursuing the measures adopted by congress in defense of the just rights and privileges of the colonies; and upon this explanation, the committee pronounced their confession and promises unsatisfactory The charges against them were sustained. The committee voted to advertise them as enemies of their country, and conclude their sentence thus: "and we hereby recommend it to all persons to break off all commerce and dealing with them, and to treat them agreeably to the resolves of congress for those who are deemed enemies of their country." The original record of the transactions is signed by John Haight, jr., clerk of the committee.

The following transaction, preserved in the American Archives, shows that the opposition to the war went still further. William Budd Lucas was a marked patriot, then temporarily living in Stamford. He was red hot against all tories, and his zeal maddened them beyond control. They therefore united with some of the same faith in Norwalk and gave him a most unmerciful whipping. For which offense they were arrested and brought to the following confession:

"Mr. Luke Raymond, Ebenezer Raymond and Billy Saunders of Norwalk in Conn. having in a cruel and unjustifiable manner been guilty of attacking, beating and mauling William Budd Lucas of Stamford, for which crime we are heartily sorry, and in the first place earnestly beg the forgiveness of said Lucas, and of all other persons whom we have offended, and furthermore we, William Starr, James Hoyt, jr. Prince Howes and Samuel Beebe of Stamford, and John Bigelow of Norwalk, having been guilty of being drawn into the riotous company above written, for which misconduct we are sincerely ashamed and heartily sorry, and humbly ask forgiveness of all whom we have offended. Furthermore, we, Prince Howes, Jas. Hoyt, jr. and Samuel Beebe aforesaid, having imprudently subscribed a certain paper said to be drawn up by Capt. Fyler Dibble, for which misconduct we are sorry and humbly ask the forgiveness of all whom we have offended. And furthermore, we, one and all, solemnly promise and declare that we will, to the utmost of our power and ability, exert ourselves in the defense of our country in opposition to the King's troops. Signed, Stamford, Sept. 15, 1775."

After these records it can scarcely be doubted that some stringent measures would be justified by the patriots of that day in putting down this opposition to their cause. Accordingly, the assembly for the state, in December of this year passed their famous act, for restraining and punishing persons who are inimical to the liberties of this and the rest of the united colonies. That act made it a treasonable offense to "libel or defame any of the resolves of the congress of the united colonies or the acts and proceedings of this assembly, which are made for the defense and security of the rights and privileges of the same." Any person found guilty was to be disarmed, and rendered incapable of holding or serving in any office civil or military, and he could be further punished by fine, imprisonment or disfranchisement.

If such legislation seems needlessly harsh, we must remember the necessity which called for it. The tories of that day were as earnest and as honest in their opposition to the independence of the American colonies as the British themselves. They not only did their utmost by tongue and pen, to oppose the patriot cause, but they openly furnished arms and men to the now declared public enemy. Whole regiments of them joined the British cause. Incidents often occurring in this town showed conclusively that either the tories must be restrained or the cause of colonial independence abandoned.

Witness the capture of the patriotic Dr. Mather and his four sons, taken from their own home, and that, the parsonage, and hurried to New York, where they could no more preach treason against their sovereign, or aid his rebellious subjects in resisting his abjured authority. Five of the eight agents engaged in this capture were parishioners of the venerable man against whom they were executing this vengeance of the king.

Witness, also, this well accredited fact. When the enemy landed at Campo Bay, May 30th, 1781, at the same time that our patriot company under their gallant captain, Daniel Bouton, were on their forced march to repel the invaders, two of the loyalist portion of the town were actually piloting the miscreants to the best farms of the neighborhood for such plunder as they could appropriate. That such opposition should greatly try and exasperate the patriots of that day and lead to severe punishment would be most natural. We shall find abundant proof of such results in many occurrences of the times, as is evident from the following case.

David Newman, a man of good repute for all that appears, had a son, Joshua, who in a freak of youthful temper early in the war had gone over to the enemy, on Long Island. Here he soon found a gentle damsel whose attractions only served to weld the bonds which already held him in the British power. The months swept on and the fair enchantress wins a pledge of marriage and the nuptial day is appointed. Not being yet fully absolved from all ties of home, the gallant Joshua ventures to brave the dangers of a return that he may have the blessing of "the old folks at home," to add to the cheer of the approaching wedding. He reaches Stamford and safely enters what had once been a safe altar of refuge for him. Eagle-eyed vigilance is aroused. The presence of the young traitor is suspected, and the swift footed ministers of the patriotic citizens are out on the search. The house is surrounded and explored, but the anxious parents, whose love was as keen and vigilant as the sharpest patriotism, had so skillfully screened or adroitly removed their "boy, still," that he could not be found. But what could the outraged citizens do? The traitor son had escaped. The father must have aided him, and he was in their power. For this offense, that of shielding his son and so giving aid and comfort to the enemy, he was arrested and thrown into the county jail. No plea of his family and no pledge of his personal loyalty could avail. Weeks and months he paid in confinement the penalty of his offense, that of holding the calls of parental affection above the demands of the public safety. Not until his jailor had testified to his loyalty and his uncomplaining readiness to suffer yet longer, if so his townsmen required, would the stern sense of the people consent to his release.

Another instance which shows how determined was the popular indignation against the loyalists towards the close of the war is found in a petition, signed Jan. 2nd, 1782, by thirty-seven Stamford and Greenwich men, in which the petitioners remonstrate against allowing "tories" who had served in the British armies to return again as citizens of either town. The remonstrance states that "since the capture of Cornwallis and his army many unprincipled wretches from us who had with arms joined the common enemy," had returned home, and that a number of them belong to the most infamous banditti, called Delancey's corps. The names of the petitioners are;—Benj. Mead, jr., Abr. Mead, Caleb Lyons, Jesse Mead, Silas Mead, jr., Eb. Mead, Isaac How, Abner Mead, Wm. Weed, Richard Mead, Abr. Weed, Daniel Bouton, Reuben Weed, Jared Mead, Deodate Davenport, Jas. Ambler, Holly Scofield, Jos. Seely, Timothy Reed, Daniel Chichester, John Mather, Sen. Webb, Samuel Young, Philip Jones, Israel Weed, Zebulon Husted, Jona. Scofield, Benj. Weed 3rd, Thaddeus Husted, Jehiel Mead, Soame Fountain, Chas. Smith, Benj. Marvin, Andrus Powers, Eli Reed, Theodore Hanford and Jona. Weed.

But as the struggle approached its close, and it began to be seen that the colonies would maintain their independence, those who had allowed themselves to oppose the struggle began to repent. They sought every opportunity to excuse and palliate the guilt of their course. How completely they had been subdued by the progress of the war the following incidents will fully show.

John William Holly, in a document dated Sept. 30, 1782, testifies that when he was fourteen years old his father went over to the British and put him under the protection of the British army. He had continued to live in New York and at Lloyd's Neck, until a month ago. He then resolved not to oppose his country longer, as his father was now dead and his widowed mother was living alone at Stamford. He therefore begs to be allowed to return, as a loyal citizen of the new government. The request was granted by the legislature. Mr. Holly afterwards became the proprietor of the Cove Mills, and a prominent and honored citizen.

Elnathan Holly a youth of nineteen years, in 1776, joined the enemy, and was employed in the army. In April, 1782, he abandoned the British service, returned to Stamford and was imprisoned. He forwards to the legislature a penitent confession, his sacred oath of future allegiance, and a fervent plea for his liberation. The petition was granted.

In May, 1782, widow Mary Wooster, pleads before the legislature the case of her son then in New York. He had been early drawn over the lines and into the British service. He had never taken up arms; and of late had lived in New York, carrying on his trade as tailor. He had made money, and is now anxious to visit his mother and make Stamford his future home. He is ready to give pledges of his loyalty to the new government and is by vote of the legislature allowed to return.

After the depredations committed by the British in the eastern part of the town, as reported in our chronological record under date of Nov. 30, 1780, the legislature appointed a committee to report all dangerous persons from Stamford. This was done, when the following names were reported; Gideon Leeds, Admer Stevens, Sam'l Hoyt 3rd, Sam'l Crissy, John Selleck, Anthony De Mill, Daniel Selleck, Josiah Scofield 3rd, Josiah Scofield, John Bates, Nathaniel Dan, James Scofield, junr., Jonathan Lewis, David Hoyt, Gideon Lounsbury and Sylvanus Seeley. Our chronological record shows that Gideon Lounsbury was acquitted of the charge. In the State Archives I found other papers respecting these tories worth reporting.

One contains an appeal from Samuel Crissy and Gideon Leeds, demanding an examination, which was granted. At the trial they brought forward such proofs of their substantial agreement with the patriots that their names were, also, erased from the black list. Thus encouraged the remainder of the list, April 29, 1782, urge upon the governor and his council their claim to be acquitted of the charge made by the assembly's committee, and demand an early re-examination. Accordingly the Governor immediately issues a warrant to the Sheriff of Fairfield county or a constable at Stamford, to summon John Hoyt, junr., town clerk, and the rest of the inhabitants to appear before the general assembly in May and show reason why the prayer of the petitioners should not be granted.

At the same time, the question of opposing the petitioners before the legislature was discussed by the select men of Stamford and by a majority vote they decided not to furnish John Hoyt with funds to prosecute the opposition. Sheriff Elijah Abel, executed his writ of summons in person, and the case went before the legislature. After examination the legislature voted to refer the petitioners to the county court, with the suggestion that if the court should see fit, they should cause the names of the petitioners to be erased from the town clerk's books and all monies expended by them in the suit to be refunded. It is probable that the court did not adopt the advice of the legislature. At any rate, the names still occupy their original position, with no line of erasure, or word of palliation.

In view of the strong feelings which these recurring collisions must produce it is not strange that the popular indignation at times broke out into acts of violence for which the law made no provision, and which the local authorities were impotent to control. Of such was that summary vengeance inflicted on that leader among our loyalists, Joseph Ferris, when our usually sober-minded citizens, after dipping him to their content in our mill pond, substituted for his comfortable home-spun, a full and close fitting wardrobe from head to toe, of nicest down, made wearable for the time being, by softest tar. Of such too was the spontaneous reception which our neighboring Norwalkers gave our loyalist townsman, Increase Holly, who had visited his brethren after his British confreres had burned the town, to rejoice with them at the success of our good King George. He had gone down, as he announced on leaving home, to bear them the olive of peace. He sorrowfully reported on his return that all he knew of an olive branch, he felt from the twigs, with which the patriot, Norwalk wide-awakes, so mercilessly tingled his exposed parts.

At the close of the war some of the most determined tories left town with such of their families as could not be content to remain here. Of those who remained the most soon yielded to the demands of the new government and rendered as loyal service as though they had aided in its establishment. The alienations which had sprung up in families and among neighbors were gradually healed, and the former mutual confidence and affection were restored; so that the grand-son of the most patriotic whig could find in the grand-daughter of the hottest tory, the most attractive and lovable maiden of his youth, and the most congenial and affectionate wife of his later years.

Fifty years after the war, when there was now no longer any bar to free intercourse between the exiles and the friends they had left behind, an occurrence took place in that part of the town which had already been incorporated as Darien, showing how strong were the sentiments of country and family still, among those who had been forced by the strife to leave. In 1838, Walter and Augustus Bates, who were among the banished loyalists, returned to the home of their childhood. Though honored and much esteemed in the home of their adoption, they still retained their youthful love for the one they had lost. By the kindness of Mrs. Seeley, of Darien, I am allowed to use the following extracts from a brief "Jubilee" which the former of those returned exiles penned, as expressive of their feelings on that joyful occasion. Doubtless many others of the refugees, retained to their death, their early love of the place and associations of their youth.

"Our two oldest brothers being dead, the remaining family eight in number were thus singularly separated—two only remained in our native town, two settled in different towns within the United States, two in the province of New Brunswick and two in Upper Canada, where we remained twelve hundred miles from each other and six hundred from our native place, until the eldest had arrived at the age of eighty and the youngest to the sixty-second year of his age. After the full term of fifty years, guided and protected by a kind Providence, we are permitted to visit our native home, the town and place of our birth, here to celebrate our jubilee with praise and thanksgiving to Almighty God for his special providence, permitting us at this time and place, to meet together, praising God in communion with our remaining relations and friends, in the same church wherein we were in infancy, by baptism, first dedicated to God by our parents.

At first view of our native town, the neatness of the village appeared as if all things had become new. The former meeting-house, of ancient architecture, pulled down and a new one in its place; the church had undergone a change for improvement; new dwelling houses, store houses, and public offices erected; and sloops and steamboats in the center of the town by a canal. On our further view we saw with regret the few old dwelling houses that remained, unrepaired, and mouldering into decay and ruin; the public burying-ground, where lay concealed the powdered remains of the deceased for more than a century past, totally demolished; a new Methodist meeting-house erected upon the consecrated ground and the ancient monuments of the tombs converted into stepping-stones. Should those monuments be thus converted?

We gaze on these objects, thus changed, with sadness and sighing; and hasten away lest their present state should weaken the images which our memory had preserved. * * * * Feasting on our anticipations we at length reach the object of our fondest wishes, the house and place of our nativity. We found the same house, but like every other object it had undergone a visible change, one part having been pulled down and improved with a chamber over it. The first appearance of the house struck our hearts with awe. * * * Melancholy gloom pervaded our memory in every part of the house; all those kind visitors who were once the free guests and fond companions of our youth started fresh to our remembrance. * * * What unspeakable pleasure did we enjoy, whenever we had the happiness to behold the countenance of one of those few known companions who still survive; with what eagerness did we embrace them; with what affection did we address them."

An incident of our revolutionary period is still preserved among us, well attested, which shows how even the tory women of that day were in no wise behind their husbands and sons in loyal courage. Mrs. Robert Nichols, who still has many descendants among our citizens, was then living on the western frontiers of the town and not far from the military lines separating the two belligerent forces. One evening she had occasion to go on an errand to a neighbor's, and as it was a time of considerable military activity, she felt the need of acting the manly, and if need be, the martial part. She accordingly donned an immense hat and overcoat which had been wont to do her absent husband good service, and with a heavy cane, also serviceable on occasions of surprize, she started on her errand. She had not gone far, before she caught a glimpse of a man's form, evidently bent on a mischievous raid over the lines into the domains of the still faithful loyalists.

He had come so near that retreat was now impossible; and with a woman's ready instinct, she took the advantage of the first charge. With as heavy voice as she could summon to her help, she hails the unknown stranger. "Who comes there?" "A friend," is the prompt reply. "A friend to whom?" continues the gruff voice of the would-be martial respondent. "To George Washington and the patriot cause." "Ground your arms and give the countersign," was the thundering charge, which instantly followed, and which was as promptly obeyed. A moment more, and the patriotic lieutenant, Josiah Smith, disarmed, stood a prisoner, before his life-long neighbor, Madam Rober Nichols—a valiant man, outwitted and now in the power of a plucky and still loyal woman.

But, thanks to the patient and heroic endurance of the patriots of those trying days, and the wisdom and energy and hopefulness of their leader, Washington, a truce was at length reached to these neighborhood estrangements and hostilities. As in our last chapter we reported the soldiers engaged in sustaining the war to its favorable end; in our next, we shall as faithfully catalogue those, who in their loyal zeal, defended, to the last, the cause of their acknowledged king.

CHAPTER XVII.

LIST OF STAMFORD LOYALISTS.

The following list embraces the names of all whom I have found reported as loyalists. For the list as here submitted I am indebted to our original manuscripts in the State Library, to the American Archives, and to Sabine's History of the Loyalists. For some of the later facts appended to several of the names, I am indebted to the notes of our townsman, the late Wm. H. Holly, Esq., who while passing a few months in 1822, in Nova Scotia and New Brunswick, visited several of their descendants.

Bates, John.

Bates, Walter, son of John and Sarah (Bostwick), and was born March 14, 1760, in the eastern part of Stamford, now Darien. In '83 he went in the Union to St. John, New Brunswick. He was for many years sheriff of King's County. He died at Kingston in 1842, aged 82 years. A sister of his, Lavinia married another loyalist, Thomas Gilbert, junr., of Berkley, Mass., who was banished after the war, and died at Gagetown on the St. John's river, New Brunswick.

Bates, William, brother of Walter, born May 1, 1758, was under Cornwallis at Yorktown; and after the surrender, he went to New Brunswick and still later to Canada.

Beebe, Samuel.

Briggs, Stephen, a farmer living out in the Farms district. His farm was confiscated, and though after the war he returned to the neighborhood, he never recovered his title to it. Yet his widow by a little cunning, secured a pension for his services.

Crissy, Samuel.

Dan, Nathaniel.

Dibble, Frederic. This name is spelled Diblee by Sabine. He was son of Rev. Ebenezer and Joanna Dibble of this town where he was born in 1753. He graduated at King's College, now Columbia, in New York. He removed to New Brunswick after the war and was made rector of the Episcopal church in Woodstock. He was a most estimable gentleman and much beloved by his parishioners. He had a large and interesting family of seven sons and six daughters. He died at Woodstock, in 1826, at the age of seventy-three. His widow, Nancy, died in the same place in 1838, aged eighty-three years.

Dibble, Fyler, born Jan. 18, 1741–2, was a practicing attorney here when the war opened. We have already reported him as captain of the first militia company of the town in 1775. It seems that in violation of his pledge then given, he went over to Long Island and entered the service of the British. Here he was captured with other loyalists in '78, and his property in Stamford confiscated. In '83 he was a deputy agent in transporting loyalists from New York to Nova Scotia. In April of this year he went with his wife, five children and two servants to St. John's, New Brunswick, when in 1784 he was granted two city lots; and where some years later he put an end to his own life. His wife was Polly, sister of Seymour Jarvis of this town. They were married here June 18, 1763, and the following children are recorded to them; Walter, born Feb. 7, 1764; William, born Jan. 14, 1766; Peggy, born Nov. 28, 1767, and Ralph, born Oct. 22, 1769.

Dibble, Walter, son of Fyler, born as above. After the war he went in 1783, to St. John in New Brunswick. He died in Sussex Vale, in 1817, aged fifty-three.

Dibble, William, brother of Walter, went also to New Brunswick in 1783.

De Mill, Anthony.

Ferris, Joseph, became one of our most active loyalists, throwing himself with all his heart into the service of his king. He raised a company, joined colonel Butler's rangers and received a captain's commission. Once during the war he was captured by his own brother-in-law but escaped. After the war he settled in New Brunswick. During the war when the British held, temporarily, Eastport in Maine, he made it his home, but on its surrender to the United States again, he returned to New Brunswick. He died at Indian Island, New Brunswick, in 1836, aged ninety-two years.

Freeze, Reuben, a notorious cow-boy who hung around Heth Stevens, and was quite officious in annoying the revolutionists.

Hanford, Thomas was a hatter, here, before the war. At the close of the war he went to St. John's, New Brunswick, where he became a prominent merchant, and where he died in 1826, aged seventy-three. His widow died there, aiso, at the age of seventy-eight.

Howes, James, deserted.

Holly, Increase.

Holly, Ebenezer.

Holly, Elnathan, in 1776, at the age of nineteen, went over to the British and served in their army until 1782.

Holly, John Wm. at fourteen years of age was put under the protection of the British, as before recorded.

Holly, Samuel met our men retiring from Norwalk and wished them success, supposing them to be British. They rode him on a rail, to record his pertinacious loyalty.

Hoyt, David.

Hoyt, James with Uriah, below, were exchanged for Peter Waterbury who had been captured here, Sept. 8, by the British.

Hoyt, Samuel 3rd.

Hoyt, Stephen.

Hoyt, Uriah.

Howes, Prince.

Jarvis, Samuel was carried to Long Island and went thence to New York where he died Sept. 1, 1780. Martha his widow, died Dec. 1, 18—. Their children sympathized with them in their loyalty and removed to the British provinces to the north. Our records have their death reported in full as follows; Martha King, died in Halifax, N. S., in 1784, in the 36th year of her age; William, died in York, U. C., Aug. 13, 1817, in the 61st year of his age; Munson, died in St. John, N. B., Oct. 7, 1825, in the 83rd year of his age; Polly Dibble, died in New Brunswick, May, 1826, in the 80th year of her age; Hannah Ingersoll, died in New York, April 23, 1829, in the 71st year of her age; Levina Todd, died in Stamford, Oct. 26, 1841, in the 81st year of her age and Seymour died in Stamford, Oct. 4, 1843, in the 75th year of his age.

Jarvis, Munson, born in Stamford in 1742. In 1783 he went to St. John, New Brunswick, when he became a prominent citizen. He was was once a member of the provincial assembly. He died in St. John in 1825, aged 83. One of his sons, Edward James, became a member of the council of New Brunswick and Chief-Justice of the Colony of Prince Edward's Island.

Jarvis, John went to Kingston, New Brunswick, where he was living in 1822.

Leeds, Carey petitions the legislature, Jan. 4, 1779, for the clemency of the state. In his plea he calls himself "one of those unhappy persons who has been over to the enemy and been in their service, and by his folly is brought into a most disagreeable and miserable situation." He claims that he could not at the opening of the contest decide what his duty was, and decided to take a neutral course, which he did, to the best of his ability. On the 20th of December, 1775, he went over to Long Island, was taken up and forced into the British service, from which he escaped Sept. 28, 1776, and found his way home again. Here he was arrested and imprisoned in Fairfield County Jail—and he now "acknowledges the great offense" he committed and hopes for merciful treatment. He also promises to be a "faithful member of the United States." The legislature would not release him.

Leeds, Gideon, a brother of Carey.

Lewis, Jonathan.

Loder, Jacob, son of Daniel and Margaret, born in Stamford, Aug. 13, 1734, and went to New Brunswick where he died at Sheffield in 1817.

Lounsbury, Gideon, arrested in 1775, on suspicion of favoring the British. Makes a humble apology and promises "to my utmost to exert myself in opposition to the ministerial troops."

Merrit, Shubael, a "cowboy" who was shot, over in Greenwich.

Mills, Jesse, had rendered himself so offensive to the patriots of the north part of the town that, he was pursued into his sister's house, which stood near where Isaac L. Jones' store now stands, on Highridge, and was wounded by a shot. He escaped from his pursuers and went to Nova Scotia.

Newman, Joshua.

Picket, David went with his wife and seven children to St. John, New Brunswick in 1783. He was a magistrate of the colony and a Justice of the Court of Common Pleas of King's County, where he died in 1826.

Rodgers, Fitch went with four brothers to St. John, New Brunswick, but returned to Stamford where he died.

Quintard, Isaac, had command of the first company of militia in Stamford, in 1775.

Scofield, James, junr.

Scofield, Josiah 3rd.

Scofield, Ezra, a brother of the patriot Captain Reuben, went to St. John, N. B., and became a prominent man.

Selleck, Daniel.

Selleck, John.

Seeley, Obadiah.

Seely, Seth, father and son, of whom the latter was a successful privateer in the war of 1812.

Smith, Joseph seems to have been one of the most active and mischievous of the "cowboys" in the vicinity of Stamford. He was without mercy, whenever he found one of the king's rebellious subjects. He felt himself justified in killing rebels anywhere and had the reputation of frequent success. He is reported as wounding Sally Dibble of Darien in the church, when the congregation were captured, because she screened a boy under her seat. She carried a handkerchief filled with the holes which his bayonet made as it pierced through it into her breast. He was himself seriously wounded, near the house of Nathaniel Weed in Darien. He managed to escape his pursuers until he reached Daniel Gorman's; and when overtaken, the rage of his captors was such that they were determined to kill him at once. On the intercession of Mr. Gorman, and on his promise that as soon as he was sufficiently recovered from the wound he had received, he should be delivered over to them for trial. But he was next heard of in Nova Scotia.

Slason, Jedidiah, went to St. John's in 1783, and afterwards to Frederictown. He was a man of considerable distinction, having been a member of the provincial parliament. He died in 1844, aged 79 years. He was quite wealthy.

Stone, William.

Stevens, Admer.

Stevens, Heth, kept a rendezvous for tories on Highridge. One loyalist was shot there.

Stephens, Henry claimed that he was over persuaded to join the enemy, went over to Lloyd's Neck and was forced into the British army, and in September 1781, deserted, reached New London and gave himself up to the authorities, and got a pass to go to Stamford, where he was at liberty for four weeks. Then the grand juror had him confined in Litchfield jail. He acknowledged his guilt, petitioned for release which was granted, when the Stamford authorities permitted it.

Tucker, Solomon, according to Sabine, was from Stamford, and went with his wife and four children to St. John, New Brunswick, in the ship Union, in the spring of 1783.

Thorpe, Edward, was " with the enemies of his country," May 15, 1781, as James Nichols, administrator on his confiscated estate testifies.

Waterbury, David, brother of Nathaniel of Middlesex parish. He went to St. John, New Brunswick, where he became a man of some distinction, and where he died in 1833, aged seventy-five years.

Waterbury, John, was with "the enemies of his country," March 15, 1781, as appears from the testimony of James Nichols the administrator on his confiscated estate. He went to St. John, New Brunswick, and was one of the original grantees of that town. He was a military man in the province at the close of the last century. He died in St. John, in 1817, at the age of 68 years. His widow was living at Mahogany, in 1822.

Whitney, Sylvanus, son of Eliaseph and Mary, born Feb. 3, 1748, was here in 1775, as our record will show. He went to St. John, New Brunswick, where he became an alderman and one of the colonial magistrates. He died in 1827, aged 79 years.

Weed, Abijah, had served in the old French and Indian war, but soon after the opening of the revolution, he deserted and went to Canada.

CHAPTER XVIII.

BIOGRAPHY.

This chapter embraces sketches of those prominent citizens of the town, who were in active life, mainly, in the first century of our history. Others, doubtless, were worthy of a place on this list, but the materials were wanting for sketches of them, other than such as has already been given in our first and second chapters on the settlers of the town.

Bishop, Rev. John, was probably educated in England. Savage says he was in Taunton in 1640, but does not mention his business. The manner of his coming to Stamford from Boston, has been already given, in our chapter on the early ecclesiastical history of the town; and both the long continued ministry of Mr. Bishop and the affection shown him in his old age by the people, are in evidence of his success in the office which he held. While here he married 1st Rebecca ———, and by her had four sons and one daughter and perhaps more. The sons mentioned in the will are Stephen, Joseph, Ebenezer, Benjamin and Whiting. The daughter, Mary, died here on the 25th day of fifth month 1658. He married for his second wife, Joanna, (Boyse), who had been the widow, first of Rev. Peter Prudden of Milford, and second, of Capt. Thomas Willet of Swanzey, who had died, as Savage tells us, on the third, though the grave-stone says, on the fourth of Aug. 1674.

The only specimen of the scholarship of Mr. Bishop, now existing, is probably that epistle of the Rev. Richard Mather of

Dorchester, written in latin, and published in the Magnalia, Vol. 1, page 458, edition of 1855.

Mr. Bishop died here in 1694, and was buried in the first burying lot, where our west park is now. The old stone which indicated the place of his grave, was removed in 1866, to a suitable base prepared for it in the Episcopal lot near St. Andrew's chapel, by the affectionate veneration of his great, great grandson Edwin Bishop, Esq.

DAVENPORT, REV. JOHN was born in Boston, Feb. 28, 1669, and was the son of John Davenport, Esq., the only son of Rev. John Davenport, the ecclesiastical founder of New Haven. He graduated at Harvard in 1687, and commenced preaching in 1690.

Our chapter on ecclesiastical matters will give a full account of his call and settlement in Stamford. The records of the town for the time he lived here, are full of testimonials to the esteem in which he was held. While here he married Martha Gould, the widow of John Selleck. They had seven children; Abigail, who became the wife of Rev. Stephen Williams, D. D., of Springfield, and the mother of an illustrious family; John of New Canaan; Martha, the wife of Rev. Thomas Goodsell, of Branford; Sarah, who married first Capt. William Maltbie, of New Haven, and second Rev. Eleazer Wheelock, D. D., the founder and first president of Dartmouth College, and became the ancestress of a talented and noble lineage; Theodore, who died early; Dea. Deodate of East Haven; and Elizabeth the wife of Rev. William Gaylord, of Wilton, Conn. His wife died Dec. 1, 1712; and that her death was deemed no ordinary event is attested by the extraordinary record of it found in Book 1, page 110, town records.

"That eminently Pious and very virtuous, Grave and worthily much Lamented Matron, Mrs. Martha Davenport, Late wife to the Reverend Mr. Jno Davenport Pastor to ye Church of Christ in Stamford Laid down or exchanged Her mortal or temporall Life to putt on Immortality and to be Crowned with

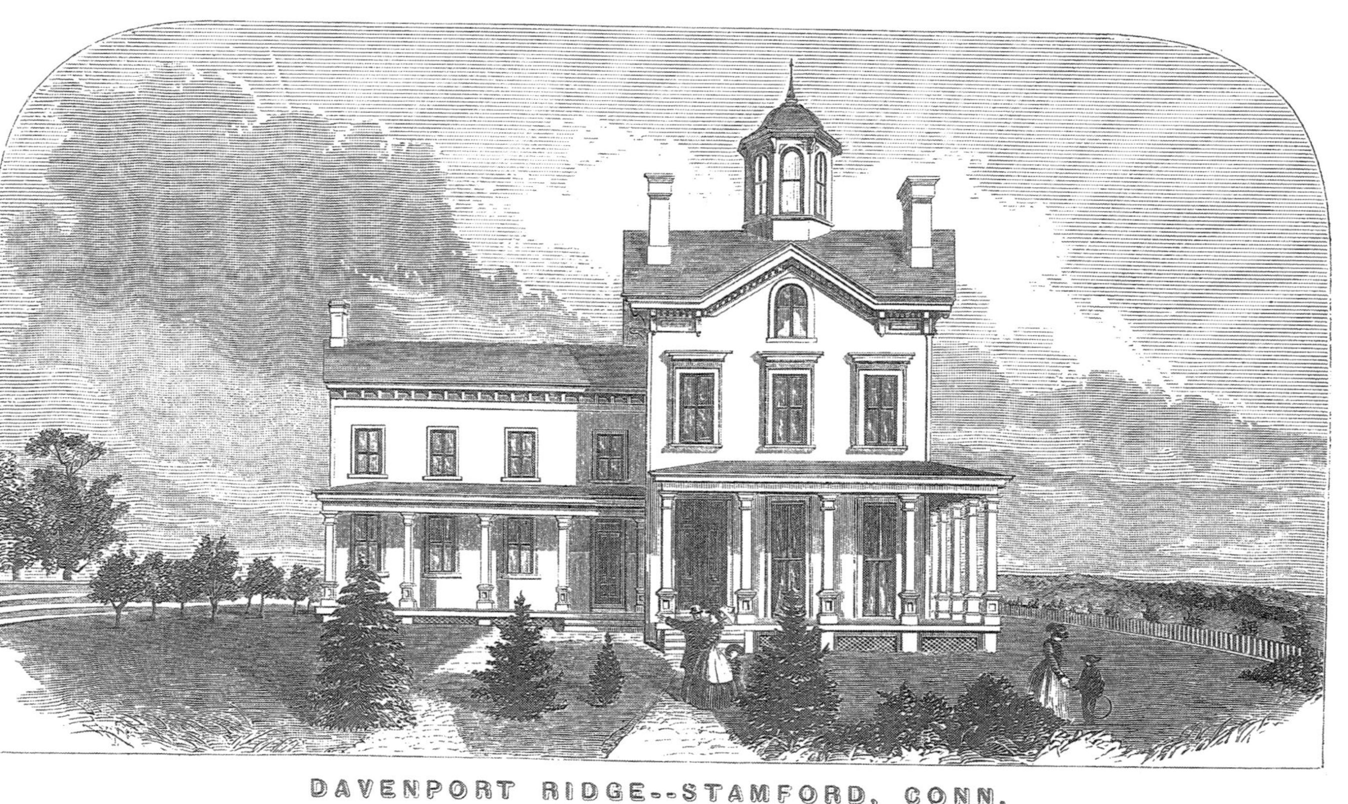

DAVENPORT RIDGE--STAMFORD, CONN.

Immortal Glory: on ye 1st Day of Decemb 1712." He married for his second wife, Mrs. Elizabeth Maltby, daughter of John Morris, by whom he had two children; Hon. Abraham, and Rev. James, biographical sketehes of both of whom will follow.

Mr. Davenport was a prominent man in his profession. He had been thoroughly educated and inherited many traits which would give him a special fitness for the work of the ministry. But few Connecticut pastors of that day had such qualifications for the sacred office. While especially eminent in the pulpit, he seems never to have lacked discretion out of it. He was equally wise in his public official administrations, and in his private influence among his people. He died here, Feb. 5, 1731. The Rev. Samuel Cooke, of Bridgeport, preached his funeral sermon, which was printed. The sermon, from the text "My father, my father, the chariot of Israel and the horsemen thereof," contains these testimonials to his eminence and worth.

"The person whose exit now calls for our deep lamentation and mourning, was both our crown and our bulwark, our glory and our defense. Our crown is fallen from our heads, and our defense is departed. We have our chariot and horsemen taken away. Wo unto us that we have sinned. It was many years since looked upon by the serious and judicious as a special favor of divine Providence, that a person of such distinction as we have now lost, was seated so near to the western limits of New England as a bulwark against any irruptions of corrupt doctrines and manners. Wo to us, our hedgewall in that respect is broken down. * * He was proof against the temptations of the smiles or frowns of others, to turn him out of the way to the right hand or to the left."

Dr. Bacon in that admirable historical discourse, delivered before the general association of Connecticut at their one hundred and fiftieth anniversary in Norwich, says of him, while characterizing the members of that memorable body of divines who met at Saybrook, in 1708, and drew up the Saybrook Platform, "John Davenport pastor of the church in Stamford, was not inferior in ability to any other member of the Synod. In his own church and town, and among the ministers and churches of that county he had a commanding influence."

DENTON, REV. RICHARD.—His name will be found among the pioneers in the settlement of Stamford. His position among them and his eminence as a Christian preacher and minister, deserves a fuller notice than was then taken of him.

Mather, in his Magnalia, has given him a high rank among the great lights of that day. With some deduction for the highly figurative language used by the Magnalia, the portrait of him by Mather is doubtless very just. He introduces him as "our pious and learned Mr. Richard Denton, a Yorkshire man, who having watered Halifax in England with his fruitful ministry, was by a tempest then hurried into New England; where, first at Wethersfield and then at Stamford, his doctrine dropt as the rain, his speech distilled as the dew, as the small rain upon the tender herb, as the showers upon the grass." He then gives us this quaint description of the man. We probably are indebted to it for all we can ever learn of his personal appearance; and perhaps our utmost research will add nothing to its estimate of his piety and scholarship.

"Though he were a little man, yet he had a great soul; his well accomplished mind in his lesser body, was an Iliad in a nut shell. I think he was blind of one eye; nevertheless, he was not the least among the seers of our Israel; he saw a very considerable proportion of those things which 'eye hath not seen.'

"He was far from cloudy in his conception and principles of divinity, whereof he wrote a system, entitled "Soliloquium Sacra"—so accurately considering the fourfold state of man in his "Created Purity;" "contracted deformity;" "restored beauty" and "celestial glory," that judicious persons, who have seen it, very much lament the churches being so much deprived of it."

"At length he got into heaven beyond the clouds, and so beyond storms, waiting the return of the Lord Jesus Christ, in the clouds of heaven when he will have his reward among the saints."

As was his wont in his brief biographical sketches of the ministers noticed in his Magnalia, Mather appends to this canonization of Mr. Denton, what he deemed an equally appropriate epitaph. Its original and the translation, I shall give as they are found in Robins's edition of the Magnalia.

"EPITAPHIUM.

Hic jaçet et fruitur tranquilla sede RICHARDUS,
DENTONUS, cujus fama perrennis erit.
Incola jam coeli velut astra micantia fulget,
Qui multis fidei lumina clara dedit.

TRANSLATION.

Here Denton lies, his toils and hardships past;
Whose name no memory of dishonor mars,
On earth a light of faith he shines, at last,
Full orbed and glorious with the eternal stars."

Of Mr. Denton's career while in Wethersfield but very little has ever transpired. Precisely what his official connection with the new church was, does not appear, from any contemporaneous account I have been able to find. Mr. Chapin's excellent and reliable account of the beginning of that church in his "Glastenbury for two hundred years," leaves the matter much in the dark. Nor do the occasional references to Wethersfield matters in the old Colony Records, much add to our information. For reasons never fully explained, the materials gathered for that new community were so discordant and infusable, as never to mingle together into a body politic or religious. Two pretty well defined parties sprang up and Mr. Denton took side with that which seems to have been the progressive and radical. He carried with him the majority of the church, but a minority only of those not connected with the church.

On reaching Stamford, an experience somewhat like that which fell to him in Wethersfield seems to have been his lot. The restless and disaffected portion of the new colony, not liking the overshadowing influence of New Haven jurisdiction, found as before, a leader in their minister, and in 1644, we find him removing with them to attempt a new settlement at "Manetos, New Netherlands," now Hempsted on Long Island. Here he labored acceptably for several years, when he returned to England in 1659, where he died in 1662 aged 76 years. He left four sons, Richard, Samuel, Nathaniel and Daniel. Richard was among the settlers of Hempstead, L. I., and Nathaniel in 1660, was living in Jamaica, where he and his squadron were authorized "to mow at the Haw-trees."

Holly, John, the ancestor, probably, of the numerous family of this name, in this vicinity, was one of the most prominent of our early settlers. He was from the first employed in the almost constant service either of the town or of the colony. In 1647, he was appointed marshal for the settlement, an office requiring a man of no inferior intelligence or business tact. He was later made collector of customs and excise here, which office he discharged to the acceptance of the general court, to which he was responsible. He was repeatedly one of the selectmen of the town, and one of its representatives in the general court. He was often appointed on responsible commissions, both by the town and by the legislature. In 1654 he was made associate judge with those worthies Law and Bell, for the court to be held at this plantation. After the union of New Haven with the Connecticut colony he was made commissioner with Law, for Stamford, Greenwich and Rye, and to assist in the execution of justice at the Fairfield County Court. It seems to have been a singular appointment, as he is next year, 1569, propounded for freeman in the Connecticut jurisdiction, where he is distinctly indicated by the title of senior. It would seem that he had shown himself so competent and useful under the New Haven administration, that he was appointed to the most responsible offices before the usual form of enfranchisement. Mr. Holly seems to have been as active in ecclesiastical as in civil and judicial matters.

The family descended from him have been both numerous and respectable. Alexander H. Holley, of Salisbury, governor of the state in 1857, was one of his great, great, great grand-sons, and Horace Holley, D.D., late President of Transylvania University, Ky., was another. The family number among their ancestry in England, Dr. Luther Halley who was born Oct. 29, 1556, in St. Leonard's parish, Shordith, London.

Mr. Holly died here, May 25, 1681, aged 63 years. A portion of the land which he received in the early allotment of lands, still remains in the hands of his descendant, our honored citizen Alexander N. Holly, Esq.

Jones, Rev. Eliphalet, was the son of Rev. John and Susanna Jones of Concord. His father had emigrated to this country in the Defence, in 1635, and settled first in Concord, from which place he eame to Fairfield in 1644, where he died in 1644, leaving six children, of whom Eliphalet, born Jan. 9, 1641, entered Harvard but did not graduate and was ordained about 1677. Savage says he was a preacher at Rye. Our ecclesiastical record shows that he was living in Greenwich when he was called, in 1672 to Stamford. Here he labored under the Rev. Mr. Bishop, probably until he was called in April, 1673, to Huntington, L. I., where he was ordained in 1676. The long period, during which he maintained his post, must be held as good proof of his faithful and acceptable service. He died June 5, 1731, leaving no children. While living in Greenwich, in 1670, he was made a joint trustee, with Joseph Mead and John Renolds all of Greenwich, of all the lands of William Grimes, also of Greenwich, to be disposed of by them in such way as, they should judge best for "inlarging of ye town of Greenwich." These trustees appropriated the lands to the use of a minister and in case there was no minister in town, Mr. Jones, as his own affidavit dated at Huntington, L. I., April 22, 1691, testifies, proposed to give the profits of the land "to helpe mainetaine such as shall bee Imployed in teaching children to Reade."

In May, 1674, the Connecticut court desire Mr. Jones "to take the paynes to dispence the word of God to the people of Rye once a fortnight on the Lord's day till the Court, October next, and then this court will take further order concerning them and for Mr. Jones satisfaction." Mr. Jones remained in Huntington, preaching and laboring with general acceptance down to his death. He is not known to have left children.

LAW, RICHARD, was perhaps the first civilian among the Stamford settlers, the acknowledged legal adviser of the community for more than a quarter of a century. His scholarly and clerical abilities gave him great advantage among the settlers. Though not one of the first twenty to inaugurate the settlement, he was at Wethersfield, arranging to join the colony at the opening of their second season in their new home. He probably took with him from Wethersfield, as his gifted help-meet, Margaret, the oldest daughter of Francis Kilborn; and their home, though not the most expensive, was to be one of the most honored of the colony. Their family, though not to remain through other generations to honor the town they were so helpful in founding, was to furnish names to give a new luster to the state whose highest civil and judicial seats they were to fill. From the first he seems to have been the scribe of the colony. His pen was equally ready for the records of the town, the church, and the courts. He was the only town clerk appointed for about twenty-four years. He was the ready lawyer, in the age preceding, technically that profession among us. He was oftener a deputy in the general court at New Haven than any other of the settlers, and apparently more in demand when there. As constable, he was noted for a fearless and tireless efficiency. He seemed to have exercised a sort of personal dis cretion in regard to prosecutions, which was not always most acceptable to parties who would dictate his official duty. John Mead once had good proof of his fidelity, never to be bribed

He had sought the help of the constable to recover damages from a neighbor for some harm done by him. The sharp-eyed official saw at a glance that there was no ground for the attachment, and refused the process. Mead scolded and threatened, but to no purpose. He then goes into court with an action against him for neglecting his official duty. But the angry plaintiff soon finds himself a sorry defendant, with but a miserable advocate. Law had him put under trial for scandalizing the church, for slanders and defamatory reports and for disturbing the peace of the church and the town. To all which nothing in extenuation could be said, and the court exculpating their officer, sentenced Mr. Mead to make full acknowledgement at Stamford, to the satisfaction of the church and Mr. Law, to pay Mr. Law ten pounds for his expense in the trial, to pay ten pounds more for disturbing the jurisdiction, and then that he and his brother or some other acceptable man, be bound over for his good behaviour. After the sentence Mr. Mead made the fullest confession and retraction, and Mr. Law was left thenceforward to prosecute his official business unhindered.

Mr. Law had married in Wethersfield, Margaret Kilbourn, by whom he had three children; Jonathan, b. 1636–7; Abigail, who married, May 11, 1665, Jonathan Selleck of Stamford; and Sarah, who married, Oct. 28, 1669, John Selleck, also of Stamford. The son Jonathan, married June 1, 1664, Sarah Clark, daughter of Dea. George Clark of Milford, and removed to Milford, where he was a man of note. His son, Jonathan, b. Aug. 6, 1674, graduated at Harvard College, 1695; was chief-justice of Connecticut for sixteen years and governor of the state from 1741 to 1750.

Mr. Law probably died in Stamford, though there is no record to show it. His will, the last document in which his name appears, bears date March 12, 1686–7. His widow had probably died before this date as no mention is made of her in the will.

There is a paper, entered on the town records in 1686, bearing date Feb. 15, 1680, which speaks of the misunderstanding under which he had given his son, Law, his land. It seems that the son removed from Stamford to Milford, and this removal was a source of dissatisfaction to the father. Still adhering to the former grant to his son, he now insists on dividing the lands which had come into his hands since that former gift, to his daughters, the two Mrs. Selleck, so that they may each have a half as much as he; for which he says "the word of God is clear, and good reason for it, and why any Christian man that loveth righteousness and equity should be against this, I see not."

MITCHELL, REV. JONATHAN, was son, not of Jonathan, as Sprague's Annals of the American Pulpit has it, but of Matthew Mitchell, the wealthiest and otherwise most noted of the lay settlers of Stamford. He was born, so Savage supposes, at Halifax, Yorkshire, Eng., and in the year 1624, according to Mather. He came with his father, in the James, from Bristol, in 1635, to Cambridge, Mass., and thence to Concord and Springfield, and in 1640 to Stamford. He remained here probably until he entered Harvard College, where he graduated, A. B., in 1647. He was ordained, Aug. 21, 1650, at Cambridge, where he labored in the ministry for eighteen years.

He was one of the early New England ministers whom the quaint Mather has immortalized in his Magnalia. He styles him the "Ecclesiastes;" "a Pastor of the Church, and a glory of the College in Cambridge, New England." In his epistle dedicatory, he calls him "blessed Mr. Mitchell," and in his sketch of the life and labors of Mr. Mitchell, he makes him the "excellent," the famous pastor" and "this best of preachers in our new English nation." The opening of his biographical sketch is worthy of a place here, as illustrating the times to which our subject belonged, and also, as furnishing us an interesting clue to his character and that of his family :—

"If it were counted an honor to the town of Halifax in Yorkshire that the famous John de Sacro Bozco, author of the well known treatise "De Sphoera," was born there; this town was no less honored by its being the place of birth to our no less worthily famous Jonathan Mitchell, the author of a better treatise of heaven, who, being descended, as a printed account long since has told us, of pious and wealthy parents, here drew his first breath, in the year 1624. The precise day of his birth is lost, nor is it worth while for us to inquire, by an astrological calculation, what aspect the stars had upon his birth, since the event has proved, that God the Father was in the horoscopes, Christ in the mid heaven, the Spirit in the sixth house, repentance, faith and love, in the eighth; and in the twelfth an eternal happiness, where no Saturn can dart any malignant rays. Here while the "father of his flesh" was endeavoring to make him learned by a proper education, the "Father of Spirits" used the methods of grace to make him serious; especially by a sore fever which had like to have made the tenth year of his life the last, but then settled in his arm with such troublesome effects, that his arm grew and kept a little bent, and he could never stretch it out right until his dying day. * * * The ship which brought over Mr. Richard Mather, * * was further enriched by having on board our Jonathan, then a child of about eleven years of age; whose parents with much difficulty and resolution carried him unto Bristol to take shipping there, while he was not yet recovered of his illness."

Mather thus speaks of his mental ability and scholarship. "The facilities of mind, with which the 'God that forms the spirit of man' enriched him, were very notable. He had a clear head, a copious fancy, a solid judgment, a tenacious memory and a certain discretion, without any childish laschete or levity in his behaviour, which commanded respect from all that viewed him. * * * Under these advantages, he was an hard student, and he so prospered in his indefatigable studies, that he became a scholar of illuminations, not far from the first magnitude; recommended by which qualifications, it was not long before he was chosen a Fellow of the College."

He first received a call to preach in Hartford, with the most flattering offer of generous aid to him in supplying himself with a suitable library. They had sent a man and a horse to Boston for him and he preached to their acceptance, June 24, 1649. On his return to Cambridge, through the entreaties of the venerable Mr. Shepard, who was providentially just about vacating by death his field of honored usefulness, he was induced to preach there as a candidate for settlement. He commenced his labors there Aug. 12, 1649, to continue them with great acceptance and success until his death, July 9, 1668.

His preaching talents were of a high order. His sermons were "admirably well studied." "He ordinarily meddled with no point but what he managed with such an extraordinary invention, curious disposition and copious application, as if he would leave no material thing to be said of it by any that should come after him. And when he came to utter what he had prepared, his utterance had such a becoming tunableness and vivacity, to set it off, as was indeed inimitable, though many of our eminent preachers, that were in his time students at the college did essay to imitate him."

Mr. Mitchell married at Cambridge, Margaret, widow of his predecessor, Rev. Mr. Shepard. Two of his sons, Samuel and Jonathan, were graduates of Harvard. One of his daughters, Margaret, married Stephen Sewall of Salem, and was mother of Chief Justice Stephen Sewall of Massachusetts.

Mitchell, Matthew, the second on our list of pioneers, and the first in point of wealth, probably, was a man of marked ability. His name is not so prominent among our early townsmen as it would have been, if he had decided to make this his permanent home, and that of his family. In the great secession of 1644, he went with his minister Mr. Denton, over to Hempsted; but probably soon repented of the move, and returned. According to contemporaneous accounts, he must have been sorely tried, as he seems to have been much reduced in his pecuniary condition, by various adverse providences. He had left his home in England to secure the freedom denied his religious faith there, and perhaps this very aim, rendered him restless, until he should attain it. His wanderings and trials are a very fair illustration of what the pioneers of our town had to endure and suffer.

Born in 1590, we find him, Feb. 24, 1622–3, a witness to the will of widow Susan Feild, whose husband William Feild, had died in North Ouram, parish of Halifax, in 1619. Here he was doubtless enjoying the instructions of Richard Denton, then curate of Coley Chapel; and it is not to be wondered at that he heartily united his fortunes with those of his minister. May 23, 1635, seems the probable date on which he set sail for the new world; and if so, he reached Boston, Aug. 17th. His first temporary home was among the pioneers of Charlestown, where he spent a winter of great discomfort. And, indeed, his troubles had preceded his landing. Two days before reaching the harbor, a furious storm had arisen, which almost dismantled their ship. The following spring he went to Concord, where a fire consumed much which the coast wreck had spared. Finding here no fitting home he next appears at Springfield, in May 1636, in the company of William Pynchon, where he and two other of our Stamford settlers, Edmond and Jonas Wood, have prominent lots assigned them. From Springfield he went to Saybrook where he stayed but a few months, when he cast in his lot with the Wethersfield planters, as before stated. Here, also, he was particularly unfortunate. On his visit to Saybrook, he had encountered that savage irruption of the Pequots and had barely escaped with his life; and in Wethersfield, his estate was doomed to suffer still more seriously, from frequent Indian raids. Other difficulties were in his way. He could not comply with some of the requisitions of the unsettled times and people among which he was called to live. He was evidently a man of positive and independent character, and was wont to assert and defend himself. He became obnoxious to a Mr. Chaplin, and in the heat of the contest, excited the displeasure of the court, which at that time was the only legislature known. His townsmen had chosen him their recorder. The court would not ratify the choice. He discharged his clerical duties, and was fined, as elsewhere appears.

At this point in his Wethersfield experience, he betakes himself with those of his fellow colonists, who had incurred like censure from the general court, to a new home. Stamford was the chosen site. His position among the settlers here is evinced by that of his name. Our pioneer list reports it. As member of the New Haven Court, and one of the judges of the local colony court, and as townsman for two years before he temporarily removed to Hempstead, he seems to have met the approval of his new townsmen. On what contemporaneous authority he is reported as having removed to Hempstead, I have not found. It is not at all unlikely that he did so; yet he must soon have returned to Stamford. He died before May 19, 1646, as is evident from the statement of the court that approved his will.

His only children of whom I find any mention were, Rev. Jonathan, (see preceding sketch), and David, who settled in Stamford, and had four sons. A list of their descendants can be found in Cothren's History of Ancient Woodbury.

Underhill, Captain John. No name among the Stamford settlers was as famous as this—equally famous for successful military feats, and for a strangely erratic social and domestic career. History transmits his character to us variously shaded, now to be envied for its self-sacrificing and brilliant achievements, and again to be deplored for its shameful humiliations.

Though here but a short time, his name deserves to be recorded among our settlers; and special mention is due to it, because it was so closely connected with the preservation of the young settlement.

His descent was from an honorable family in Warwickshire. His earliest years must have exhibited more than the ordinary restlessness of boyhood. Though we have no account of his childhood, we may be assured that they were no ordinary feats of mischief and of daring which were his pastime. Nothing less than a mock broad sword, or a mimic battle, could have met and satisfied the deepest longings of this child-hero; and so, as soon as his years would let him, we find him ready for the deed and daring of the thickest fight. That was no unmeaning pupilage through which he went in the English service, under such a leader as the gallant Essex in his wars with Spain. That was, to the young soldier, no useless lesson which he learned in the fierce and successful storming of Cadiz. And those later days of service in the ranks with veterans who had grown old and wise in war, were full of hints for his judgment and stimulants for his courage, preparatory to his career in the new world. Nor were those successful struggles of the Dutch, in which he shared, and from which they arose to a merited independency of their haughty Spanish masters, without many a lesson to him on the fundamental question of his personal rights and responsibility. So that by the time the way was open for him to seek a home for himself and his, across the Atlantic, he had received, in some sort, a providential training for a special and needed work.

What special reasons induced him to leave England, are not given by the historian. That his spirit would brook with much patience even slight restraint, whether upon his conscience or practice, either in religion or in politics, was not to be expected; and the probability is, that greater freedom than the staid policy of the fatherland allowed, moved him to the change. But without such a reason, the very restlessness of his excitable and roving disposition, would have tempted him to try the novelties, while the utter recklessness of his fearless soul, would have taken richest pleasure in braving and conquering the dangers of the yet savage wilderness.

We find him in 1630 in Boston, then a new settlement, enrolling himself among the pioneer founders of New England; and that he was deemed worthy of position among them, is evidenced by his appointment to responsible offices, civil and military. The old "Ancient and Honorable Artillery Company" of the Bay state bears testimony to his military standing; and the general court of Massachusetts honored him as their metropolitan deputy.

But he was soon found to be most serviceable in the field. The exposed colonists were perpetually harassed and endangered by wily and hostile Indians; and Underhill was more than a match for them. He was inferior to them, neither in celerity, nor in cunning; he was greatly their superior in intelligence, judgment aud skill. So signal were the services which he rendered, that as early as 1632 he received a pension of thirty pounds; and thenceforward he is one of New England's most reliable defenders against their most dreaded foe.

The Pequod war soon enabled him to show his courage and his skill. Under the resolute and prudent Mason, he performed prodigies of valor at the storming of their principal stronghold on the banks of the Mystic All the intrepid heroism of his nature found room for play; and the boldest savage of that most untamable tribe quailed before him, whenever he moved about among the falling and the fallen of their race.

And, now, we begin to find developing another phase of the hero's character. He had become professedly a Christian. His religion, as might be expected, was in earnest. Zeal, whether according to knowledge or not, was its most noticeable characteristic; and he began to suspect and denounce those who could not sympathize and work with him. The Boston clergy were too tame to suit him. Their only zeal was that of the scribes and pharisees or that of Paul before his conversion. Mrs. Hutchinson's piety, and Wheelwright's liberty, and Vane's polity had much more in them to suit his tastes. When, therefore, these were condemned by a majority of the Boston authorities, he could do no less than to utter his protest, and he accordingly signs the petition to have Mr. Wheelwright restored. For this, he too, is disfranchised and given permission to depart. We next find him the governor of the new colony at Dover, but not to hold his position long. Gov. Endicott, writes a member of the colony, "how ill we should relish if they should advance Captain Underhill whom we have thrust out for abusing the court and feigning a retraction, both of his seditious practice and also his corrupt opinions, and after denying it again." This letter put the Dover colonists on their good behavior and led to the removal of Underhill. Underhill, himself, seems to have lost his spirits, and descended to the humblest apologies and earnest entreaty for forgiveness.

But his offenses, extending even to repeated adulteries, as was then believed, were not to be borne, and his sentence was banishment.

We find him next in England. While here he issues from the press, his history of the Pequod war, entitled "News from America, or a new and experimental Discovery of New England; containing a true relation of warlike proceedings these two years past, with a figure of the fort or palisado, by John Underhill, a commander in the wars there."

In 1639 he again appears in Boston, occupying literally "the stool of repentance," with the white cap covering his head, bewailing his past insolence and crimes, and promising amendment. The church accept his confessions, and the court restore him to their favor.

During the summer, in which our Stamford fathers were taking possession of their purchase, we find him again the subject of legal process in Boston, and this time, it would seem, without law or right. He was arrested by the order of the governor, without charge of any offense committed since he had been pardoned both by the church and the court. He is dismissed. The same farce seems to have been repeated in the following year, and with a like result.

But the suspicions and persecutions which awaited him in the Massachusetts colony, rendered a home there intolerable to him. He had already made trial of our Connecticut air and soil, and was not averse to them. The Dutch further to the west, despite his attachment to the loving damsel, who had followed him from his Holland campaign, hither, would have suited him well enough, had he not been compelled to own allegiance to the

States General and the Prince of Orange; and for a similar reason he would not join the English settlers on Long Island. Refusing a handsome offer from the Dutch governor, who would gladly have secured his services in his incessant collision with the Indians in his colony, he decides to make Stamford his future home. Furnished with an outfit and a pinnace, by the church, this versatile man finds his way, with his family into the Stamford harbor; and in October of our second year he takes his place among the fathers of the new settlement.

How favorable an impression he made here, is shown in his appointment the next spring as deputy to the New Haven court; and the opinion of his character held at New Haven appears in his appointment by the general court, with gentlemen Mitchell, Ward, and Robert Coe, as the local court, auxiliary to the general court, "for the more comely carrying on of public affairs." Thus, before the end of his second year in Stamford, he was fairly installed in citizenship and in high official position.

We have seen in the previous history how much the new colony were indebted to him for their safety in the midst of suspicious and hostile savages. No one more than he held in check the inflamable passions of resident Indians; and none in all the region had a name so full of terror to neighboring tribes. When, therefore, savage tribes stole down from the north and threatened the entire destruction of the Dutch settlements, to whom else should the endangered colonists look for help? And when the scattered settlements on the Island, from Manhattan to Montauk were in danger of extinction, who, if not he could be entrusted with the management of their defense? And both the English on the Island, and the Dutch, both on the Island and on the main land, between Stamford and New Amsterdam, were loud in their praise of their great captain, who so signally wrought out deliverance for them.

It was while engaged in chastising the Indians on the Island that he seems to have formed the purpose of making it his future home; and we find him as early as 1660, established in his new home in Oyster Bay, where he died in 1672.

CHAPTER XIX.

STAMFORD IN 1800.

Connecticut, at this date, had more than quadrupled the number of her towns reported in 1700;—from 27, having increased to 118. But Stamford, meanwhile, had gone forward in population, from the little scattered community of 585 souls, to the respectable township of 4465—a growth nearly eight-fold in the century, and the growth in wealth, had been even greater than in population; while the advance in facilities for travel, and in all the arts which minister to the social well being of a community, had been still more rapid than in wealth.

The territory had not yet suffered excision; though the citizens of the eastern part of the town were beginning to think of caring for themselves. The northern end of that portion had already concerted a plan for speedy secession. But we find the town exceedingly loth to surrender a single foot of the territory, or a single vote of the subjects that for more than a century they had ruled and cared for as inalienably their own. The citizens entered upon the contest with those portions of the town which asked permission to leave the old jurisdiction, and set up for themselves under new auspices; and the struggle was long and earnest until the secession of a part of New Canaan and the whole of Darien was finally carried.

New York was not yet so accessible as to stimulate very noticably the business longings, and educate the business talents of our young men. The days of the old stage-coach had indeed been for years wearing themselves out in the humdrum style of those quiet and sober times; and Stamford was simply a well-to-do town, whose honest and industrious people were mainly content with such gains and show, as they could win from the soil, or as they could coin from the sobered prosecution of their varied handicraft.

In making up our estimate of the condition of the town at this date, let us first see who are occupying its varied offices of honor and trust. The list we shall report, without giving the offices assigned to the several names. Captain Isaac Lockwood leads our citizens, evidently, as appears from the uniformity with which, at this period he is called to preside in our public meetings; and with Nathan Weed, jr., he also represents the town in the state legislature. John Hoyt, jr., is still, as for the last twenty-five years, the faithful clerk of the town, and his large, fair, hand-writing will be easily legible, as long as the accurate records shall be preserved. Following these names, stand the long list of those who in one way and another were found worthy to serve the town of their nativity or adoption. The list is worthy of reservation. It reports to us the names of the fathers and grandfathers of the present citizens of the town, as they sought to do their duty here, sixty-eight years ago.

LIST OF TOWN OFFICIALS FOR THE YEAR 1800.

Josiah Smith,	Isaac Quintard,	Jacob Scofield,
Cary Leeds,	Jeremiah Palmer,	John Davenport, 3rd.
Amos Weed,	Zadoc Newman,	Warren Scofield,
Isaac Penoyer,	David Smith, 3rd.	Rufus Newman,
Stephen Bishop,	Jeremiah Knap, jr.,	Warren Hoyt,
Jesse Hoyt,	Josiah Dibble,	William Weed,
Samuel Hoyt, 3rd.	Ebenezer Webb,	Gold S. Pennoyer,
Jona. Bates,	Nath'l Webb,	Elisha Stevens,
Stephen Selleck, jr.,	John Nichols,	Joseph Smith,
Samuel Whiting,	Thos. Lounsbury,	Nath'l Waterbury,
Nath'l Clock,	Thaddeus Hoyt,	Elisha Leeds,
Amos Lounsbury,	Jas. Buxton,	John Waterbury, 3d.
Smith Weed,	John Lounsbury,	Nathan Seely,
John Wm. Holly,	Bradley Ayers,	John Bell,
Robert Scofield,	Abishai Weed,	David Foster,
Isaac Smith, jr.,	Enoch Stevens,	Nathan Reed,
Ezra Lockwood,	Epenetus Hoyt,	Nathan Bouton,
Charles Knapp,	Reuben Jones,	Josiah Smith,

John Nichols,	Sylvanus Knap,	Nathan Seely,
Joseph Bishop,	Isaac Lockwood,	Israel Weed,
Jona. Brown,	Joseph Waring,	Benjamin Brush,
Charles Weed, 3rd.	Jesse Hoyt,	Samuel Mather,
Enoch Comstock,	Shadrach Hoyt, jr.,	Enos Waterbury,
Stephen Bishop,	Hoyt Scofield,	Gold Smith,
Benj. Weed, jr.,	Wm. Waterbury, 4th.	Abraham Davis.

So many and such are the names, recorded in 1800 to transact the business of the town.

Let us next see what were the religious condition and privileges of the town at this date. There were standing within the Stamford limits, in 1800, six church edifices. In the oldest, the first Congregational, Rev. Daniel Smith, a young man had just entered upon his long ministry, and both as preacher and teacher was laying good foundations for his work. The Episcopal congregation were still worshiping in their first church, standing on the rocks, south-east from their present church on Main street. They were still in sorrow over the recent death of their first rector, Dr. Dibble, though hoping much from the opening ministry of Rev. Calvin White, who had come here to his aid in 1798. The Baptists were rejoicing in their new meeting-house, so upright and square, overlooking the Mill-pond on River street. The patriarch of their denomination, Ebenezer Ferris, was still with them and with the Rev. Marmaduke Earl, in charge over the congregation at the Bangall church, was providing for the spiritual training of both branches of the denomination. Two or three Methodist preachers officiated within the limits of the township, though as yet no church edifice had been built for their worship—the private dwelling of Mr. Isaac Reed, their pioneer, still accommodating all who wish to attend their meetings at the center of the town. In North Stamford, which by this time had outgrown the old title of Woodpecker ridge, a good congregation were edified by the youthful ministry of their third pastor Rev. Amzi Lewis. In Middlesex, (Darien), the venerable Moses Mather, D. D., the same who for his revolutionary zeal was taken nineteen years before from his own pulpit and marched over the British lines into New York, was still doing good service in his ministerial work.

Thus instead of the simple church and its solitary pastor of 1700, the opening of this century gives us six church edifices with six settled pastors and the gradual preparation for at least three other places of worship.

Our schools were under the management of three ecclesiastical societies; and the whole territory had been divided into twenty-seven districts, and parts of three others so as to bring the school within convenient distance of all parts of the town. In parson Smith's house, still standing south of the Baptist church, and then the imperial mansion of the town, were thus early the rudiments of a town and boarding school, in which, for many years, many of the youth of the town and not a few from New York, received the finish to their preparation for college or business. Another of these institutions was soon to be opened under the auspices of a son of the town, Frederick Scofield, who graduated in 1801, and began here his career as teacher. The children of the center of the town in District No. one, which then extended from Mill river to the Noroton, were accommodated in that little square structure, with its slight cupola on its top, now standing across Bank street from the Congregational church. The play grounds for these children were all that triangle now inclosed by Main, Atlantic and Bank streets, the school house being then the only building on the entire opening. Some of our oldest citizens of 1868, remember to have used those grounds for their mimic navies in summer and their ringing skate steel in winter. But that was before they were needed for the various business uses to which this last half century has wrested them.

Let us look now at the business of the village, that part of the town now in the Borough. We shall find here four little stores, in each of which we might have bought whatever the frugal habits of that day needed for use, of dry goods or groceries, not excepting even the "good creature," which then had not been voted contraband. These stores were standing, the first just east of where the Union House now stands, next to

Smith Weed's house; the second, on the south-west corner of the lot where Mr. S. W. Smith's, new brick block stands, and was in the hands of that early woman's rights practicioner, Mrs. Munday, where some of our oldest citizens now living bought their first stick of candy and took their first lessons in commercial life; the third, where our citizens Hurlbutt are now carrying on their tailoring business; and the fourth, on the corner of south street, where Chas. Williams, Esqr., now lives. Where the Rippowam Woolen Mills stand, then stood the village grist mill, which for 158 years had been maintained as the chief and most important business institution of the town. On the corner of parson Smith's lot, about where our jeweler Weed has his handsome front, stood what was called a hat shop, the age of factories not having yet dawned. The only other building used for business purposes, within the present borough limits, was the slaughter house of the town, standing then, where Dr. Trowbridge now lives, near the north-west corner of the old burying lot. Of the seventy-seven families then residing on this territory, only one remains in 1868, in actual occupancy of the same lot and residence, and that is our citizen Isaac Quintard. On all this territory, there are no signs of an "Algiers" or "Dublin," of canal or of railroad. Our thoroughfares were one street, east and west, nearly coinciding with our present Main street; and one north and south where Atlantic and Bedford streets are now. Besides these, on this territory, was only a lane from the gate, then standing on the corner south-east of St. John's Park—leading over to the cove and down to Shippan point by the Indian Cave, which itself has disappeared in the progress of blasting; and what was then called west south street, now south, from the bridge on Broad street, down to the Landing. Broad street, was opened eastward, only to Atlantic street. All other parts of the territory from Norwalk to Greenwich were as well supplied with roads as the village itself, and since that date about one-half of the roads in the rest of the town have been opened. The business of the town was largely agricultural—the saw-mill, the grist-mill and the tannery being the extent, as yet, of our other business enterprizes. Darien, North Stamford, Long-ridge and "Bangall" constituted four business centers, each of which was no mean rival to the enterprize of the village itself. The old burying-ground of the first pioneers, still held sepulchral sway over the very ground where our main street now runs; and but for the new era of steam, soon to dawn, the Stamford of 1868 would but little exceed the sketch which indicates its growth in 1800.

CHAPTER XX.

SEPARATE CHURCH ORGANIZATIONS.

In this chapter we shall give such account, as the materials within reach will enable us to do, of all of the churches which have been organized on the territory, which down to about the first of the last century was under the spiritual care of the only church then in existence here. We shall commence this cata logue with our record of that First Church of Christ in Stamford, and at the point in its history where our seventh chapter leaves it.

FIRST CHURCH OF CHRIST IN STAMFORD.

The first known records of this church, distinct from the town records, were those begun by Mr. Welles, at his ordination, Dec. 31, 1746. He prepared the folio in which the records were to be kept, as if for a permanent depository of all the doings of the church in Stamford. Its title page, in large round hand, reads:

" Notitia Parochialis Stamfordiensis
or.
Stanford Church records,
Begun Jan. 1st, A.D. 1747.

By Noah Welles, who under the conduct of divine providence was called to office by the church and society in said Stanford, and by ordination fixed in the work of the gospel ministry there. The day of my ordination and solemn investiture according to divine institution, by fasting and prayer with the imposition of the hands of the presbytery, the elders of the churches of

Christ in the western association of Fairfield County; the Rev. Messrs. Noah Hobart, John Goodsel, Benjamin Strong, Jonathan Ingersol and Moses Mather, was Dec. 31. 1746.

N.B. In the following records the year begins with the 1st day of January, being the day after my ordination."

The first record made is that of all the names of those who were in full communion in the church at the time of his ordination. That list, just as it appears on the third and fourth pages of the records is as follows:

Jonathan Hait, Esq., Deacon,
Samuel Hait, Esq., Deacon,
Jonathan Maltbie, Esq.,
Benjamin Hait,
Samuel Blatchley,
Samuel Scofield,
Benjamin Weed,
Lieut. Daniel Weed,
Stephen Ambler, Deacon,
Joseph Bishop,
James Bishop,
Benjamin Bunnel,
Jonathan Waterbury,
Jonathan Clauson,
Ebenezer Hait,
John Scofield,
Thomas Waterbery,
Miles Weed,
Nehemiah Bates,
Abraham Davenport, Esq., Deacon.
David Bishop,
Captain Bishop,
E. Bishop,
Joseph Webb,
Lieut. Nathanael Webb,
Nathan Hait,
Nathan Bishop,
Benjamin Weed, junr., Esq.,
Daniel Weed, junr.,
Daniel Weed, 3rd.,
Joshua Lounsbery,
John Scofield, junr.,
Nathaniel Stevens,
Epenetus Lounsbery,
Josiah Scofield,
Charles Scofield,
Reuben Scofield,
Israel Bordman,
Zebulun Husted,
Nathan Scofield—Bapt.
Abraham Hait,
Peter Knap,
Benjamin Jones,
Ebenezer Scofield,
Charles Bishop,
Miles Scofield,
Lieut. John Bates,
John Weed,
Ebenezer Weed, jr.,
Timothy Curtis,
Josiah Holly,
Joseph Judson,
Epenetus Webb,
Benjamin Hait, junr.,
Ensign Charles Knap,
David Hait,
Jagger Hait,
Hezekiah Weed,
(1769,) Joseph Scofield,
Ensign Israel Weed,
Thomas Potts,
Jonas Scofield,
Jeremiah Hait,
Gideon Lounsbery, Episcopal.
Capt. Amos Weed,
Nathan Lounsbery,
Joseph Hustead,
Nathanial Cressy,
Reuben Weed,
Joseph Finch,
Jonathan Garnsey,
Lieut. Hezekiah Weed, jr.,
Ezekial Roberts, Quaker.
Samuel Weed,
Whole number 75 Males.

Madam Davenport,
Hannah, Dan, We of David,

Sarah, wife of Nathan Scofield,
Ruth Bishop,
W'w of Deacon Hait,
W'w Burnham,
Mary, wife of Lieut. Eb. Weed,
Elizab. we of Lieut. Danl. Weed,
W'w Hait,
Mrs. Blatchely, we of Saml.
Elizab. W'e of Benj. Hait,
Millescent, W'e of Col. Hait,
Experience, W'e of Sam'l Ferris,
W'w Blatchely, W'e of Abr'm Hait,
Rose, W'e of Joseph Weed,
Mary, W'e of Sam'l Hait, Esq.,
Deborah, W'e of Stephen Ambler,
Wife of Lieut. Waterbury,
W'w Bishop, of Capt. Bishop,
W'w Blackman, w'e of Josiah,
W'w Martha Leeds,
Azubah, W'e of Simeon June,
W'w Hannah Thorp
Sarah, W'e of Jona. Maltby, Esq.,
Mary, W'e of Chs. Sturges,
Elizabeth, W'e of Jona. Clauson,
Mary Bishop,
Sarah, W'e of Josiah Scofield,
Deborah, W'e of Lieut. N. Webb,
Elizab. dau. of Lieut. D. Weed,
Hannah Slason,
Mary, W'e. of Lieut. Ezra Smith,
Elizabeth Jessup,
Mary, W'e of Josiah Scofield,
Joanna, W'e of Miles Weed,
Hannah, W'e of Jos. Lounsbury,
Susanna, W'e of Nehem. Bates,
Hannah, W'e of Abr'm Hait,
Sarah, W'e of James Bell,
Rebecca, W'e of Samuel Weed,
Sarah, W'e of Jno. Lockwood,
Hannah, W'e of Samuel Weed, jun.,
W'w Susanna Waterbury,
Mary, W'e of Benj. Weed, jun.
Marg. W'e of Ebenr. Hait,
Lydia, W'e of Seremiah Hait,
Abigail, W'e of Reub. Scofield,
Sarah Hait,
Lydia, W'e of Reub. Weed,
Mrs. Sarah Slayd,
Abigail, W'e of David Dibble
Wid. Abigail Clauson,
Kezia. W'e of Daniel Weed, 3d,
Ruth, W'e of Nathan Brown,
Anna, W'e of Nath'l Brown,
Abigail, W'e of Zab. Hustead,
Mary, W'e of Peter Knap,
Susanna, W'e of Dan'l Weed,
Mary, W'e of Ebenezer Scofield,
Mary, W'e of Chris'n Sturgis,
Hannah, W'e of Sam'l Scofield,
Rachel Lounsbury, W'e of J. Scofield,
Abigail Lounsbury,
Deborah, W'e of Jonath. Garnsey,
Bethia Brown.
Sarah, W'e of Dan'l Lockwood,
Rebecca, W'e of Jos. Gales,
Hannah, W'e of Lieut. Sam'l Scofield.
Susanna, W'e of Timothy Curtis,
Sarah, W'e of Capt. Knap,
Mrs. Hannah Wright,
Martha, W'e of Jos. Smith, now of B. Weed, Esq.,
Mercy, W'e of Jona. Weed,
Mercy, W'e of Quinton Patch,
Sarah, dau. of Jonas Weed,
Elizabeth Hunt,
Eliz. W'e of Sam'l Scofield,
Mary Holly,
Deborah Webb, now We of Dan'l Smith,
Mary, W'e of Charles Buxton,
Abigail, W'e of Wm. Blanchard,
Abigail, W'e of Richard Webb,
Rebecca, W'e of Jona. Ayres,
Deborah, W'e of Jos. Husted,
Kezia, W'e of Jas. Roberts,
Thankful, dau. of Mrs. Weed,
Martha, W'e of —— Waring,
Hannah, W'e of Jas. Scofield,
Elizab. Bishop,
Esther, W'e of Dan'l Whiting,
Mary Bouton,
Bethia Scofield,
Mary Lounsbury,
Sarah, W'e of Gershom Mead,
Mary, W'e of Sergt. Jno. Scofield,
Mary, Dau. of Sergt. Sam'l Scofield,
Mrs. Hannah Mather,
Hannah Dan, W'e David,
Mary, W'e Benj. Jones,
Whole No. 99 Females. Total 174.

The above list comprises probably all the resident members of this first church of Stamford in 1746.

Dr. Welles continued here until his death in 1776. Under his ministry there was a steady growth of the church, without any very marked season of revival; the largest number added in any one year being twenty, in the year 1769. In all, during his ministry, there were added to the church 173, of whom only 61 were males. He baptized during the thirty years of his ministry here, 1365. That no more additions were made to the church may be ascribed to the increase of membership in other churches during this period. We shall see in the record of the several churches established on the same ground, that while the parent church held her own, the cause of religion was extending through the rapid multiplication of churches, all of which were thoroughly evangelical. To estimate truly the progress which religion was making, therefore, during this period of the town's history, it will be necessary to examine the establishment and growth of the several churches of the same name and those of different names, which sprang up on the same ground occupied for about a century by this first church alone.

Very few incidents occurred during Dr. Welles' ministry, the entire records of the church for that period being found on eight pages of the church journal. These records are mainly those of cases of church discipline, about which there is nothing striking or instructive. They only serve to show us that the church of that day was not altogether remiss in her watchfulness. If not yet perfect, she had no little regard for the purity of her name, and the unworthy were not allowed, unwarned and undisciplined, to bring reproach on this fair heritage of the Lord.

The year after Dr. Welles' settlement, was made memorable by the advent of a bell for the church, the first of which our records make mention. The enterprising pastor, it would seem, started a subscription, to procure this aid to him in his work, and so far succeeded as to secure a vote of the society, in 1748, to make up the deficiency, and furnish all the means for hanging the bell and clock in the meeting-house. The three town notables of that day. Col. Jona. Hoyt, Capt. Jona. Maltby, and Mr. Abraham Davenport, were made a committee to "manage that affear." A few years later, 1762, the society add a hundred pounds of new metal to the bell, and have it run anew. The clock seems to have been a bill of expense and trouble to them, and it was soon removed.

Another innovation was introduced in 1747. The society, probably out of regard to the wishes of their new pastor, voted to change the form of their service of song in the sanctuary; and this change took place, both in the first church at the Center and in the new church in Middlesex parish, now Darien. The vote of the first society is: "Per vote, the society agree to sing according to regular singing, called ye new way of singing, in ye public worship of God." The vote in the Middlesex society was: "Yt Mr. Jonathan Bell, or any other man agreed upon to sing or tune ye salm in his absence, in times of publicht worship, may tune it in ye old way or new, which sutes you best."

This change from the old to the new way of singing had been introduced in 1721. The eight or nine tunes brought over with the pioneers "had become barbarously perverted," and Rev. Thomas Walter, of Roxbury, Mass., composer in that year, published "The Grounds and Rules of Music Explained; or, an Introduction to the Art of Singing by Note." The treatise "contained twenty-four tunes, harmonized in three parts."

In 1750 one other innovation seems to have completed the changes which were deemed of absolute need. After due deliberation, doubtless, "the society agrees that Doctor Watteses avartion of ye psalms shall be introduced into ye prisbeterian congration."

The following vote, passed Dec. 10, 1770, in society's meeting, is preserved, to show how lenient the society were towards those from whom legally they might collect taxes. That the allusion to names may be understood, it must be known that at a previous meeting, the persons named, in the northern part of the town, had been excused from paying their rates, in part, if they would pay them at Poundridge. The society vote Mr. Welles' rate, two pence a pound, "deducting therefrom only what is above ordered to be abated to Thomas Potts and John McCollum, and the other inhabitants of this society who live above them, and also such rates of poor persons in this society as the society committee may think proper to abate."

Once, only, during Mr. Welles' occupancy of the parish was the church called upon to record its vote upon the mere question of purity of doctrine. The erratic course of the Rev. James Davenport, a native of the town, had engaged the notice of the church, and about a year after Mr. Welles' settlement they had become divided on the question of inviting him to preach, on occasions of his visits to his friends. Without taking the responsibility upon themselves, they voted that the reverend association of the western district of Fairfield county be desired to convene and settle for them their duty in this matter. The reverend gentlemen met according to request, April 6, 1748, at the house of Mr. Bostwick. The church were represented on the occasion by Col. Jonathan Hoyt, Capt. Jonathan Maltbie, Abraham Davenport, and Stephen Ambler. After hearing the case stated, the clergy, finding that the objections to Mr. Davenport's officiating in the pulpit of his native town not so formidable as to threaten serious disturbance and divisions if he should be suffered to do so, gave, probably, the only advice they could safely give: "that the said Mr. Davenport be sometimes invited, as per record of association may appear."

One case brought before the church may show how anxious they were to maintain the sacredness of the Sabbath. Ebenezer Weed, on his own confession, had traveled several miles on the Sabbath, and taken off the skin of a dead horse. His defense was that it was a work of necessity. The church deliberated, and finally "concluded to take further time to consider whether the action was a breach of the fourth commandment or a work of necessity." At a later meeting, Mr. Weed offered a satisfactory confession of the offense above alluded to, and also of having been guilty of " drunkenness," and was continued, by the approval of the church, in Christian fellowship.

A serious cause of offense during the administration of Mr. Welles was evil and censorious speaking; and the offense was sharply rebuked, or, it even led to the suspension of offending members. But the offense which oftenest disturbed the peace of the church, and called for most constant watchfulness, was that of intemperance. Drunkenness was a crime not to be overlooked, and there was no offense to which it did not lead. We find, therefore, the church occasionally scandalized by the presence of this evil, but mainly, efficient in checking it. In all, during the thirty years of Dr. Welles' administration, there were but eleven cases of discipline reported on the records. These are probably all that occurred worthy the notice or action of the church. When we take into account the entire number of church members represented by these delinquents, 422, and also the almost universal use of intoxicating drinks, even to excess, we must acknowledge the rare fidelity and purity of the church.

Dr. Welles died in 1776, after the struggle of our revolution had fairly begun; and the church was left without a pastor until its close. A blank occurs in the church records for this entire period, and the society and town affairs had now become so distinct that the town records give us no light upon the condition of the church. There was, doubtless, preaching here during those years of trial and strife, and a maintenance of all the ordinances of religion; but the presumption is, that other and more stirring themes engaged and ruled the thoughts and feelings of the people

The last record in the fair handwriting of Dr. Welles bears date December 8, 1775, and simply preserves the appointment of Stephen Bishop as deacon in the church.

The regard of the society for their deceased pastor is shown in their vote to continue his salary to his widow so long as the "Rev. Elders" in the western district shall see the pulpit supplied. And in 1779 they still further vote to raise, by subscription, enough to make up the depreciation of the currency occasioned by the progress of the war, or the committee were to draw upon the society fund.

Several candidates, it would seem, officiated here after Dr. Welles' decease. The church has no record to show that they invited either of them to settle. The society, in 1780, make application to Rev. Mr. Kettletas to supply the pulpit, if possible; and from baptisms performed during this interval, he probably preached some months.

The peculiar language employed in the records of the society of date March 24, 1777, would suggest that they were not prepared to settle any one as pastor. By 1781 they had evidently become tired of being without a settled minister, and formally voted to endeavor to settle one. They vote, also, to apply to Rev. Mr. Searl to accept the pastorate.

But in August of this year they are more successful in their attempt. They unanimously vote to settle Rev. John Avery. They vote him a hundred pounds annually, for three years, in silver or gold, and to give him three hundred pounds also, in three equal payments, and after the third year to give him one hundred and twenty-five pounds annually.

The society's records supply an omission in those of the church. They copy the doings of the church for November 28, 1781, which show us that "Mr. John Avery being present, and after discoursing at large on church government, said church, by an unanimous voice, voted to give said Mr. Avery a call to a settlement in the gospel ministry, and to take the pastoral charge of said church, expecting to be led and governed by the rules laid down in the Saybrook Platform and practice of the consociated churches in this State."

The Rev. John Avery was ordained January 16, 1782, and the record is again resumed.

A period of severe trial for the church had just been passed. Without the care of a faithful pastor, and that in a time of war, the church had greatly suffered. Every interest of religion had been exposed, and the exposure had left its marks.

Not that none were left faithful and true. The church of Christ remained. There were still not a few whom years of comparative spiritual abandonment and the evil passions which war engenders could not seduce from the precious faith.

But it cannot be disguised that these years had seriously lowered the standard of piety in the majority of the church, and left too many of the less established Christians a prey to their spiritual enemy. The sad proof of this degeneracy is abundant in the records which Mr. Avery, a faithful and effective pastor, is obliged to make during his short pastorate. The most favorable result, which a careful examination of all the evidences in our reach has forced upon us, is, that at the end of our revolutionary period this ancient church exhibited about five-fold the irregularity and looseness in morals which marked her previous career. Under the searching preaching of Mr. Avery, and the earnest and effective discipline which the church now maintained, these evils were gradually corrected.

For the four years after Mr. Avery's ordination only fifteen new names were added to the church. But the seed which he so faithfully and industriously sowed during those years of patient waiting and working, began now to spring up. The sower began at last to reap. The next year, 1786, added forty-seven new members to the church. It may also indicate the increasing success of Mr. Avery's labors, and the growing fidelity of the church, that the same year also records the baptism of sixty-one of the children of the church.

Mr. Avery continued to preach here until September, 1791, in which month his death occurred. The last records made by his hand are of September 4th, in this year, the one enrolling Abraham Smith as member of the church, and the other witnessing the marriage of John Larkin and Elizabeth Hoyt.

Nearly two years passed before his place was permanently

supplied. And here, too, we must learn of the movements in the church during the interval between Mr. Avery and his successor, from the society records alone. It seems the church and society had agreed, in hearing Mr. Jonas Coe, as yet only a licentiate preacher, and, liking him, had called in the advice of the Association of the Western District of Fairfield County. The committee appointed by the association, Revs. Moses Mather, Isaac Lewis, Robert Morris, and John Shepperd, heard Mr. Coe preach, and examined him "on the most important points of divinity," and expressed their "entire approbation of the society's improving Mr. Coe, for the purposes" of a settlement. This approval is dated April 4, 1792. On the 11th of the same month the society unanimously vote Mr. Coe a call to settle, on a salary of one hundred and fifty pounds; and the committee were to write to Mr. Coe and to the Presbytery of New York, to inform them of the proceedings. The church, on the 13th of the same month, after listening to Mr. Coe, vote, also, unanimously to approve the call. The answer of Mr. Coe does not appear in the records of either the church or society.

In the following spring, March 21, 1793, the church, after "conversing at large upon church government, with Mr. Daniel Smith," who had probably been supplying the pulpit for some time past, unanimously voted to give him a call to settle. To this course the committee of the association also gave their advice. On the 25th of the same month the society unanimously approved the vote of the church, and voted also the salary of one hundred and fifty pounds.

In answer to this call, Mr. Smith was ordained pastor of the church, June 13, 1793. He had come to the field well commended, to commend himself still more fully, in a long and successful ministry.

There were no violent changes in the church and society during the ministry of Mr. Smith. His own urbanity would exempt him personally from violent opposition, and his easy courtesy disarmed what opposition might arise, of its most effective motive. During the earlier part of his ministry his salary had been raised by taxation. That the people became restive under that mode of ministerial support the following transaction attests.

For five years, ending with 1806, quite a list of unpaid taxes had accumulated, and the next year Augustus Lockwood is appointed a special collector, with instructions forthwith to levy upon the estates of such as failed to meet the arrearages. In the prosecution of his duty he seized a horse of William Waterbury, 4th, and sold it under the ordinary warrant. The defendant turns plaintiff, and institutes a suit against the collector for the recovery of his horse. The society stand by their agent, as appears from the following vote, of December 6, 1809: "Voted, unanimously, that this society will indemnify Augustus Lockwood, in the suit that William Waterbury, 4th, has commenced against him, which is now pending in the Superior Court, on account of horse which said Augustus Lockwood took from said Waterbury, by virtue of warrants for society taxes, of which said Augustus was collector." In 1811 we find a heavier tax than usual levied—five cents on a dollar—and the excess over the usual rate, which had been about two and a half cents only, seems to have been charged to the above suit. The vote states that it "is granted for the purpose of defraying the necessary expenses of the society, and for discharging the demand Augustus Lockwood has against said society." The last tax voted by the society seems to have been in 1835, the expenses of the following year having been met by a subscription.

Another event of this period indicates a change which has taken place in the mode of warming our churches. In 1817, the society vote to purchase "an iron stove, sufficiently large to keep the house comfortable, and set up the same in the meeting-house; and that the committee sell the brick composing the present stove to the best advantage." The record states that the "brick of the stove" sold to Sturges B. Thorp, for five dollars. To make this record intelligible to those who are accustomed only to the modern furnace, we will attempt to exhibit the interior of the meeting-house as it was, no longer than fifty years ago. The house stood, as the most of my readers will remember it, where our cosy, little, ornamental park now lies, in the center of our village. You enter the sacred precincts through the tower, which was built in front of the main building, and which, at the time to which we are referring, was surmounted by a spire.

Opening the double doors, connecting with the audience room, you enter an arena of little square pews. An aisle leads you up to the deacon's seat, directly beneath the stiff and solemn pulpit, which fronts the entrance, and which stands up as a stately sentinel, commissioned to take note of all which transpires in tho remotest corners of the room. The front of the room, over the entrance, and both sides, are darkened by wide galleries, around which stretch two tiers of seats, and still further back, beyond a narrow aisle, a row of square pews, lining the entire wall of the house, save the two openings near the front corners for the stairways. On the lower floor you have the four walls of the room lined with pews, excepting the entrances on the front and on the middle of both sides, and the center of the rear, or north end, where the pulpit stood. Within this row of pews was a generous aisle, sufficiently wide in these ante-days of crinoline for two persons to walk abreast; and this aisle enclosed the two center parallelograms of pews flanking the center aisle.

But when, in the progress of improvements, it became necessary to introduce some apparatus for warming the room, no place was found for the innovation. No chimney had been built in the house, since such a thing as fire for the church had never been contemplated. Not yet had stoves been cast which could promise to furnish the warmth for so large a space. But thanks to the meddlesome spirit of invention, a "Russian stove" was devised, and forthwith a place is prepared for it. Taking out the outer sides of two pews from the south-west corner of the west parallelogram of pews, and the seat and partition which separated them, a space of about six by twelve feet was made for the new experiment, and the construction begins. Cart-loads of new brick, as if for some modern edifice, are duly deposited at the side door. Masons are seen, busy as never before in the sanctuary. The floor is removed from a portion of the cleared space, and solid stone work, the foundation for the huge, oven-like structure, is laid even with the floor. Then the inner walls of the vast central oven, six feet in length and three or four in width, arise, arching over at the hight of three feet, with flues coursing their skillfully arranged circuits among the mass of solid brick-work, fully two feet in thickness, enclosing them, until the huge pile stands ready for use. Friday morning—the first Friday in December after the work is done—has come. Winter has fairly set in. The Sabbath is drawing on, and the sanctuary must be made ready for the comfort, now, as well as the worship of God's people. The fire is kindled in the new "stove," with solid logs of solid wood, and is to be renewed and kept aglow, day and night, until the time for Sabbath service.

All day it takes to warm up that mass of brick, and at night the added fuel serves to prolong the heat, and soften slightly the chill in the great room, never before modified save by the summer air or by the glow of warm breathing and beating hearts. All day Saturday, all the night which brings in the Sabbath, and all the morning of the holy day, the faithful committee—and no names are more faithful than those honorables, Davenport, and Knapp, and Lockwood—ply the huge oven with selectest fuel, and lo! when the sharp Sabbath air cuts all about that meeting-house, you might have felt, on entering it, only the pleasant and bracing chillness of an early autumn air. A great triumph had been won. The "Russian stove" became, thenceforth, until the more recent iron stove and furnace took its place, a necessity in God's house.

One other incident, occurring in the time of the edifice in which this Russian stove was built, gives us a lunatic's idea of the peculiar pulpit which was built in it. The old "barrel" pulpit, with a single pair of stairs, had been removed, and a larger one, with stairs on both sides, took its place. Peter Hoyt, known for many years as "Crazy Pete," entered the church, as usual, on the Sunday morning following this exchange. He had scarcely caught sight of the two-fold ascension to the pulpit, when a singular fancy seized him. Grasping, with indignant vehemence, his hat, he started for home. As he pressed on, his indignation grew. A neighbor, who met him, rallied him on getting through service so soon. Peter, with no room in his soul for any other feeling than that of his outraged orthodoxy, exclaimed: "Never go to that old Presbyterian meeting-house again, as long as I live! Only think of it! Who ever heard such doctrine before? Two ways up to Heaven! I'll never stand that pulpit doctrine, anyhow."

Before closing our record of the first society of Stamford, two illustrations of the legal authority of that venerable society, in the time now gone, to return no more, should be given. They illustrate not the power of the society more than the spirit and sharpness of the men whom it had to manage.

Captain William Waterbury, the only son of the General David Waterbury, who had been eminent for his loyalty both to the civil and ecclesiastical authorities over him, signalized the opening of the present century, in this usually quiet place, by a persistent refusal to pay the annual society's tax. He claimed that as he did not receive anything from the society,—no tangible commodity, temporal or spiritual, there was no reason why he should be set upon for his purse. Patiently, the good-natured collector, Augustus Lockwood, Esq., reasoned the matter with him, showed his authority to collect, and in the name of the great State itself threatened his suit. The refractory subject still refused, and calmly awaited the execution. True to what was then thought to be the right, as well as the law of the case, the execution was issued. A mare was attached, an old mare, which the owner told the officer would yet kick to the full satisfaction of the society, if they dared to take her. Before the process was served the mare had been spirited away, and could not be found. The officer, however, not to be foiled thus, seized upon a similar one and sold her, and thus the tax seemed to be paid.

Now was the time for the Captain's offensive. He sued out a writ of replevin, and the society vote to back their faithful collector in the legal contest. The lawyers enjoyed the game, and both the contestants were quite willing to foot the bills. Nor did the plucky parties cease the play before each had inflicted on the other a bill of expense of about a thousand dollars apiece.

Nor did the resolute captain forget or forgive, even then, the presumptuous claim of the society. A half score years roll on, and a meeting is notified, for the sale, at auction, of a certain lot of land, which "parson" Smith greatly desired to buy. The neighbors who were interested in the transaction gathered at the appointed hour, the good parson among the first. The cool, imperturbable Captain Waterbury was also on hand, walking about, as if to pass away an unemployed hour, and get the news of the day.

The auctioneer begins. The lot is offered, and a long suspense awaits a bid. The neighbors, supposing the parson would like the lot, were evidently not disposed to anticipate him. At length the parson bids, and another long pause ensues. No volubility of the man at the hammer could tempt a higher bid. "Going, going,—gentlemen, I can't dwell, I shall strike it off for the mere song named, unless you speak quick,—going—going—go—

"Five dollars an acre more," slowly, but very coolly, said the captain, just in time to save the fall of the hammer.

Another pause, and then another call for bids, until the anxious parson took from the captain his chance. Now the utmost ingenuity of the auctioneer could not induce for a long time a higher bid, and the "going, going, going," and the significant flourish of the hammer at the very last moment of grace, roused once more the consciousness of the still cooler captain, as he

CONGREGATIONAL CHURCH, CORNER OF ATLANTIC AND BANK STREETS.

still more deliberately interposed again: "Five dollars an acre more, if you please, auctioneer."

Thus gaining, the hammer rises again, and a still louder call for bids. Not to lose a good chance thus, the parson raises upon the last bid, and again it hangs. Just in season to anticipate the final "gone," the captain, consciously pleased, and not without a chuckle, which the discerning might have noticed, adds, "five dollars an acre more."

Once more the excited parson advances, and now the auctioneer has no art by which to tempt another bid. His utmost eloquence is in vain. With a twinkle in his eye, not altogether unused to humor, the roguish captain quietly relieves himself: "I have to say, auctioneer, I don't want that lot. It's not in my line. It's only that old mare that wasn't mine, that's kicking yet."

One Obed Scofield, also, a blacksmith, who din't use the meeting-house or the minister, thought he should not be taxed. He, too, defied an execution, which finally came. He pointed out his "Scott's Bible" as the first article which the sheriff must sell. At the appointed time for the sale the books were struck off to the good Mrs. Scofield, who valued the good book at a higher rate than her industrious husband. But how was the good woman to pay for the books? Evidently by drawing upon her husband, and to him the sheriff was accordingly sent. Anticipating just such a result, the sharp blacksmith had prepared for it. He coolly hands over to the sheriff a copy of the legal posting of his wife, and the officer finds himself tricked, at once, out of both the tax and the books.

Since Mr. Smith's day no marked change has taken place in the condition of this church. The old church edifice becoming antiquated in appearance, and uncomfortable, from its exposed position in the very center of the rapidly increasing village, was sold in 1857, and used as a place of worship the last time, September 19, 1858. A new house, built on the corner of Atlantic and Bank streets, was dedicated September 23, 1858.

The following is the list of ministers who have served this church from its organization:

RICHARD DENTON, 1641-4. (See page 272.)

JOHN BISHOP, 1644-94. (See page 269.)

JOHN DAVENPORT, 1694-1731. (See page 270.)

EBENEZER WRIGHT, ordained tn 1732, and died here in May, 1746.

NOAH WELLES, D. D., ordained Dec. 31, 1746, and died here, Dec. 31, 1776. (See later biography.)

ABRAHAM KETTLETAS, preacher in 1780. He was licensed by Fairfield East Association, in 1756.

JOHN AVERY, ordained Jan. 16, 1782, and died here, in September, 1791.

DANIEL SMITH, ordained June 13, 1793, and died here, 1846. (See later biography.)

JOHN W. ALVORD, installed colleague with Mr. Smith, March 16, 1842, and dismissed Oct. 14, 1846.

ISAAC JENNINGS, installed Sept. 1, 1847, and dismissed April 28, 1853.

JAMES HOYT, preacher from June, 1853, to January, 1855.

HENRY B. ELLIOT, installed Dec. 4, 1855, and dismissed July 6, 1858.

JOSEPH ANDERSON, was called Dec. 9, 1858, installed March 27, 1860, and dismissed Feb. 26, 1861.

LEONARD W. BACON, pastor elect, from Nov. 17, 1861, until January, 1865.

RICHARD B. THURSTON, the present pastor, installed Oct. 3, 1865.

CONGREGATIONAL CHURCH, OF DARIEN.

This church was duly organized at a meeting of the consociation of Fairfield West, June 5, 1744, when the following persons were enrolled as its members: Rev. Moses Mather, David and Martha Tuttle, Thomas and Mary Reed, Edmund and Elizabeth Waring, John and Hannah Reed, John Raymond, Daniel and Elizabeth Reed, John and Mary Smith, John and Katherine Waring, Samuel and Mehitabel Brinsmayd, Eliakim and Anne Waring, Nathan and Mary Reed, Isaac Bishop, Joseph Waterbury, Nathan and Sarah Sellick, Joshua and Anne Morehouse, Samuel Bishop, Charles and Susannah Weed, Theophilus and Sarah Bishop, Nathaniel and Sarah Bates, James and Elizabeth Scofield, John Reed, Jr., and wife, Desire; Elias and Mary Reed, Elijah Jones, Sarah, wife of Samuel Reed; Sarah, wife of Thomas Reed; Elizabeth, wife of Samuel Richards; widow Rachel Raymond, Rebecca Raymond, widow

Martha Reed, Elizabeth Reed, Joanna, wife of Jonathan Bates; Abigail, wife of David Bates; Mary, wife of Eliaseph Whitney; Mercy, wife of Ebenezer Brown; Mercy, wife of John Pettit; Rebecca, wife of Jonathan Crissy; Elizabeth, wife of James Slason; Hannah, wife of Deliverance Slason; Mary, wife of David Weed; Abigail Andrus, widow sarah Crissy, and Jona. Bell.

Under Mr. Mather the church was greatly prospered. The records kept by him, and still preserved, show, that down to October, 1803, he had baptized 921 persons; down to October, 1804, he had solemnized 361 marriages, and admitted to the church 258 members. In addition to those admitted to full communion with the church, 161 persons publicly "owned the covenant."

Dr. Mather recorded, during fifty-six years of his ministry, 766 deaths in his parish.

The organization of this church was a very simple process. After the council had examined and approved Mr. Mather as the pastor elect of the church to be constituted, and twenty-one of the brethren, whose names are on the preceding list, had exhibited their credentials of church membership in the several churches to which they then belonged, and had, before the council, "entered into a solemn covenant relation with each other, according to the constitution of the churches in this government; the council acknowledged them as a particular church, and as a member of this consociation." After thus constituted "a particular church," they formally chose Mr. Mather to be their minister, and the ordination service was immediately performed.

The first meeting-house of this parish stood until 1838, when it was taken down, and the present substantial brick church was built.

The ministers of this church have been:

MOSES MATHER, D. D., ordained and installed June 6, 1744, and died Sept. 21, 1806.

WILLIAM FISHER, ordained and installed July 16, 1807, and dismissed March 31, 1819.

EBENEZER PLATT, ordained and installed in September, 1825, dismissed in August, 1833, and died here April 7, 1863, aged 68 years and 5 months

B. Y. MESSENGER supplied the pulpit one year.

ULRIC MAYNARD, installed June 24, 1835, and dismissed April 24, 1838.

EZRA D. KINNEY, installed Aug. 8, 1838, and dismissed May 3, 1859.

JONATHAN E. BARNES, ordained and installed Aug. 21, 1860, and died here, May 31, 1866.

F. ALVORD was installed Dec. 26, 1866.

NORTH STAMFORD CONGREGATIONAL CHURCH.

This church was organized June 4, 1782, and consisted of twenty-two members, as follows:

Benjamin Weed, Ebenezer Weed, Zebulon Husted, Amos Weed, Israel Weed, Joseph Ambler, John McCullum, Ebenezer Dean, Miles Weed, Reuben Scofield, Mercy Hoyt, Elizabeth Ambler, Abigail Weed, Kezia Dean, Mary McCullum, Mercy Hoyt, Jr., Prudence Weed, Sarah Seeley, Elizabeth Scofield, Rebecca Ayres, Rebecca Curtis, and Rebecca Beedle.

Previously to this date, the celebrated Dr. Samuel Hopkins, of Newport, R. I., who had left his parish when the British took possession of the town, in 1776, and who had come to Stamford in 1778, to supply the pulpit of his deceased classmate, Dr. Welles, had been also supplying this pulpit for about a year and a half. He left in 1780, and the church was supplied with temporary preachers until March 23, 1784, when SOLOMON WOLCOT was ordained its first pastor. He continued to labor here until his dismission, June 21, 1785.

The other ministers of this parish have been:

JOHN SHEPPERD, ordained June 27, 1787, and dismissed June 11, 1791.

AMZI LEWIS, installed June 17, 1795, and died here April 5, 1819.

HENRY FULLER, installed June 6, 1821, and dismissed Jan. 23, 1844.

NATHANIEL PIERSON, preached here from April, 1844, to January, 1846.

WM. H. MAGIE, from January, 1846, to January, 1849.

WM. E. CATLIN, from March, 1849, to March, 1850.

F. E. M. BACHELOR, for several months in 1850 and 1851.

LIVINGSTON WILLARD, installed March, 1852, and dismissed in June, 1856.

JOHN WHITE supplied the pulpit from May, 1857, to October, 1858.

W. S. Clark, installed in April, 1859, and dismissed in 1861.
H. T. Ford, in 1862.
Roswell Smith, in 1863 and 1864.
H. L. Teller, ordained May 15, 1866, and dismissed in 1868.
Josiah Peabody, began preaching in the spring of 1868.

LONG RIDGE CONGREGATIONAL SOCIETY.

About the year 1840, a union church was built on Long Ridge, which the Congregational portion of the community secured in 1842, when they organized a church and society. The names of the members of the church were Isaac Ayres, Jared Holly, Charles E. Smith, William L. Holly, Alfred Ayres, Ransford A. Ferris, Polly Holly, Harriet M. Holly, Sally Scofield, Harriet E. Ayres, Hannah R. Raymond, Mary W. Smith, Ann M. Holly, Lydia Ferris, Clarissa Smith, and Phebe Scofield.

Rev. Frederick H. Ayres was engaged to supply the pulpit, commencing his ministry Nov. 6, 1842, and preaching until 1853.

From that time meetings have been kept up for the most of the time, the church having enjoyed the labors of the following ministers, none of whom have been installed: Mr. Perry, Augustus B. Collins, John Smith, Ezra D. Kinney, Dennis Platt, — Timloe, and — Gilbert.

EPISCOPAL CHURCH.

St. John's.—The first allusion which I have found to the presence of Episcopalians in Stamford, is in a letter from the Rev. Henry Caner, of Fairfield, dated March 15, 1727–8, and addressed to the Secretary of the "Society for Propagating the Gospel in Foreign Parts." I am indebted for this letter, as for many of the following quotations, to that thoroughly exhaustive "Documentary History of the Protestant Episcopal Church in the United States of America," edited by Francis L. Hawks, D. D., LL. D., and Wm. S. Perry, A. M.

In this letter, which is a report of his mission, Mr. Caner informs us that among his other labors he had preached several times, during the preceding winter, in Stamford. The same letter shows us that the field in which Mr. Caner was then laboring embraced, besides Fairfield, the following towns and villages: Poquonnuck, Greensfarms, Greenfield, Norwalk, Stamford, Greenwich, Chesnut Ridge, Newtown, Ridgefield, and Danbury. At Newtown, only, did Mr. Caner have any assistance, sharing the labors of that parish with Rev. Mr. Johnson, of Stratford. He also tells us that in "most of the above-mentioned places there are seven, ten, or fifteen families professing the Church of England;" and that "the taxes strained from members of the church for the support of dissenting teachers amount to £100, which is £40 sterling, of which Fairfield pays about half. * * * Notwithstanding this discouragement, the church grows and increases very much."

In another letter, found in the same work, in 1728, Mr Caner intercedes with the society to appoint him their missionary, to serve "from Fairfield to Byram river," with permission to "reside sometimes at one of these places and sometimes at another." This proposal was made to meet the provision which had been made by the State government, allowing all Episcopalians who lived near enough an Episcopalian minister to attend constantly his preaching, the privilege of paying their ecclesiastical tax to him rather than to the Congregational clergy.

In 1738, a very earnest and lengthy plea was sent to the General Assembly of Connecticut, asking that the members of the Church of England in the State might be excused from paying for the support of the Congregational mode of worship. This plea has attached to it the signatures of 636 Episcopalians in nine towns. Fifty of these names are from Stamford and Greenwich. They are, Gershom Lockwood, Samuel Mills, Caleb Knapp, John Lockwood, Wm. King, Henry Jones, Benj. Knapp, James Knapp, Jos. Knapp, Jeremy Peck, Hez. Lockwood, Jonathan Lockwood, Jonathan Austen, Thos. Johnson, Thos. Ballis, David Reynolds, John Avery, John Johnson, John ———, Jas. Wilson, Benj. Young, Rob. Arnold, John Burley,

Nath'l Hubbard, Peter Demill, John Finch, Benj. Day, John Hicks, Mills Riggs, Israel Knapp, Chas. Southerland, Richard Charlton, Sam'l Morine, Isaac Quintard, Jos. Barton, Nath'l Lockwood, John Kirkham, Nath'l Worden, Thos. Roberts, and Abraham Rundal, Jr. The above list is preceded by this memorandum:

"Under the care of Rev. Mr. Wetmore. The subscribers belonging to Greenwich and Stamford to be annexed to the general address of the members and professors of the Church of England, in the colony of Connecticut, To the Honorable General Court, in May, 1738 ; which address having been communicated to us, the subscribers, we hereunto sign our names."

In addition to the above-named address, these Stamford petitioners drew up a plea of their own, of more than three closely written foolscap pages, urgently demanding at least a partial exemption from the tax imposed upon them, to support a ministry which they could not approve. They asked that, at least, they might be allowed to join with those of their own church, in a neighboring colony (Greenwich), and that they might use their tax for the support of the ministers of their own choice in that colony, "provided, always, that the said miuister's settled abode and residence be within five miles of this colony, and that by officiating alternately in each colony he performs divine service at least twelve times in the year in this colony." In addition to the preceding names, this special petition has the following,—Abraham Nichols, John Matthews, and Nath'l Worden, Jr.

The petition was negatived in both houses of the legislature. In 1740, the Rev. James Wetmore was preaching in Stamford once in four weeks, and this seems to have been the only Episcopal service held at that time in the town.

The following votes of the town give us our only knowledge of the progress made by the Episcopalians at this time. The first was under date of Dec. 2, 1742, and is in answer to an appeal made by the Episcopalians for a grant of land, on which to build:

"The town agree to put in a committee to view the place by Mr. Eliphalet Holly's, where the professors of the Church of England have petitioned for setting a church house, whether it may be granted without damage to the town, and to make return to the adjourned town meeting ; and Ensign Jonathan Bell, Sergeant Nathaniel Weed, and Joseph Bishop, to be the court, for the purpose aforesaid."

The result of the examination made by the committee appears under date of Dec. 10, 1742:

"The town agree to give the professors of the Church of England a piece of land, to set a church house upon, on the hill between the widow Holly's house and Nathan Stevens' house—the piece of land to be 45 feet long, east and west, and to be 35 feet wide, when the committee shall lay it out; the committee to be Ensign Jona. Bell, Sergeant Nathaniel Weed, and Joseph Bishop."

The lot granted, as above, to the Episcopalians, was the south-east corner of the present lot held by St. John's parish, in front of their parsonage. It was at that time a rude ledge of loose rock, and bounded east and north by an almost impassable swamp, so that, in all probability, its alienation to the new proprietors did not materially "damage" the town. On this lot the first church was built. Of the date of its corner-stone, or completion, we find no record. It was so far finished in March, 1747, that it could be used.

Mr. Wetmore seems to have been succeeded by the Rev. Henry Caner, of Fairfield, who, with his brother Richard, of Norwalk, and a Mr. Miner, supplied the Episcopalians with what preaching or service they had down to the commencement of Mr. Ebenezer Dibble's long and successful ministry.

In a letter from Mr. Caner, in 1744, alluding to a petition from the people of Stamford, Greenwich, and Horseneck, for a minister to reside among them, we find this charge, for which, in view of the age to which it belongs, we can believe there was too much necessity: "These people have been much persecuted by the dissenting government, for when they would have rewarded the Rev. Mr. Wetmore for his monthly attendance in officiating among them, by paying their proportion of the rates, according to an express law of the colony, they were prevented by a very oppressive judgment of the court."

In 1746 we find Mr. Caner, of Fairfield, bitterly lamenting the want of ministers for both Norwalk and Stamford. He reports both places as losing ground, for want of "a more constant service" than he can supply.

The following letter deserves a place in our local history; partly as illustrating the religious movement of the age, and still more as our introduction to Mr. Dibble, who bore so conspicuous a part in the progress of the Episcopal church of the town:

COLONY OF CONNECTICUT,
STAMFORD, March 25th, 1747.

Reverend Sir:—We, the subscribers, churchwardens and vestrymen of St. John's Church, in Stamford, with the unanimous concurrence, and in behalf of all the professors of the Church of England, in the towns of Stamford, and Greenwich, in Connecticut, beg leave to represent to the venerable society the state of our church, and with humble submission request their patronage, and that the effects of their extensive charity, which hath brought the means of salvation to many thousand souls, may preserve us and our posterity from wandering in error and darkness, and guide our feet in the ways of peace, by assisting us to procure a settlement of the worship of God among us, according to the pure doctrines, and wholesome rites and usages of the Church of England, which we highly reverence and esteem. We have struggled with many and great difficulties in advancing to the state in which we now are, to have a church erected, and so far finished as to be fit for our assembling in it, and with accessions to our number of professors sufficient to be enabled to purchase a glebe, and to pay twenty pounds sterling per annum to a minister, which we have obliged ourselves to do, by subscription, under our hands, and hope to make some additions, so the whole may be worth thirty pounds sterling per annum, which is the most that we are able to perform at present, and too little for a decent support for a minister. We have been much oppressed by the Dissenters among whom we live, who, under protection of the laws of the colony, have obliged us to pay taxes to their minister, and to build them meeting-houses, even when we had obliged ourselves to contribute, according to our abilities, to reward ministers of the Church of England for coming to preach among us, and administer to us the Holy Sacraments; and several have been imprisoned, and others threatened with imprisonment, to compel them to pay such taxes; and we could get no relief from the courts of justice here. This has made us very desirous to obtain a minister in orders among us, which is the only means to obtain exemption from such taxes, according to the express words of the colony act. We, therefore, exerted ourselves to the utmost of our abilities to assist Mr. Miner to go for orders, who was taken by the French, on his passage, with the Rev. Mr. Lamson, and afterwards died in England, which proved a very melancholy disappointment to us; and before, we had contributed considerably to assist Mr. Isaac Brown, when he went home for orders, with hopes that he might have been sent to us, but were disappointed by his coming back for Brook Haven. Since Mr. Miner's death we have applied ourselves to Mr. Ebenezer Dibble, by the advice of Reverend Mr. Caner and others. This gentleman has read prayer and sermons among us, to our very great satisfaction, for near a year and a half, and being willing to go home for holy orders, and to return to us, to be our minister, we have again exerted our utmost power to obtain a glebe, subscribed for his support annually twenty pounds sterling, and do assist him further to defray the expense of his voyage. We have applied to the Reverend Clergy to represent our state, who all of them approve well of Mr. Dibble, and having given him testimonials to the Lord Bishop of London, we earnestly hope he may obtain holy orders, and humbly entreat the venerable Society to compassionate our circumstances, and admit Mr. Dibble to be their missionary to us, with such salary as they may think fit to allow, which we hope will contribute to the glory of God, and to the salvation of many poor souls, and we, your poor petitioners, as in duty bound, shall ever pray for the enlargement of Christ's kingdom by the extensive charity of your venerable Society. We are, Reverend Sir, your most obedient, &c.

JOHN LLOYD,
THOMAS YOUNGS, } Church Wardens.
And others.

The Rev. Mr. Miner referred to in the above letter was probably the Rev. Richardson Miner, a Congregational clergyman, settled in 1730, in Unity, late North Stratford, and now Trumbull, who, in 1742, declared in favor of Episcopacy; was dismissed March 21, 1743–4, and went to England for orders, and died there.

The result of the above appeal was the admission of Mr. Dibble to priest's orders some time in the year 1748, and his return to Stamford. Here he, at once, entered with all his heart, upon the work of his ministry, as rector of St. John's parish, where he spent the rest of his honored and useful life.

It was in this year, also, that Mr. Caner, who had labored with marked success in Fairfield, Norwalk and Stamford, was appointed to the King's, Chapel, Boston, and on leaving he gives this estimate of the progress of Episcopacy in this vicinity. He had come to this mission in 1727, when he found in Fairfield 12 communicants, and left 68; at Norwalk, none when he came, and 115 when he left; and 20 at Stamford. The next year Mr. Dibble reports 16 communicants in Stamford.

In 1757, Mr. Dibble reports his parish, united and prosperous. He says: "We have sundry accessions to the church since my last of the 29th of September." It will illustrate the times to add from this letter the statements,—"I preached, last Christmas, to a numerous assembly. Multitudes of the dissenters came to church, and behaved with great decency. Seven heads of families have declared conformity since my last account, in Stamford, and some at Horse Neck and Stanwich."

The following plea to the Connecticut Assembly explains the disabilities under which the Episcopalians were laboring, and proved one of the steps which at length led to their recognition as a distinct denomination, entitled, in their own way, to support their own worship:

"Your memorialists, being desirous to enjoy the worship of God according to the liturgy and discipline of the Church of England, to which we conscientiously thought it our duty to conform, did, several years ago, undertake to build a church for divine worship, and engaged our present worthy incumbent, then not in orders, to read prayers to us, and afterwards sent him home to England, for orders, who accordingly went, and soon returned in orders to us, we having laid ourselves under obligations to pay him a considerable sum annually, towards his support, and for his expenses in going home, all which undertaking laid us under a considerable burden, which, however, we cheerfully endorsed, but soon finding we were unable to advance monies requisite to carrying on these designs, we ventured to borrow a considerable sum of money, in New York, for the purposes aforesaid, which, together with some benefactions procured for that end, we laid out in building our church, hoping we should be able, in a few years, to repay the same. * * * But, soon after these transactions, the nation became involved in a dangerous and expensive war, * * * and not being by law empowered to tax ourselves, our church must still remain unfinished, and we are scarcely able to support our incumbent, who has a numerous family: Wherefore, we humbly take the liberty to request the favor of your Honors to grant us liberty to set up and draw a small lottery, of about £2,000, lawful money, subject to a deduction of fifteen per cent.; * * * we are strongly encouraged and almost assured, if we obtain this favor of your Honors, that we shall be able to sell the most of the tickets in New York, Boston and Philadelphia, and consequently bring money into the colony, rather than carry any out; and we conceive there is no danger of its being a prejudice to the public, or to any particular person."

May 9, 1759. EBENEZER DIBBLE, *Clerk.*

JOHN LLOYD,
PETER DEMILL,
EBENEZER HOLLY,
JOHN BATES, } *Vestry.*

EPHRAIM SMITH,
SAMUEL JARVIS, } *Church Wardens.*

How this petition was treated by the Assembly the following complaint of the Rev. Mr. Dibble sufficiently attests:

"But, alas, no such favor could be obtained, not even to draw a lottery in the government, if we should not offer a ticket for sale in it. And why? Not because it is repugnant to their principles, for they have given countenance to public lotteries, even to repair broken fortunes of private persons, and to help build up and establish an Independent College in the Jerseys, when they could obtain no such favor in their own province. But, alas, this was too great an act of favor to the Established Church."

In September, of this year, Mr. Dibble reports to the secretary of the society the peaceful and united state of his people in all parts of his extensive mission. The French war, however, was seriously interfering with accessions to the church, in Stamford the enlistments into the public service even diminishing the church; and what was still more trying, was the death of "twelve heads of families—seven males—some of them the best ornaments of religion." He reports this year thirty-nine communicants.

The next fact of interest occurring in connection with this church in Stamford, I find recorded under date of April 16, 1765. John Lloyd, the same, doubtless, whose name appears as one of the vestry of the church, in 1759, in consideration of £343 6s. 11d., received from St. George Talbot, Esq., of Barn Island, N. Y., makes over "to the venerable Society for the propagation of the gospel in foreign parts" two tracts of land—one of eighteen acres one rood and twenty-three rods, in Northfield, on the west side of Mill river; and the other of four acres, twenty-nine at North street, bounded south by North street, west by Church of England parsonage, and east by highway. These lands, by the terms of the surrender, were "to be and inure to the use of the missionary, for the time being, the rector or incumbent of St. John's Church, and his successors, as the glebe lands of the Church of England in said Stamford."

The following record shows how far the "ruling order" of that day was disposed to recognize and aid the Episcopalians.

At the meeting of the Congregational Society, held Dec. 15, 1772, it was voted that two collectors shall be appointed, the one to collect the rates belonging to the "Presbyterians" (Congregationalists), and the other those belonging to the "Church of England within this society." Jonathan Waring is appointed for the Congregationalists, and Abijah Bishop for "that part of the ministerial rate that belongs to the Rev. Ebenezer Dibble." The records of the Darien Congregational

Society still preserve the receipts which the Rev. Mr. Dibble, of Stamford, and Rev. Mr. Leaming, of Norwalk, gave to the society's collector for their part of the rates.

The following is a specimen of one of these receipts:

"STAMFORD, Jan. 5, 1779.

Mr. John Bell, and Mr. Samuel Richards, and Mr. Gershom Richards, Soliciting Committee in Middlesex parish, 1778:—Please to discharge your collector, Mr. Jonathan Bell, Jr., on account of the rates he was to collect of the professors of the church. It shall be accepted in full of all demands upon your society in the year 1778, said rate made up on list, 1777.

Test., EBENEZER DIBBLE.

The foregoing is a true copy of the original.

Test., GERSHOM SCOFIELD, Society Clerk."

And in 1786, we find the following witness to the temper of the town regarding the claims of the Episcopalians. The vote shows that the citizens were not yet ready to make extravagant concessions to the new order:

"Per vote: Whereas, Capt. Nathaniel Webb and Alexander Bishop, in behalf of themselves and the rest of the Episcopal Church in Stamford, made application to this town to grant them liberty to erect a decent fence around their church, at the distance of one rod from said building, the Selectmen are hereby directed to view the circumstances thereof, and order and direct therein as they shall think proper therein."

Under the administration of Mr. Dibble and his successors, the parish was greatly prospered. Their first house of worship answered for the use of the congregation until 1843, when the present church was built, where it now stands. This, in its turn, was soon found too small, and was enlarged, in 1855, to its present dimensions. But even this enlargement was not found to answer the needs of the parish long; and May 14, 1860, they were called to lay the corner-stone of their new mission chapel, St. Andrew's, between Washington avenue and Northfield street. The only rectors of this period were Revs. Jonathan Judd and Ambrose S. Todd. From the summer of 1858, the labors of Dr. Todd having become too great for his failing strength, the parish employed an assistant, Rev. Walter Mitchell, then in deacon's orders, and who was ordained priest April 27, 1859.

Dr. Todd continued in the rectorship of the parish until his death, June 22, 1861; and his assistant, Mr. Mitchell, was instituted rector Nov. 13, 1861. Under his rectorship the church was increasingly prosperous. He was assisted by Rev. F. W. Braithwaite. On the resignation of Mr. Mitchell, in 1866, Rev. William Tatlock entered on the rectorship, Aug. 30, 1866. He is assisted by the Rev. Joseph W. Hyde. The continued prosperity of the parish is evinced by the building of Emmanuel Church, at Shinoh, in 1867, to meet the wants of the northeast part of the parish.

The following is the list of the clergy who have officiated in this parish, as far as the records of the church and contemporaneous history have furnished their names:

James Wetmore, 1735–1741.

Henry Caner, 1744–1747.

Ebenezer Dibble, D. D., 1747–1799. (See later biography.)

Calvin White, 1798.

J. H. Reynolds, S. Wheaton, and Ammi Rogers, the latter of whom was degraded from the ministry, by Bishop Jarvis, in 1804.

Jonathan Judd, instituted rector October 10, 1810, and resigned in 1822.

Bennet Glover.

Ambrose Todd, D. D. (See later biography.)

Walter Mitchell, instituted rector Nov. 13, 1861, and resigned Feb. 4, 1866.

William Tatlock, instituted rector, August 30, 1866.

St. Luke's, Darien.—The Rev. W. H. C. Robertson, an English gentleman, commenced preaching in 1854, in the chapel which was more recently used by the Presbyterian Church. In August, 1855, the Episcopal parish was regularly organized. James E. Johnson was chosen senior, and Ira Scofield, junior Warden. John W. Waterbury, Edward A. Weed, and Isaac H. Clock, were appointed Vestrymen. The cornerstone of the present church was laid August 11, 1855, by the Rev. Dr. Todd, of Stamford, to whose jurisdiction this part of Darien had previously belonged. It was consecrated by Bishop Williams, March 27, 1863.

The rectors of St. Luke's have been:

W. H. C. Robertson, from the organization of the parish, in 1855.

GEORGE D. JOHNSON, instituted September, 1861.
LOUIS H. FRENCH, August 2, 1863, the present incumbent.

ST. ANDREW'S CHAPEL.—The corner-stone of this chapel, between Washington avenue and Northfield street, was laid May 14, 1860, and the house was finished and consecrated May 8, 1861. The persons who have officiated at this chapel have been THOMAS W. PUNNETT, who, in November, 1861, accepted the rectorship of St. Paul's Church, Staten Island, and ARTHUR MASON, NATHANIEL E. WHITING, and F. WINDSOR BRATHWAITE, who was ordained deacon in St. Andrew's Chapel June 17, 1862, and ordained priest June 17, 1865. About the same time, St. Andrew's was organized into an independent parish, and Mr. Brathwaite was called to be rector. This is a free church.

EMMANUEL CHURCH, SHINOH.—The corner-stone of this church was laid June 29, 1867. This neat, Gothic structure, of stone, was built by the Missionary and Benevolent Society of St. John's, as a chapel of the parish church. It stands on the New Hope road, about three miles from the village; and religious services are held here by the rector of St. John's and his assistant.

BAPTIST CHURCHES.

The records of the Baptist Church and society are preserved much more fully than those of the other denominations in town. The first item of information respecting the Baptists is a statement made in 1769, by Ebenezer Ferris. He had united with the Congregational Church, here, with his wife, Abigail, Feb. 12, 1769, and by Oct. 27th, of the same year, he had become so far convinced of the invalidity of his baptism as to seek immersion, at the hands of Elder Gano, of New York city. His own statement of the change is as follows:

"Having been some time exercised in mind, in disputes upon religious subjects, searching the Scriptures, for understanding, and becoming convinced that the Baptist, in their practice, are agreeable to the order of the gospel, (I) made application to the Baptist Church in New York, under the pastoral care of Elder Gano. Desiring to unite with them in the privileges of the gospel, after being examined, they manifested their freedom. Was baptized Oct. 27, 1769, and received into church fellowship."

From the same records we learn that Elder Gano, in April, 1770, preached here, and baptized Nathan Scofield and John Ferris, of Stanwich, the former having been a member of the Congregational Church from the settlement of Dr. Welles, in 1647. In June he came again, and baptized Nehemiah Brown and David Wilson, of Horseneck, and Moses Reynolds, of Stanwich.

In the following March, 1770–1, the persons above-named, as being baptized "with Moses Fountain, a Baptist, who lately came to this place, having joined the church of New York, our number seven was by said church considered as a branch of the same, residing in Stamford; and to have the privilege of having ordinances of the gospel administered here by the Elder Gano, and to receive into church fellowship such persons as should be judged meet subjects by this branch and the Elder."

It was further provided that Mr. Gano should preach here once a month, for six months; upon which the branch "agreed to meet statedly on Lord's-day, for public worship, at the house of Moses Fountain. Begun first, in April, 1771."

The following persons were baptized during this year: Oliver Sherwood, of Horseneck; James Winchel Elizabeth Davis, Hannah Ferris, Rebecca Reynolds, of Stanwich; Elizabeth Rowel, of Horseneck; Mindal Smith, of Bedford; William Brundage, and Nathan Sutton, of Horseneck—making the number, at the end of 1771, sixteen.

In July of this year Ebenezer Ferris had been chosen deacon. The record states that of the above persons Mindal Smith had been previously baptized.

The Congregational Church records of 1772, have this vote in them, the first allusion to the existence of the Baptists which these records contain: "Samuel Youngs shall be exempted from paying society rates as long as he continues in thi society, a Seventh Day Baptist."

Another vote of the Congregational Society, Dec. 27, 1773, is worthy of preservation. It abates the society rates for the year 1771 of the following Baptists: Moses Fountain, Nathan Scofield, Ebenezer Ferris, Nathan Scofield, Jr., Daniel Scofield, Samuel Clason, Joshua June, and the widow Sarah Mead. At the same time they abate the rates of 1772, of the following additional names: Joseph Webb, Jr., Daniel Turney, Stephen Longwell, Peter Mead, Jesse Smith, and John Lockwood, Jr.

The above names are probably all which constituted the pioneers in the Baptist movement in this place.

Deacon Ferris purchased a piece of land, in October, 1771, for a church site, for which he paid £4 10s., York money; and on this site the frame of the first Baptist church this side of New York was raised, June 11, 1772. The same frame stands on the same lot, in the Bangall district, to this day. It is the only surviving representative in town of the almost universal type of the "Lord's house" which prevailed in New England a hundred and fifty years ago.

On the 6th of November, 1773, those Baptists who were living in this vicinity were organized into a separate church, Elder Gano being present, and giving them "the right hand of fellowship." The list of the new church numbered twenty-one names. They are Ebenezer Ferris, Ezariah Winchel, Nathan Scofield, John Ferris, Nehemiah Brown, Sylvenus Reynolds, Gabriel Higgins, Joseph Webb, Jonathan Whelpley, Moses Reynolds, John Higgins, Elizabeth Brown, Mindal Smith, Hannah Ferris, Rebecca Reynolds, Mary Reynolds, Elizabeth Davis, Mary Miller, Sarah Higgins, Esther Smith, and Hannah Tyler.

The ministers who labored here for the next ten years were Elder Coles, 1773; Thomas Ustic, 1775; President Manning, of Providence, 1775, and Robert Morris. Mr. Morris had been licensed by the church to preach, in 1776, but he became loose in his doctrinal views, and in 1780 his license was withdrawn, and he was excommunicated. In October, of this year, Elkanah Holmes, of Nine Partners, came here and took the charge. His family followed him the next spring, and he continued here until October, 1784. Mr. Ferris, who had well discharged the office of a deacon, was also thought worthy of the ministerial office, and accordingly, in October, 1783, he was licensed to preach, and on the 3d of the next July he was ordained formally to the work of the gospel ministry.

The Baptist Church seemed from the first to prosper. It established branches in the lower part of the town, in Salem, Bedford, Yorktown, and Sing Sing, N. Y. In December, 1784, they dismissed twenty-five of their members, to constitute the church of Salem, N. Y., and Elder Holmes was transferred to the charge of that new church. Elder Ferris remained in charge of the Stamford church for the rest of his life.

In 1787 they dismissed seventeen, to constitute the Baptist Church of Bedford, N. Y. In October, 1788, they dismissed thirty-two, to constitute the Church of Courtland Manor, N. Y., and in 1790 they dismissed thirty-four, to be organized into the Church of Mount Pleasant (Sing Sing), N. Y. The records show that after these several dismissions there still remained on the list of the Stamford church thirty-nine communicants.

The Baptists in the lower part of the town becoming more numerous, demanded a place of worship nearer than the one on Fort Hill, and accordingly, on the 24th of June, 1790, they raised the second Baptist house of the town, on the lot on River street, a few rods south of the bridge. This house—similar in form to that on Fort Hill—gave way, in 1856, to a neat church, and this, in 1860, on the completion of the present elegant house on the corner of Broad and Atlantic streets, was converted into the block now overlooking our village pond.

In June, 1791, the Stamford parish being so large, and the work in the vicinity so burdensome, Marmaduke Earl, who was a licensed preacher at Scott's Plains, was invited to come to the assistance of Mr. Ferris. He removed to Stamford the next month, and entered upon his labors. In February, of the next year, Mr. Earl made a formal proposition to the church, if they wished him to remain another year, to provide for him a home, by fitting up the parsonage, and allowing him forty pounds a year, with the privilege of teaching school. This proposal the church and society accepted. Before the year had closed Mr. Earl had taken exceptions to the action of the church upon doctrinal points, and a long and spirited contest commenced.

Mr. Ferris, who was, to the last, sustained by the church, commenced his labors in the new building on River street, in 1792, and the old church on Fort Hill was for a while held by the opposition, and was finally, in 1806, transferred to the Long Ridge Baptists, and became the Second Baptist Church of Stamford.

There have been from this church five members licensed to preach, four of whom were afterwards ordained to the work of the ministry. They were Robert Morris, who, being licensed in 1776, soon proved himself unworthy of the trust, and his license was withdrawn; Ebenezer Ferris, Greenleaf S. Webb, Frederick Smith, and Henry Little.

The following record we preserve here, as too illustrative of the devotion of a member of this church, and of the wants of the earlier age to which it belongs, to be lost:

"Oct. 8, 1797. Died, at Norwalk, Sybil Whitehead, aged 116, as published in the public prints, a member of this church, baptized and added, Oct. 5, 1780, which must have been in the 99th year of her age. She lived at Norwalk, where she taught a school, and for years frequently attended public worship with the church in this place, which was thirteen miles distance. Came on Saturday and returned on Monday, horseback. The last time she came was May, 1789. She came nine miles on foot, and returned on foot, in the 99th year of her age—said person having never been married. FREDERIC SMITH, Clerk."

The ministers of this church who have officiated since Mr. EARL'S co-pastorship with Mr. Ferris have been:

FREDERICK SMITH, co-pastor, from August, 1807, to February, 1817.
GREENLEAF S. WEBB, co-pastor, from June, 1816, to April, 1821.
JOHN ELLIS, pastor, from December, 1822, to October, 1836.
WILLIAM BIDDLE, from October, 1836, to January, 1839.
JAMES M. STICKNEY, from April, 1839, to April, 1842.
ADDISON PARKER, from April, 1843, to April, 1845.
HENRY H. ROUSE, from November, 1845, to April, 1848.
JAMES HEPBURN.
J H. PARKS, to the union of this and the Bethesda Church.

In 1848, the Bethesda Baptist Church was organized, by sixty-two members from the First Church. They built on the corner of Atlantic and Cottage streets, where they continued a separate organization until the two were happily re-united in 1858.

On the organization of the Bethesda Church, in 1848, Mr. Rouse became the pastor of the new church, where he continued to officiate until January, 1857.

ALANSON H. BLISS succeeded him, and remained until the re-union of the two churches, in October, 1858.

At the union of these two village churches, disposing of the two lots and church buildings which they owned, they purchased a lot on the corner of Broad and Atlantic streets, and erected the elegant brick structure which now stands there. Its corner-stone was laid in August, 1859, and the house was dedicated.

Its two pastors have been PHILIP S. EVANS, installed in Nov., 1858, and resigned in 1865, and EDWARD LATHROP, D. D., who was installed Feb. 22, 1666.

METHODIST CHURCHES.

MAIN STREET.—There seems to have been no record of the early Methodist movement in this vicinity, and it is doubtful whether any was made for several years after this denomination began its labors here. The earliest records, now existing, are those begun in 1830, by Rev. Daniel De Vinne, who was then stationed here. He introduces his records with a historical sketch, from which I take the following statement:

"The first regular society of the Methodist Episcopal Church, in this town, was formed about the year 1788. What circumstance led our ministers to this place, who was the first preacher, or who formed the first class, cannot at present be ascertained. But it is most probable that it was the Rev. SAMUEL Q. TALBOT or PETER MORIARTY, who traveled on the New Rochelle circuit. The next year, 1789, the Rev. JESSE LEE and ANDREW VAN NOSTRAND were appointed to Standford circuit. On their arrival at this place they found kindred spirits, who

BAPTIST CHURCH, CORNER OF ATLANTIC AND BROAD STREETS.

had drunk at the same fountain with themselves. Sister Elsie Scofield, who is now (1830) living, had been awakened by his ministry in this village, at the house of Mr. Gurnsey, some years previous to 1791, the time at which she joined the infant society in this place. Mrs. Martha Reed, who had been awakened by the ministry of the Rev. Freeborn Garretson, in Shelburne, Nova Scotia, settled in this village in 1790. Immediately on her arrival she attached herself to the class, which consisted of about twelve, over which one Enos Weed was placed as leader. The stated meetings were held at the house of a Mr. Lockwood, now owned by Mrs. Smith, near the present Methodist Episcopal Church; and the preachers were entertained by General Waterbury, near the harbor, whose wife and sister were members.

Mr. Isaac Reed, who, during the Revolutionary war, had become a Christian, joined the church, at the same time, with his wife, and invited the congregation and ministers to hold their public meetings in his house. In this place the ark of Methodism rested for nineteen years; and this excellent family subjected themselves, during all this time, to the inconvenience of accommodating, almost weekly, meetings, supporting the preachers and their horses, and also furnishing more than their quota of traveling expenses.

After frequent petitions, the town, which was at that time under the influence of the Congregational order, granted to the "Fanatics" a place—a mud-hole—on the commons, on which to build a church. About 1813 the church was finished and dedicated, and six years after was cleared of debt."

Such, probably, was the origin of this enterprising denomination of Christians in this village. Our town records show that the selectmen were empowered, Feb. 17, 1814, "to give a lease, for ninety-nine years, to the trustees of the Methodist Society, of a spot of ground near the dwelling-house of Fred. Hoyt, on the west side of the old burying-ground, for the purpose of erecting a meeting-house." This must have been the "mud-hole" referred to in the preceding statement. It was a little to the east of the present site of the Methodist church on the park; and the frame of that first church still stands on River street, the second house from the corner of Park place.

The only names on the record of this church for thirty years are the following: Martha Reed, Elsy Scofield, Lanney Garnsey, Jonathan Brown, Ezra Garnsey, John Thompson, William Waterbury, Lois Waterbury, Hannah Brown, Richard Scofield, Hephzibah Scofield, Joseph Selleck, Phebe Selleck, Solomon Smith, Polly Smith, Isaac Wardwell, Jane Weeks, Mary Trowbridge, Joanna Augusta Devinne, Nancy H. Lockwood, James H. Trowbridge, Phebe Adams, Nancy Knapp, and Margaret Valentine.

From such beginning, so recently made, to quote from the records of the movement, the Methodist "Cion continued to grow, notwithstanding the shade of public sentiment and the rude attempts of the bulls of Bashan to devour it."

The second Methodist church built in the village was finished and dedicated Oct. 12, 1843. It stood north-west of the first house, where it was used by the society until 1859. It still occupies mainly the same ground, on the corner of River street and Park place, having been turned round and converted into tenements.

The present Methodist church was dedicated Feb. 16, 1859. This denomination has made very rapid progress, as our notice of several congregations in town will indicate. Yet its growth was not very marked until about 1855, since which its progress has probably had no parallel among our congregations.

The following list of the ministers of this denomination who have been located in Stamford, embraces all whose names have been recovered, with the dates of entering upon their labors here:

1788. S. Q Talbot and P. Moriarty.
1789. Jesse Lee and Andrew Van Nostrand.
1790. Freborn Garretson. 1812, Samuel Luckey.
1813. Thomas Drummond and Benj. Griffin.
1814. Phineas Rice and Benj. Griffin.
1815. Coles Carpenter and Theodosius Clark,
1816. Theodosius Clark and Aaron Hunt.
1817. John Reynolds, two years.
1819. John M. Smith and Samuel D. Furguson,
1820. Elisha P. Jacob and John M. Smith.

1821. John B. Matthias, two years.
1822. Eli Denniston, two years. 1823. Jarvis Z. Nichols.
1824. Nathaniel Porter and Noble W. Thomas, two years.
1825. Cyrus Foss.
1826. Elijah Woolsey, two years, and Luman Andrews.
1827. Samuel U. Fisher, two years.
1828. Daniel De Vinne, two years. 1829. Edward Oldren.
1830. Samuel Corcoran and Daniel I. Wright, two years.
1831. Henry Hatfield, two years. 1832. John Lovejoy.
1833. E. Hibbard, Abraham S. Francis, and Geo. Brown.
1834. Oliver V. Ammerman and Charles Stearns.
1835. Richard Seaman and Zachariah Davenport.
1836. A. S. Hill, two years, and D. B. Ostrander, Jr.
1837. Wm. Gothard, two years. 1838. Edward Oldren, two years.
1839. S. J. Stebbins, two oears. 1840. John Tackerbury.
1842. George Brown. 1844. Peter C. Oakley.
1846. Aaron Rodgers. 1850. Friend W. Smith.
1852. Albert Nash. 1854. Samuel Smith.
1856. George Dunbar. 1858. Robert M. Hatfield, D. D.
1860. L. S. Weed, D. D. 1862. Thomas Burch, D. D.
1864. E. G. Andrews, D. D. 1867. Wm. C. Steele.

HIGHRIDGE.—From the historical sketch, drawn up by Mr. De Vinne, in 1830, we learn that this organization, then called the Duntown Church, is the oldest Methodist church on the Stamford circuit. We learn, also, that the Stamford circuit is the oldest circuit in New England. It appears that one Henry Eames, who had been converted under Wesley's preaching, in Ireland, came to this country and settled in the south part of Poundridge. He soon gathered about him a number "of the sons, in the gospel, of his spiritual Father, and invited them to his house." These became the nucleus of a church and society.

Some time in the year 1787, the Rev. Samuel Q. Talbot, stationed on New Rochelle circuit, came to these neglected parts, preached in several places, and formed several in a class, some of whom remain to this day" (1830).

The first house of worship built by this society stood just across the Stamford line, in Poundridge, where the church held their meetings until 1841, when the present chapel was built or them on Highridge. The only two names now on the records of the Dantown church, for the year 1787, are Samuel and Ruhamah Dann. In 1797 these two are added: Sarah Selleck and Hannah Deforest; and in 1799 these four: John Slauson, Rhoda Slauson, Enoch Stevens, and Ruhamah Bishop.

It will appear from these records that we had organized here a Methodist church, enjoying the ordinances of the gospel at least two years before the time when, according to Dr. Bangs, "the first seeds of Methodism were sown in Connecticut." This church was earlier by two years than that society in Stratford which is called the first in Connecticut, consisting of three women, and which was formed Sept. 26, 1789.

The Stamford circuit was already organized before 1790, the year in which the three circuits of New Haven, Hartford and Litchfield were established; and when, according to the "Contributions to the Ecclesiastical History of Connecticut," there were but four Methodist ministers in New England. The ministers of this church have been the same as those who have officiated at Hunting ridge and Poundridge.

Darien.—That there were meetings of this denomination in Darien as early as 1788 is testified by the certificates of that date, which Samuel Quinton Talbott gave to Joseph Waring, Jr., Gershom Raymond, and Edward Raymond. Cornelius Cook also gives similar certificates, in the same year, to Ezra Slason and Jesse Waring. These certificates testify that the five gentlemen above-named were considered as "members of the Methodist congregation." During the next six years the following ministers give similar certificates to relieve the bearers from the legal obligation to pay their ministerial rates to the Congregational treasurer: Jesse Lee, Daniel Smith, and John Clark, and the number of such certificates is nine.

Longridge.—My account of this church is also taken from the records of the Stamford circuit, as made out in 1830, by Mr. De Vinne: "About the year 1809, Mrs. Phebe Mead moved into this neighborhood, and finding no religious meetings, invited the Methodist ministers to come and preach at her house. The first who accepted the invitation and preached was Daniel Welpley, a local preacher. Some time after him the Rev. Eben Smith occasionally visited the place and preached.

When the Rev. John Reynolds was appointed to this circuit, he preached here some time statedly, although it was even to a single family. About the year 1819, when the Rev. John M. Smith traveled, the preaching was moved to the school-house, in which place it has continued ever since;" that is, until 1830.

Bangall Chapel.—This chapel was built before 1834, and is supplied with preaching by such ministers of this denomination as are living in the vicinity.

Hunting Ridge.—This chapel, making the sixth place of worship for this denomination within the territory of the ancient Stamford, was built in 1850, the Rev. Walter W. Brewer having previously labored successfully for two years in gathering a congregation on the Ridge. Mr. Brewer subsequently made the Ridge his home, where he died, in 1868, much esteemed for his piety and usefulness. Since then, the following ministers have been stationed here, the most of them for two years each: Miles Olmstead, Joseph Heuton, John A. Silleck, Harvey Husted, T. D. Littlewood, William Crawford, William Ross, ——— Monson, and ——— Maguire.

UNIVERSALISTS.

Longridge Society.—For the following facts, respecting this society, I am indebted to Rev. Eber Francis, formerly of this town:

During the Revolutionary war, Richard Sibley, a Universalist, came from Long Island and settled on Longridge; and, so far, as is known, he was the first resident who openly avowed Universalist sentiments in the town. Solomon Glover, of Newtown, Connecticut, a few years later, came down occasionally, and preached in the school-house on the Ridge. Mr. Ferris, Mr. Dykeman, Mr. Babbitt, and Thos. F. King were successively employed as preachers on the circuit to which Longridge belonged. This Mr. King was father of the late lamented lecturer and preacher, T. Starr King, of San Francisco. From the removal of Mr. King, in 1825, to 1832, there was no stated preaching here. Rev. Shaler J. Hillyer was settled here at this date, preaching a part of the time, also, at North Salem, N. Y., in which place he finally settled, and where he still remains.

The formal organization of the society bears date April 27, 1833. Fourteen persons gave in their names to constitute the society.

Of them the late Ebenezer Dean, Esq., was chosen Moderator, and Smith R. Sibley Clerk. The first committee were Geo. Lounsbury, William Todd, and Aaron Dean.

In October, 1834, the present house of worship having been completed, it was formally "dedicated to the worship of Almighty God," with appropriate solemnities, the Rev. Dr. Sawyer, of New York, preaching on the occasion. For years this was the only house for public worship in that part of the town.

Second Universalist Society.—For the following facts I am indebted to the Rev. Eben Francis, who was pastor of this church about three years:

For a number of years there had been irregular preaching here by ministers of the Universalist denomination, when in the spring of 1835 the Rev. F. Hitchcock accepted a call to settle here. He was succeeded by Rev. S. J. Hillyer, who also remained but a short time, and was succeeded by Rev. B. B. Hallock. The society was not organized until 1841; at which time thirteen persons subscribed the constitution. Its committee were,—Wm. H. Potts, Wm. E. Young, and James B. Scofield. In 1844 the society took steps towards building, having thus far mainly depended upon the Town House for a place to worship. They purchased the corner lot, on which their church now stands. The church was dedicated Feb. 5, 1846, during the ministry of Mr. Hallock. The following ministers have succeeded Mr. Hallock:

J. J. Twiss, J. H. Moore, two years; C. H. Fay, two years;

Asa Countryman, one year; Eben Francis, about three years, and J. Smith Dodge, Jr., who is still the occupant.

CATHOLIC CHURCH.

The first Catholic services in Stamford, of which we have any account, were held by Rev. John Smith, in September, 1842, in the house of P. H. Drew, in West Stamford. At that date there were but three Catholic families in the town. Services were held there, monthly, until 1846. Mr. Drew removing to the old "Webb Place" on South-St., services were there held, first, by the Right Rev. Bishop Tyler. Here the meetings of this denomination were continued, by several ministers, until the church on Meadow-St. was built in 1851. Since then, the Catholic population has increased very rapidly. The church has been once enlarged, and the present necessities of the congregation call for still greater enlargement, for which provision is being made.

The following priests have been stationed here:

James Brady, 1850—1854.

Edward Cloney, 1854—1857.

James Reynolds, 1857, and died here Oct. 20, 1858.

James O'Neil, from Sept. 1858 to the present time. He has been assisted by the following curates, Edward O'Neil, who died while in this office, Christopher Dugget, and his present assistant, curate Eugene Gaffney.

FRIENDS MEETING.

How early the movement was started which led to the Friends' meeting in Darien, I have been unable to learn. From a work published in 1844, embracing the biographies of Catherine Seely and Deborah S. Roberts, who were themselves Friends, we learn that their grandmother, Catherine Selleck, was the first member of the sect in Stamford. The opening of a Friends' meeting at a private residence is thus described by Miss Roberts. "After seriously weighing the subject, on the 21st of 6th month, 1828, and on the 1st day of the week, we convened at the house of Uncle Wyx Seely, and quietly sat down together in the capacity of a religious meeting for worship. It was held in the sick room of my dear cousin C. Seely, and was the same one in which our worthy grandmother Catherine Selleck, the first member in this place, sat down in the same way, herself alone. At length others joined her and finally a meeting was allowed." The first "minister" they had, was probably a woman by the name of Griffin; and the only preacher who was located there was probably one of the resident members, Mr. Samuel Bishop, who died in 1852, a lineal descendant of Rev. John Bishop, the second pastor of the first Congregational church of Stamford. The Friends built a small, square meeting house in 1811, and for a few years held in it their simple service. But the meetings were long since abandoned, nothing being left as a witness to the fact of such an attempt, save the old square frame in which the meetings were held.

FIRST PRESBYTERIAN CHURCH OF STAMFORD.

The first records of any movement towards organizing a Presbyterian church in Stamford, are found among the records of the Congregational church. After the communion service of Jan. 2, 1853, in a church meeting, the following members of the Congregational church called for letters of dismission from the church, to constitute a Presbyterian church about to be formed.

Augustus R. Moen, Alexander Milne, George Elder, James D. Haff, Luke Baker, Hiram Warner, James Robinson, John Holmes, Mrs. Sophia A. Moen, Miss Cornelia A. Moen, Hannah E. Elder, Mrs. Mary E. Haff, Mrs. Almira Baker, Mrs. Sophia Warner, Miss Elizabeth M. Warner, Mrs. Georgette A. Robinson, Mrs. Catherine Helmes.

Letters of dismission were voted to these members of the church according to the rules of the church, Jan. 16, 1853. During the next few weeks similar letters were given to the following members of the Congregational church:

Wells R. Ritch, Mary Ann Sturges, Elizabeth Sturges, Mrs. Amzi Ayres, Miss Matilda Moen, Mrs. Sarah A. Ritch, Miss Sarah L. Ritch.

This church was organized Feb. 25, 1853 with twenty-six

members. It has since then added about 250 to its membership, and is one of the wealthiest of our churches. Its ministers have been:

J. L. CORNING, installed Apr. 19, 1853 and resigned Oct. 15, 1856. He is now settled in Poughkeepsie.

R. R. BOOTH, D. D., installed Mar. 4, 1857, and resigned in Feb. 1861, to accept the pastorate of the Mercer St. Presbyterian church in New York.

JAMES P. LEEDS, preached very acceptably one year.

DWIGHT R. BARTLETT, installed Apr. 14, 1862, resigned, in Feb. 1864.

SAMUEL P. HALSEY. installed, Mar. 8, 1865 and resigned Feb. 7, 1867.

A. S. TWOMBLY, installed, Apr. 30, 1868.

MISSION CHAPEL.—This chapel of the First Presbyterian church grew out of a movement, organized in 1859, to supply a local want in the Wescott neighborhood. It is situated on the "Cove" road, and was built in 1868.

FIRST PRESBYTERIAN CHURCH OF DARIEN.

This new organization was made Nov. 4, 1863. The following list of members were from the First Congregational church in Stamford:

Isaac Weed, Benjamin Weed, Rufus Weed, Mrs. Sally Weed, Mrs. Mary Weed, Mrs. Phebe Weed, Mrs. Hannah Weed, Miss Mary Weed, Miss Rebecca Weed, Mrs. Sarah W. Crissey, Mrs. Abigail W. Bishop.

The following were from the First Presbyterian church in Stamford:

William A. Cummings, and his wife Louisa Cummings.

Mrs. Anna E. Ballard and Mrs. Martha Harris, from First Presbyterian church, New York City.

Lewis E. Clock and his wife Eliza, Miss Eliza Clock, and Mrs. Hannah Waterbury, from the Congregational church of Darien; and Miss Fanny Kennedy, from the Methodist Episcopal church of Stamford.

This church commenced worshiping in the chapel which had been built here, a quarter of a century ago, as a Union chapel, for all evangelical denominations. This church is under the care of the fourth presbytery of New York city. Their new church, a beautiful structure of light colored brick, was dedicated May 31, 1866.

Their only pastor has been the Rev. JAMES WM. COLEMAN, who was ordained and installed here Mar. 6, 1864.

UNION CHAPEL, NEW HOPE.

This house was built in 1858 for the use of a Sunday school, and for evening services for that part of the town, and was dedicated Thursday, Jan. 27, 1859. Services have been held here, somewhat irregularly, conducted by clergymen of the five evangelical denominations in town. There is no church organization connected with the chapel. A Sabbath School has been kept up here for the most of the time since the house was built, as there had been in the district school house for years before.

UNION CHAPEL, TURN OF THE RIVER.

This house was built for the use of this neighborhood as a convenient place for holding the meetings of the Sunday school which had been previously held in the school house. It was dedicated in 1860, and has since had in it Sunday evening services conducted by the brethren of the vicinity, or by some one of the ministers of the town.

CHAPTER XXI.

EDUCATION.

Among the founders of Stamford were a few men of literary culture. But neither the age, nor the country in which they had grown up, nor their family means, nor the tempestuous times which had otherwise engrossed their earliest attention, had allowed the majority of them the advantages of scholastic training. Gifted they were in intellect, men of strong, sound sense, thoughtful, accustomed to self-reliance, and fertile in devices for their personal improvement and prosperity, and they could not overlook the claims of their children. Indeed, the New England fathers, and our pioneers were among them, saw that the only way to establish here, and perpetuate a society which could satisfy either their tastes or their hopes, would be through a more careful and thorough, and general education of their children than might have been necessary in the mother land. A necessity seemed to be laid upon them to look after all the resources at their command; and to none of them did they turn with a wiser forecast than to those which their very intuitions told them were awaiting development in the hearts and minds of their children.

How soon our Stamford fathers reared their first school house, where it stood, what its size, and how furnished, are interesting facts now beyond our reach. The record of that incipient school enterprise here is lost. Its influence upon the generations which have succeeded has been incalculable.

Of one thing we may be certain. The first school house here had no needless room in it, no uselessly expensive adorning, and no special provision in its furnishments to minister to the ease and promote the effeminate languor of the children to be educated in it. It was set up by the hard and self-denying labors of the parents for the place of the hard and protracted work of their children—not for five hours a day, four or five days in the week, but for eight and ten hours, for each of the six working days of the week.

The fundamental laws of the New Haven jurisdiction required under severe penalties every town to provide means for the early instruction of their children. The parent who should allow himself to neglect his child's education, was to be duly warned by the civil magistrate. If he did not at once atone for his neglect, he was to be fined ten shillings for the first offense. If the neglect should be continued, in three months the fine should be doubled; and if then the guilty parent should refuse to do his duty to his children, the law would take from him their care and find a guardian who should better educate and govern them, "both for public conveniency and for the particular good of the children."

It seems that some towns did not provide for the education of their children. Accordingly, in 1657, the New Haven court ordered, "that in every plantation where a school is not already set up and maintained, forthwith endeavors shall be used that a schoolmaster be procured that may attend that work, one-third part shall be paid by the town in general as other rates, the good education of children being of public concernment."

In 1660 it was added to the fundamental law of the colony under the same penalty before noticed, "that the sonnes of all the inhabitants within this jurisdiction shall be learned to write a leegible hand, so soone as they are capable of it."

Nor was the theory of the Connecticut jurisdiction any less exacting in its demands for the general education. When Stamford was brought under this jurisdiction, the fundamental law of education still read much as that in New Haven had done. There could be no mistaking its terms. "The select-men of every town in the several quarters and precincts where they dwell, shall have a vigilant eye over their brethren and neighbors, to see, first, that none of them shall suffer so much barbarism in any of their families, as not to endeavor to teach, by themselves or others, their children and apprentices so much learning, as may enable them perfectly to read the English tongue, and knowledge of the capital laws, upon penalty of twenty shillings for each neglect therein."

It was stilll further provided, that every town having fifty householders in it, should "forthwith appoint one within their town, to teach all such children, as shall resort to him, to write and read, whose wages shall be paid, either by the parents or masters of such children, or by the inhabitants in general."

Under such laws, Stamford could do no less than make full legal provision for the education of the young. The one central school house was early built, and to it, all the first generation of the town children were sent. And it came to be a settled principle that all classes, alike, must sustain, and receive their education from the town school. They made no provision for a superior education for a favored portion of the community; but seem, as occasional records show, to have made the needed provision for educating the children of the most "worshipful" part of the settlers, and then by penal motives, held the poorer class to the necessity of using them. Our very first record which refers at all to the school, indicates the existence in that early day of a better philosophy than has since then prevailed in our State.

It bears date, December 24, 1670, and is as follows: "ye towne hath agreede to hyr mr bellemy for a scoole Master for this yeare;" and as if to show that they were in earnest, and meant to discharge their full responsibility in that important trust they add: "ye towne doth graunt and agree to putt doun all peety scools yt are or may be kept in ye toune, which may be preiudicial to ye general scoole." "The toune hath graunted Mr. Mathew Bellemy a home lot of about one acere & halfe & he is hereby Ingaged to bouild a habitable house upon it within two years, before he alienate it to any one, or els to throw it up to ye toune again."

Whether Mr. Bellamy found the post too difficult to fill, or the pay too small for his support does not appear. We find the next spring, arrangements made for a new teacher, and the lot which had been assigned to Mr. Bellamy, transferred to a Rev. Wm. Clements. The votes passed respecting the new teacher, will indicate somewhat the literature of the day, and the propriety of a prompt and thorough trial of the master's vocation.

On the 31st of the 11th month, (January) 1670, it was voted in town meeting "that Mr. Rider be admited in to the town for a time of triall to keep school as a comite apointed for that end shall agree with him, and if after triall the town aprove him and he like to stay they may after acomidate him according to their capacity as they se good. Mr. Seleck, Fra. Brown and Jonathan Bell are chose to treat, and, if they can, so agree with Mr. Rider to teach school in the towne."

On the 2nd of 2nd month, (April) 1671, the town grant to Mr. Rider "so much timber of the ould meeting house as may build him up a room to the school house of about ten or twelve foot square, and in case he doth remove it shall return to the town."

Mr. Rider evidently did not suit the town, as the next year we find this record: "voted, the towne is not minded to hier Mr. Rider any more." At the same time the following vote shows how careful the town authorities were to see that the school master was paid for his services. "By vote, the town inioyne all the children that went to anny other scoole this last yeare, except only such that went only to larn to knitt or sowe, shall paye their proper fiiers, (fares) to the scoole master."

The above records, a literal transcript of the original, are themselves a very good exponent of the rude provisions made for the town school of that day. There seems to have been, as yet, only a single public school; and from the preceding record, the town was apparently accommodated by a room of ten or twelve feet square. This pioneer school room, for it could hardly be called a house, stood probably not far from where the old square school house of the first district in Stamford has so long stood, on the corner of Bank and Atlantic streets, a little to the east of the last one built there, now used as a dwelling house. Here were laid the foundations of whatever education the first two generations of the Stamford children received.

At this day, we can have no adequate conception of the extreme difficulty attending those early educational measures. So completely were the energies and resources of the settlers taxed to supply their physical wants, that we could hardly blame them for neglecting altogether those of their intellectual and social natures. And yet there was among them so clear a discernment of the need and worth of education, that no pains were spared to secure it for their children. Every one of those to whom would soon be entrusted the entire control of the new community here formed, must at least be so far taught as to learn "to read perfectly the English tongue," and write a legible hand. The civil magistrate was to make it his first concern to see that this result was reached.

Once, at least, each year, should he personally visit every family suspected of neglecting this duty, to call him to account. If no application should be made for the teacher's post, he was authorized to appoint some one, in whose competency he had confidence, and forthwith summon him to this work. And why should not some officer be required to "attend this duty of the town?" Was not every citizen liable to be called upon to serve the town in other departments of the public service, and was not the refusal to respond a finable offense? Why, then, should this, the most important of all the public interests be neglected, when citizens could be found competent to attend to them? Accordingly we find our highest civil dignitary making annual arrangements for the education of the young—teaching them himself at his own house, requiring some competent citizen, to arrange for the same needed service at his home; next engaging some applicant to perform this duty in the "scoole" house, built for the "better entertainment" of "scollers" on the corner of the town plat; and finally, as was his duty, when it came to be a necessity, choosing some one from some other pursuit, and requiring him, for a season, to serve the town as its official teacher. Such a summons, I think, must have been issued in 1680 to Stephen Bishop, probably a son of the pastor; and at the end of the year, the town, unwilling to impose excessive labors upon its officials, grant him a release from the service.

Thus the education of the young was managed by the town for about a century from its settlement. The first and second school rooms of course had to give way to larger, as the town increased, and by 1690, in September, we find on record a vote to build a new house. The old school house, which had been built of the remains of the old meeting house, and must therefore have been a much nobler structure and of nicer finish than the old rude germ of riven logs, and plank covering, which it had succeeded, was "by outcry" sold to the same Steven Bishop who had once, at least, been its acknowledged master. It may show us the times, at least thus much, to report the value of the sale, "twenty shillings and sixpence," but we must also report that the town reserved for their own use "ye dore hings and flores." It ought, perhaps, also to be added that the school house, now sold, had been quite recently improved by the addition of a stone chimney, a luxury which had doubtless been denied the home-warmed children in their home-made clothes, down to 1685.

The progress of the town had now become such that the one school house was thought to be too small for their accommodation; and the people at a distance from the center were beginning to feel the need of schools nearer to their own homes. Little schools were held for a few weeks at a time in two or three localities distant from the center. Temporary schools, also, sprung up to minister to some local want for some peculiar class of pupils; and it became a question what school or schools should receive the sanction or support of the public, at the public expense.

So, in 1702, the town were called in midsummer to settle this question. They vote as follows: "ye town doth say that they doth accept ye present scoole kept by ye person, (Samuel Holly then town clerk,) to teach to reade English and to write and arrithmitick—is a scoole according to lawe"—the simple meaning of which probably is, that reading, writing and arithmetic were the branches for which the law enabled them to make provision; and so they could sustain Mr. Holly's private school. The town meeting arrange also for the following schools, in addition to the town school at the center.

"Ye towne doth give liberty to ye people of ye east side of norwoaton Riuer, and ye people on ye west side side of ye mill riuer, to hire a woman scoole on boath sids ye sd riuer; and that ye mony collected in ye cuntry Rate shall be distributed to each scoole; yt is to say, to ye three scooles; on in ye middle of ye towne and ye other two above sd, according to ye heads in said scoole; and ye Rate to be paid by ye heads yt Goes to sd scools."

We now have provision for these three schools, but the records show that even this number was deemed too great, and that the muliplication of schools was strenuously opposed.

As early as 1702, we have seen a private school was established, probably to teach higher branches than the town school admitted. By the colony law a grammar school had been established in Fairfield for this part of the colony, to which the advanced pupils of the town had access; and it was probably to fit pupils for this county school or to aid those who could not attend it, that the private school had been opened. From time to time the town testified their approbation of the new school, and their confidence in "master Holly," by appropriations from the "county fund."

But it would seem the native teachers were not specially in favor with the town. In 1708, the committee, who were the select men of the town, were definitely instructed to hire "a stranger who is not a inhabitant to keep schoole upon Tryall." The support of the schools at this period was raised by a tax of 40 shillings on the 1000 pounds in the town list, and this was to be collected by the school committee when such were appointed and at other times by the selectmen; and if this were not sufficient, as in Stamford, it was increased by an assessment on scholars. In 1705 this additional assessment the town declare by vote "shall be paid by the scollars that goes to scoole."

But a permanent division of the town for school purposes took place in 1716; when it was voted in town meeting, that "all east of Benj. Hickox and all east of Noroton river, and all west of Mill river, shall have the privilege of their own county money for the encouragement of schools among themselves."

In 1722 the town granted to the inhabitants "north of Thos. June's and Stephen Bishop's jun." the same privilege as was allowed those east of the Noroton and west of the Mill river in 1716. The next year, however, we find the money divided into three parts, to be "E Qaull according to the lists;" but any family might send their children to either of the schools by paying there his proportion of the money.

In 1727 the Newfield people, as far north as Nathaniel Brown's, and as far south as Nathaniel Holly's, were allowed their school money; and the people on the west of Mill river were empowered to divide their money and build a school house "between Clement Buxton's and Benj. Green's where they can do it with the least damage to the public."

In 1734, the "Simsbury" people down to the Sequest, and over the river to "Tanton," are allowed their proportion of the school money.

This year marks a new era in the administration of the schools. They are now provided for, not in the town meeting as heretofore, but in the ecclesiastical Society meeting. By this meeting, orderly warned, Dec. 26, 1734, three committees are appointed to take care of the schools; the first consisting of Eliphalet Holly, Mr. Jona. Maltby, and Ebenezer Weed;

the second, of Capt. Jonas Hoyt, Joseph Waterbury, and Nathaniel Weed, and the third of Ensign Knapp, John Penoyer, and Nathaniel Webb. Though the record assigns them no restricted territory over which their respective jurisdiction is to extend, the names would leave us to assign to the first committee the center of the town, between Mill and Noroton rivers; to the second, all east of the Noroton, and to the third, all west of the Mill river.

Two years later three committees are again appointed, when the members are located as follows: Thomas Skelding and John Holly, middle of the town; Justice Wheeler, Jona. Clason and Moses Knapp, over Mill river; and Capt. Jona. Hoyt, Nath'l Weed, and Jona. Bell, over the Norcton river.

In 1739, the town give permission to "the inhabitants of the middle portion of the town to set up a school house on the west end of the town house, and the town's committee to stake out the place for them."

In 1744 the Simsbury people were allowed to use their part of the school money if they choose to do so at home, if not, it must go to the people on the west side of Mill river.

At this time, and for some years later, the school committee seem to have been appointed as one body, yet selected doubtless with reference to their residence in the different parts of the town. In 1747 this committee consisted of Ensign John Holly, Sergeant James Bell, Peter Demill, Col. Jona. Hoyt, Lieut. David Waterbury, Eb. Scofield, Monmouth Lounsbury, Miles Weed, Timothy Curtiss, Benj. Weed, jun., Sergt. Jona. Clason.

Books were in these days a somewhat rare article—and of course the day for the general distribution of newspapers had not yet come. But that the good people of the state who were supposed to be thoroughly instructed in divine law, might also have no excuse for remaining ignorant of our human code, the laws of the state had been printed for their use, and in the town meeting of 1756 we find this vote to secure their distribution: "the town agree that the law books shall be distributed into all parts of the town according to their lists of estates, to say £1,000 and a little more to a law book." To carry this vote into effect, Col. Jona. Hait, then, perhaps the most eminent man of the town, is appointed to make the distribution. The number of books thus furnished for distribution in the town was seventy.

That this work was not very thoroughly done, and that it was still felt to be an important measure for the town, we find proof in additional legislation passed in 1761; "that Col. Hait and Mr. Abraham Davenport shall divide the law books; viz.: law books according to act of assembly, by the first of March next."

And, as though the town felt themselves under still further obligations for the enlightenment of the people, they pass this additional vote: "that Col. Hait and Mr. Davenport shall divide the Confessions of Faith, by the first day of March next, on August list, 1760."

One more vote shows how earnest the town had become in this matter of circulating especially legal science among the people; viz.: "that every person that has got any of the law books and refuseth to deliver them to the committee appointed to divide them, shall incur the penalty of twenty shillings, lawful money."

This last record would suggest that this second division of the law books was simply a re-distribution of them, so that other citizens also could have access to them. And may it not be, that thus early we have in this town transaction, the hint of a town circulating library.

In 1772 a committee of whom Abraham Davenport was chairman, was appointed to report at the next annual society's meeting, some proper division of the society into school districts. This report was not recorded, but in 1775 it was voted that the school monies raised in the Society shall be delivered to committees of the respective districts in sd society according to their lists." The process of districting went so far, that the same territory which in 1716 needed but three districts, had been divided into not fewer than twenty-eight, leaving still, fragments of other districts, connected with those of the neighboring towns.

Stamford, it must be confessed, down to a date quite recent, had not been noticeable for any very marked eminence in education. The earlier attention given to this subject by the fathers, was certainly creditable to their times. The list of professional men, who from the settlement of the town, have here exercised their gifts. will compare favorably with that of our most advanced New England towns. We have had men of eminent ability in every profession. But from our comparative distance and isolation from the educational center of the state; from the somewhat urgent call on our young men to the exciting commercial temptations of the national metropolis; from the unfortunate dependence which the last two generations came to put upon the generous school fund, which instead of an aid and stimulus to the improvement, was too generally accepted as the sufficient support of our town schools; and from that unrecognized yet prevalent delusion among the wealthy, that the expensive education of the few would save a people from the reproach of neglecting the many, it followed that the town had educationally fallen behind many of her sister towns, and private schools came to be the main dependence of the citizens for the education of their children.

Dr. Dwight, in his Travels, probably did the town no injustice, when near the close of the last century he writes: "both religion and education have always been here at a low ebb; yet for many years there have been several good private schools, in which, however, children from New York are almost the only pupils."

As, however, the center of the town began to fill up, on the opening of the railroad through it, it was soon found that our public school at the center, was not doing the proper work of such an institution. The accommodations for pupils were neither sufficient in extent, nor suitable in character. After continued deliberation over the matter a new graded school was established in 1852, in a beautiful, and, as was supposed, ample structure at the east end of Broad street. This building was erected under the direction of J. D. Warren, Theodore Davenport, and Edwin Bishop. On the burning of this building in 1866, provision was made for a much ampler and more durable structure of brick on the same site. This elegant building was dedicated to school uses May 18, 1867. No more creditable school building has yet been erected for public school uses in the state. It is thoroughly finished in the best and latest style, and heated by the best steam heating apparatus in use. Its capacity is equal to the generous accommodation of eight schools of fifty pupils each; and the space occupied by it exceeds that of thirty-two just such structures as the pioneers of the town required for the first school house designed for the children dwelling on more than forty times the territory for which this provides.

It was the intention to raise the range of studies in the higher department of this school to embrace all those included in the regular course preparatory to college; and a number of students already have been fitted for college.

The present committee of the district are John D. Ferguson, Esq., L. H. Hurlbutt, M. D., and Thomas G. Ritch, Esq.

The Principals of this central school, thus far, have been: E. A. Lawrence, Rev. E. B. Huntington, Henry Balcam, Samuel Coburn, W. C. Ginn, and Alden P. Beals.

STAMFORD ENGLISH AND CLASSICAL BOARDING SCHOOL.

Among our private school enterprises, none have been more successful than that of James Betts, Esq. Mr. Betts is a native of Wilton, in this State. He opened a private school in North Stamford in 1838, but soon removed to his present location on Strawberry Hill. Here his career, from the first, has been one of great success. About five hundred youth have gone from this institution either to college or into business.

Mr. Betts is a deacon in the Congregational church, and earnestly alive to everything which promises to promote the welfare of the town. Though principal of a private school, he takes a deep interest in the public schools of the town; believing that the public school should be good enough for the richest families, as well as cheap enough for the poorest.

STAMFORD INSTITUTE.

Another successful school of the town is that established in 1850 on South street, by RICHARD E. RICE, Esq., a graduate of Yale in 1839. He was born in Saybrook, Conn., Feb. 8, 1810, and after his graduation, spent some three years in mercantile pursuits at the south, and subsequently located himself in Stamford, as above. While here he was chosen deacon in the Congregational church. His health giving way, he sold his school to WALLACE C. WILLCOX, of St. Louis, Mo. Mr. Willcox is also a graduate of Yale college, and a native of New Haven. Under his vigorous management the school has greatly prospered. Like his predecessor, Mr. Willcox was chosen deacon in the Congregational church.

GEO. B. GLENDINING'S SCHOOL.

Another school, which for several years has been well patronized, both by attendance from the town, and by boarding pupils, is that of GEO. B. GLENDINING, Esq., on the corner of Washington avenue and North street. Mr. Glendining is an English gentleman, educated at Oxford. He was engaged for years in a successful school in Troy, N. Y.; afterwards in Seymour, Conn.: and since 1853, in Stamford. The demand for admission into his school, has for several years exceeded its accommodation for pupils.

MISS ANNA WEBB'S SCHOOL.

This excellent school was commenced in 1854 and has continued to merit and receive the confidence of its patrons. Its average number of pupils is about thirty.

MISS AIKEN'S YOUNG LADIES' SEMINARY.

This institution was opened in the fall of 1855, in the commodious boarding house, on Henry street. From the first it has won a good name for the thoroughness of its instrucuction in all the essentials to a complete school education. In 1862 it was removed to Clark's Hill where under the efficient administration of Miss AIKEN, who has now associated with her, Mrs. Williams in the boarding department, the school has assumed the character of a permanent and flourishing institution. In all the qualities of an excellent young ladies seminary, very few in the country can surpass it.

THE MISSES SCOFIELD'S DAY SCHOOL.

This flourishing school for misses was opened in 1862 by Miss KATE SCOFIELD, eldest daughter of Edwin Scofield, jr., so long our Town Clerk. Since then the school has greatly increased, and Miss Scofield has associated with her her sister EMMA, under whose joint supervision it is becoming one of our most successful schools.

CLARK'S HILL INSTITUTE.

W. C. GINN, a graduate of the Wesleyan university at Middletown, Conn., opened this private school for boys,—both day and boarding pupils, in 1859. His accommodations are designed for a school of about twenty-five pupils.

CATHOLIC SCHOOL.

In 1862 this school was opened, for the children of Catholic parents, on Meadow street, near the Catholic church. The number of children in attendance has been about two hundred, under two teachers.

CHAPTER XXII.

WAR OF 1812—'15.

This war began in the vicious claim of England to the service of every subject born within her dominions, however long he might have been a resident and citizen of other countries, and ended in the effective denial, both on land and on the high seas, of any such authority over American citizens. Fought out, largely, on the sea, the war excited here comparatively little local concern or interest. Our records show no public meetings or action with reference to the war. Probably none was needed. Our citizens, however, were called on for such service as their position justified; and they heartily responded to the call. The town enrolled men and kept them in readiness for service when the needed emergency should come; and the most that our record proposes is to register their names and service. My first list is found on the following "muster roll of a company of infantry under the command of David Waterbury, Capt. in the 37th Regt. of the U. S., commanded by Lieut-Col. Aaron Benjamin, from the 31st Oct. when last mustered to the 31st Dec., 1813." The roll was furnished for use in this History by Charles Brown, Esq., son of John Brown, the first lieutenant on the roll.

On the back of this muster roll, in very distinct and ambitious chirography, is inscribed, in the captain's hand, "Don't give up the Ship." "Lawrence." "David Waterbury."

David Waterbury, Capt.;
John Brown, 1st Lieut.;
Henry Hoyt, 2nd Lieut.;
Samuel Keeler, 3rd Lieut.;
Samuel Keeler, jr., Ensign;
Alanson Holly, Sergt.;
Nehemiah Rose, Sergt.;
Lewis Jones, Corp.;
Wm. Jones, Corp.;
James Sandford, Drummer;
Nathan Champlin, Drummer;

David Brown,
Wm. H. Buel,
Joseph Clock,
Elisha Crab,
Ebenezer Dennis,
John Dean,
John A. Dickens,
James Forbes,
Elisha Fish,
Shadrack Ferris,
Lysander Fancher,
George A. Fox,
Charles French,
Charles Gill,
Warren Huchins,
Joel Hoyt,
Daniel Johnson,
Reuben Knapp,
John Larkin,
Moses Mountcalm,
Benjamin Odle,
Harry Provost,
Isaiah Rogers,
Charles Rowlson,
Amos Stickland,
William Stevens,
J. W. Shallenburg,
Selleck Scofield,
Oliver J. Smith,
David Tucker,
Samuel K. Weeks,
Isaac Wilmoth.

Our second list is that found on the following muster roll, now in the Controller's Office in Hartford. It is the roll of Captain Elijah Reed's Company in the 34th Regt., commanded by Nehemiah Lockwood, and bearing date Sept. 8-13, 1813 It has on it the following minute, probably in the handwriting of the Captain:

"The enemy appearing hostile in the Sound by the verbal order of Nehemiah Lockwood, Esq., Lieut.-Col. comt, I called the Company into service on the 8th of Sept., 1813 and on the 13th, by his verbal order dismissed them."

Elijah Reed, Capt.;
Jas. Clock, Lieut.;
Ralph Hoyt, Ens.;
Selleck Weed, 1st Sergt.;
John Street, 2nd Sergt.;
Abr. Tibbet, 3rd Sergt.;
David Camp, 4th Sergt.;
Holly Bell, 1st Corp.;
Roswell Reed, 2nd Corp.;
Jacob Wardell, 3rd Corp.;
Isaac Bishop, 4th Corp.;
Geo. Weed,
Isaac Warren,
Seely Slason,
Isaac Bouton,
Chas., Brown,
Lewis Waterbury,
Scudder Weed,
Chas. Weed,
Lyman Seely,
Henry Smith,
John M. Nash,
Raymond Mather,
Fred. Smith,
David Scofield,
Nathan Nash,
Samuel Street,
Leander Hoyt,
Ezra Hoyt,
David How,
Jas. B. Weed,
Walter B. Hoyt,
Marza Scribner.
David Weed,
Joseph Wood,
Jacob Little,
Chatman Smith,
Andrew Bixbee,
Samuel Holden,
Benj. Little,
Jonas Weed,
David Holly, drummer, not on duty;
Joseph Scofield, absent;
Peter Stevens, appeared, but excused for ill health;
Alvah Scofield, not called on;

Isaac Weed,
Henry Weed
John L. Webb,
Hervey Waterbury,
Samuel Waterbury, lived remote ;
Thos. Robertson, not called on ;
John A. Scofield, not called on.

Our third list is that of the company in command of Captain Peter Smith, then lieutenant. The following roll is now in the Controller's Office in Hartford. It is headed with this minute,

"Co. 3, commanded by Peter Smith, lieutenant, Col. Samuel Dean's regiment, September 8-12, 1813."

The company was called out on the appearance of a hostile fleet, and was stationed for four days on Shippan Point. They were allowed twenty cents a day by the government—the lieutenant, commanding, having received sixty cents a day.

Isaac Knapp, Sergt. ;
Jas. Webb, Sergt. ;
John Selleck, Sergt. ;
Luther Knapp, Sergt. ;
Chas. S. Gaylor, Corp. ;
Andrew Webb, Corp. ;
Elisha Hawley, Corp. ;
Darius Lockwood, Drummer ;
Lewis Lockwood, Fifer ;
Isaac Ferris,
Solomon Garnsey,
John Andrews,
Moses W. Smith,
Smith Knapp,
Benj. Hoyt, jr.,
Thos. Weeks,
Isaac Nichols,
Wm. Waterbury, 6th,
John Hanchaw,
Wm. W. Scofield,
Jas. Hoyt. jr.,
Josiah Austen,
Alanson Provost;
Epenetus Scofield,
Annanias Hoyt,
Wm. Scofield, jr.,
Eber Smith,
Drake Studwell,
Jas. Smith, jr.,
Elisha Scofield,
Gilbert E. Waterbury.

The following are still other names of our townsmen who were in the service. Their names have been collected from various sources, such as seemed entitled to credit.

John Billings, who is still living on Longridge, was at New London.
John Dan and Jonathan Dan, were also at New London.
Reuben Dibble, son of John, was for twenty-three months a prisoner in the famous Dartmoor prison.
Stephen Haight, of North Stamford, then living in New York, was in regular service.
Alanson Holly, enlisted and served.
Amasa Lounsbury was in the navy.
William W. Lounsbury was taken prisoner at New Orleans, in 1812.
Harvey Scofield at New London, in 1812.
Samuel Sherwood, at New London.
John Sherwood, son of Matthew, was in Canada.
John Burgess.
Elisha Leeds.
Noah Lockwood.
Solomon Scofield.
Ezra Stevens.
Lewis Waterbury.
Sylvanus Meed.
James Sniffin.
James Weed.

Tyler Mead was in service at Saratoga.
Squire Palmer was sergeant at New London.
Samuel Provost was pensioned for service.
Scudder Weed.
Henry Sniffin.
Silas Weed.
Rufus Weed.

Among the natives of Stamford who rendered good service during this war was also NATHANIEL WEED, Esq., now of Darien. At the opening of the war he had just become well established in business; but at the call of the government he consented to accept a captaincy in the army. At the close of the war he had reached the rank of colonel, and won a good name for his uniform promptness and efficiency at every post. (See later biography.) Harvey Weed, brother of Nathaniel, was also in service in this war. He was a lieutenant and was appointed paymaster. Like his brother, he was living in New York. He is now residing in Newburg, N. Y.

Captain WILLIAM SKIDDY, now an honored resident here, was an active participant in the naval struggles of the war. At its opening, he was before the mast. He was midshipman on board the Hornet, captain Nicholas Biddle, in the successful fight with the Penguin; and the following graphic account from his journal will be of sufficient historical interest for insertion here. It has never before been printed. The squadron in which the Hornet sailed consisted of the President, Hornet, Peacock, Tom-Bowline, and a private armed merchant brig.

"The ships were prepared for sea by the middle of December (1814) but were so closely watched by a much larger squadron in the offing, New York harbor that no opportunity presented of sailing until the 13th of the following January; when all the ships except the President, succeeded in getting to sea with orders to rendezvous at the island of Tristan d'Acanha, on the coast of South America, and there await the order of the President."*

We will now leave the journal to tell its own story.

"Nothing material took place until the 15th of March, when we arrived off Tristian d'Acunha, in latitude 37 south, and longitude 11 west. Our first lieutenant, D. Conner, had just landed, when the signal was made to return, there being a strange sail in sight bearing down for us. We hove to,

* Perkins' Later War.

and were getting dinner (it was duff day), while she was running down. The "duff" was hardly swallowed, when the drum beat to quarters; this required but a few minutes, and all was ready for action, every eye watching the stranger. He soon luffed to on our weather quarter, about pistol shot off, hoisted the British flag, and gave us a gun; this we did not notice, waiting for him to shoot ahead more.

He now gave us the first broadside, and as soon as the guns flashed, ours were in operation, and in five minutes I perceived the blood running from his scuppers a stream, and as he almost stopped firing, our little captain ordered us to cease. The enemy thinking we were disabled, renewed his fire, and, of course, we soon convinced him of his mistake. He then, as a dast alternative, ran his bowsprit between our main and mizen masts, with the intention of carrying us by boarding. I was stationed with the first lieutenant in the third division on the quarter deck, (three after guns each side), and was now commanding this division, the first lieutenant having been severely wounded at the commencement and carried below. The jib halyards being shot away, the fore-tack was hauled down to veer the ship. The enemy was now fast of us, and all hands called to repel boarders. We were then hand to hand, and the enemy soon driven back. We were now on the enemy's bows, and it required all the exertions of our captain and officers to prevent our men from boarding them; had they gone, the enemy would have suffered very much. Their men were now (heaving the cry for us to board,) running below, and left their first lieutenant, McDonald, alone on the forecastle. Many muskets were levelled at him, but were prevented by our officers from firing on so brave a man. He then asked our leader, the second lieutenant, Lieutenant Newton, the name of the ship, and was answered, 'U. S. sloop Hornet,' when he waived his sword and walked aft.

Our ship in shooting ahead, carried away his bowsprit, tore away all our mizzen rigging, and the enemy lay across our stern. Our captain was standing on the arm-chest aft, speaking to them, when their foremast fell along the lee waist. The marines in the fore-top clung with their muskets to the rigging as the mast fell, and as soon as down, jumped forward, fired, and wounded our captain, the ball passing through his neck. They undertook to rakes us with their bow guns, then opposite our stern. I was standing in one of the stern ports (being open), looking directly at them, and only about twelve feet off. We were then all hands aft to prevent their boarding, and certainly expected to see many of us fall at that fire. Had those guns been well directed, many of us must have been killed, but fortunately at that very moment the sea lifted our ship's stern, and the balls went under the counter in the water.

Our ship now came round on the other tack, [port] and I played my division of guns into them, raking them fore and aft. They again cried quarter, and our captain ordered me to cease firing.

She proved to be H. B. M. sloop-of-war Penguin, Captain Dickinson, who was killed during the action, by a ball through the heart. She mounted nineteen guns,--sixteen thirty-two pounders, two long nines, and one twelve pounder on the forecastle. They reported fifteen men killed, and twenty-eight wounded, They had a number of men on board from the Medway, seventy-four, and was sent expressly to cruise for the young Wasp privateer. We made out by the rolls on board of her, twenty-five killed, and several of those wounded died.

The Hornet was the same length, one foot less beam. The size and number of guns, except the twelve pounder on her forecastle. We had one man killed, and eleven wounded, and all in the after division--my division. The poor fellow that we killed, was a six-foot marine that was firing over my head, and the first I perceived was his brains on my shoes ; and in turning, I observed the top of his skull taken off by a ball. As he was much in the way, I shoved him through one of the ports overboard.

The first lieutenant was also wounded, standing by me. I carried him out of the way of the guns, and had him sent below.

The most painful was the heart-sickening sight after the fight, of all those poor fellows who, only a few minutes ago, were well and joyful, now mangled by different kinds of balls and splinters. Groans were heard from all quarters. We were now employed getting the prisoners on board, unbedding and bending sails, repairing rigging, and replacing, soon as possible, all damages. This called us from the dying groans of the wounded. The surgeons were all employed amputating limbs and dressing wounds. The prize taken in tow, and night visited the dismal scene. Several died during the night, and were committed to the deep without any ceremony, and the captain, Dickinson, was buried the day after with the honors of war ; his own officers and marines officiating.

Penguin's number of men	158
Hornet's " "	130
Difference in men	28

In addition to the above account, we have only to add that a number of our townsmen during this "war of the sea," laid the foundation of their fortunes in privateering. How many of them were thus favored, and to what extent their fortunes were increased, we are without records to show.

CHAPTER XXIII.

PHYSICIANS AND LAWYERS OF STAMFORD.

PHYSICIANS.

MOEN or MOENE, JACOB, is the first member of the medical profession whose professional title I have found on our records.

The first record in which this name occurs, bears date Mar. 4, 1701-2. In regular town meetings, " by voat ye town do grant to Mr. Jacob Monen, chirgaim, (chirurgeon,) that peese of land in Rocky neck which ye town had of Stephen Bishop upon exchange, for his incouragement to build on upon conditions that he settle among us."

Another bears date Oct. 6, 1707. In it, Jacob Moon sells land to David Smith, and the "Majesties' justice," Samuel Peck, before whom he witnessed the sale, calls him Doctor Jacob Moene. I find an earlier record in which Jacob Moon and Mrs. Abigail Selleck were recorded as married Jan. 11, 1704-5; and subsequently several children are recorded to them. On the 10th of October, 1707, Dr. Jacob Moen, chirurgeon, desiring to remove to New York, acknowledges receipt from John Gold, jun., on account of his father, John Gold, sen., yeoman, one gray mare, one quarter of mutton, and twelve pounds of flax. This receipt is signed, Doctor Jacob Moene. This name is spelled by the recorder Moon as well as Moen; and it is subscribed by the Doctor himself, neither the one or the other, but Moene. When he came hither and how he succeeded in his profession, we know as little as we do concerning the orthography of his name.

DREW, JOHN, is the second name on our records which bears

this professional title. He married here, Feb. 4, 1714, Elizabeth, a daughter, probably, of one Joseph Green. Mrs. Drew is on record as having died Mar. 25, 1716; and of Dr. Drew, nothing further appears on record.

Bishop, Ebenezer, stands third on the medical list. This name is found on page 58 of the records of births, marriages and deaths, Book No. I. The record informs us that Doctor Ebenezer Bishop dyed on October ye 4th day, 1743. The same record gives us the death of Thomas, a brother of the doctor; of Mrs. Sarah Jefferey, his sister; and Sarah, his mother.

Hubbard, Nathaniel, is our fourth recorded "Doctor;" and the first mention of his name with its professional title, is in the year 1748, when he is reported as a member of the school committee. It is still remembered by some of our oldsst citizens that a physician of this name once lived in the house on South Street, just north of the residence of John Furguson, Esq. It is also remembered that he was spoken of as a man of unusual skill in his profession; that he was a very active and energetic man; that he was remarkably prompt and forcible both in speech and act; and that his unusual force of character and expression, together with his inexorable practical applications, left the impression that he was a man of unfeeling and cruel harshness. He probably is the Nathaniel Hubbard who married, May 18, 1733, Mary Quintard. They had a son, Nathaniel, who was b. Apr. 29, 1745. In 1853 he sells land lying on the road to Stanwich.

On our list of physicians should be found the names of several "ancient" dames of the town, in whose hands for the first hundred years probably was the most of the medical practice known here. It is hardly probably that they were ever matriculated, M. Ds., as this branch of the medical faculty was yet to come, nor were they, probably, professionally taught the healing art; yet they exercised such gifts and skill of healing as came to them when the necessity for such practice arose.

That the profession was honorable in these early days is plain from the honorable mention made of it in the records, as witness the following: "Mrs. Sarah Bates, a useful and skillful midwife, departed this life in Stamford in the evening of the eighteenth day of February in the year 1711-12."

PEREZ FITCH, who graduated at Yale in 1750, stands next on the list. He was born in Canterbury, a son of Major James F. Fitch and great grandson of Rev. James Fitch, the first minister in Norwich. He married here Sept. 4, 1753, Mrs. Martha Coggshall; and they had children recorded to them; Martha, b. July 20, 1754; William, b. Oct., 10, 1756; Abigail, Mar. 29 1760; Kate, baptized in 1763; Betsey, b. Oct. 4, 1765, and Samuel, b. Aug. 20, 1768.

Dr. Fitch united with the church here, by letter, Sept. 9, 1759; and Martha, his wife, July 6, 1760. In 1757, Capt. Perez Fitch is ordered to sit in the fore pew in the meeting house, which fact sufficiently indicates the social position of the family at that date. Dr. Fitch died before 1776; and of course we have no citizens now left who have any personal knowledge of him or of his professional standing. We have those still living, however, who remenber to have heard him spoken of as a very affable and pleasant gentleman; as urbane and courtly as his competitor, Dr. Hubbard was, forcible and rough. After his death his widow married, Aug. 8, 1776, the Hon. Abraham Davenport, of this town.

COGGSWELL, JAMES, son of the Rev. Dr. James and Alice (Fitch) Coggswell, of Windham, Scotland Society. After studying medicine, he was settled for a while in Preston; and on the opening of the revolutionary war he was commissioned a surgeon. In the practice of his official duties, he was stationed in this vicinity, and while the war was going on, he married here, August 8, 1776, Elizabeth, third child of Hon. Abraham and Elizabeth (Huntington) Davenport. While here he seems to have been active, both in the affairs of the church and those of the town. On the death of Dr. Welles, in 1776, he was appointed on the committee of supply for the church. In 1779, while the war was still going on, the town voted him liberty "to set up a small pox hospital at the house of Capt. Reuben Scofield, and at such other houses not within one mile of the heart of the town, after liberty first obtained of the neighborhood; and all such hospitals to be under the inspection of the selectmen." Dr. Coggswell remained here until after the war. His wife died, November 15, 1779, and he married the second time, May 18, 1783, Mrs. Abigail Lloyd, by whom he had children—James, John, Sarah, and Harriet. He removed from Stamford to New York city, where he became eminent both for professional skill and for his unobtrusive yet effective piety. His first wife left one daughter, Alice, who became the wife of the Rev. Dr. Samuel W. Fisher, of Greenbush, N. Y., and the mother of Rev. Dr. Samuel W. Fisher, Pres. of Hamilton College.

Hough, Walter, was stationed here as surgeon during the revolutionary war, having his post at the fort on Fort Hill, on the lot on which John Clason, Esq., has recently built. He remained here some years after the war. He married Patty, a daughter of Dea. Daniel Lockwood, and lived about a mile south of the fort. While here, his son John was born, August 17, 1783. After the birth of this son, the family removed to Canterbury.

Hubbard, Nathaniel, was the son of Henry Hubbard, and was born March 4, 1772, in Greenwich, Stanwich Society, a short distance west of the Stamford line. After being licensed to practice medicine, he located himself first in Greenwich, and then for a short time in Carmel, N. Y., and in 1796, he established himself at what has since been known as Hubbard's Corner, in the west part of Stamford. He soon became known as a successful physician, and his practice rapidly extended. For quite a number of years his business was very great, and his health was seriously impaired. His nervous system was so much deranged, as to require him to abandon, at length, his practice. In the vigor of his manhood he was noted for a remarkable memory, and for unusual powers of observation. Our records give us a partial report of his marriage. "Dr. Nathan iel Hubbard and Mary Hubbard were married by Mr. Platt Buffet, pastor of the church in Stanwich." The important point of such a record, the date, is omitted. The children of doctor and Mary, his wife, are registered as follows: Arch, b. in Greenwich, October 14, 1798; Henry, b. in Carmel, N. Y., August 17, 1800; Alexander, b. in Stamford, June 3, 1804; Mary, b. October 28, 1806; John Wheaton, b. May 26, 1808; George Mackay, b. June 10, 1810; Eleanor, b. October 10, 1812; Sarah Thomas, b. February 17, 1815, Cornelia, b. May 16, 1817; William, b. July 24, 1719; and Francis, b. August 17, 1821. Dr. Hubbard died in Stamford, June 27, 1855.

TOWNSEND, PLATT, is reported here in 1763. The town assigned land to him, and made over to him an old highway that went from the "landing place" to Totomok Point, provided he would secure to the town a good road to said landing, through his land. He married here, April 26, 1760, Elizabeth, daughter, probably, of Nathaniel and Mary Quintard Hubbard, who was born here, May 18, 1743; and had a daughter, Elizabeth, b. April 25, 1763. In 1777, he deeds to Charles Wright, of Hartford, the Tatomoc bottom lands: three islands in Stamford harbor, near Rocky Neck and Jack's and Grassy islands, near Shippan. In this deed he is said to be of Greenwich.

WILSON, JOHN, is reported as being a native of the town. He commenced practice here about 1760. He was evidently much respected in town; and during our revolutionary war was one of the most influential of our citizens. He remained here until 1796, when he removed to New York city, where he died in 1802. He had four sons. John, who became a physician, and was settled in New York city; Stephen, also a physician, of New York city; James, who was a physician of Westchester county; and Henry, b. October 10, 1763, a physician, who settled in Bedford. He had also two daughters—Phebe, b. September 9, 1765, and Mary.

After the death of the mother of the above children, he married again, June 16, 1787, Mrs. Elizabeth Holly. Our town records, under date December 7, 1784, thus report him to us:

"Upon application made by Dr. John Wilson, praying liberty to carry on the innoculation of the small pox under proper regulations. Voted, That the town grant the above request, and authorize the civil authority and selectmen to grant liberty to said Wilson to carry on innoculation under the direction of said authority, as the law directs."

WILSON, JOHN, JR., was with his father in business here for some years, and then went to New York city. While here, he married, August 12, 1778, Lydia Quintard. The births of two of his children, are recorded here—John Quintard, b. February 3, 1781; and Isaac, b. April 22, 1783. He became somewhat eminent in the city.

SMITH, ISAAC, was here in 1780, and as late as 1789, as physician. He was son of Nathaniel and Abigail Smith, and married Abigail Waring.

DARIUS KNIGHT, brother of Dr. Jonathan Knight, of Norwalk, was a teacher in this town, and afterwards a practicing physician for a couple of years. He was located in Darien.

JAMES KNIGHT, son of Dr. Jonathan Knight, of Norwalk, settled here in the practice of medicine, and died soon after wards, in 1818.

SAMUEL WEBB, was born here, March 7, 1760, and was son of Col. Charles Webb, who so distinguished himself in our revolutionary war. He graduated at Yale, in 1779, and soon established himself here in the medical profession. He became eminent in his profession, and eminent also in civil life. He represented Stamford in the state legislature several times, and was one of the most active citizens in all measures which promised the social welfare of the community.

He had studied medicine with Dr. John Wilson, an eminent physician of the town. He married December 15, 1781, Mary, a daughter of Dr. Wilson, and by her, had Charles, b. September 29, 1782, who became a seaman, and died in China; John

Wilson, born August 3, 1784, who was also a seaman and captain, and who died of yellow fever in New Orleans; Henry Wilson, b. November 28, 1786, and became an eminent physician in New York; William, who died in Lima, Peru; Mary and Betsey who died single in Stamford; Cornelia, who died single in Indiana; Caroline, who became the wife of William H. Holly, Esq., and who is still living; Angeline, and Catherine, who married a Morehouse, of Indiana. On the death of his first wife, he married a Miss White, of Ballstown, N. Y., and had by her, James A., who was in the whale fishery, hailing from Nantucket, and was lost; Lucy P., who married a Mr: Shaw, and now lives in Nova Scotia; Fanny, who married a Mr. Royce, and died in Nova Scotia; and Elizabeth, now Mrs. Thomas, of Sacramento, Cal. Dr. Webb occupied the house still known as the "Webb house," on Atlantic street, where he died, December 29, 1826.

WARREN PERCIVAL, son of Dr. Percival, of East Haddam, where he was born, April 5, 1783. Three of his uncles and four of his brothers were physicians. He studied with his uncle James, father of the poet Percival, and on being licensed to practice medicine, located himself in Middlesex parish, Stamford. Here he remained until his death in 1851, having practiced his profession for forty-six years. He was always a careful but successful practitioner, and died regretted by all his old friends and patrons. In 1809, Dr. Percival married Sarah, a daughter of Major David Street, and by her had two children, the eldest, a daughter, who married Dr. Chauncey Ayres; and the other, a son, who died in 1854. Dr. Percival survived both his children; but his widow is still living on the old homestead in Darien, in 1868.

SAMUEL LOCKWOOD, was one of ten children of Ezra and Anna (Davis) Lockwood, of Stamford. His parents had moved to Watertown where he was born in July, 1787. In 1801, the family returned to Stamford. After studying medicine with Dr. Elton, of Watertown, he graduated at the New York Medical College, and soon opened an office here, on the north side of Park place, where Mr. Swartwout now lives. His practice be came quite extensive, and he at once rose to eminence in his profession. He was also much esteemed as a citizen. On retiring from active business in 1838, he removed to the homestead of his father and grandfather, and built near it the residence now occupied by Israel Minor.

He married Helen Sheddon, a native of Scotland. His children were, Robert, John, William, Ann, Francis, and Helen, now Mrs. Phyffe, of New York, the only surviving member of the family.

JOHN AUGUR came to North Stamford as a teacher, about 1800, and was successor of Rockwell & Foote. He was a good physician, and remained here until his death, April 16, 1827, aged fifty years. His widow continued to reside in the house he left, until her death, in 1865.

SAMUEL BEACH came to Stamford in 1827. He at once enrolled himself as member of the Congregational Society, and in 1830 was chosen deacon of the church. He was very active in the church, and was a popular man in the community. He removed to Bridgeport in 1834, and was one of the victims of the Norwalk railroad disaster of May 6, 1853.

WILLIAM TURK, about 1805, a choir leader in the Congregational church, and was thought skillful in his profession. He had been a surgeon in the United States navy, to which he returned when he left his practice in Stamford.

—— ROCKWELL, was several years in North Stamford, and went to New York city.

BENJAMIN ROCKWELL, son of above, became a physician, and after practicing with his father, went to New York.

URIAH TURNER, an intelligent man and skillful physician was here a few years, and went to New York.

A few other names have appeared, for a brief time, on the list of practicing physicians in the town, of which I have been unable to learn any other facts. Their names have been, FOOTE BANKS, CHILDS, TUCKER, and CLOSE.

NATHANIEL D. HAIGHT, a native of Peekskill, N. Y., graduated in medicine at Pittsford, N. Y., in 1825, and came to Stamford in 1826, settling first at North Stamford, but soon removing to the village, where he has had an extensive practice ever since. He married in 1824 Phebe Dauchy of Ridgefield. They have had three children; Wm. B., now in the drug business in Stamford; Bradford; and Mary E., wife of Samuel H. Holmes of Stamford.

CHAUNCEY AYRES, born in New Canaan, Ang. 14, 1808; graduated in medicine at Yale in 1831. He first opened an office in Greenwich, and later in New York, but after a few months settled permanently here in 1834, where he has secured a good practice. His first wife was daughter to Dr. Percival, of Darien; and their children were a son, now engineer in the U. S. N., and three daughters. His second wife was Mrs. Julia A. Simpson, of Brooklyn, N. Y., by whom he has three children.

HARRISON TELLER, settled in 1843, in Stamford, and after ten year's practice, went to Brooklyn, N. Y. His wife and two daughters were members of the church in North Stamford in 1848.

SAMUEL SANDS has practiced medicine for several years in Darien, where he still resides.

ROBERT LOCKWOOD, son of Dr. Samuel above, was a native of the town. He studied medicine with his father, and took his diploma from the New York Medical College. He engaged here in the practice of medicine, and in the drug business, but died at the early age of thirty.

LEWIS RAYMOND HURLBUTT, is a native of Wilton. He graduated at Yale in 1843, was tutor from 1847 to 1850, when he received his medical diploma. He came to Stamford in 1852, and from the first took a high rank in his profession. He married Matilda, daughter of Augustus R. Moen, of Stamford, and has had seven children.

WILLIAM H. TROWBRIDGE, son of James H., of Danbury, graduated in medicine at Yale in 1835, and located himself here in 1851. Excepting the period he was in the service of the government as army surgeon he has been in successful practice.

JOSEPH HOWE, a native of Bedford, N. Y., where he studied medicine. He settled in North Stamford in 1853, where he died of consumption, after a successful practice of eight years, Nov. 2, 1861. He was a worthy christian gentleman, as well as a good physician.

GEORGE HUNTINGTON, a graduate of Albany Medical College was here a few months, and went to Portage City, Wis. He was surgeon in the Union army during the late war.

GEORGE W. BIRCH, a native of New York city. He studied medicine in Brookfield, Conn., and graduated M. D. at Yale in 1858, and settled first in Reading, and in 1861 came to North Stamford, as successor to Dr. Howe. He has this year, (1868) removed to the Borough of Stamford and opened his office on the corner of Atlantic and Broad Streets.

RUSSELL Y. GRISWOLD, graduated at Williamstown College in 1832 and in medicine at Pittsfield, Mass. He commenced practice in Lanesboro, Mass., and in May, 1859, settled in Stamford.

B. KEITH, came to Stamford from New York city, where he had been for many years a medical practitioner. His specialty is in the treatment of chronic diseases.

PIERRE R. HOLLY, son of Wm. Welles Holly, of Stamford, graduated at Yale in 1852. After a practice of a few years in the West Indies, and in Greenwich, Conn., he settled, here, in his profession in 1860.

JAMES H. HOYT, a native of New Caanan, graduated in medicine at the College of Physicians and Surgeons, New York and practiced in that city one year, and afterwards in Greenwich. He came to Stamford in 1867 and went into partnership with Dr. Haight.

LAWYERS.

The following embraces all whom I have found accredited to Stamford, at any time, as lawyers. The list begins in 1797, when the State Register reports the first two on the list.

JOHN DAVENPORT, the first child of Hon. Abraham and Elizabeth (Huntington) Davenport, was born in Stamford, Jan. 16, 1752. He graduated at Yale in 1770. His scholarship is indicated in his appointment to a tutorship in 1773. Entering on the legal profession, he was soon called to take an important place among the revolutionary patriots of that day. With a major's commission he was employed in commissary department, and his duties here were often onerous and difficult. When the patriot cause was suffering for the want of a suitable public interest in the welfare of the new nation just ordained by the declaration of independence, he was appointed by the Assembly of the state as one of a commission to visit the principal towns and arouse the people to a just sense of their dangers and move them to corresponding exertions.

On the death of his brother James, in 1799, he was chosen to take his place in the national Congress, and held his seat in the House of Representatives until 1817, when he declined a re-election. He was a member of the Congregational church in Stamford, of which he was appointed deacon in 1795. This was the office in which his eminent goodness was best shown. He was, to his death, an example of earnest, living piety, whose fruits were ever manifest in the character of a benevolent, fervent and exemplary christian. His death occurred Nov. 28 1830.

His wife was Mary Sylvester Welles, daughter of the Rev. Dr. Noah Welles, of Stamford. They were married May 7, 1780. Their children were, Elizabeth Huntington, who married Judge Peter W. Radcliffe, of Brooklyn, N. Y.; John Alfred, who recently died in New Haven, Conn.; Mary Welles, who married James Boorman, Esq., of New York city; Theodosia, who died in her twenty-second year; Theodore, still,

1868, a deacon in the Congregational church of which his great grandfather was so long a pastor; Rebecca Ann, who died young; and Matilda, now the wife of Rev. Peter Lockwood, of Binghamton, N. Y.

JOEL T. BENEDICT, son of Rev. Mr. Benedict of North Stamford, after a short practice of his legal profession became a preacher.

JAMES STEVENS, was the youngest child of David and Mary (Talmage) Stevens, and was born July 4, 1768, in that part of Stamford, Ponus Street, which has since been incorporated with the town of New Canaan. He became a lawyer, and opened an office in his native town, in the village of Stamford. He was a man of considerable native talent, and joining heartily n the democratic movement, then inaugurated, he won his way to a seat in the house of representatives of our national congress. He was in that famous congress which passed the "Missouri Compromise," and gave his vote for that measure. He represented Stamford thirteen times in the state legislature, and was much in public life until his death, which took place Apr. 4, 1835.

A brief obituary of him in the *Sentinel* of that date, says;

"Mr. Stevens has been extensively known as a kind neighbor and friend, as a politician of sterling integrity, and as an inflexible advocate of democratic principles. He has represented this town in both branches of the legislature of this state; was for some time a judge of the county court; has been a representative from this state in the congress of the United States."

While here he married in 1813, Mary, fourth daughter of Thaddeus Hoyt. They had two daughters, Mary H. and Ann C. Stevens, both of whom are still living.

MINOR, SIMEON H., was son of —— ——, of Woodbury, where he was born, in 1777. He was descended from that Thomas Minor who was born at Chew Magna, England, April 23, 1608. Came to New England in 1630, and settled in New London in 1645, where he died in 1690. He was a prominent man among the settlers in eastern Connecticut. His family name dates back to about the middle of the fourteenth century, when the Third Edward bestowed it upon Henry the Miner, of Mendippe Hills, Somersetshire, England, for his prompt efficiency in furnishing him an escort, as he embarked on that famous invasion of France, in which he won the battle of Crecy, against so great odds.

John Minor, third son of John, of New London, was born in 1634, so Cothren, in his History of Woodbury, says, went to Stratford, and thence to Woodbury, and was a leading man for years.

Simeon H., of Stamford, was probably a great, great grandson of this second John. On being admitted to the bar, he settled in Stamford in 1831, and spent here the rest of his life.

He rapidly won a high position at the Fairfield county bar, of which he was a prominent member until his death, August 2, 1840. The *Stamford Advocate*, of the same week, pays a high tribute to his professional ability. "Possessed of a strong mind, and sound legal judgment, no member of the bar commanded a greater share of practice, until his health began to fail him, than he. For fourteen years he discharged the office of state's attorney." He represented the town in six sessions of the legislature, and was judge of probate several years. In the discharge of all official duties he was prompt and efficient.

He married, in Stamford, May 31, 1812, Catherine Lockwood, of Greenwich. They had three children: James Hinman, b. November 17, 1813; William Thomas, b. October 3, 1815; and George Albert, b. June 19, 1817. His wife died, March 29, 1819.

Frederick Scofield, son of Benjamin, and brother of our venerable townsman, Selleck Scofield, was born, August 13, 1778. He graduated at Yale, in 1801, and entered the legal profession, and for a few years had an office here. He subsequently became a teacher in Philadelphia, where he died in 1841.

Wood, Joseph, was a descendant in the sixth generation, of

Jonas Wood, one of the pioneers of the settlement in Stamford. Joseph Wood, second, a great grandson of the pioneer, removed from Hempsted to Stanwich, where Joseph was born, March 24, 1779. His father David, son of the above Joseph, second, was among the respectable farmers of Stanwich, a man of intelligence and piety. His mother, Sarah Ingersoll, was noted for her cheerful and amiable disposition.

Brought up on his father's farm, he acquired habits of industry, and being of an inquisitive turn of mind, he commenced in his seventeenth year fitting for college. He graduated at Yale in 1801, and devoted himself to the legal profession. His law teacher was Judge Chauncy, of New Haven. He was admitted to the bar of New Haven, when he selected Stamford as the field for commencing his professional career. Here he opened an office in 1803, where he continued to practice until 1829. During his stay here, he was held in esteem as a good citizen, and honorable in his profession. He represented the town in the state legislature, and was judge of probate several years.

While here, he married, May 10, 1809, Frances, second daughter of Chief-Justice Oliver Ellsworth. She was born in Windsor, August 31, 1786, and died March 14, 1868, in New Haven, much revered and loved for her many excellent qualities both of her head and heart. Their children, six in number, were all born in Stamford. Their residence was the stone house, which has recently been transformed into the elegant mansion of our enterprising townsman, George A. Hoyt.

Frances Wolcott, their oldest daughter, was born, March 25, 1810, and is now the wife of Rev. S. Cowles, of Gowanda, N. Y.

Oliver Ellsworth, b. April 14, 1812, resides in New York city, where he has for years been well known in business circles.

George Ingersoll, b. May 20, 1814, graduated in Yale, in 1833, and is a congregational minister.

Delia Williams, b. September 20, 1820, is now the wife of Prof. C. S. Lyman, of Yale College; and William Cowper, b.

November 10, 1822, married Miss Lawrence, of Brooklyn, L. I., and is now living at Joliet, Ill.

In 1826, Mr. Wood removed to Bridgeport, thence to New York city in 1837, and from this city, in 1841, to New Haven, where he spent the remainder of his life. Here he stood among the first citizens of the classic city, in intelligence and social worth. He joined Dr. Bacon's church in 1843, by a public profession of the faith he had long cherished; and the confidence he won for his Christian character is best shown by his selection to fill a deaconship in that ancient church in 1848.

After his removal to New Haven, he was appointed judge of the county court, in which office he showed eminent qualities as jurist. His stern and sterling integrity never forsook him here. He was still later chosen to the office of the city clerk. His tastes were especially literary. While in New York he had edited an agricultural periodical. He had also gathered largely the materials for a memoir of his father-in-law, but never published it.

He died Nov. 13, 1856, during a session of the literary club at the residence of Rev. Pres. Day, just after an interesting discussion in which he had taken part.

Benjamin T. Shelton is reported as a practicing lawyers here in 1812.

Chalres Hawley was born June 15, 1792, in what is now the town of Monroe, formerly Huntington, and still earlier Stratford. His ancestors were among the early settlers of that old town, and both on his father's and mother's side,they were among the most respectable and honored of the settlers. Joseph Hawley, the progenitor of the family in this country, came to Stratford, probably with the pioneers of the town, and for many years was a leading man in the new colony. He represented the town several times in the state general assembly. In his will in 1689, he gives to his son Samuel all his "buildings and lands in Parwidge, Derbyshire, in old England," indicating thus, no doubt, the early English locality of the family.

On his mother's side, Mr. Hawley was descended from William Curtiss, another of the prominent settlers of Stratford. He also numbered among his Stratford ancestors, Henry De Forest, who fled from France on the revocation of the edict of Nantes, in 1655, and Richard Booth, the ancestor of another honored line.

Thus Mr. Hawley is found to belong to the best names of which our country can boast. From a record of his ancestry, gathered by him with much pains and care, we learn the following facts. His great, great grandmother, Bethia Booth, was born in 1658, and lived until 1759. At the time of her death, her grandson, Milton Hawley, the grandfather of Charles, was twenty-four years of age; and at the date of his death in 1819, Charles was twenty-six. Thus it was made possible for Mr. Hawley in 1865, to report from the lips of his grandfather, the the story which he had learned from the lips of his grandmother, of events coming under her personal observation, as far back as 1665.

Possibly so rare an opportunity of learning the family story, may account for one of the most marked characteristics of Mr. Hawley's later years, his strong family affection.

Mr. Hawley graduated at Yale college in 1816, and entered on the study of law in the Litchfield law school. On being admitted to the bar, he established himself in Stamford in 1819. From the first, his diligence in business, and his zeal in working, won the confidence of the public. That he might fit himself locally, for his profession, he made himself early familiar with the records and traditions of the town; and even became so much interested in these gleanings for professional use, as to form a plan of the history of the town. But he rose so rapidly in his profession that he found himself obliged to abandon this attempt; and so the opportunity of presevering much of the material for such a history, which then existed, was forever lost to the town.

Giving himself wholly to his professional work, he soon

placed himself among the first jurists of the State. From the very beginning of his professional career he was thorough, exact and exhaustive in whatever cause he undertook. His sense of right and justice was as keen as his discriminations of falsehood and truth; and this made him one of the most persistent and inexorable of advocates. A cause accepted by him became a bond on his conscience; and he could do no less than his best in its management.

He was never a politician, yet few men of the age had more carefully studied the whole science of government. Without seeking or wishing office he represented his adopted town in seven sessions of the state legislature, and once represented his senatorial district in the state senate. Once, also, he served the state as its Lieutenant-Governor.

But his tastes and aims were pre-eminently professional; and his success and reward, both in professional eminence and in substantial wealth, were very great. His estate was one of the largest ever gathered in the town, and it was as solid as it was large.

Of Mr. Hawley's fine literary tastes almost every plea he made for the last half of his professional career; and indeed his most ordinary conversation on ordinary topics, gave most abundant proofs. His language was exceedingly terse and exact, rising often under the glow of earnest feeling, to a high degree of strong and fervid eloquence.

In his religious experience, Mr. Hawley's record is peculiarly one of the conscience and heart. Educated early in the faith of the Congregational church, to the day of his death he accepted and cordially endorsed that faith. Without ever making a public profession of religion, few men have given better evidence of the control of religious principles; and both his lips and his life modestly, yet unequivocally assured those who knew him best, that his was the faith of Jesus.

Mr. Hawley was married Jan. 28, 1821, by the Rev. Jonathan Judd, rector of St. John's church in Stamford, to Mary S., daughter of David Holly, Esq., of Stamford. Their children were; Charles Augustus; Martha Coggshall, now Mrs. Brantingham; Jane De Forest, now Mrs. Windle; Marianna Clarke, now Mrs. Charles W. Brown; Emmeline Smith; Elizabeth King ; Maria Adelaide and Francis Milton. (See list of graduates.) With the exceptions of Mrs. Windle, and Maria who is dead the family are all now living in Stamford.

ALFRED A. HOLLY, son of John Wm. and Rebecca (Welles) Holly, of Stamford, graduated at Union college in 1818, was admitted to the bar, and began practice here. He soon left the profession, and since then has been connected with the Stamford and Savings Banks of the town.

JOHN BISSEL, was a student of law in the office of Charles Hawley, and after being admitted to the bar, opened an office here, but soon went to New York city.

JOSHUA B. FERRIS, a native of Greenwich, graduated at Yale in 1823. He commenced life in Stamford as a teacher, and afterwards, when admitted to the bar, opened here an office. He has been successful in his profession, taking high rank as an advocate among our Connecticut lawyers. He has represented the town in the state legislature, and his district in the senate He was for years judge of probate and state's attorney. He married in 1823, Sally H. daughter of Wm. B. Peters, Esq., and grand daughter of Rev. Dr. Peters, of Hebron. Their children have been: Harriet, who died young; Samuel J., who was lost at sea; Isadore W.; Joshua B., who was drowned; Elizabeth J., now Mrs. Wm. R. Fosdick, of Stamford; Mary, L., now wife of Rev. E. O. Flagg, of New York; Samuel P. now major in the U. S. A. (see Stamford soldier's memorial); and Henry J., now in the insurance business in New York.

MINOR, WILLIAM THOMAS, LL.D., the second son of Simeon H., of this town. See preceding sketch. He graduated at Yale, in 1834, and studied law with his father. After being admitted to the bar, he commenced practice in his native town where he has continued to reside. He has always been popular at home; and his townsmen from the first have looked to him

Very Respectfully Yours

William T. Minor

WM. T. MINOR LL.D.

LATE GOVERNOR OF CONNECTICUT.

as a leader for them in all local movements for the prosperity of the town. He has represented the town in the state legislature seven times; and once, his district, in the state senate. In 1855, he was chosen governor of Connecticut, and re-elected the next year. He received in 1855 the honorary LL.D. from the Wesleyan University at Middletown. In 1864 he was appointed by President Lincoln consul-general to Havana, which office he resigned in 1867.

He married here, April 16, 1849, Mary C., daughter of John W. Leeds, Esq., of Stamford. They have had five children, of whom only two are now living—a son, Charles W., now in the university of Munich, Bavaria, and a daughter.

On returning to his native town, he was chosen to represent the town in the state legislature; and by the legislature he was appointed judge of the superior court of the state.

HENRY A. MITCHELL, of New Canaan, was here in 1842 and 1843. He was judge of probate, and went to Bristol, where he still resides.

JAMES H. OLMSTED, a native of Ridgefield, came to Stamford as a teacher and student at law. He was admitted to the bar, and located himself here, where he has been successful in his profession. He married here a daughter of Col. Lorenzo Meeker, and has had four children.

FRANCIS M. HAWLEY, son of the Hon. Charles, a native of Stamford, graduated at Trinity College, studied law with his father, was admitted to the bar in 1864, and opened here a law office.

CURTIS, JULIUS B., son of Nicholas Curtis, of Stamford. After practicing in his profession for several years in Greenwich, Ct., removed to Stamford, in 1866.

CHILD, CALVIN G., son of Asa Child, Esq., a native of Norwich, Ct., graduated at Yale, 1855; was a practicing lawyer in New York city until 1866, when he formed a business partnership with J. B. Ferris, Esq., of this place.

CHAPTER XXIV.

LATER BIOGRAPHY.

AMBLER, DAVID, son of Stephen and Deborah Ambler, was born in Stamford, April 29, 1739. He spent the first thirty-four years of his life in his native town, and won here a good name. In 1766 he united with the Congregational church. Our records, both church and town, show him to have been an active and efficient man, and when he removed to Woodbury, he soon won for himself there the reputation of a thorough, practical man, and was held in great esteem and honor. He was probably a grandson of our Abraham Ambler. He married in 1761, Olive A., sister of Rev. Benjamin Wildman, of Southbury, and in 1773, removed to Bethlehem society, then in the town of Woodbury, but since incorporated as a separate town. He represented his adopted town in ten sessions of the state legislature. Cothren's History of Woodbury says of him:

"He had for a long period the supervision of the town affairs in the section where he resided; was an efficient magistrate, and during the revolution rendered important services to the country, as committee of safety and in procuring and forwarding supplies to the army. He died January 8, 1808."

His widow moved to Bridgewater, N. Y., where she lived many years with her daughter. They had ten children.

BELL, THADDEUS, was the son of Thaddeus and Mary (Leeds) Bell, and was born in Stamford, March 18, 1758–9. He was early brought forward into public life, and for a period of a half century, was one of the most noted men in the town. For eleven

Eng.d by Geo. E. Perine N.Y.

Respectfully yours
A. Bishop

sessions he represented the town in the legislature, and was much of his life employed in public business, for his town and county. But he is best known as one of the most earnest of our revolutionary patriots. The following tribute to his services in that struggle, is from the pen of G. C. Hathorn, Esq., late of Williamsburg, who married a daughter of Mr. Bell.

"He was attached to the coast guard during the revolutionary war, and for a considerable portion of the time was orderly sergeant in the company to which he belonged. He was present on several noted occasions in the war, such as the burning of Danbury, he being one of the small number who compelled the British forces to retreat precipitately through Saugatuck, now Westport, to Compo, the place of their embarkation. He also participated in an attempted defense, on the firing ot Norwalk by the British, and was among the number who reinforced the brave Gen. Putman after his famous descent on horseback of the precipice now known as "Put's Hill." He remembered having seen the holes in the General's hat produced by a ball fired at him in his daring descent, and often reiterated the exclamation of brave "Old Put" when he in turn became the pursuer, and waving his sword shouted, "come on brave boys." He was also, with a number of his fellow parishoners, and their venerable pastor, Doctor Mather, taken unarmed from the house in which he was worshiping on the Sabbath by a band of tories and British, and conveyed to New York, where he suffered imprisonment for upwards of four months, among felons of the lowest grade. His own brother died on his way home, and he himself was so low and emaciated that he was unable to walk and had to be carried to his home and family upon a litter."

Mr. Bell married here, May 4, 1780, Elizabeth How. Their children were: Hannah, b. September 14, 1781; James, b. October 7, 1783; and Sarah, b. May 6, 1787. He died, after a useful life, in great peace, and with a firm hope, October 31, 1851.

BISHOP, ALFRED, descended from our second minister, Rev. John Bishop, was son of William and Susanna (Scofield) Bishop, and was born here, December 21, 1798. His boyhood was noted for nothing more than its quiet and respectful deportment. At an early age, he commenced his self-reliant career as a teacher in one of our public schools. He taught but a short time, when he went into New Jersey with the intention of spending his days in farming. While thus employed, he made presonal experiments with his pick ax, shovel, and wheelbarrow, from which he accurately estimated the cost of removing various masses of earth to different distances. In this way he prepared himself for the great work of his life, as canal and railroad contractor. Among the public works on which he was engaged, and which constitute the best monument to his name, are the Morris canal, in New Jersey; the great bridge over the Raritan, at New Brunswick; the Housatonic, Berkshire, Washington and Saratoga, Naugatuck, and the New York and New Haven railroads.

He removed from New Jersey to Bridgeport, Ct., where he spent the rest of his life. It is not claiming too much for him to say, that this flourishing city owes much to his enterprise and public spirit. Mr. Bishop readily inspired confidence in his plans for public improvements, and at his call the largest sums were cheerfully supplied.

But in the very midst of his extensive operations, and while forming plans for still greater works, he was suddenly arrested by his last sickness. From the first he felt that it would prove fatal; and now, still more than while in health, he displayed his remarkable talents in arranging and planning all the details of a complicated operation. In the midst of great physical suffering, he detailed with minuteness the necessary steps for closing up all his extensive business engagements, laying out the work for his executors, as he would plan the details of an ordinary contract for a railroad. He then, in the same business manner, distributed his large estate. One quarter of it he disposed of in gratuities, outside of his own family, partly to his more distant relatives, partly to his personal friends who had been unfortunate, and partly to strictly benevolent uses. His pastor was remembered with a hundred dollars annuity. The American Bible Society received $10,000, and the Female Benevolent Society, of Bridgeport, $5,000. After thus distributing one-fourth of the estate, he entailed the balance upon his wife and children.

Mr. Bishop married Mary, daughter of Ethan Ferris, of Greenwich, and had three sons, all born in New Jersey.

Ethan Ferris, who was educated at Yale, and took his maser's degre e at Trinity, took orders in the Episcopal church, and has had charge of a parish in Bridgeport, Ct., where he established St. Luke's college for the education of orphans and destitute boys.

William Darius graduated at Yale, 1849, and has once represented his district in the national congress, and is now president of the New York and New Haven railroad; and Henry, who was educated at Trinity college, Hartford, and now lives in Bridgeport. The widow, who is now traveling in Europe, still occupies the elegant residence built by her husband, on Golden Hill, in Bridgeport.

DAVENPORT, HON. ABRAHAM, was born in Stamford, in 1715, the eighth child of the Rev. John Davenport, by his second wife, Mrs. Elizabeth (Morris) Maltby. He graduated at Yale in 1732, and we soon find him at home filling such offices in the gift of his townsmen, as the most promising young man of the times were allowed to hold. Our town records, from that date to the end of his eminent and honored life, are full of witnesses to the esteem with which the people regarded him, and the universal trust reposed in him. In the most trying period of our history, that of our revolution, he seems to have been the one to whom the town looked for counsel and defense. No man has ever served the town as one of its selectmen as long as he. He also represented the town in the state legislature for twenty-five sessions, and at several of them was clerk of the house. He was state senator from 1766 to 1784. He was judge of probate for several years, and at his death was judge of the county court. He was, also, very active in religion, being a deacon in the Congregational church from 1759 to 1789.

In 1776 he and his son John and Thaddeus Burr, were sent to the army under Washington, to assist in "arranging it into companies and regiments," and to commission the officers appointed by the assembly for the battalions raised by the state. He was likewise empowered to arrest and bring to trial persons suspected of irresolution or disloyalty.

In 1777 he was one of the committee of safety for the state; and he was always consulted by Governor Trumbull and General Washington as one of the wisest counselors in our most trying days.

He married his first wife, November 16, 1750, Elizabeth, daughter of Colonel Jabez Huntington, of Windham. Their children were: John, whose biographical sketch will appear in its place; Abraham, who died in infancy; Elizabeth, wife of Dr. Cogswell, whose record is among our physicians; James, whose sketch will follow in its place; and Huntington, who died in childhood. After the death of his first wife, December 17, 1773, he married August 8, 1776, Mrs. Martha, widow of Dr. Perez Fitch, of this town.

The following is the estimate in which he was held by a man as competent to judge as the eminent Dr. Dwight. The testimonial deserves a place in our local history.

"Col. Davenport was possessed of a vigorous understanding and invincible firmness of mind, of integrity and justice unquestioned, even by his enemies; of veracity exact in a degree nearly singular; and of a weight of character which for many years decided in this county almost every question to which it was lent. He was early a professor of the christian religion, and adorned its doctrines by an exemplary conformity to its precepts. He was often styled a rough diamond, and the appellation was, perhaps, never given with more propriety. His virtues were all of the masculine kind; less soft, graceful and alluring than his friends wished, but more extensively productive of real good to mankind than those of almost any man who has been distinguished for gentleness of character. It would be happy for this or any other country, if the magistracy should execute its laws with the exactness for which he was distinguished. Col. Davenport acquired property with diligence, and preserved it with frugality; and hence was by many persons supposed to regard it with an improper attachment. This, however, was a very erroneous opinion. Of what was merely ornamental, he was, I think, too regardless; but the poor found nowhere a more liberal benefactor, nor the stranger a more hospitable host. I say this from a personal knowledge, acquired by a long-continued and intimate acquaintance with him and his family. While the war had its principal seat in the state of New York, he took the entire superintendence of the sick soldiers, who were returning home; filled his own house with them, and devoted to their relief his own time and that of his family, while he provided elsewhere the best accommodations for such as he could not receive. In a season when an expectation of approaching scarcity had raised the price of bread corn to an enormous height, he not only sold the produce off his own farms to the poor, at the former customary price, but bought corn extensively, and sold this also, as he had sold his own. His alms were at the same time rarely rivaled in their extent.

"Two instances of Col. Davenport's firmness deserved to be mentioned. The 19th of May, 1780, was a remarkably dark day. Candles were lighted in many houses; the birds were silent, and disappeared; the fowls retired to roost. The legislature was then in session at Hartford. A very general opinion prevailed that the Day of Judgment was at hand. The house of representatives being unable to transact their business, adjourned. A proposal to adjourn the council was under consideration, when the opinion of Col. Davenport was asked. He answered:

"'I am against an adjournment. The Day of Judgment is either approaching, or it is not. If it is not, there is no cause for an adjournment; if it is, I choose to be found doing my duty. I wish, therefore, that candles may be brought.'

"The other instance took place at Danbury, at the court of common pleas, of which he was chief-justice. This venerable man, after he was struck with death, heard a considerable part of a trial, gave the charge to the jury, and took notice of an article in the testimony which had escaped the attention of the counsel on both sides. He then retired from the bench, and was soon after found dead in his bed.

"To his private friends Col. Davenport extended his acts of kindness, as if they had been his children. I say this from experience. Of his country, and of all its great interests, he was a pillar of granite. Nothing impaired, nothing moved his resolution and firmness, while destined to support in his own station this valuable edifice. He died, as he had long wished to die, in the immediate performance of his duty, November 20, 1789, in the seventy-fourth year of his age."

Rev. JAMES DAVENPORT, was the younger son of Rev. John Davenport and his second wife, Mrs. Elizabeth (Morris) Maltby. He was born in Stamford in 1716 and graduated at Yale in 1732. In 1738 he became pastor of the church in Southold, L. I. Here he labored with great acceptance, about two years. He was regarded as a man of much promise, warm hearted, zealous, sound in doctrine, and faithful to the sacred responsibilities of his office. Earnest and impressive, he was eminently fitted to move the masses in any community, and his opening ministry gave promise of great influenee and usefulness.

Soon after his settlement the gifted and earnest Whitfield came to this country, and by his impassioned eloquence stirred the hearts of all christian believers with new and strong impulses. Even cold hearted christians were warmed to the earnest fervor of religious zeal. Mr. Davenport could not resist those moving appeals. He yielded to the spell of the great pulpit orator, and his enthusiasm know no bounds. He became restless under ecclesiastical restraint. He could no lo nger content himself to work on the narrow field of his limited parish. He felt himself called to go forth and stir up unfaithful churches, and arouse from their slumbers the masses of the impenitent, who seemed to him to be on the very verge of ruin. Calling his people together, he gave them notice of the new call he had received, and after a lengthy and impassioned expostulation with them for their worldliness, he turned away, burning with a zeal which would brook no hindracce to achieve elsewhere readier triumphs in his master's cause. He soon joined the Tennents and Whitfield and even incited them to greater fervor in their holy work. In Pennsylvania, New Jersey, New York, Connecticut and Rhode Island, wherever listeners could be gathered, and where could they not be found flocking around any banner sustained with such gifts and such zeal, this earnest apostle labored, in season and out of season, rashly at times, no doubt, yet with constant witnesses to his power. Wherever he went he was thronged. Even ministers, who deprecated his irregularities, were moved often to admiration of his spirit and success. Warm-hearted and impulsive men called him "the angel of the Lord." Sober-minded and careful men acknowledged the power they were unable to resist. Abundant testimonies are on record to the triumphs of his eloquent zeal. Whitfield, himself, felt rebuked by his heavenly spirit, and the ardent Tennent was stimulated by him to intenser earnestness in his self-consuming work. His brethren in the ministry every where yielded to him the palm for an ardor and efficiency in winning men to Christ, which was beyond their reach. Towns which had never before been visited with what could have been called a revival of religion, were swayed by his impassioned plea, as the forest by the winds. Strong men and children bowed themselves down together, trembling with terror, or melting in tenderness and love. But it was not long before Mr. Davenport found that not even his eloquence could plead his cause against the fears of his brethren, who were set to guard the orthodoxy and the ecclesiastical proprieties of these churches. It was rumored that he was becoming intemperate in his zeal; that he was undermining the confidence of the churches in their ordinary means of grace; that he was sowing broadcast, seed most fruitful of divisions in the churches, and apostacies from the faith, and of the wildest and most lawless fanaticism. Gradually his ministerial brethren began to distrust and denounce him. In his turn he became censorious. If he could not preach to the people, he could find occasion to pour his invective upon their ministers. He could cast contempt upon the profession of piety which did not approve and aid his plans. He could forge his hottest anathema for those who sought to moderate his zeal or to limit his influence.

And the opposition which his erratic career aroused against him, went still further. A petition to the governor and assembly, at Hartford, was sent from the parish of Ripton, in Stratford, by Joseph Blackleach and Samuel Adams, charging that Mr. Davenport had come into their parish between the twenty-first and twenty-fifth of May, 1742, and with "one Pomeroy," and several "Eletarate" men, had acted in a strange and unaccountable manner, with many expressions unwarranted from the word of God; did affright and terrify the people, and put them into the utmost confusion, contention, hate, and anger among themselves. This charge and plea the general assembly deemed worthy their notice. They issued a warrant to Samuel Talcott, sheriff of Hartford county, to arrest both Davenport and Pomeroy, afterwards Dr. Pomeroy, who for half a century was the minister of Hebron, where he had been ordained in 1735. A law had just been framed by the assembly, in view of the great excitement attending the great revival of 1740, against all fanatical excesses and gross irregularities. The assembly found that Mr. Davenport had been guilty of "great disorders." Yet in consequence of some indications of partial insanity, by reason of his "enthusiastic impressions" and impulses," he was dismissed with no further punishment. They also decided that Mr. Pomeroy had done nothing "worthy of stripes or death;" and he, too, was dismissed. Mr. Davenport continued to labor "in season, out of season," through the rest of this and the following year. His feelings, which had been his master, gradually yielded to the dictates of his taste and judgment, which were constitutionally right. In 1746 he was regularly dismissed from his charge in Southold, L. I., and soon settled in Hopewell, N. J. Here he labored with general satisfaction, until 1755, when death put an end to his somewhat checkered but by no means useless life. He had three children: John, who graduated at Princeton in 1769, and became a Presbyterian clergyman; James, and Elizabeth, who married a Mr. Kelsey, of Princeton.

DAVENPORT, HON. JAMES, the fourth child of Hon. Abraham and Elizabeth (Huntington) Davenport, was born in Stamford, October 12, 1758, and graduated in Yale in 1779. Like his father and his elder brother John, he was an earnest patriot, and during the revolution was employed in the commissary department. His tastes were especially literary; and though much in public life, having been a lawyer by profession, with the office of the judge of the court of common pleas, a member of the state legislature in both houses, and a member of the national congress, he still found time to make himself one of the most intelligent men of his times, upon all subjects that received the attention of scholars and thinkers. He was a fellow of Yale college from 1793 until his death. The following testimony of Dr. Dwight, himself one of the most learned men of the day, is worthy a place in this tribute to one of the most gifted men of the town.

"Few persons in this country have been more, or more deservedly esteemed than the Hon. James Davenport. His mind was of a structure almost singular. An inferior constitution precluded him to a considerable extent, from laborious study, during his early years; and, indeed, throughout most of his life. Yet an unweraied attention to useful objects, a critical observation of everything important which fell under his eye, and a strong attachment to intelligent conversation, enabled him by the aid of a discernment almost intuitive, to accumulate a rich fund of valuable knowledge. With respect to conversation, he was peculiar. The company of intelligent persons he sought, with the same eagerness and constancy, as the student his books. Here he always started topics of investigation, fitted to improve the mind, as well as to please, and in this way gathered knowledge with the industry and success with which the bee makes every flower increase the treasure of its hive. I never knew the value of intelligent conversation and the extent of the coutributions, which it is capable of furnishing to the stock of public knowledge possessed by an individual, exhibited more clearly and decisively. than in his example. At the same time his own conversation was so agreeable, and intelligent, and his manners so engaging, that his company was coveted by all his numerous acquaintance. His life, also, was without a stain; and on his integrity, candor, and justice, his countrymeu placed an absolute reliance. With these qualifications, it will not be a matter of wonder, that at an early period of his life, he was employed by the public in an almost continual successiion of public business: or that he executed every commission of this nature. He died in the thirty-ninth year of his age of a paralytic stroke, brought on by a long continued, and very severe chronic rheumatism. Few persons have been more universally or deeply lamented."

He had married May 7, 1780, Abigail Fitch, who died in November, 1782. He married his second wife, November 6, 1790, Mehitabel Coggshall. The only child of his first wife, Betsey Coggshall, became the wife of Charles W. Aphthorp, of Boston. By his second wife he had three children: Abigail Fitch, born November 18, 1791, who was the wife of that gifted pulpit orator, Rev. Philip Melancthon Whelpley, the pastor of the first Presbyterian church in New York city; Mary Anne, born November 16, 1793, the wife of the accomplished scholar and Christian minister, Rev. Matthias Bruen, of the Bleecker street church, New York city; and Frances Louisa, born November 10, 1795, the wife of that eminent preacher and theologian, the Rev. Dr. Thomas H. Skinner, of New York.

He died August 3, 1799.

Ebenezer Dibble, who became the principal pioneer in the Episcopal movement here, I have supposed to be the son of Zachariah and Sarah (Clements) Dibble. If so, he was born July 18, 1706. He graduated at Yale in 1734, and the same year was licensed to preach by the Fairfield East Association.

We hear nothing further of him,—except that the First Society, of Stamford, passed a special, and apparently an exceptional vote, in 1741, giving him a vote in Society meeting—until we find him seeking orders in the Episcopal church. This appears in 1746, in a letter of Dr. Johnson, of Stratford, who writes, "I have heretofore desired leave for Messrs. Dibble and Leaming to go for orders." But the next year, in a letter to the Bishop of London, after stating that he is alone in the ministry on the seacoast, for a distance of a hundred miles, and that his burden is insupportable, he complains that no leave has yet been granted to any to go home for orders, "though there are five or six valuable candidates."

Under date of December 27, 1747, the secretary of the Society grants liberty for Mr. Dibble to go home for holy orders, and to take charge of our (Stamford) church, with that of Norwalk;" the conditions being "that Stamford should pay ten pounds sterling annually for his support; and Norwalk should give security for twenty pounds more, with the actual possession of their glebe."

In the letter which gives us these items of intelligence, dated April 26, 1748, the churchwardens of Stamford urge their plea for the entire services of Mr. Dibble, on the ground that they appreciate his labors more highly than the Norwalk people, because he had already read service "among us steadily for two years and a half," and because "we have great esteem and regard" for him. They add, using their own italics, "we shall be very much gratified if we can obtain from the venerable society's great charity, his being appointed their missionary for *our* church." Again in this letter they say, "our people, from a hearty affection to Mr. Dibble, resolved cheerfully to undertake the expense of his voyage, and we have effectually secured the payment of twenty pounds sterling per annum to the society's missionary, according to our bond in Mr. Dibble's hand, and promise hereby to put him in possession of our glebe, which is better than that of Norwalk." If, however, the society should still think it better to keep the two parishes united under Mr. Dibble's care, they gracefully add, "we humbly submit, and shall be heartily thankful for any share in Mr. Dibble's ministry."

Mr. Dibble reached Stamford ,October 25, 1748, after having taken orders in England. In his first report to the secretary of the society, November 14, 1748, he mentions the cordial reception he met with on his return home. He speaks also of the offense which his course had given the Norwalk people, alluding probably to his unwillingness to accept the united charge of the two parishes.

Of Mr. Dibble's laborious service in his profession, we have abundant proof in his reports to the society. His zeal and labors must have been quite apostolic, extending to Norwalk, Ridgefield, and on the "oblong" between New York and Connecticut twenty, or thirty miles," at the same time, faithfully ministering to the spiritual wants of his own parish.

In 1752 he received a call to the parishes in Newtown and Reading, with a larger salary than he was getting here. This call he refused. A similar call came, also, in 1760, from Rye, but could not tempt him to leave the Stamford parish.

On the opening of the revolution Mr. Dibble, as a matter of course, opposed the revolutionary move. As early as October 18, 1768, we find him in one of his reports to the society using this language:

"With pleasure I can inform the venerable board, of the peaceable, flourishing, increasing state of my parish, and of their firm attachment to our happy constitution, both in church and state, nothwithstanding party rage never ran higher; and under the specious pretence of civil and religious liberty, every art is used to throw us into all imaginable confusion, and to prejudice his majesty's subjects against the conduct of the government in being, and our religious constitution in particular. We hope in God for better times."

His position in 1775, on the opening of actual hostilities, is thus shown in another letter, of the 5th of April, of that year.

"We view with the deepest anxiety, affliction and concern, the great dangers we are in by reason of our unhappy divisions, and the amazing height to which the unfortunate dispute between Great Britain and these remote provinces hath arisen, the baneful influence it hath upon the interest of true religion, and the well-being of the church. Our duty as ministers is now attended with peculiar difficulty—faithfully to discharge the duties of our office, and yet carefully to avoid taking part in these political disputes, as I trust my brethren in this colony have done, as much as possible, notwithstanding any representation to our prejudice, to the contrary."

While thus opposing the revolution with conscientious earnestness, I find no evidence that he was ever seriously endangered in his person and family, by what, he still spoke of as an unjustifiable rebellion. His personal popularity was probably his defense. Mr. Seabury, who afterwards became bishop, in speaking of the Episcopal clergy of Connecticut says: "I believe they are all, either carried away from their cures, or confined to their houses, except Mr. Dibble, who is gone to Sharon to be inoculated for the small pox,—possibly hoping thereby to enjoy a few weeks respite from persecution." However it may have been during the war, at its close he came forward and carefully acknowledged his allegiance to the new government and remained until his death a faithful churchman, and a successful and popular minister.

Testimonials to the gentlemanly bearing and christian character of Mr. Dibble are abundant. He was held in very high esteem by Christian people of every denomination. One of the lay patrons of the Episcopal Church who spent large sums of money and devoted much time to the welfare of the church he loved, who had made a tour of the churches with him in 1762, bears witness to the unwearied and unceasing labors in which he endeavored "to serve the interest of true religion and our holy church:—whose services I find universally acceptable, and his life agreeable to his public character."

The following record, on the monument in St. John's Church, is a just tribute to the worth of this successful minister of Christ:

"As a missionary of the 'Society for the Propagation of the Gospel in Foreign Parts,' he entered upon the duties of his sacred office October 16, 1748, and continued to discharge them in this capacity, with great fidelity and zeal until the close of the revolutionary war. Subsequently to this period he fulfilled his duties unconnected with the society in England until 1799 when he died full of years, in peace with God and charity with man-rector of St. John's parish 51 years.

He became endeared to all by his unwavering devotion to their best interests, his holy life, unremitted zeal in the name of Christ and his church."

Of the family of Dr. Dibble I have found on record only the following: A gift of land to Dr. Dibble in 1752, for his wife, Joanna from Jonathan Bates, calls her "my loving daughter," thus preserving for us her parentage. The only children recorded to them, which I have been able to find, are: Ebenezer, born December 19, 1737; Joannah, born June 15, 1739; Fyler, born January 18, 1741; and Frederick, born in 1753.

FULLER, REV. HENRY, was born August 11, 1789, in Vershire, Vt. He graduated at Middlebury college in 1812, and studied theology with Dr. Asa Burton, a somewhat famous theological teacher of Thetford, Vt. He was ordained to the work of the ministry, as pastor of the united churches of Smithtown and Freshpond, L. I., October 23, 1816. He was next installed pastor of the Congregational church in North Stamford, June 6, 1821, where he continued until January 23, 1844. He was a very acceptable preacher and pastor while here. After his dismission, he removed to Huntington, L. I., in 1845, where he resided until his death, September 2, 1867.

Of his children the oldest, Amanda, born in Smithtown, died in North Stamford, at the age of twenty-three years. The other children were born in North Stamford. They were: William Henry, Hannah Maria, Edward Thurston, who died in infancy, and Edward Thurston. The latter graduated at Yale college in 1857, and died while a member of the Princeton theological seminary, November 7, 1859, at twenty-four years of age.

GAY, ROYAL LEAVENS, was a native of Stafford, Conn., where he was born, November 4,1780. He came to Stamford in 1811, and settled on Shippan. His intelligence and practical tact and strong good sense soon won the confidence of the citizens, and almost from the first he was entrusted with their most important offices. Few men have ever served the town with more marked ability, or more to the credit and approval of the town; and when, in the winter of 1856–7, he was obliged from increasing years and infirmities, to ask relief from the cares of office, he was not permitted to vacate the places of trust he had so well filled, without most gratifying witnesses to the esteem he had won. An elegant service of silver, consisting of four pieces, suitably inscribed, constituted the tribute of his fellow townsmen who had known him longest and best. Both the pitcher and salver testify to his "long and faithful service," and the "personal esteem and appreciation of his public service," by his fellow citizens. One of the goblets has the simple inscription, "Selectman twenty years"; and the other, "Treasurer fourteen years." One passage from the presentation address, made by his excellency Governor Minor, so clearly expresses the sentiment of the community regarding Mr. Gay's official career, that its insertion is due to the memory of the man whom it honors.

"Your friends have witnessed with high gratification your career in public office for the last quarter of a century, being assured that the honesty, integrity, and impartiality which have ever characterized your discharge of public duty, have proceeded from a good heart and an honest desire for the best interests of the public."

Besides these offices, Mr. Gay represented the town in the state legislature. He was, also, an efficient officer in the ecclesiastical society (congregational) of which he was a faithful member. Indeed, there was nothing which could promote the civil or social welfare of the community in which he was not interested and which he did not most cordially support.

But the death of this useful and honored citizen soon came; and deep and hearty was the mourning of the afflicted town. At a meeting of the Warden and Burgesses of the borough, June 23, 1857, two days after his decease, resolutions were passed, expressive of the universal sorrow felt at his death. They testify to the great loss which the borough and the town; the poor and the afflicted had experienced. They honor his public career as one of unswevering fidelity; and his private life as "courteous, full of brotherly kindness and charity which never failed."

Mr. Gay married in Tolland in 1811, Sally Shepherd. They had five children;—Ann Elizabeth, who married Edmund Lockwood; William S., who died in infancy; William who has been successful in business as one of the Stamford Manufactury Company at the Cove; Edward, who died young, and Theodore, who died at nineteen years of age. The first Mrs. Gay, who was a most excellent woman and a devoted christian, died January 16, 1822. Mr. Gay married for his second wife her sister, Ann Shepherd, by whom he had one son, Edward, who is still living in Stamford, where he is held in honor. The second Mrs. Gay, an estimable lady, died in Stamford, December 18, 1851, aged 66 years.

Holly, William Henry, son of Isaac and Levinia (Bishop) Holly, was born here, May 5, 1798. His life was mainly spent in his native town, and the most of it in such services as gave him prominence in public affairs, and made him more familiar with the history of the town than any other man of his time. Descended in the seventh generation from John Holly, the pioneer of this name, he seems to have inherited his ancestor's business character, and to have reproduced the same style of public life. He was for several years judge of probate for his district, which office he held to the last year of his life. He was also assistant assessor under the national revenue law. He died very suddenly, June 29, 1867. He married here, Caroline, daughter of Dr. Samuel Webb. He left at his death three daughters: Gertrude, Caroline, and Angie.

HOUGH, REV. JOHN, D. D., was the son of Dr. Walter and Martha (Lockwood) Hough, and was born in Stamford, in the house occupied by Malthy Smith, Esq., 1783. He graduated at Yale in 1802, and commenced the study of theology with Dr. Moses C. Welch, of Mansfield, Conn., and subsequently studied with Rev. Joel Benedict, of Plainfield, and Dr. Hart, of Preston. He was also in the first class of theological students under the teaching of Dr. Dwight. He was licensed to preach by the Windham Association in 1805, and was appointed missionary to Vermont the next year. He was ordained in Vergennes, Vt., March 12, 1807, where he preached until 1812. In November of this year he was appointed professor of Greek and Latin in Middlebury college, and for twenty-seven years he here made proof of his fitness for teaching the classics and theology. His biographer in the *Congregational Quarterly*, of October, 1861, says of him: "He was eminently successful as an instructor." In 1839 he resigned his professorship, and went West, where he spent the next ten years in preaching. Losing his sight in 1850, he spent the remainder of his life with his sons. He died at Fort Wayne, Ind., July 17, 1861.

He married November 19, 1812, Lucy, daughter of David Leavitt, of Bethlehem, Conn., by whom he had two sons: John, who graduated at Middlebury college in 1838; and David Leavitt, who graduated in 1839. Mrs. Hough died at Fort Wayne, February 11, 1859.

HOYT, ABRAHAM, son of Benjamin, who was the son of Benjamin, who was the son of Simon the pioneer, was born in Stamford, in 1704. He was a man of solid and substantial worth, and was much in public life. He was also an active member of the Congregational church for a good many years. He married here, November 27, 1729, Hannah Bates, by whom he had the following children: Abraham, born October 13, 1732, and died young; Isaac, born September 15, 1734; Ezra, born April 23, 1737; Silas, born March 2, 1738–9; Sarah, born February 3, 1740; Thaddeus, born January 26, 1742; Rachel, born August 7, 1745, and died same year. He married for his second wife, June 3, 1748, widow Hannah Blachley, by whom he had two children: Mary, born August 22, 1750, and died November 17, 1754; and Bates, born July 7, 1754. His descendants are very numerous, and they have been as enterprising as they are numerous.

Hoyt, Amos, was the son of Peter and Sarah Hoyt, and was born in 1762, and died September 10, 1793. He was a young man of great promise. His mind was of a high order, and his opportunities for improving it had been seduously improved. He entered Yale college in 1788, and graduated with honor in 1792. He was among the most promising and popular members of his class.

Many years after his death, the late Thomas S. Williams, of Hartford, was pleased to recall his many excellent traits, and to acknowledge his own personal obligations to his good will and kindness. To be praised by such a man is no slight honor; to be counted among the benefactors of such a man, is to have earned fame. This young man, so gifted and so honored, did not live to fulfill the high expectations of his friends. His gravestone shows that he had just completed his academic and professional studies when he died, away from his friends, in Glastonbury. His remains were buried in the Hoyt burying lot, on Hope street road, where his simple memorial stone testifies to the parental affection which could not leave his previous remains to lie in a stranger's grave.

The Stamford ancestors of this member of the Hoyt family, according to their historian, were: Peter, David, Benjamin, Benjamin, Benjamin, and Simon, the pioneer.

Hoyt, Edwin, the son of Abraham and Sarah (Knap) Hoyt, was born in Stamford in 1804. His grandfather was that captain Thaddeus who was so prominent among the patriotic civilians of the town during our Revolutionary period; and who at his death had gathered one of the largest estates of the town. Among his descendants have been several who have followed the venerable patriot in wordly success; yet among them all, and they are quite numerous, none has attained greater eminence in all those special qualities which constitute the successful business man than the subject of this sketch. And I think, too, none of the sons of the town has better illustrated the leading spirit of the town, or is more exactly its business representative than he. Receiving, here, the substantial rudiments of such an education as the boys of an industrious agricultural people acquire, he found his way, still a youth, into New York; and there, beginning at the fouudation, built for himself firmly, the basis of what has since been one of the most solid business characters in the metropolis. As clerk, diligent, active, studious, faithful, he soon won esteem and confidence. As partner in the successive firms of Hoyt & Fearing; Hoyt & Bogart; Hoyt, Tillinghast & Co.; and Hoyt, Spragues & Co,, he has in each successive advance steadily increased his reputation. The great crisis in commercial and mercantile life, in which so many splendid fortunes have been wrecked, have only the more triumphantly shown his great energy and tact. At these periods his resources never fail. In the fearful crisis of 1837, when every movement around him foreboded disaster to his house, he calmly examined his ground and resolved, even under circumstances which would have appalled almost any other man in the business circle to which he belonged, to go on. With wonderful courage and an activity as astonishing as it was successful, he provided for large amounts of the maturing paper of a long list of heavy debtors, and, though suffering heavily, came all the stronger out of the trial. Since then, his house has stood second to none in the metropolis.

With all his promptness and energy in business, and with a self-reliance which never fails him in an emergency, Mr. Hoyt is still one of the most quiet and modest of men. He lives in and for his business, and his success has fully justified this habitual and life long devotion. Mr. Hoyt married Susan, daughter of Governor William Sprague, of Rhode Island. They have had four children. all now living; Sarah, Susan Sprague, William S. and Edwin. The family occupy during the summer their

Eng^d by Geo. E. Perine, N.Y.

Isaac L. Hoyt

ISAAC L. HOYT

Capt. 10th Conn. Vols.

beautiful residence on the East River in Astoria; and for the winter, their elegant mansion on Fifth avenue. With all his devotion to business, Mr. Hoyt has maintained a deep interest in the family name in the town of his nativity, which his career has so honored.

Isaac Lockwood Hoyt, the son of Thaddeus and Rebecca Hoyt was born in that part of the town which has since been incorporated as Darien. On the breaking out of the late war he cheerfully entered the Union service, though at great personal sacrifice.

In his first term of service, three months, he won for himself the love and confidence of the entire company. Though not in command, it is not too much to say that he was the man in the company to whom they had cause to look for advice and help; and under whom they would gladly trust themselves, if the country should again call them to the field.

Accordingly, after a few weeks of rest from the severe service they had seen, when the question was raised, who shall take another company of our sons into the field, he seemed to be the one to whom all our people turned. With unaffected modesty he urged his sense of incompetency. He had received no special military training and he felt no military ambition. He had already sacrificed much, but with every interest of his country still at stake, he could not long hesitate. He accepted the command to give himself thenceforth to his country. He was in the Tenth Connecticut, a regiment destined to win no mean honors for the state, whose name and fame they were proud to bear. In the famous Burnside expedition into North Carolina, they were not a whit behind the bravest regiment under their gallant commander, and Captain Hoyt's company was never wanting where daring was needed. The zealous patriotism, and the calm and deliberate devotion of their captain were, also, shared by the men. But he was not long to command his company. The local fever seized upon his healthy frame and he was forced to yield. Though warned again and again of his danger, he would not ask for a furlough while his company needed his care.

He risked his own life that he might care for them; and cheerfully paid the price of his whole-souled devotion. His death occurred on board the New Brunswick, at Newbern, N. C., March 20, 1862. His remains were taken to Darien, where they were interred in the pleasant cemetery on the western slope of the Ridge on which he had spent his days. This patriot son of Stamford went to his grave amid the sincerest tokens of sorrow which a grateful people could pay to his honored and cherished memory. Our history elsewhere will show, that before the war he had been honored by his native town, having served his townsmen both as their selectman and as their representative in the state legislature.

HOYT, JAMES HENRY, fourth son of Billy and Sarah (Wood) Hoyt, was born in Stamford April 14, 1809. See sketches of Abraham and Thaddeus Hoyt.

His father was a farmer, and his early educational advantages were those of the sons of our ordinary New England farmers. At the age of seventeen he was apprenticed to the cabinet-making business, and at the close of his minority he took the business of his former master into his hands. He soon connected with this business the lumber trade. It will illustrate his enterprise thus early in his business life, that while engaged in this trade he imported the first cargo of hard coal ever brought to Stamford.

In 1831, the canal extending from the harbor up into the center of the village was opened. Mr. Hoyt united his business with the drygoods and grocery trade of his two brothers, William and Roswell. Leasing the canal for five years, they purchased shipping and did their own carrying trade, and imported their own West India goods. In this business he continued with varied success until the expiration of their lease, when he resumed the lumber trade, in which he continued until the New York and New Haven Railway was projected. In the building of this great thoroughfare he entered into contracts for grading portions of it, building bridges, and furnishing ties. All of these contracts were promptly and acceptably

Eng^d by G.E. Perine &Co N.Y.

SUP^T N.Y. & N.H. RAIL ROAD

executed. On the completion of the road, at first built with a single track, he contracted to supply it with fuel, and when the second track was laid, he was a heavy contractor for the work. From this statement it will be seen that Mr. Hoyt, from the very beginning of this great public work until it had fairly established itself as an efficiently-managed enterprise, had been connected with it in such ways as to make him familiar with its character and wants. He had enjoyed a good opportunity of watching the management of the road under its chief engineer and first superintendent, Mr. R. B. Mason, subsequently connected with the Illinois Central Railway; and also under its second superintendent, Geo. W. Whistler, jr. That he had not neglected the opportunity thus furnished him is evidenced in the unanimity of the choice which called him to the superintendency of the road on the resignation of Mr. Whistler in 1854. Still better evidence has been furnished in the increasing success which has attended his administration during the fifteen years he has held this onerous and responsible post.

His entrance upon the office was signalized by a sudden blow, which, under a less efficient administration, would have doomed the road to a partial or total suspension. But, despite the extensive Schuyler frauds, and the preceding catastrophe at the the Norwalk bridge, the stock of the road has steadily risen from about 90, its market price when Mr. Hoyt entered upon its superintendency, to over 150. Nor is it more than the truth will warrant, to affirm, that no one who has been connected with the road from its opening to the present time, is its advance more certainly due than to Mr. Hoyt. His unwearied care and painstaking devotion to the interests of the road from the time of his first contract; his minute attention to the least defect, either in the road-bed, or bridges, or rolling-stock, or in the habits or manners of the employees on the road, with his prompt remedy for it, or as faithful and prompt a reference of it, if not within reach of his authority, to the board of directors, have made him first among our eminent railway superintendents; and he has not been without abundant testimonials, both from his own board of directors and from the employees of the road, to the esteem and affection in which he is held.

In his private life Mr. Hoyt is eminently a domestic man. His home, when not in his business, is emphatically in the bosom of his family. He married January 31, 1838, Sarah J. Grey, of Darien, and they had five children, three of whom are now living. It was a very severe stroke which bereaved him of his wife. He had entrusted to her the entire administration of his domestic matters, because his official duties required all of his strength. He only asked, what in the stress of his care and responsibility he so much needed, a quiet and restful home, in which he could find the repose that should refit him for his work. And it was just such a home that he found, under her administration, always ready to welcome him.

In politics Mr. Hoyt has always been with the democratic party. Though not an aspirant for office, he has represented his native town and his senatorial district in the state legislature. He was a principal mover in the organization of the Stamford Savings Bank, of which he has been for several years the president.

As a practical business man, Mr. Hoyt stands among the first of his townsmen. He has reaped the rewards of his earnest and honorable enterprise, both in a most excellent business reputation, and in the still more tangible token of a handsome worldly estate.

HOYT, JONATHAN, for several years, about the middle of the last century, stood at the head of our public men, and was especially prominent during the period of the French and Indian war. He was equally eminent in civil and religious and military affairs. As early as 1747 he was a deacon in the Congregational church. As one of his majesty's justices, he officiated at many of the marriages of the town, and is recorded as the "worshipful" Mr. Hoyt. He attained in military service the rank of colonel; and from the positions assigned him in trying days he must have been held in confidence and esteem. As evidence of his reputation we find this characteristic vote of the society, December 23, 1731; "per vote ye Society do agree and Desire Capt. Jonathan Hait to set in ye foremost pew in y e meeting house."

HOYT, THADDEUS, son of Abraham and Hannah (Bates) Hoyt, was born in Stamford, Jan. 26, 1742-3. His entire life was spent in his native town, where he became a man of influence, and, for the age in which he lived, of quite considerable wealth. During the revolutionary war he was one of the most earnest and efficient advocates of independence. He married April 28, 1766, Hannah Holmes. Their children were Frederick, born Jan. 24, 1767; Hannah, born Oct. 16, 1768, who became the wife of Joshua Scofield; Abraham, born Oct. 16, 1770; Thaddeus, born Oct. 21, 1772; Billy, born July 30, 1774; Darius, born Jan. 30, 1776; Rebecca, the wife of Capt. John Brown; Mary, the wife of Hon. James Stevens; Betsey and Bates.

LEEDS, FRANCIS RANDOLPH, was the son of Sylvester and Susannah (Watson) Leeds, and was born in Stamford, June 18, 1835. He was early employed in the Stamford bank, where he won for himself a good reputation for accuracy, faithfulness and skill. He was eminently gifted with those traits of character which make the business man popular; and few young men were ever more universally esteemed than he.

In 1862 he was authorized to raise a company of volunteers for the service of the government in suppressing the great Rebellion. His ranks were rapidly filled up, when he received a captain's commission and left with his men for the seat of the war. Having already in his southern travels been attacked by the fever, he became again an easy prey to the insidious foe. He came north to recruit his impaired strength; but, impatient to join his command, he again left for that purpose, Jan. 2, 1863. He here joined his company at Pensacola, Fla., only to be struck down, this time fatally, by the relentless disease. He died at Pensacola, Feb. 17, 1863, deeply lamented by his command, who seemed to love him with an affection truly fraternal. His remains were brought home and interred in the new cemetery.

LEEDS, JOHN, was the son of Cary and Mary (Giles) Leeds, and was born in Stamford, July 31, 1764. He was a merchant and farmer, living in New Hope district. He was long an earnest and active member of the Episcopal church, and a most estimable citizen. His death, which took place Sep. 15, 1831, was felt to be a "public as well as private loss." He was one of those meek and quiet men whose lives are filled with unnoticed, because unobtrusive deeds of kindly good will. He was esteemed as a model in those graceful excellences which most endear to us our most trusted and prized companions. His integrity could not be questioned, and his personal friendship was courted as an honor and cherished as a blessing. He married, Dec. 6, 1796, Honor Williams, daughter of Moses and Martha (Robins) Williams, of Rocky Hill, Conn. Her paternal grand parents were Jacob and Eunice (Standish) Williams. This Eunice Standish was daughter of Thomas Standish of Hartford, the son of Alexander of Roxbury, Mass., the oldest son of the famous colonial captain Miles Standish. Their children were John Williams, (see following sketch), Jacob W. and Harry, the last two of whom are dead. Mrs. Leeds died, August 22, 1849, aged 83 years.

LEEDS, JOHN WILLIAMS, son of John and Honor (Williams) Leeds, was born in Stamford, August 18, 1797. He has always resided in his native town, where he has been held in deserved esteem. His business has been mainly mercantile and financial: and his success has placed him among the first men of the town. On the opening of the Stamford bank in 1834, he was chosen president of it, and has held the office until now. As a business man he ranks rather with the cautious and prudent than with the venturesome and daring, and his success has justified his business career.

He married Eliza, daughter of Elisha Leeds, and has had nine children, of whom six are living; Charles Henry, well known as one of the proprietors of the extensive Cove Mills; Sarah Elizabeth, wife of Gov. Wm. T. Minor of Stamford; Mary Cath-

Eng^d by G. E. Perine & Co. N.Y.

Yours Resp^y Jno W. Leeds Pres^t

JOHN WILLIAM LEEDS

[illegible]

erine, wife of Dr. Samuel Lockwood, dentist, of New York city; Josephine Eliza; Edward Francis, and Emily Irene.

LOCKWOOD, ISAAC, son of Isaac and Rebecca (Seely) Lockwood was born in Stamford, Nov. 4, 1762. Like many others of the sons of the town during the last half century, he commenced his life as a seaman. He soon abandoned his sea-life, returned to Stamford and settled down, on what was then the old turnpike, in the old Lockwood homestead, now occupied by George Hubbard, Esq. Here he spent the rest of his days. He was soon found ready and efficient in aiding forward every needed enterprise of the town, and rose rapidly to his place among the first citizens. At the beginning of this century, no man stood higher than he in the public esteem. For nineteen years he did good service as one of the select men of the town, and represented the town in eight sessions of the state legislature. He was characterized for his promptness and punctuality. It was a proverb that Capt. Lockwood's rambling pony was the best time piece in the town, never failing to appear with her rider at the post office at the appointed time.

MATHER, JOSEPH was the second son of Rev. Moses Mather, D. D., of Middlesex Society, Stamford, (Darien,) where he was born, July 21, 1753. He united with his father's church, Aug. 9, 1778. He was a young man of much promise, and soon attained a position of influence among the citizens of the town. He distinguished himself early as a warm advocate of the independence of the American colonies; and of course, like his patriotic father, he was a constant mark for the shafts of British and tory vengeance. He lived about two miles to the north of the village, and his house was used as a depository for the more costly treasures of the citizens who were more exposed to the raids of the enemy from Long Island. But, removed as he was from the center of the parish, he was easily found and greatly harassed by his former neighbors, who had now gone over to the enemy. No less than forty-four of his father's parishioners were at one time during the war, just across the Sound on

Lloyd's Neck, more bitter against patriots than the king's troops themselves.

He married, May 29, 1777, Sarah Scot, of Ridgefield. Their children, eight of whom are still living, (1862,) were Hannah, born June 2, 1777; Sarah, born March 28, 1780; Moses, born May 21, 1782; Raina, born May 4, 1784; Clare, born July 31, 1787; Joseph, born Sept. 30, 1789; Nancy, born Jan. 27, 1792; Betsey, born March 23, 1794; David Scott, born Dec. 14, 1795; and Phebe, born Nov. 27, 1798. At his death he left these ten children, forty-five grandchildren, forty-eight great-grandchildren, and one great-great-grandchild.

Mather, Moses, D. D., was the son of Timothy Mather of Lyme, Conn., where he was born March 6, 1719.

He graduated in Yale in 1739, and was settled over the church in Middlesex Society of Stamford, now Darien, June 14, 1744, having begun to preach there April 19, 1742. Here he remained a faithful and successful preacher and pastor until his death, Sept. 21, 1806—more than sixty-four years—which fact of itself is ample testimony to his usefulness. His ability is also testified in the works which he left, which though not numerous, evince his solid learning and his deep piety. He won his doctorate from the College of New Jersey in 1791. From 1777 to 1790 he was a Fellow of Yale College.

But the doctor will be best known for his earnest and active patriotism during the struggle which won our colonial independence, of which our account of that struggle will furnish ample proof.

The following testimony from Dr. Dwight's "Travels" is abundantly corroborated by all that we hear of his character from those who remember him, or from those who heard their parents dwell upon his precious memory.

"Dr. Mather was a man distinguished for learning and piety, a strong understanding and a most exemplary life. His natural temper was grave and unbending. His candor was that of the Gospel,—the wisdom which is from above—which, while it is 'pure and peaceable' is also 'without partiality."

S B Provost

Dr. Sprague's "Annals of the American Pulpit" contains an interesting letter from Rev. Mark Mead of Greenwich, which gives us the following delineation of his personal appearance and social character.

"He was a man of about the middle stature, rather slender than otherwise, of a pleasant expression of countenance, and free and easy in conversation. Dr. Mather, though generally a poor man, had a rich vein of humor, of which there still remain many traditions. A man in his parish who pretended to be a sort of half Quaker, half infidel, and who was a member of the vigilance committee in the revolution, as he was riding in company with him on horseback, said to him, 'Your Master used to ride an ass, and how is it that you ride a horse?' 'Because," said the doctor, 'the asses are all taken up for committee men.'

"Dr. Mather used to wear a long, rounded, Quaker coat, with very large brass buttons from top to bottom. The Quakers, at that time, used to wear buttons made of apple tree, and just enough to fasten their coats. The same man mentioned above, on meeting Dr. Mather one day, said to him, 'Moses, why does thee wear so many buttons on thy coat.' 'To show you,' said the Doctor, 'that my religion does not consist in a button.'"

Nor is the Dr. scarcely less to be remembered for the family which he left. Soon after his settlement, Sept. 10, 1746, he married one of his parishioners, Hannah Bell, by whom he had three children—John, born Sept. 20, 1747, Hannah, born May 20, 1751, and Joseph, born July 21, 1753. His wife died April 23, 1755, and he married again, Jan. 1, 1756, Mrs. Elizabeth Whiting, also a parishioner, by whom he had only one son, Noyes, born Septemher 1, 1756. His second wife died Dec. 18, 1757. He married for his third wife, Rebecca, Raymond, of Norwalk, Aug. 23, 1758, by whom, there were recorded to him four children; Moses, born Nov. 13, 1760. Raymond, born Jan. 31, 1763, Isaac, born Dec. 6, 1764, and Samuel, born Dec. 19, 1765. Of the above children, Hannah married Philo Betts and had eleven children; Joseph married Sarah Scott, of Ridgefield, and had ten children, six of whom, now venerable both for years and personal worth, it was the author's good fortune to meet at the homestead of their father in the summer of 1862; Noyes married and had nine children, and Samuel had five.

Of the ten children of Joseph, eight had families, and their children to the number of fifty-five are enrolled in the "Genealogy of the Mather Family."

In 1855, Rev. Mr. Kinney, then pastor of the church in Darien, makes this interesting record for Dr. Sprague's "Annals of the American Pulpit:"

"I think that more than half of those who compose my congregation on the Sabbath, and nearly our whole choir of singers are his (Dr Mather's) descendants. Two of his great-grandsons have recently been ordained deacons of this church."

PROVOST, STEPHEN BISHOP, son of Daniel and Elizabeth (Bishop,) was born in Stamford, April 23, 1792. His mother was daughter of deacon Stephen Bishop of the North Stamford Congregational church, who was grandson of Rev. John Bishop, the second pastor of the first church of Stamford. Mr. Provost has spent the most of his life in his native town, where he has been successful in business, and much respected and honored, as our official record will show. He married, April 5, 1821, Catherine, daughter of Christopher and Elizabeth Tillman, of New York. Their children have been; Stephen Henry, now a merchant in New York city; Christopher Tillman; David R., now in California; Mary Catherine, the late Mrs. Edward Scofield; Elizabeth Jane, now Mrs. Hiram Taylor, of Stamford; and Julia Francis, who died young.

QUINTARD, GEO. W., eldest son of Isaac Quintard and his wife, Mrs. Clarissa (Hoyt) Shay, was born in Stamford, April 22, 1822. He went, still young, into New York city, where he was engaged a few years in the grocery business. He married, Feb. 15, 1844, Frances, daughter of Charles Morgan, Esq., later proprietor of the Morgan Iron and Ship Works, corner of Ninth-st. and East River. Disposing of his grocery business, he entered the firm of his father-in-law, then T. F. Secor & Co., Mr. Secor being the foundry-man of the firm, and Mr. Morgan the financier. Afterwards, under the title of the Morgan Iron Works, in company with his father-in-law, and later with his brother-in-law, Hon. F. M. Merrit, of Stamford, and

Geo W. Quintard

still later as the sole proprietor of those extensive works, Mr. Quintard laid the foundation of the great business prosperity which has placed him among the leading men of the city. During the recent war he was largely employed in furnishing engines for the war ships needed in the United States Navy, and rendered timely and important aid to the Union cause. Since the war he has retired from the iron business, and is now president of one of the southern lines of steamship transportation. He is also connected with various other business boards in the city. His summer residence is in Rye. He has two children.

Quintard, Charles Todd, brother to the above, was born in Stamford, Dec. 22, 1824. He graduated M. D. at the University of New York in 1846, having been a student of Dr. Valentine Mott. After spending a few months in the Bellevue Hospital, and as physician to the New York City Dispensary, he removed to Georgia. Here he soon won reputation in his profession and as a medical writer, and in 1851, he was called to the chair of physiology and anatomy in the Memphis Medical College.

Devoting himself, meanwhile, also, to theological studies, under the direction of Bishop Otey of Tennessee, in 1855 he was admitted to orders. At once, he entered on the rectorship of Calvary church, Memphis, from which he went, in 1858, to the church of the Advent, Nashville. Under his successful ministry of four years, this church advanced from thirty-six to about three hundred communicants. His progress in his new profession of theology was rapid, as in that of medicine, and in 1866 he received his doctorate in Divinity, and was chosen Bishop of Tennessee, to which office he was consecrated by the General Convention of the Protestant Episcopal Church in the United States, in Philadelphia.

Quintard, Edward A., brother to Geo. W. and Charles T., above, is also a native of Stamford, where he was born in 1826. He went to New York as clerk to the Scranton Coal Company. Since then he has been largely engaged in the coal business, making for himself a good name and an eminent place, among the leading firms in his branch of business. He is extensively engaged also in mining coal. For a number of years he has spent his summers in Stamford, and in 1867, he built on Clark's Hill, a fine family residence of stone, one of the most imposing as well as costly of our many elegant Stamford homes. He married for his first wife, Matilda Gillespie, of New York city, who died leaving two children. He married for his second wife, Mary, daughter of captain William Skiddy, of Stamford, by whom he has two children.

Reed, Elijah, son of Jesse and Mercy (Weed) Reed, was born in Stamford, Middlesex parish, in 1778. In his thirty-sixth year he became a christian, and devoted himself with singular earnestness, to the duties of the christian life. He was chosen deacon of the church in Darien; and from that time he felt himself to be a servant of the Lord. There was no call which the church could make upon him to which he did not respond. In season and out of season, he embraced opportunities, or created them, for doing good. The Bible was his daily companion; and from its treasury, he never failed to draw timely instructions for all classes whom he met. No man practiced a more rigid self denial than he, that he might do good. None cultivated all the graces of the spirit more than he. None evinced a deeper interest in the welfare of Zion, or in the spiritual condition of impenitent men than he. And no one had more faith in the divinely appointed means for the recovery and salvation of men.

This good man died Nov. 16, 1851, when, and as he would have wished to die, on the morning of the Lord's Day, with all the peace and joyful hope which that day had been wont to bring him. Mr. Reed was only the fifth generation removed from the John Reed whom we have enrolled as the pioneer of the family in the town. The line of the ascent will be John, Thomas, and Thomas, the second son of John, as above.

RICHARDS, JAMES, D. D., was born Oct. 29, 1767, in New Canaan parish, a short distance east of the old line between Stamford and Norwalk. While still a boy, he came to Stamford village and engaged himself as an appren tice to the cabinet making trade. He proved a faithful appre ntice, yet found time in his leisure moments for reading and study ; and at length formed and executed the purpose of fitting himself for college. While in Stamford he became a teacher in one of our village schools. He was also the subject of a re vival of religion, and united with the Congregational church here, Sept. 17, 1786. In 1739 he entered Yale college, and received, in 1794, the honorary degree of A. M. He studied theology with Dr. Dwight, and was licensed to preach by the Fairfield West Association in 1793. The same year he was settled in Morristown, N. J., as pastor of the First Presbyterian Church there. He soon gave proofs of that strong good sense and efficiency in all that he attempted, which at length gave him the enviable reputation which he won and retained. From Morristown he was called to Newark in June 1809, to succeed that prince among our pulpit orators, Dr. E. D. Griffin, who had then accepted his professorship at An dover. Here Mr. Richards became very eminent in his profession, both as preacher and pastor. In 1823 he was called to the chair of Christian Theology in the Auburn Theological Seminary. He died in Auburn, N. Y., Aug. 2, 1848.

SKELDING, DEA. THOMAS, was son of James and Mary Skelding, and was born in Stamford, Feb. 6, 1773. The year after his marriage he removed to Troy, N. Y., where he soon attained eminence among the enterprising men of that flourishing city. He was equally eminent in business and religion. Brought up a Congregationalist, after his conversion, he united with the Baptist church in Troy in 1806, and proved himself one of the most faithful and devoted of chri stians. He was chosen deacon of this church in 1812; and when, in 1822, he removed to New York, he was at once called to the same office in the South Baptist Church of that city, then just organized. Here he labored with a growing zeal until his work on earth was done. On the second Sabbath of December, 1830, while enjoying the usual services of the sanctuary, he was struck with a sudden paralysis which almost deprived him of motion and speech. He was taken home, where he languished many weeks, but partially recovering the use of his limbs and of his voice. In July of the next year he visited his friends and kindred in his native town; and while here, surrounded with the grateful reminiscences of his early days, in the family of his brother James, he peacefully and in joyous hope closed his earthly career Aug. 1, 1831. His obituary in the *Baptist Repository*, gives us a very pleasant impression of the cheerful and beneficent piety of this good man: "In wealth he was an example to the rich," and when deprived of his earthly possessions, his cheerful trust in God still "taught the poor to be humble, submissive and thankful."

Smith, Rev. Daniel, was the son of Peter and Mary Smith of New Canaan, where he was born Aug. 3, 1764.

He graduated at Yale in 1791, and the same year united with the Congregational church in Sharon. After studying theology with the Rev. Cotton Mather Smith of Sharon, whose youngest daughter he married, he was licensed to preach, Oct. 2, 1792, by the Litchfield North Association, and ordained pastor of the First Congregational church in Stamford, June 13, 1793. Here he labored in word and doctrine with very great acceptance down to a very advanced age. He was a man, who is remembered still by many of the citizens of Stamford, both in the denomination to which he belonged, and in others, as one of unusual good sense and wisdom. Few pastors ever endeared themselves more to their people than he. His hold on his people was fully and most promptly shown, when in 1839, after a ministry of forty-seven years, he recounted his labors, acknowledged his growing infirmities, and asked to be relieved from a portion of his cares. Their reply is found in the following resolution:

"That we recognize in our pastor a diligent servant of Christ, one who, for the long time he has ministered to us in holy things, has ever exhibited a happy union of prudence with zeal; and one who, in all his intercourse with us and his ministrations to us has cultivated those feelings which most endear a pastor to his flock. And we earnestly entreat our God that he may long be spared to watch over us, to instruct us and to pray for us."

In addition to the labors of preacher and pastor, Mr. Smith conducted a private school in his own house for many years; and many of the youth of the town recall with affectionate interest the days of their pleasant pupilage under his kindly care.

He married for his first wife Mary Smith, as above, July 9, 1793, by whom he had two children, Julia Ann, born April 5, 1794, and Thomas Mather, born March 7, 1796..

He married again June 14, 1801, Catherine, daughter of David Webb, of Stamford. Their children were David Webb, born April 11, 1802, lived single and died in Stamford; Mary Elizabeth, born Oct. 28, 1804, and married Fitch Rodgers, of Stamford, and still survives to occupy the house which her father left; James Augustus, born Aug. 1, 1807; Edward William, born Sept. 2, 1813, who graduated at Yale in 1835, and studied law; and John Cotton, born April 6, 1811, graduated at Yale in 1835, and was studying medicine when he died.

Smith, Thomas Mather, oldest son of Rev. Daniel, (see preceding sketch,) was born in Stamford, March 7, 1796. He graduated at Yale College in 1816; and after spending a year with his uncle, Hon. John Cotton Smith, he entered the theological seminary, where he graduated in theology in 1820. In 1822 he was ordained to the work of the ministry, and settled over the Third Congregation church, in Portland, Maine. He, also, was settled as Congregational pastor at Fall River, Mass.; at Catskill, N. Y.; and at New Bedford, Mass. While here, his views of church polity changing, he embraced the Episcopal theory, and was ordained deacon, by Bishop Smith, of Kentucky; and the next year, priest, by Bishop Eastman, of Massachusetts. In 1845, he was appointed Milnor Professor of Systematic Divinity at Kenyon College, Gambier, Ohio. In 1850 he was honored with the degree of Doctor of Divinity, by

Bowdoin College. He remained at his post in Kenyon College until 1863,—discharging its duties, which were often very exacting,—having embraced at times those of president of the institution, with great acceptance and success. On his resignation, in 1863, he was honored as Emeritus Professor.

The following testimony is borne to his character by his classmate, Rev. Dr. W. C. Fowler, of Durham, Conn. He says,

"What struck me was his fine social nature. Perhaps the reason of this was, that his mother and my mother were first cousins, through their grandfather, Rev. William Worthington. He always met me as a cousin, frank, confiding, affectionate. The movements of his mind were easy and natural, not requiring any special excitement to bring them into play. His emotional nature was healthy and easily stirred, but also controlled, so far as I saw, by the proprieties of time and place. He was always a good scholar, with the power of being a better one. In short, I think he showed, while in college, in perceptible embryo, the same mental characteristics, which in subsequent life were so finely developed and matured."

Mr. Smith married, Sept. 26, 1822, Mary G. eldest daughter of Rev. Dr. Leonard Woods, of Andover, Mass. They had six children, three of whom died in infancy. His son, John Cotton Smith, graduated at Bowdoin College in 1847; studied theology at the seminary of which his father was a professor, and is now a popular preacher of the Episcopal denomination in New York city. He, also, has been honored with a doctorate of divinity.

Smith, James W., oldest son of Philander and Clarissa (Holly) Smith, was born on Longridge, July 8, 1810. He fitted for college under the late Hawley Olmstead, Esq., of Wilton, having the work of the ministry in view. His physician thinking his health would never allow him to be a preacher, dissuaded him from the attempt, and he devoted himself to the study of medicine, graduating at the New York Medical College; and was commissioned by the American Board as physician to their Sandwich Island mission in 1842. While engaged in the work of his profession as missionary physician, he was also called to the office of lay preacher; and such was the urgency of the calls upon him, that he was, in 1854, ordained as pastor of the church in Koloa, on the island of Kauai. Here we soon find him in full charge of the missionary work at his station, and gathering around him and training faithful native helpers.

We next find him so strongly endeared to his people, that they are ready to propose supporting him, themselves. Accordingly we find him, in 1851, asking a release from the service of the Board, and since that date he has been supported by the people whom he was appointed to lift up out of the degradation of heathenism. During his residence on the island he has filled several important offices, and in them all has commended himself to the people.

He married Millicent Knapp, of North Greenwich, a sister of the two excellent christian ministers, Revs. Horton, and Jared D. Knapp. They have had nine children, of whom seven are still living; William Owen, Jared Knapp, Alfred Holly, Emma, Lottie, Melina and Juliett.

SMITH, TRUMAN, a native of Roxbury, Conn. He graduated at Yale in 1815, and entered the legal profession, in which he became one of our most eminent jurists and advocates. Entering upon public civil life, he became as representative and senator from Connecticut in the United States Congress,—one of our ablest statesmen. In 1853 he removed to Stamford, where he has since then resided. His first wife was Maria Cook, of Litchfield, who died April 20, 1849, leaving one daughter, Jenny P. now Mrs. George A. Hoyt, of Stamford. His second wife was Mary A. Dickenson, by whom he has had six children.

On the organization of the Court of Claims, to decide cases arising under the various acts growing out the rebellion, Mr. Smith was appointed one of the judges, holding the office until the court terminated. No generation of Connecticut jurists or statesmen has furnished us an example of more diligent and successful working, or of more uncompromising loyalty to the welfare of the people.

STEVENS, EDWIN, was the son of deacon David and ——— Stevens, of Ponus street, in what is now New Canaan. He was born July 4, 1802, and graduated at Yale with honor in 1828. He was also tutor in Yale in 1831 and '2. In 1831, he was licensed as preacher by the New Haven East Association, and became a christian missionary. He commenced this service as chaplain to our seamen in the East, and for three years had his home in Canton, laboring in season and out of season for the temporal good of this long neglected class. In 1838, he was transferred from the support of the Seaman's Friend Society, to that of the American Board of Foreign Missions. He started in March of this year, with those apostolic missionaries, Rev. Messrs. Gutzlaff and Medhurst, on a tour up the coast from Canton. They ascended the Min, four days journey, without opposition, but on the fifth day their course was arrested by hostile demonstrations from the natives. They were fired upon, and two of their company, which numbered eighteen souls, were wounded, and the attempt to proceed further was postponed. The time had not yet come for that populous territory to be opened to the intercourse of foreigners, and they, the teachers of a new religion. They succeeded in retreating down the Min, and coasting along the shore; and, stopping where allowed, they distributed books and held such conferences with the natives as might promote their work. In Shantung, alone, in two days, they succeeded in distributing 1,000 volumes of religious works, and wherever they could come in contact with the people, not over-persuaded by the presence of suspicious officials, they found a readiness to entertain their message and receive their books.

But the government were soon on the guard, and the movements of the missionary party were effectually arrested. Their voyage was the first ever made by missionaries along that coast for the purpose of evangelizing those teeming millions, without first conciliating them by the gift or sale of opium. On the temporary interruption of their labors, Mr. Stevens applied himself with very great success to the mastery of the Mandarin, the national language of China.

In December, 1836, he started on board the Himmaleh, to

visit several of the islands in the Indian archipelago, to examine the spiritual condition of the people and distribute among them such books as he might be able to induce them to take. In the prosecution of this pioneer missionary work, he touched at Singapore on the 15th of the month. The fever of that climate suddenly seized him, and terminated his life, Jan. 5, 1837.

His co-laborers in the field where he so prematurely fell, agree in testifying to his great worth. His loss was deeply felt by them. They had proved his great excellence. His scholarship and his deep-toned piety were alike needed, and they felt that the loss of them was irreparable. Their testimony of him is:

"He possessed a mature judgment and remarkable decision of character, a holy intrepidity in facing dangers that came in the path of duty. From his conversion, the Bible was his constant companion. 'Christ, our rock, was pre-eminently his theme. Accuracy characterized him as a Chinese student. His knowledge of the Bible and critical study of it, marked him out as an invaluable assistant in the future revisions of the Scriptures into Chinese; and to this his own attention seemed to be turned."

TODD, AMBROSE SEYMOUR, D. D., son of Rev. Ambrose and Lavinia Todd, was born in Huntington, Conn., Dec. 6, 1798.

He was ordained deacon in the Episcopal church, July 15, 1820, and priest, June 30, 1823, by Bishop Brownell, and instituted rector of St. John's church, Stamford. For nearly forty years he remained in charge of the St. John's parish. With more than ordinary ability in the pulpit, he showed great tact and wisdom in his pastoral oversight of his charge. Few men have secured more universal esteem. Few pastors have won so much regard and confidence, at the same time, from both their own and other denominations. His death occurred here June 22, 1861.

The following extract from the funeral address, delivered by Bishop Williams, is a fitting testimonial to his ministerial fidelity and success:

"This ministry, with its trials and its cheer, our brother exercised faithfully through more than twice a score of years, and—what is specially remarkable in these days of change—for almost the entire period in a single cure. And he was permitted to live to see great fruits spring from th s long-continued and faithful labors. What was the one cure, thirty-eight years ago, forms to-day five parishes, with seven churches and chapels duly consecrated, served—till he himself was removed—by seven clergymen.

"In this immediate parish, the humble edifice that in the beginning more than served its needs, has given place to this in which we meet to-day; and this has been once enlarged itself, and there is added to it now another house of God. Thirty-six years ago, the number of those who gathered to the Lord's table, in all the cure, was ninety; to-day, the roll comprises the names of near five hundred.

These are some tangible and visible results, whose testimony comes before us to-day, and whose witness is laid up on high. But, brethren, how much more is there which is not written, which cannot be written here—which man's eye can never see, of which man's lip can never speak, and which, after all, is the true and living history of this, as of every other faithful pastorship! The unwritten story of the spiritual lives of the generation of this people that has passed away; the sermons preached; the baptisms and eucharists administered; the young trained and led on to confirmation; the sick visited and prepared for death; sinners pointed and brought to the blood of Jesus; the pastoral counsels, the priestly labors, the ministrations to the poor and the afflicted, the public service, and the work from house to house—what a history do all these make up—what a testimony do they bear!"

Nor is the following testimony, from the excellent discourse preached on the Sunday following his death, by his assistant and successor, Rev. Walter Mitchell, less beautiful or illustrative of the character and influence of the man:

"Thirty-eight years are this day completed since he knelt before the same altar where, thirty-six years before that, *his* father had knelt, to receive, at the hands of Bishop Seabury, the commission to preach and to baptize. Thirty-eight years are this day fulfilled, during which his life has been all your own. Its story is better known to you than to me; for what I have but heard, you—at least many of you—have seen and felt. Yet I may allude to facts, long since occurred, which may have passed from your memories. At the time of his coming, the town of New Caanan was within the same charge, and for one or two years it was his constant custom to mount his horse, at the close of the second service here, and to ride over roads far less easy of travel than at present, to repeat his ministrations at that distant station. In addition to this, his cure extended over what is now Darien on the east and Greenwich on the west. And that was then no nominal labor. As I have gone with him upon his more distant visitings, there would scarcely be a house at which had he not at some time held services. For every funeral, almost every occasion at which believers were called together, was then held to be a fit time and place for the pastoral voice to be heard. Through the whole extent of this and the neighboring townships—a territory as wide as the See of many a primitive bishop—there is hardly a place not associated with his labors.

During the period of his ministry, he preached more than four thousand five hundred times, exclusive of extempore addresses and funeral discourses; performed over four hundred funeral services; baptized over five hundred infants and more than one hundred adults, and presented for confirmation three hundred and twenty-six persons. He also fulfilled the duties of Trustee of the General Theological Seminary and of the Berkley Divinity School, at Middletown, of this diocese, and represented the diocese as a delegate to the eventful General Assembly of 1844. The degree of Doctor of Divinity was the same year conferred on him by Columbia College. He was the first to propose and to organize the county meetings of the clergy of Fairfield county, and to his efficient aid and counsel, they owed, for many years their success.

WATERBURY, DAVID, Jr., son of John and Susanna Waterbury was born in Stamford, Feb. 12, 1722. His prominence as one of the military actors in our revolutionary struggle will justify the space which our sketch of him must occupy in our town history. We probably had several citizens engaged with the patriots in that memorable contest, who in many respects were his superiors; but he attained, and, as we are increasingly convinced, not without merit, a rank in the service higher than any of them.

That he had already seen service in the French and Indian War has been elsewhere shown. That he was ready at the opening of the revolutionary struggle to enter heartily into the service of the patriot cause, is most abundantly evinced by the responsible military offices he accepted and honored. Our first introduction to him as a military officer in the revolutionary war, we have through the following letter from Gen. Lee:

NEW HAVEN, Jan'ry ye 16th, 1775.

SIR:—It is with the greatest concern that I am informed you have received orders to disband the men whom you had engaged. The important news from Canada renders it necessary that they should without loss of time be re-assembled. I must request therefore that you will immediately call 'em together. I will myself answer for the measure to the Continental Congress. I entreat and conjure you therefore that they may be re-enlisted and equipped for service with all possible expedition. As to the arrangement of your officers you shall receive instructions before the men can be assembled. For God's sake lose no time. Every thing, perhaps the fate of America depends upon your expedition.

I am sir, your most obedient servant,

CHARLES LEE,

To Colonel Waterbury, Stamford. Major General.

Early in March we find Col. Waterbury with his regiment recruited, and ready to march from Stamford. He preceded them himself to New York, to prepare for the coming action. The colonel finds at Kingsbridge a deputation of citizens, earnestly pleading with him not to enter the city, as the enemy had sworn to fire it, if revolutionary troops should be found in it. But the Connecticut men had enlisted for the fight, and under their leader they were not inclined to cede any part of the domain to the rule of King George's troops: and we ac-accordingly find him quartered in the upper part of the city.

On the sixth of March he is still in the city and is ordered to send down from the upper barracks, Wm. Lounsbury and others confined there for spiking our guns beyond King's Bridge. They were sent down, according to orders and on being tried and found guilty were remanded to the same confinement.

We next find him at the head of his regiment, a thousand strong, leaving Harlaem the third Tuesday of July, 1775, for Albany. August 28th, he embarks from Ticonderago for Isle aux Noix, fourteen miles below St. John, toward which the army were now moving. The object of the campaign was the permanent occupancy of Crown Point and Ticonderoga, they having just been taken from the British, who had held possession of both forts since the memorable campaign of 1759.

On his return from his northern expedition in January, 1776, Col. Waterbury was ordered by President Hancock to raise five or six hundred men and go over to Long Island to capture tories who had refused to vote for deputies to the convention to be held in New York. It appears that when he had gathered his quota of men his orders were countermanded. A letter of the colonel is preserved in the American Archives to President Hancock, dated New York, Sept. 15, 1775, asking for indemnity for his expenses for the preparations then made. Though he seems not to have pursued the tories on the Island, he had done very efficient service among their sympathizers in Westchester county. Great complaint was made of his severity towards that class of traitors. He seems to have shown them no mercy. One of the reasons given by citizens in this vicinity for going over to the enemy was the excessive rigor of Colonel Waterbury. So Elisha Davis, of Greenwich, testifies for himself, when he made a plea for the restoration of his estate. In February, 1776, Colonel Samuel Drake, of Westchester, made, an appeal for thirty guns, two pair of holsters, nine cutlasses, and three pistols, which the officious colonel had taken from suspected citizens within his jurisdiction, by orders from General Lee. The following testimony regarding the colonel bears date March 2, 1776, and shows us how jealous he was of every hindrance to the progress of the Revolution: "Jos. Cheeseman, of New York, testifies that this day being on board a boat in Peck's Slip, he heard Col. Waterbury say that he had for some time thought that things would not go well unless the city of New York was crushed down, and that it must be done by their people before things would go well." (Am. Archives, vol. v.)

That this sensitiveness to the toryism of the day did not disqualify the colonel for his military position, the following order shows:

CAMBRIDGE, March 15, 1776.

SIR:—You are to proceed with the regiment under your command to Norwich, in Connecticut. His excellency expects you will preserve good order and discipline upon your march. * * * The general, depending upon your zeal, experience and good conduct, is satisfied that on your part no vigilance will be wanting.

Col. D. Waterbury, jun. HORATIO GATES, Adjutant General.

The following correspondence exhibits still further the estimate in which Colonel Waterbury's services at this period were held:

LEBANON April 29, 1776.

SIR :—David Waterbury. jun., of Stamford, Esquire, Col. of a regiment from this colony in the northern department the last year, and at the taking of St. Johns and Montreal, and lately in the service at New York with major general Lee ; at all times behaved with bravery and honor. When you have a vacancy in the army answerable to his rank, I do heartily commend him to your kind notice and regard.

I am with great esteem and regard, sir, your obd. humble servant,

To his Excelleney Gen. Washington. JONA. TRUMBULL.

NEW YORK, May 13, 1776.

SIR :—Gov. Trumbull has been pleased to mention you to me as a proper person to succeed to the command of a regiment lately General Arnold's. If you incline to engage in the service again, I shall be obliged to you for signifying as much, in order that I may lay the matter before congress for their approval.

I am, sir, with great respect, your most obd. servant,

To Colonel David Waterbury, of Stamford. GEO. WASHINGTON.

In his reply to this proposal of Gen. Washington, the colonel complains that he had not hitherto received the promotion which was his due, and while he asked no further commission, he pledges his readiness to volunteer his services at any moment when they may be needed.

The general assembly in their session of June, 1776, appointed Col. Waterbury a brigadier general "in the battalions of militia now to be raised to reinforce the continental army in Canada."

On the 5th of July, at the head of the first division of the continental forces, he reached New York, sharing the command of that division with General Wadsworth. With all possible dispatch the men are hurried to the scene of the opening campaign on Lake George.

The general himself reports from Skeensborough, July the 15th, where he is forwarding troops to Ticonderoga, as fast as they can come up.

Under date of July 18th, he again writes to Washington as follows :

"DEAR SIR : I received your favor of the 16th, and your honor may rest assured that I shall execute the orders as far as lies in my powor ` I would inform your honor there are no troops arrived yet. I have had intelligence of their being on the march to this place, and I hope they will soon arrive. I have a small party now clearing out Wood Creek and a small party building a place proper to keep a guard on the hill east of the mill; and the rest are employed in getting timber for the carpenters and mills, and on guard. I have not men sufficient to begin the fortifications on the west side of the mill. Your honor will see by the returns that there are but few men here; but what there are I shall endeavor to keep well employed; and as soon as others come in, I shall do the same by them. I have picked up all the axes, and the blacksmiths have overhauled them. I shall stand in great need of tools on the arrival of troops.

Sir, I shall with pleasure receive your orders as you see cause to send them, and hope I shall be able to put them into execution agreeably to your honor's expectation. DAVID WATERBURY, jr."

From this time, until early in September, he remained here in command, exercising the utmost dispatch in drilling and transmitting recruits. His labors must have been very great, as his letters and special dispatches of that period evince. A large number of these letters are preserved in the American Archives; and it is not saying too much of them to claim that they show the general to have been an earnest patriot and a faithful servant of the people in that day of their great struggle. The only one of these letters which our space will allow us to use is that of August 31st. It discloses both the humanity and the fidelity of the general. It was addressed to his superior officer, General Gates.

SIR:—Col. Woodbridge and his major have been detained in this neighborhood fourteen days, in consequence of having been inoculated, and not bringing certificates that they were properly cleansed; and they grow uneasy that they are kept back. I shall be glad to know if your honor intends I shall let them go forward to Ticonderoga. If not I shall be glad to have some instructions how to act concerning them.

I am, dear general, your honor's most obd. humble servant,

DAVID WATERBURY, Jr.

That the general was held in high esteem among the highest officers in the army is abundantly attested, by the army correspondence of that day. Under date of Aug. 7, 1776, General Schuyler thus writes to him from German Flats:

"I thank you for your attention, and the information you gave. My long stay here very much distresses me. It is however a great alleviation of my anxiety that you are at Skeensborough, and I am confident you will expedite the work as much as possible. I am, dear general, sincerely your most obedient humble servant, PHILIP SCHUYLER."

Under date of Aug. 18, 1776, General Gates, then in command of the northern army, thus commends and endorses General Waterbury: "As he is an able seaman and a brave officer, I intend that he shall join General Arnold with the rest of the squadron, the instant they can be armed and equipped. As General Arnold and he are upon the best terms, I am satisfied no dispute about command or want of confidence in each other will retard the public service."

And, again, Aug. 20th, General Schuyler thus writes to General Gates: "I am extremely happy that General Waterbury is to join General Arnold. I know him to be a good man as well as a good officer."

General Waterbury was appointed, Sept. 2nd, second officer in the fleet under General Arnold, then in Lake Champlain; and on the eighth, he started for Ticonderoga to take this new command. On the second of the following month he sailed from Ticonderoga with two galleys to join the fleet.

On the fourteenth, a letter from Sir Guy Carleton to Lord Germain introduces General Waterbury to us as a prisoner. He ends his account of their victory with this exultation: "We have taken Mr. Waterbury, the second in command, one of their brigadier generals."

The following dispatches also show him to be a prisoner of war, yet show in what esteem he is held by his superior in command.

SARATOGA, Oct. 18, 1776.

SIR:—General Waterbury, who is prisoner on his parole, is on his way from Albany to Connecticut. I have advised him to go directly from Albany to you. He is capable of giving you that information you requested in your last favour to me. He is not only a brave and good officer, but a candid and honest man, uninfluenced by any unbecoming prejudices. He will also acquaint you with our affairs at Ticonderoga.

I am, most respectfully, sir, your obedient and very humble servant,
To the Hon. Jona. Trumbull. PH. SCHUYLER.

Oct. 23, 1776.

General Waterbury has entreated me to recommend him to congress to be exchanged for General McDonald, or any other officer. I wish it to be accomplished. PH. SCHUYLER.
To John Hancock.

A lengthy letter from General Waterbury, dated Stamford, Oct. 24, 1779, and addressed to President Hancock, giving his account of his capture, is preserved in the American Archives.

The general was soon exchanged. I do not find that he was afterwards in any special engagement, though he was continued in command.

He returned to his native town, where he was held in honor by his townsmen. He served the town as selectman, and as representative in the state legislature. His residence was on the west side of our harbor, where his business was that of a farmer.

He died June 29, 1801, and was buried in the old burying lot, on the west side of Mill River. His widow, Mary, died Nov. 7, 1810, aged 77 years. They left one son, William, who was a man considerably in public business of the town, known as William Waterbury 4th. He left, also, one daughter, Mary, who died single, at twenty-six years of age.

WATERBURY, CHARLES, son of Jonathan B. and Betsey (Weed) Waterbury, was born here, in November 1819. He learned the saddler's trade in Bridgeport, but on the opening of the New York and New Haven Railroad, he engaged in the service of the railroad as baggage master. He afterwards served as baggage master, conductor and assistant superintendent on the Naugatuck road, until he was appointed, in 1843, its superintendent, which office he held until his death in 1868. Few men in these offices, have commended themselves more fully to the traveling public than he has always done. Modest and retiring in disposition, he was nevertheless a prompt and most efficient business man. The Waterbury dust-excluding ventilator, which a few years ago added so much to the comfort of passengers over his road, during the summer months, was his invention, and from the sale of the patent he realized a handsome sum. Mr. Waterbury was also an earnest christian man, and has been for years connected with the second Congregational church in Bridgeport. His funeral, which was atteuded in Bridgeport, on Sunday Sept. 6, 1868, was a marked tribute to his private and public worth. He married Cordelia Lockwood, of Greenwlch, who survives him. They had no children.

CHARLES WEBB was the son of Charles and Mary Smith Webb, and was born here, Feb. 13, 1724. He became early prominent in civil and military affairs, as the town records abundantly show. In 1757 he was chosen selectman for the first time, and was afterwards re-elected nineteen times. In 1758 he was chosen for the first time to represent the town in the state legislature, and was re-elected to the same office twenty-three times. . At this date he had become so prominent as to be entitled by vote to the third pew in the meeting house. He was also a military man, having attained, in 1760, the rank of captain. On the opening of the revolutionary war, he was at once looked to as one of the leaders of the town in opposition to the demands of the crown. We find him in the state legislature, and at home, speaking for the war; and when at length the war had been declared, we find him entrusted with posts of weighty responsibility, both in civil and military life.

In May, 1775, he was sent by the Continental Congress on a tour of military investigation to Ticonderoga, of which he made a satisfactory report on the 8th of June following. In July of this year the legislature commissioned him colonel, and he is put in command of a regiment of the state militia, and is stationed at Greenwich. In September he is ordered to New Haven, and in Oct. 23, he writes from his camp, Winter Hill, that he has now prepared his command for any service to which General Washington may call them.

He was in the battle of White Plains, Oct. 28, where he won for himself the reputation of an excellent and bold officer. The following certificate from the colonel is preserved in the American Archives.

HARTFORD, June 16, 1777.

"I hereby certify that in the action at the White Plains, on rhe 28th of October, 1776, the regiment then under my command, in obedience to my orders unslung and laid down their packs to engage the enemy; and the enemy overpowering and gaining the ground, said packs and the baggage of the regiment fell into the hands of the enemy without the default of the losses and by the merit of the chauce of war.

CHAS. WEBB, Col. 19 Regt.

Considerable loss of clothing and arms was sustained by the regiment under my command in the action and retreat on Long Island in August last, none of which, so far as came to my knowledge, appeared to happen thro any neglect or disobedience of orders of the loosers; also on York Island Sept. 15, 1776, said regiment were ordered by Gen. Scott to unsling their packs to engage the enemy, which we did accordingly, and the enemy advanced; and precipitate retreat being ordered, said packs fell into their hands and without any neglect or cowardice of the owners, so far as I could judge.

Hartford, June 2, 1777."

He was also at the battle of White Marsh, December 1777, where his regiment received the attack of the Hessian force. The struggle was very spirited, and his regiment lost eighty-four killed on the field and a large number wounded.

As an officer, Colonel Webb was marked for his promptness and efficiency. He was a strict disciplinarian. Thoroughly in sympathy with the revolutionary movement himself, he could accept nothing less than a whole-hearted earnestness in all who were engaged in its support. He tolerated no patriotism which suspicion could touch.

He married here, July 16, 1747, Mary Holly. Their children were, Charles, born Dec. 30, 1750; Sarah, born May 2, 1753; Hannah, born May 28, 1756; Samuel, born March 7, 1760; and Isaac, born July 28, 1766.

The son Charles was with his father in the revolutionary army, and was killed on a gun boat in the Sound but a short distance from Stamford harbor. He had married here, Feb. 15, 1772, Elizabeth Smith, and had a daughter, Betsey, born Oct. 16, 1772.

WEED, CHARLES A., son of Smith and Mary (Youngs) Weed, was born in Stamford, May 13, 1826. He had been living in Richmond about nine years, when the southern rebellion opened, and had about fifteen thousand dollars invested in his business. As he would not renounce his allegiance to the government of the United States, the local authorities took possession of his property and gave him a few hours to leave the city with his family. He accepted the terms and removed his family again to Stamford, preferring even poverty, if it must be so, to treason.

When at length in the progress of our Union armies, Gen. Butler had taken possession of New Orleans and the surrounding country, Mr. Weed was at liberty to avail himself of the advantages offered to loyal citizens. He had been despoiled by the rebellion of his entire property, and the chance was now offered to him to wrest from the rebellion many times his loss.

He found on reaching New Orleans, in July, 1862, the large plantations of the neighborhood covered with crops, which the fugitive planters had sown, now neglected and in danger of being utterly lost. Under governmental protection he went to the work of gathering in the crops. He hired the negroes who had been abandoned by their masters, giving to the government one half of the products secured, and abundantly indemnifying himself for the loses he had sustained in Richmond.

Since then he has been engaged in business in New Orleans, where he has had an extensive commission house under the firm of C. A. Weed & Co. His enterprise is also shown in other ways. He found the old New Orleans *Crescent* in a bankrupt condition, purchased it, and substituting for it the New Orleans *Times*, has built up the largest and one of the most successful newspaper enterprises of the South. He was also the original mover of the First National Bank of the city,

Eng^d by G. E. Perine & Co N.Y.

C. A. Mead

and the largest stockholder in it. He was offered the presidency of it, but refused. He, also, projected the New Orleans Fire Insurance Company, which has also grown to be an institution of great local value.

Mr. Weed is now erecting a family residence on Noro ton hill, one of the most commanding sites in his native town, which is to be for the present, the summer, and which he intends to make the permanent residence of his family. He married in 1826, Abigail S. Lounsbury, daughter of Samuel Lounsbury, and has four children, three sons and one daughter.

WEED, EDWARD, son of Philo and Abigail ——— Weed, was born in the north part of the town, July 17, 1807. In 1817 his parents removed to the town of Denmark, New York, where from the frontier condition of that neighborhood, but few privilges could be enjoyed.

At the usual age he commenced learning a trade; but on his conversion, in his eighteenth year, longing to do all in his power to win others to the Saviour, he left his trade and began studying in the hope of becoming a preacher. In two years he had fitted himself to teach, and engaged for the winter of 1826–7 in a school in Boonville, N. Y. Dnring this time he was very actively engaged in christian labors, and showed a zeal and skill which promised much future usefulness. The next summer he entered the Oneida Institute, then just established on the manual labor plan, where he remained four years. He spent also three years in Lane Seminary from its opening in 1832, when he showed himself an honest christian scholar.

Among the questions discussed at the literary society of the students, that of anti-slavery forced itself upon their attention. It elicited the intensest interest, and became so engrossing as to excite the fears of the trustees of the seminary; and they soon prohibited its further discussion. Several of the students, of whom Mr. Weed was one, left the seminary, and spent some time in the careful study of the interdicted subject, and became henceforth zealous and effective champions of the slave.

He was licensed to preach by the Chilicothe Presbytery in November, 1835, and entered upon this work with a zeal almost apostolic. He soon engaged in lecturing upon anti-slavery, and was employed by the Ohio State Anti-Slavery Society. In this field of labor he was unwearied, through evil report as well as good, counting not his own life dear unto him, if by its sacrifice he might help the oppressed. He labored on, amid opposition and ridicule and persecution, until the spring of 1838, when he was invited to the pastorate of the free Presbyterian Church of Mount Vernon, Ohio. Here he labored with great acceptance until the year 1842, when he accepted a call to Paterson, N. J. While connected with this church he labored extensively as a revivalist in many other churches, and was greatly blessed. In January, 1842, he was, greatly to the sorrow of his church and people in Paterson, dismissed, that he might take charge of the free Presbyterian Church in Brooklyn, N. Y. He returned to his former charge in Paterson, after an absence of fifteen months, was installed and continued to labor among them until his health failed in the spring of 1849, and he was obliged to ask for a dismission. Hoping to recover his strength, he accepted a kind invitation from captain Knight, of the ship New World to take the ocean trip with him on his next voyage to Liverpool. While in England he made many warm friends who ministered to his comfort and supplied all his earthly wants. But no care from them and no solicitude of the dearer ones he had left behind, could arrest the progress of his disease. It was decided by his physicians that he could not long live, and he resolved to return and die among his friends at home. He reached home Dec. 22, 1850, and lived until Jan. 20, 1851. On the 23rd he was buried in Paterson amid the tears of an affectionate family and an endeared people. He had been greatly beloved for his great excellence of character, and the mourning was now most heart-felt, because his great usefulness had so soon ended.

Mr. Weed married for his first wife, Nov. 5. 1836, Phebe Mathews of Mexicoville, N. Y. She died Dec. 12, 1843. He married for his second wife, Sept. 9, 1844, a Miss Porter, of Whitestown, who survived him. He had four children, to whom allusion is made in his memoir; Benjamin, Josephine, Edward and Albert.

WEED, ENOS, was one of the most erratic characters that Stamford has produced. He was the son of Enos. He was a man of considerable originality, thinking independently of books, and practicing, in everything, with no special regard to the rules or usages of customary practice. He went into medicine, and became somewhat noted as a medical adviser and practitioner, but, in his own way. He went into letters, and constructed a spelling book with many novelties, both in the alphabet employed and in the orthography.

He went also into religion and theology. Following no school or sect, he struck out for himself, and became a preacher, whom, though the orthodox could not wholly endorse, they could not utterly condemn. It may be due his memory to note the fact that with all his eccentricity, he was counted worthy, in 1790, of being appointed leader of the first Methodist class established in Stamford; and that he was an authorized local preacher in that denomination.

A single specimen of his genius and spirit is here inserted, taken from an old paper to which he sometimes contributed, and probably nothing which the historian could write, would so effectually set this unique son of the town so exactly before the reader as this autobiographic waif:

My name is Enos Weed, and junior too,
Which is something more,
It shows that Weeds have grown before.
Long as you see this in the paper,
From place to place I mean to caper,
And pick up all the cash I can,
Conforming to my present plan,

How large the "pile" was, which his capers gathered, history does not show.

WEED, NATHANIEL, son of Hezekiah and Rebecca (Knapp) Weed, was born in Stamford, Oct. 1, 1785. He is a descendant probably in the sixth generation from Jonas Weed, whose name occurs among the pioneers of the town. At the early age of fifteen years he went into New York city, where he engaged as clerk until he should become of age. Before this period arrived he had won such confidence in his business integrity and skill, as to secure flattering offers to engage in new business enterprises; but he characteristically decided to fulfill his engagements with his employer to the end of his minority. When his time was out and he had enjoyed a visit to his parents for a few days, his former employer proposed engaging him still longer, as a clerk. His prompt answer was, "I shall be no man's clerk hereafter. I can manage for myself, and if it must be, with a buck and saw, I can still do better than to clerk it longer." With this spirit he entered the dry goods business, and success was with him.

In 1827 he was chosen president of the North River Bank, and soon organized the Ocean Bank, of which he was for years president, and which he left in 1850, greatly to the regret of the directors. He still has among the cherished memorials of his business life the elegant vase which they gave him on his retirement from that office.

Retaining his interest in the town which gave him birth, he built the elegant mansion which he still occupies in Darien, only a few rods east of the place on which he was born. Here, since 1850, he has lived, respected and honored in a graceful old age.

He married, first, Hannah Smith, of New York city, in 1810, by whom he had a son, Harvey A., who graduated with first honors of his class in Columbia College, New York, and became a lawyer; and a daughter, Caroline, who died at the age of tweuty-six.

Mr. Weed married for his second wife, in 1840, Mrs. Mary (Smith) Weed, a younger sister of his first wife, and the widow of his younger brother.

Weed, Samuel, son of Ananias and Sally (Brown) Weed, was born it Stamford in 1794. He fitted for college at the North

Eng^d by Geo. E. Perine N.Y.

Nathl. Weed

NATHANIEL WEED.

LATE PRESIDENT OF THE OCEAN BANK NEW YORK.

Salem Academy, and entered Yale College in 1809. He graduated with his class in 1813, taking a good stand in a class containing such names as Geo. E. Badgor, L. L. D.; Elias Cornelius, D. D., of whom he was the room mate while in college; Norris Bull, D. D.; David B. Douglass, L. L. D.; William T. Dwight, D. D.; Prof. Alexauder, Wm. Fisher, Charles Hawley, Esq.; Augustus B. Longstreet, L. L. D.; Elisha Mitchell, D. D.; Prof. Denison Olmsted, L. L. D., and Dr. George Sumner.

He commenced the study of theology with Rev. Ebenezer Philips, of East Hampton, L. I., and after being licensed to preach, supplied the church in Babylon, L. I., for a year. While here he received a call to settle in North Stamford, his native parish, and had decided to accept it. Being already under appointment to the general assembly of the Presbyterian Church at their first session in Philadelphia, he started to attend the meeting and was taken with the sickness from which he never recovered. He died in Philadelphia in June, 1820.

WEEKS, JONATHAN DIBBLE, was the son of Lewis and Sarah (Guire) Weeks, and was born in Stamford, Feb. 2, 1811. His youth was spent in comparative poverty. His advantages were only those of the poorer boys of our poorer rural school districts. But he had in him that which gives the poorest boy a certain passport to most substantial prosperity and wealth. Industrious, honest and persevering, he was equally faithful to himself and his employer.

The talent entrusted to him, thus faithfully used, was soon more than doubled. Beginning as an apprentice in the rolling mills at Rippowam foundry, he went, at about the age of twenty, into the employ of Davenport & Layton, at Roxbury mills, where he soon became an equal partner with John A. Davenport.

During his apprenticeship, by unwearied application, he had made such progress in his studies that he had read the necessary Latin and Greek for admission to college at his twentieth year; and had, also, by his industry and economy, besides contributing to the support of his father's family, laid by what he supposed would enable him to take a collegiate course, preparatory to the study of law, in which profession he hoped to spend his life. But unexpected sickness thwarted this cherished plan, and regretfully, yet with earnest purpose, he still gave himself to the business which Provideuce seemed to appoint him. After a successful career at the Roxbury mills he became joint partner with the Davenport Brothers, in the extensive rolling mills at Stillwater. Here he spent the rest of his life. In the duties of his extensive business, whose business was mainly entrusted to his care, and in quiet and private acts of his noble generosity, he accomplished great good.

He was universally beloved by the many laborers who were in his employ. They were all mourners when he died. Multitudes of the poor of his native town were the objects of his generous benefactions. He seemed most pleased in giving, and, to those who most needed it.

He never married, but he found or made for himself a home in the family of his younger brother, James William, where he found all that he wanted in a home. Here he enjoyed himself, and here he was the joy of those whom he spoke of as his own family. Nothing could fempt him to leave it. For the last eleven years of his life he had not spent a night away from the home he so much loved.

Here he gave himself to his business and reading. In both he was diligent and thorough. Every hour was employed, and well employed. His reading was carefully selected. He could not be entertained by the fashionable light literature of the day; he needed something more substantial. History, biography, philosophy and science, were the works which engrossed his time, and in them his reading was quite extensive.

Two characteristics prominent in his whole life, made him one of the most beloved and trustworthy men of the town. He was conscientious and benevolent. After he had reached manhood, learning that a school bill of his boyhood had never been paid, he carefully enquired after every possible arrearage of those early years, and cashed them with full interest. His benevolence was unbounded, and much of it was unknown. Though he gathered a handsome estate, he had, while living, the truer joy of distributing in benefactions, where he knew they would do good, probably a still larger amount.

His sudden death occurred Jan. 21, 1804, and the multitudes who gathered at his funeral were the best witnesses a good man could have, to the esteem in which he was held. Uuaffected and universal mourning attested the public bereavement.

WELLES, NOAH, D. D, was born in Colchester, Jan. 23, 1718, and graduated at Yale College in 1741. His scholarship is indicated in his appointment as tutor in his Alma Mater in 1745. After receiving his license to preach he was settled as pastor of the Stamford Church, as our chapter on ecclesiastical matters, shows, Dec. 31, 1746. We have already in our history been obliged to report his success in the work of the ministry here. He attained a high rank among the ministers of Connecticut. He was chosen a Fellow of Yale College in 1774, and received the degree of D. D., the same year from the College of New Jersey.

Dr. Dwight thus testifies to his ability and standing.

"Dr. Welles was early distinguished for his talents. His imagination was vivid and poetical, his intellect vigorous, and his learning extensive. His manners at the same time were an unusually happy compound of politeness and dignity. In his conversation, he was alternately sprightly and grave, as occasion dictated, and entertaining and instructive. At the same time he was an excellent minister of the Gospel; exemplary in all the virtues of christian life; an able preacher; a wise ruler of the church; and an eminently discreet manager of its important concerns. He was one of the three chosen friends of the late Governor Livingston of New Jersey, to whom he addressed, when young, a handsomely written poem, prefixed to his Philosophic Solitude."

Dr. Welles was somewhat fond of theological controversy. And as his ministry was in that period in which Episcopacy was working its way into the colonies, and particularly into Fairfield County, he felt himself called upon, in virtue of his office here, to defend the church organization to which he was attached. His discourse on Presbyterian ordination, printed in 1763, at the new printing office, near the Royal Exchange, by John Hoyt, was an able justification of his authority as a minister of the church of Christ. It had been preached on two successive Sabbaths to his own people. Subsequently, he published a still more lengthy, and perhaps still more spirited defense of the authority of the Congregational clergy, and of the polity of the Congregational Church. Though earnestly entering into their discussions, he was never diverted by them from the great work of his profession; nor was his spirit ever soured by them towards the Episcopal clergy or the denomination. The work just named stirred up considerable denominational feeling among the Episcopal clergy, and called forth from the earliest clergyman of that denomination here, the Rev. James Wetmore, a work of some spirit entitled; " A Vindication of the Professors of the Church of England in Connecticut, against Invectives contained in a sermon by Noah Hobart, of Stamford, Dec. 31, 1746." The name Hobart in the title of the work is of course a mistake of the printer, for Welles. (See Wetmore Family.)

Dr. Welles, married in 1751, Abigail Woolsey, daughter of Rev. Benjamin Woolsey, of Oyster Bay, by whom he had the following children: Sarah, born Nov. 9, 1752; Mary Sylvester, born Oct. 20, 1754; Theodosia, born Oct. 22, 1758; Abigail, born Oct. 12, 1760; Noah, born Oct. 3, 1762; Betsey, born Feb. 23, 1765; Rebecca, born July 5, 1767; William, born Jan. 22, 1769; Melancthon Woolsey, born Dec. 9, 1770; Apollos, born Oct. 10, 1773; John and James, twins, born April 7, 1776. Dr. Welles died Dec. 31, 1776, and his wife Oct. 28, 1811, aged 81.

CHAPTER XXV.

MISCELLANEOUS TOPICS.

UNION LODGE.

This is one of the oldest institutions of the town, and deserves its place in our history. Its charter bears date, Nov. 18, 1763; and was issued by "Geo. Harrison, Esq., Provincial Grand Master of the most Ancient and Honorable Society of Free and Accepted Masons in the province of New York." It authorizes Sylvanus Waterbury, "our worshipful and well beloved brother," "to form a lodge, to choose his wardens, and appoint other officers, with the consent of the brethren assembled in due form, to make masons, as also to do all and every such acts and things appertaining to said office, as usually have and ought to be done by other masters." He is to pay over to the Provincial Grand Lodge at New York, out of the first monies he shall receive, three pounds and three shillings sterling, to be applied to the use of the Grand Charity. This lodge was designed for Stamford and Horseneck, (Greenwich,) and parts adjacent.

The records of the lodge from 1763 to 1780 are lost, the only name of the members for that period, preserved, being that in the charter, Sylvanus Waterbury. Since then there have been four hundred and sixty names added to the membership.

The worshipful masters of the lodge, according to the records preserved have been, Sylvanus Waterbury, John Anderson, Israel Knapp, Jabez Fitch, Wm. Bush, Isaac Reed, Sturges Perry, Samuel Bush, Noyes Mather, Alexander Mills, James Stevens, Isaac Lockwood, Samuel Keeler, Simeon H. Minor, Benj. Huested, Isaac Bishop, Charles Hawley, Erastus Weed, John W. Leeds, fourteen years; Peter Brown, Sands Adams,

A. A. Holly, nineteen years; W. H. Holly, Roswell Hoyt, H. Bulkley, Philip L. Hoyt, T. J. Daskam, John A. Scofield, James H. Olmstead, and Dwight Waugh.

RITTENHOUSE CHAPTER.

This chapter of royal arch masons was chartered at a grand chapter of royal arch masons held in New Haven, Oct. 18, 1810, on a memorial presented to them by JAMES STEVENS and sundry other brethren, now residing in, and adjacent to, Stamford. The officers installed by the chapter are the most worshipful brother JAMES STEVENS, H. P.; the right worshipful brother, ISAAC LOCKWOOD, K-g.; and the right worshipful brother EZEKIEL LOCKWOOD, S--e.

The high priests of this order have been: James Stevens, Isaac Lockwood, Simeon H. Minor, Joseph Keeler, Wm. J. Street, Charles Hawley, John W. Leeds, Nathan Camp, Wm. Holly, Smith Scott, Geo. B. Glendining, Luke A. Lockwood, and James H. Olmstead.

ROADS.

At this day we have no conception of the difficulties connected with travel in the early period of our history.

For many years the travel was on foot or on horseback; and the roads were only meandering paths, such as afforded easiest progress for the weary feet. For many years they were marked hardly more than to clear off the trees and bushes, and this was done by each landowner before his own lot. How rapidly these paths or roads were laid out we have no means of knowing. One peculiarity of the highway of that early day was the fact of a gate across the road, wherever a side road entered the main one of the settlement—so that for several years, one could not probably have traveled a half mile in any direction from the center of the town, without meeting one of these gates. After a few years, by special action in town meeting, these gates were removed, generally on petition of some of the outsiders who found them a serious annoyance.

The following vote of 28th, 2d month, 1682, is a sample of the votes providing for the support of these highway gates:

"Joseph Stevens is to have on acre and half of land joyning to ye north of his lot in consideration whereof he is to keep and maintain ye lower south field gate; and ye sd land is bound for ye maintaining thereof. Also the sd Stevens is to keep & maintaine ye rocky neck gate for ye same quantity of land yt before was laid to it & ye land to stand bound for ye gate as aforesaid: goodman Dean & Joshua Hoit are apointed to lay it out."

The following vote is curious, as showing how even the great coast-route thoroughfare must have been subject to a similar obstruction. It bears date, Jan. 1764. "By vote ye town doth own the prosecution yt hath bine made upon ye state of John Pettit or ye fins for the deffects in a pece of fence by Grinwich bars, markt I P, and neglected by him, viz. John Pettit."

These gates, bars and fences across the roads were found exceedingly troublesome; and when other reasons could not induce their removal, resort was sometimes had to the strong arm. Thus, in 1726, we find this record: "the town by vote agree that they will stand by and justify those men that have been employed by the proprietors to pull down the fence that was set up across the highway near Thomas Stevens."

Without prosecuting the research further, it is due at least to the entertainment of future readers of our town history, that we attempt to sketch the final touches to the great thoroughfare of the town. From the first, the route between New Haven and New York ran through Stamford, mainly where the main road now lies. Yet, from local impediments, it was much more crooked, than now. Our engineering skill had not yet come to test its ability, in the encounter with very formidable granite bluffs, nor with what seemed the bottomless marshes and impenetrable swamps of our impracticable surface. And so it happened, that as business grew, and demanded greater expedition,—as wheeled carriages succeeded equestrian or pedestrian locomotion, and felt more than they, these deviations from a right-lined course, our enterprising townsmen gave themselves no rest until they had done what seemed to them possible, towards leveling and straitening their roads.

Especially on those roads built for the daily passing of the heavy stage coach, did this improvement seem indispensable. Such was our main road through Stamford. The entire population in Eastern Connecticut, and so on all the way to Providence and Boston, were interested then as now, in shortening the distance and the time over the route. They had succeeded in satisfying themselves with the old roads until about 1795, when the call for thorough improvement began to be heard. The state legislature appointed commissioners, with almost absolute authority, to go over the road and lay out a new turnpike for greater expedition in travel. All along on the road between New Haven and Greenwich, there arose dissatisfaction and opposition. In Stamford there seems to have been no very earnest objection to the route adopted by the committee until, in their zeal for reform, they decided that the interest of the traveling public demanded a strait road through the village. But here they found themselves arrested by the old burying lot which, from the earliest remembrances of the towns people, had been held sacred for the rest of their dead. This lot covered the ground between the old "Washington House," or Webb Tavern, and the corner occupied by the Methodist Church; and the old turnpike had followed the present route of Park Place till it enters River street. The enterprising committee insist on laying out the new turnpike right across that hallowed spot. The town opposed, and for years kept the committee and the legislature at bay. But the world moves on and by 1805, enough of our townsmen had been drawn into the current to approve and second the measure. John Davenport even took stock in the sacrilegious enterprise, and we find his name at the head of a petition for the summary and authorative opening of the desired road. The town oppose and the corporation persevere. The legal authority is granted, and the invasion begins. Entering the burying lot, just south of the east end of our present Park Place, they plowed strait across, as the present Main street runs, to the Methodist Church, where they again entered the old turnpike. Removing carefully the grave stones and exhuming the remains beneath, they commence the thorough grading of the new road. In spite of the mutterings, which betokened serious hostility to the daring act, the corporation go on in their work. Night overtakes them, and they are obliged to rest. But now is the time for the opposition. Team after team of Stamford oxen, sturdy and true to the sturdy and true men who drove them, filed on towards the newly opened road. Immense rocks were hauled right across both ends of the opening; and when "Uncle Thad," the same who thirty years before had so delighted his townsmen by shaking his tory neighbor, was satisfied that the turnpike corporation would have a job sufficiently discouraging to remove the obstructions, the men and teams were withdrawn to rest for another night's work, if it should be necessary.

Twice more this game was played, but the influence of the age and the strong arm of the law were alike against it, and the opposition of the town had to yield. The road was finished ; but the feeling of some of the opposition, at the head of whom were such leaders of the people as Captain Isaac Lockwood and Captain Thaddeus Hoyt, was so deep, that no pressure of business could ever prevail on them to drive over those few rods of what, to the day of their death, they looked upon as desecrated ground.

NEWSPAPERS.

In April, 1829, Stamford took a new step forward in her progress. A printing office was opened here and the *Stamford Intelligencer* was issued. The editor not succeeding to his satisfaction, Wm. H. Holly, Esq., at the solicitation of some of the citizens of the town, and under a pledge of pecuniary support, started a new paper, Feb. 16, 1830, under the title of the *Stamford Sentinel.* From that date to the present, the town has not been without its weekly paper. Mr. Holly continued in charge of the paper under the title of "Sentinel," "Democratic Sentinel" and "Farmer's Advocate," until June 27, 1841. It is not too much to say for the paper that its management was marked by great ability. As a pioneer paper, few of its day equaled it.

Alfred W. Pearce succeeded Mr. Holly, under whose editorial care it continued until Sept. 29, 1841, when Henry Nichols succeeded him. The last paper issued by Mr. Nichols, which I have found, bears date March 26, 1842, and in June of the same year the "Farmers and Merchant's Advocate" was issued under the editorial management of the former editor, Wm. Henry Holly.

In May, 1848, Edgar Hoyt and Andrew J. Smith took charge of the paper, and enlarged with the simple title of the "Stamford Advocate," which it has since retained. On the dissolution of the copartnership between Mr, Hoyt and Smith in June, 1849, Mr. Hoyt assumed full control of the *Advocate* until 1860, when Wm. S. Campbell, who proved an efficient editor, became proprietor. There were few papers in the state more ably managed, than the *Advocate*, while in his hands. He soon took into partnership with himself, Wm. W. Gillespie, the foreman in his printing department. On his death, Mr. Gillespie formed a new partnership with Rev. James J. Woolsey, which was dissolved in the spring of 1868. Mr. Gillespie immediately organized a new firm, W. W. Gillespie & Co., introduced steam as motive power, and greatly enlarged his facilities for carrying on all departments of his business. How satisfactorily the paper is managed, and how necessary it is found to be to the town are seen in the increasing subscription list, this having more than trebled during the last three years.

STEAMBOATS.

As early as 1825, the Oliver Wolcott was put on the Stamford line, and for years made trips every other day to New York. But the town has been mainly supplied by boats which touched here on the route from ports further east. In the spring of 1849, the Steamboat Norwalk, running between Norwalk and New York stopped at Stamford. And since then, successively, the Ella, and Stamford, and Shippan, have done a large part of the freighting between New York and Stamford. At first, at low tides, the boats landed on the west side of the harbor, but a short distance above the present residence of our venerable deacon Theodore Davenport; but in 1856, the brothers Knapp—James E., of New York, and John B. of Richmond Hill, opened the channel to their new dock at the foot of South street, to which point the boats have continued to run until now. For several summers, the only steamboat which accommodated Stamford stopped at Portchester.

CANAL.

This work was due mainly to the energy of Alfred Bishop. (See Later Biography.) It was deemed the beginning of better days for the town, when in 1833, this feat was accomplished. The first sloop which cleaved its waters was our "Mayflower," and we may be sure its young captain, not yet among our oldest citizens, Rufus Wardwell, Esq., felt no little pride as he pioneered our local commerce. Those warehouses which lined the terminus of the canal, were doubtless looked upon as the beginning of no slight commercial prosperity. But a readier avenue to the great commercial center was destined at no distant day to be opened; and our commercial warehouses were doomed to decline into the work shops and low tenements, which we shall have to await the coming of a better time to remove.

Two years after it was opened, our local paper, the *Sentinel*, thus speaks of its possibilities:

"Through the perseverance of a single individual, a ship channel has been opened, and the enterprising Messrs. Wm. and R. Hoyt & Co., have despatched the schooner James Star with a full freight for the West Indies, The value of this canal to this vicinity, is not yet fully realized, but every day unfolds to the skeptic new evidences of its utility.

The schooner in due time, about six weeks, returned, "nine days from Eleuthall, well laden with fruit, copper, dye woods,

&c., proving a profitable experiment for the adventurers." The editor acknowledges his obligations to the captain for a handsome present of pine apples.

STAMFORD SHIP CANAL COMPANY.

Joseph B. Hoyt and Joseph D. Warren in the winter of 1867–8, conceived the plan of opening a permanent ship canal, from the harbor up, so as to connect easily with the railroad. They accordingly purchased the needed land, controlling both sides of the proposed canal, and entered, in the spring of 1868, upon the work. Beginning in the bed of the old canal, about sixty rods below the Depot of the New York and New Haven Railroad, they are digging some nine feet below the present bed of the canal and opening a channel, down to the harbor, eighty feet wide; making as they go, solid land as far as the material thus removed will extend, on each side of the channel, for building and business uses. When successfully completed, this enterprise promises a large addition to the facilities which the town will offer, for mechanical and manufacturing purposes.

RAIL-ROAD.

That was a new and exciting day for our quiet villagers, when in 1844, a special town meeting was called to consider the petition of the Housatonic Railroad Company for a road from Bridgeport to Byram river along the Long Island shore. The town came together May 7th, and after considering, variously, the strange proposal, agree, with a singular unanimity, in favor of the road, and instruct their representatives in the assembly to favor it. But, as is the fate with most novel enterprises, this was doomed to delay; and the restive and ambitious citizens of the town had to wait four years more for the fulfillment of their desire. But the fulfillment came, and when, in 1848, the great thoroughfare between Boston and New York was opened, under date of Dec. 19th of that year, we find in the *Stamford Advocate*, then edited by Edgar Hoyt, Esq., the following graphic note on the wonderful event of the first appearance of the iron horse among us:

RESIDENCE OF JOSEPH B. HOYT, NORTON HILL, STAMFORD.

"The citizens of the village, as well as the horses, cattle, &c., were nearly frightened out of their propriety on Wednesday afternoon last, at about five o'clock, by such a horrible scream as was never heard to issue from any other than a metallic throat. Animals of every description went careering round the fields, snuffing the air in their terror, and bipeds of every size, condition and color, set off at a full run for the railroad depot. In a few moments the cause of the commotion appeared in the shape of a locomotive, puffing off its steam and screaming with its so-called whistle at a terrible rate. Attached to the locomotive were a lumber and a passenger car, and the latter, we believe, is one of the most splendid description now in use on any road in this country. * * * They have not yet commenced running regularly to this place, and it is not probable that they will do so until the road is finished to New York, which will probably be about the latter part of the present week or the first of next."

By January 1st the road had been completed, and the year 1849 was inaugurated by what was deemed a great marvel, the actual transit of three trains, daily, the whole distance from New Haven to New York and back again. The trial trip had been made on Monday, Dec. 25, and a single passage, in the account of that trip, from the pen of William H. Holly, Esq., who was one of the honored passengers of the occasion, is worth preserving in our history of the times :

"The train had to remain at Coscob Bridge some three hours for the last rails to be laid over it, and the delay gave ample opportunity to the surrounding people to come in and witness the wonderful feat. The general impression among them seemed to be, that the first train that attempted to cross this elevated pass would also be the last. All sorts of old women's stories to frighten the children had been put in circulation regarding the safety of this bridge, and many a spectator expected to see our splendid locomotive, elegant car, and confiding attendants and passengers plunged into the deep below.

Ten minutes before two o'clock, P, M., Mr. Mason, chief engineer of the company, gave the word, 'all ready.' Our prancer was let loose. Every skeptic's heart rose to his mouth. Breathless anxiety pervaded the multitude on each shore. The train moved majestically along and the next minute the western shore received its ponderous weight, and the welkin rang with the shouts of the congregated people."

Probably no event in the history of Stamford has had more to do in shaping the future of the town than the opening of this great thoroughfare. Very soon after the road was built, all fears of an unfavorable result upon the prosperity of the town were dissipated. We were soon seen to have been made a suburb of the great city. Our talent could find a much readier field for its use in the city, and the wealth and talent of the city a much more attractive home here. The sons of Stamford who had previously been wont to go to the city to make their fortunes, could now return to invest and enjoy them here. Now, and hereafter, without changing their residence for a week, our sons can avail themselves of all the aid which the city can give.

The following postscript in the *Stamford Sentinel* of June 6, 1836, may indicate how much we may have gained, in time at least, from this iron track:

"Just arrived, sloop Mary Flower, Bell, nine, days from New York, via. Cow Bay, where she was detained by the inspector of the weather. Hands all well, but rather meager in countenance for want of fresh provisions and ordinary exercise. Left New York, where it formerly stood. Business brisk. Spoke two hundred vessels or more bound up, awaiting favorable weather."

And what gain the railroad has made upon its own beginning, we shall easily see in comparing the time table of 1849, with its three daily trips, with that of 1868, furnishing us with thirteen. Nor is it foreign to our record to add, that much of this marked progress has been due to the long and successful superintendency of our townsman, the Hon. James H. Hoyt.

NEW CANAAN AND STAMFORD RAILROAD.

This new enterprise was chartered in 1867, with a capital of $100,000, with the privilege of increasing it to $200,000. Its track was so far completed that an excursion train was run over it, July 4, 1868. Already we have evidence of the stimulus which this road has given to the north east part of Stamford, as well as to the business of New Canaan, by whose capital and for whose special interest it was mainly built.

CEMETERIES.

In the meeting of the society, held Dec. 24, 1747, a committee consisting of Col. Jona. Hoyt, Capt. Jona. Maltby and Mr. Abraham Davenport was appointed "to seek a proper place for a burying ground and purchase it at the society's charge.

DEPOT OF THE N. Y. & N. H. R. R., AT STAMFORD, 1867.

This is the first record of any action taken by the town regarding places of burial. For more than a century the main question in choosing a place for the graves of a family had been, where is the most convenient place. Much was made of the funeral service, but little heed was given to the place of sepulture. Accordingly, all over town we find the scattered graves of the departed generations—the number of society and neighborhood and family burying grounds on the old territory having increased to nearly one hundred; and during the first century, the number of single graves, opened in places now unmarked and unknown must have been very much greater. With literal truth we live and tread among the graves of the former generations. Our principal street opened its way through thick graves. Our middle aged citizens remember the little hill just east of the Methodist church, where slept the remains of several generations of our departed. This was undoubtedly the spot chosen in 1747, as above, for the town burying ground. At that time the town street at the center of the plot where the Congregational meeting house stood, turned to the north west, making what is now Park Place, and then turning to the north, up to what is now Broad street, crossing Theal's Bridge and so over Palmer Hill towards Greenwich. When Main street was straitened, by order of the committee of the assembly, it entered the burying lot at the east end of where our west Park is, and crossed it to the corner where the Methodist Church is, leaving two small burying lots on each side of a street four rods in width. As late as 1807, the town grant permission to the citizens of Stamford old Society to fence in the burying ground betweeu the house of Enoch Hoyt and Andrew Newman, reserving two rods each side of the old cart path through the burying ground, as laid out by the assembly's committee. If, however, they should find the road running through Enoch Hoyt's garden, thence west over the burying ground, they were to proceed no further. After the road was opened, and it was done by the strong hand, we find a vote authorizing Isaac and Enoch Lockwood

Isaac Wardwell and Isaac Hoyt and associates, to fence in the burying ground north and south of the turnpike, and the ground to be used for nothing but burying lots. Some twenty years later, the remaining grave stones were removed to the burying lot on Northfield street, and the old hill leveled, the church being removed across Park Place to the corner.

But a new order, we trust, has been inaugurated in the opening of the

WOODLAND CEMETERY.

This beautiful rural cemetery occupies a portion of what, in the earlier records of our town, was denominated Rocky Neck, and still later, the "Uplands." To the east and south, it lies on the east cove of our harbor, and under the skillful engineering of Mr. Hathaway, it is fast becoming one of the points of attraction in the town. The tract of about forty acres had been purchased for this use by an association of gentlemen, who organized themselves for the purpose, in August, 1856. The entire stock of the association, $20,000, was subscribed by sixty-three citizens of the town, and they chos for their first official board the following gentlemen: President, Charles Williams; Treasurer, William Skiddy; Secretary, H. M. Humphrey, Directors, George L. Brown, Wells R. Ritch, William Pitt, Henry Taff, J. B. Hoyt, Theodore Davenport, James L. Lockwood, Oliver Hoyt, and George A. Hoyt.

Under their direction the grounds, substantially enclosed, were skillfully laid out by their engineer, B. F. Hathaway, and so far worked as to authorize a formal dedication of the cemetery, July 29, 1861. The following gentlemen participated in the exercises of the dedication: Prayer by Rev. P. S. Evans, and reading of the Scriptures by Rev. Wm. C. Hoyt. Rev. J. S. Dodge furnished an original hymn—which was sung. Rev. Mr. Weed, of the Methodist Church, and Rev. Mr. Francis, of the Universalist Church, made appropriate addresses. Rev. Mr. Mitchell, of the Episcopal Church, read a poem, and the Hon. Wm. T. Minor made the presentation address. The services were closed by a prayer and benediction from Rev. Mr. Booth, of the Presbyterian Church.

STAMFORD BANK.

This bank was incorporated in 1834, with a capital of $100,000, on condition that the bank should pay a bonus of $5,000 to the Wesleyan University of Middletown, in two installments. There were 363 subscribers to the stock of the bank, of whom 84 were Stamford residents.

John W. Leeds was chosen President, and he has retained and honored the post down to the present time. The Bank has had the following cashiers: J. F. Henry, Edward Hill, Samuel K. Satterlee, Charles K. Rockwood, Douglass R. Satterlee, H. M. Humphrey, Francis R. Leeds, and Joseph L. Leeds, its cashier since 1863. The character of the bank is pretty well shown in the fact that when, in 1861, permission was given to increase the capital stock $90,000, in one week from the opening of the subscription, $144,000 was pledged. In 1865, the bank became the Stamford National Bank.

FIRST NATIONAL BANK OF STAMFORD.

This bank was established in 1863, with a capital of 200,000. Under the presidency of H. M. Humphrey, M. D., formerly of the Stamford Bank, with its cashier, Charles W. Brown, it has established itself in the confidence of the public. During the temporary absence of Mr. Humphrey, Joseph B. Hoyt, Esq., and Welles R. Ritch, Esq., have been acting presidents.

STAMFORD SAVINGS BANK.

This institution was organized July 21, 1851. Its presidents have been Theodore Davenport, Charles Hawley and James H. Hoyt. Its vice-presidents, Joseph D. Warren, James H. Hoyt, and John W. Leeds. Its treasurers, Chas. G. Rockwood, Samuel K. Satterlee, Francis R. Leeds and Alfred A. Holly. That the institution has been successful is evidenced in its rapidly increasing deposits.

STAMFORD BOROUGH.

This was incorporated in the spring of 1830. An enumeration of the population had been made the preceding summer, when, within the limits of the proposed borough, the following results had been reached: families, 92; inhabitants, 663; white males, 354; white females, 283; free colored males, 10; free colored females, 14; and two slaves.

The petition for incorporation was headed by David Holly, Esq. The persons named in the act to call the first meeting of the borough were, Charles Hawley, Simeon H. Minor, Theodore Davenport, and Seymour Jarvis.

The officers chosen for the borough for the first year were, for warden, Simeon H. Minor; clerk and treasurer, Seymour Jarvis,, burgesses, John W. Leeds, Wm. H. Holly, Charles Hawley Esq., John S. Winthrop, and David Hoyt; street commissioners, Isaac Quintard, sen., Sands Adams, Fitch Rodgers, Smith Scott, and Peter Smith, jun.; agent, J. B. Ferris.

In 1850, so great had been the irregularity and confusion in the names of streets in the borough, that a formal meeting was held and a committee appointed, with authority to make a selection of names, and submit them to a subseqnent meeting. That committee consisted of J. W. Leeds, James H. Hoyt, Wm. H. Babbitt, Edwin S. Bishop, Andrew Perry, and H. J. Sanford. Their report recommended, mainly, the names which the streets then opened, now bear. The growth of the borough has been very rapid in population and wealth. From 1840 to 1850, the population of the borough gained about 133 per cent., and that of the entire town about 42 per cent.

The following is the entire list of wardens, to the present time: Simeon H. Minor, two years; Charles Hawley; J. W. Leeds, four years; Wm. H. Holly; Sands Adams, two years; Theodore Davenport, five years; Ezra Scofield; Henry H. Waring; H. J. Sanford, six years; Geo. E. Waring; James H. Hoyt; Chauncy Ayres, three years; Jona. M. Hall; Wm. T. Minor; Albert Seely; Charles Williams, two years; Geo Elder; H. K. Skelding, three yrs.; Wm. P. Jones and E. Gay, two yrs.

FITCH'S HOME FOR SOLDIERS.

This institution, situated about a half a mile east of the pres ent Stamford line, in the town of Darien, was chartered in 1864, to provide for the disabled soldiers of the twelfth senatorial district of the state. It takes its name from its founder, Benjamin Fitch, Esq., of Darien, who has contributed towards its endowment and support, something over $100,000. It was found that it was not needed for disabled soldiers, and in February, 1865, the trustees, Hon. Morgan Morgans, Joseph B. Hoyt, and Charles Starr, of Stamford; Wm. A. Cnmmings and Charles Brown, of Darien; E. C. Bissel, of Norwalk; Stephen Hoyt, of New Canaan; M. B. Pardee, M. D., of South Norwalk; Charles Marvin, of Wilton, and P. Button, of Greenwich, decided to open here a home and school for the orphan and destitute children of our fallen or disabled soldiers. Rev. E. B. Huntington, their agent, gathered into the Home by the end of May, twenty-seven of these children, where the most of them have since been supported. Others have been added to their numbers, making the entire number thus far supported about sixty. Mr. Fitch, in addition to the buildings used for the ordinary uses of such an institution, has given to the Home a fine brick building for a library, and a gallery of paintings and statuary. At his own expense, mainly, he has gathered here over two hundred paintings, making a very showy gallery, costing not far from $50,000.

When no longer needed for the soldiers or soldiers' children of the twelfth senatorial district of the state, the funds of the Home are devoted, by the charter, "to the support of aged and infirm persons of said district, and to the support and education of orphan children of said district."

FIRE COMPANIES.

In 1815, on petition of Sands Seeley, Lorenzo Meeker and James H. Minor, they, and such other citizens of Stamford, not to exceed thirty, as might unite with them, were chartered under the title of the Rippowam Fire Company. By special act of the legislature of 1855, the Rippowam Company was authorized to increase its number to sixty members.

STAMFORD FIRE ENGINE, NO. 2.

In 1854, Andrew Perry, Edwin Bishop, G. K. Riker, T. J. Daskam, Geo. E. Scofield, Jesse A. Reed, J. N. Webb, Theodore Lockwood, Wm. Lavender, Francis Dauchy, Theodore Hoyt, Wm. W. Smith, C. F. Peck, Theodore Davenport, jr., and Charles B. Finch, and such other citizens as might unite with them, not to exceed forty, were incorporated as the "Stamford Fire Engine, No. 2."

Of the efficient character of this company, and their machine, we have ample testimony in the results of the national trial of fire engines in Albany, Sept. 30, 1859. Thirty-six engines were entered for the trial; and Stamford, No, 2, stood second on the list, being excelled only by No. 3, of Brooklyn.

STAMFORD GAS LIGHT COMPANY.

This company was organized in 1858, on a capital of $20,000, which has now reached $52,500. Their works are located on Mechanic street, near the depot. The first board of directors were, H. K. Skelding, president, Geo. A. Hoyt, Geo. L. Brown, Geo. Scofield, Wm. Gay. John W. Leeds, treasurer. Charles Pitt is now president, and Edward Gay; treasurer and superintendent.

CRYSTAL LAKE ICE.

In 1855, John B. Knapp, Esq., formed an artificial lake, in what was called the Ladden brook, crossing the "turnpike" a few rods east of the Greenwich line, for the purpose of securing ice for the town. Commencing in the winter of 1855, with a stock of about 400 tons, the demand has increased steadily, until now, when its buildings will hold about 5,000 tons, and the one horse wagon of 1855, has been succeeded by the heavy teams now traversing every part of the village.

MILL RIVER ICE COMPANY.

Charles E. Smith, Esq., and sons, in the fall of 1866, converted what had been an old pottery, standing on the west bank of the "mill pond," into an ice house, where he now stores about 1,800 tons, yearly.

COVE MILLS.

In 1791, William Fitch secured permission to build a dam across the Noroton Creek, at a place called Noroton Gut. The terms were: that he should build a mill within seven years, and thereafter grind and bolt as other mills do; that after three years, he should, every summer, draw off the water, giving notice to the inhabitants that they may take shell fish therein; that he should keep a good scow in the mill pond, sufficient for carrying 2,000 bushels of grain, which should always be free for the use of the town; that he should build a good wharf below the dam; and that he should make good any damage to individuals who have property above said Gut—the damage to be assessed by three indifferent, judicious men.

The next year John W. Holly moved over to the Cove, then called the *Pound, and, in company with Mr. Fitch, commenced building the dam and mills. It will indicate the great change which has taken place since that date to state that there was no house between the one now occupied by Robert Walsh, Esq., at the south east corner of St. John's Park, and the one which Mr. Holly built at the Cove. Nor was there any road, excepting the path leading from the east-field gate, where Elm now crosses Meadow street, through open fields or the old forest, over to the Pound.

Under Mr. Holly, in his two mills, was carried on, for years, a heavy flouring business. He also added to this the grinding of dye woods. After the death of Mr. Holly, his son, Wm. W., rented, and afterwards sold the mills to John and Henry Sanford, who had already commenced the preparation of dye woods in Greenwich.

In 1844, they organized the Stamford Manufacturing Com-

*This name is still attached to the rocky headland now so much resorted to by our summer pleasure seekers, and was given to the locality from the fact, that in the autumn of the year, the town herds which had been roaming over these common grounds during the warm months, were taken, by being driven down to this point, as into a pound, over the narrow neck of land which has since been cut by the mill canal.

pany, which from that date have done here, the heaviest business in the town. They purchased, also, the flouring mill of David Holly, at the mouth of Mill river, and, also, own mills in other towns. The business carried on by this company has been that of grinding dye woods, spices and barytes, and also the making of extract of licorice. The present company consists of Charles H. Leeds, president; H. J. Sanford, J. C. Sanford, Sanford Brown, John W. Leeds, Wm. Gay, E. F. Leeds, A. W. Bissel, and S. K. Satterlee, directors.

In August, 1655, these works at the Cove were destroyed by fire. They were immediately built of brick, and are now fire proof.

STILLWATER AND ROXBURY ROLLING MILLS.

In 1825, Mr. Wm. Lacon, an Englishman, started the Roxbury rolling mills, and soon associated with himself Dea. Theodore Davenport. Subsequently, these works were owned and improved by J. A. Davenport and J. D. Weeks, as a rolling and wire mill. On the organization of the Stillwater Company, in 1835, consisting of Dea. Theodore Davenport, J. D. Weeks and J. A. Davenport, they purchased the farm which had been owned by Joseph Watson, of Stillwater, and built the heavy rolling mills still in operation there; carrying on, also the works at the Roxbury mills. Since that date, both of these localities have been used by the Stillwater Company—the one at Stillwater as a rolling mill for the manufacture of iron and steel, and that at Roxbury, for making wire. The present owners are Dea. Theodore Davenport and his sons, and Jeremiah N. Ayres.

WOOLEN MANUFACTORY.

Near the beginning of this century, Samuel Wheaton improved the water power on the Mianus, just above Bangall, as a site for a woolen mill; using it for carding wool and dressing cloth. In 1826, Benjamin Mathews purchased the property, and, for years, added to the former business, that of weaving woolen goods. The property is now owned by J. F. Mathews, son of the former owner, and E. June, and is used for the manufacture of woolen yarns.

STAMFORD STOVE FOUNDRY.

This enterprise had its origin in the iron foundry established by Geo. E. Waring, having its first location on the west side of Bedford street, just south of where Spring street now enters it. On building the elegant cottage on the corner of Bedford and Broad streets, Mr. Waring removed his works down to the rolling mills of David Holly, purchasing the entire mill privilege and property. The Holly Rolling Mill had succeeded the carding and grist mills of the brothers Thorp, and these works occupied the site of the earliest mill privilege granted to the Webbs. In 1848, Mr. Waring formed a partnership with J. B. Scofield, J. M. Hall, and Isaac Wardell. The next year, Joseph D. Warren took Mr. Hall's place in the firm, and after the withdrawal of Mr. Waring, the other three gentlemen, under the firm of J. D. Warren & Co., removed the works over to the head of the canal, where it is now situated. In 1867 they greatly enlarged their business facilities, and are now employing between fifty and sixty men.

PHOENIX CARRIAGE MANUFACTORY.

This company was organized in 1860. John B. Reed, who had been in the business a number of years before, united with Grant Judd, E. P. Whitney, Isaac G. Traphagen and Benjamin U. Lyon, and located their works on the east side of Gay street, where their iron work is still done. Soon finding their room too small for their works, they commenced building, also, on the west side of the street. In 1858 they purchased the old Congregational Church, then standing where the triangular park now is, in the center of tho village, and removed it to the rear of their ware room on the west side of Gay street. By introducing two floors, they divided the building into three stories, giving them a great amount of room for their business. Since then, they have been engaged successfully in the manufacture of all descriptions of the better styles of carriages, employing from thirty to forty men. There has been but a single change in the firm since its organization, resulting from the removal by death of Mr. Traphagen in 1855. Mr. Reed has, from the beginning, been the financial agent of the firm.

STAMFORD WOOLEN MILLS.

These extensive works occupy the grounds formerly occupied by the earliest grist mill of the town; and more recently by the Rippowam Iron Foundry. They are now owned by Harding, Smith & Co., who commenced, in 1867, the manufacture of woolen goods. John A. Smith, one of the proprietors of the firm resides here, and has the management of the works. They are now employing about one hundred and fifty persons in the establishment.

LONG RIDGE SHOE FACTORY.

The shoe business has been carried on at the Ridge for nearly half a century. Under George W. Todd, Scofield & Todd, and Scofield, Cook & Co., it had grown to be quite an interest of the locality. Some ten years ago, our enterprising young townsmen, Cook & Lounsbury took hold of it, and have done here an excellent business. They employ about fifty hands, and with the aid of machinery are able to turn off about 20,000 pairs of shoes a year. The time needed for sewing on the sole of a shoe with their stitcher, is somewhat less than a half minute.

UNION FIRE-BRICK AND DRAIN-PIPE WORKS.

In 1845 Charles Anness, Esq., began these works on the west bank of Mill river, opposite Harding & Smith's woolen mills. His brother Samuel succeeds him in the business here, having removed the works in 1862 to Water Side, where he now employs in the business about fifteen hands.

SHIRT FACTORY.

C. D. Jones has been for years engaged, quite extensively, in the manufacture of shirts and draws on High Ridge. The work, here, is done mainly for the New York market, and has employed a large number of operatives.

NEW ENGLAND MANUFACTURING WORKS AND COMPANY.

This joint stock company was organized in 1868, with a capital of $60,000, for manufacturing machinists' tools. They are now operating by steam on Main street, near South, but have found it necessary to enlarge their works; and have purchased and are building at the foot of South street, near Knapp's Dock. Robert Fairchild is president; G. W. Bishop, the patentee of the articles now manufactured, is superintendent, and J. E. Law, treasurer.

BROAD STREET STEAM PLANING AND SAW MILL.

This enterprise was started in 1864 by Richmond Fox and John St. John. Since the death of Mr. Fox, in 1867, Harvey Hoyt has been one of the partners of the firm. There has been done, here, in connexion with their lumber yard, a few rods north on Bedford street, a heavy lumber business.

CONCENTRATED MEDICINE LABORATORY.

These works were opened here in 1865, by B. Keith & Co., for the preparation of organic medicines. They are located at Water Side, and require about five hands to carry them on

CANAL STREET STEAM MILL.

This work was begun here in the spring of 1868, by Edgar Studwell and B. Franklin Hobby. It is designed as a saw, planing and grist mill, and is now worked by Hobby, Stivers & Co.

WOODSIDE PARK.

This Park has just been opened by its proprietors, the brothers T. I. and S. H. Ferris, jun. It lies on the west side of Mill river, about a half mile north of the village, and has an excellent, circular track, a half mile in length.

TELEGRAPH.

1848 added the Telegram to the former facilities to Stamford business; and we are sure no little curiosity was excited here, by the arrival of this noiseless messenger. At first, the telegraph office was opened in the building next east of the

Union House, but was removed to the Depot, where it has been ever since. The business has increased until it has come to be a necessity to business itself, twelve wires supplying us with instantaneous reports of important changes, from every point on telegraph routes. Its present manager is J. K. Butler, with two assistants.

CAMPHOR AND WAX FACTORIES.

These works were established here in 1856, by Charles H. Phillips, Esq., of New York, for refining camphor and bleaching wax. They are located about a mile and a half north east from the village, at our "New Hope," and are among the most extensive refineries in the country, employing not far from twenty-five hands. To the rear of these works, on the banks of the Noroton, Mr. Phillips has laid out and worked to a charming perfection, one of our completest gems in landscape culture. Everything about it—its summer house, fish ponds, fountains, statues, lawns, shrubbery and walks,—is as near perfection as human skill can make it; and altogether constitutes one of the most attractive localities in the town.

SLAVES.

"Jack, Son to Rose, a servant of Samuel Bush of Greenwich, said Jack, being the property of Isaac Quintard, deceased, was born on June 20, 1788."

STAMFORD, April 6, 1797.

This is to certify, that, I, widow Mary Selleck of Stamford, do freely give Nathaniel and Africa Chloe his wife, a certain negro boy, by the name of Harry, their son, formerly belonged to me.

Charles A, Belding, }
Anna Belding, } MARY SELLECK.

The records above are specimens of those which remind us of an institution never again to be revived in Stamford. They are here preserved as a part of the history of the earlier times in this old puritan town.

APPENDIX. A.

THE PATENT.

Whereas the generall court of Connecticutt hath formerly Granted unto the proprietors Inhabitants of the town of Standford all those lands both meadow and upland within these abutments upon the sea at the south, east on the fiue Mile Brooke between Standford aforesaid & Norwalke from the mouth of the sayd Brook till it meet with the cross pass that now is where the country roade crosseth the sayd path, & from thence to run up into the country till Twelve miles be run out upon the same lyne that is between Stratford and fayrefield; and upon the west Tatomak Brooke, where the lowermost path or road that now is to Greenwich cutts the sayd brooke & from thence to run on a straight lyne to the west end of a lyne drawne, from the falls of Standford Mill river which sayd lyne is to run a due west poynt towards Greenwich bounds a meat mile & from the west end of sayd line to run due north to the present county roade towards Rye and from thence to run up into the country the same line that it is between Norwalk and Standford to the end of the bownds, the sayd lands having been by purchas or otherwise lawfully obtayned of the Indian native proprietors, and whereas the proprietors, the aforesayd Inhabitants of Standford in the colony of Connecticutt have made application to the Gouernor and company of the sayd colony of Connecticutt assembled In court May 25, 1685, that they have a patent for confirmation of the aforesayd lands so purchased and granted to them as aforesayd & which they have stood seized and quietly possessed of for many years last past without Interruption now for a more full confirmation of the aforesayd tract of land as it is butted and bounded aforesayd unto the present proprietors of the sayd township of Stanford, in their possession and enjoyment of the premises; KNOW ye that the said Gouernor & company assembled in GENERAL COURT according to the commission granted to them by his Ma'tie in his charter have given & granted & by these presents do give, grant, ratify and confirm unto Mr. John Bishop, Mr. Richard law, Capt. Jonathan Silleck, Capt. John Silleck, Lieut. Francis Bell, Lieut. Jonathan Bell, ensign John Bates, Mr. Abraham Ambler, Mr. peter ferris, Mr. Joshua Hoyte, and the rest of the sayd present proprietors of the township of Standford their heirs, successors and assigns forever, the aforesayd parcell of land as it is Butted and Bounded together with all the meadows, pastures, ponds, waters, rivers, islands, fishings, Huntings, fowlings, mines, minerals, Quarries and precious stones upon or within the sayd tract of land and all other proffitts comodities thereunto belonging or in any wayes appertaining and do grant unto the aforesayd Mr. John Bishop, Mr. Richard lawe, Capt. Jonathan Silleck, Capt. John

Silleck, Lnt. francis Bell, Lnt. Jonathan Bell, ens. John Bates, Mr. Abraham Ambler, Mr. peter ferris & Mr. Joshua Hoyt & the rest of the proprietors Inhabitants of Standford their heirs successors and assigns forever that the aforesayd tract of land shall be forever after deemed, reputed & be an Intire Township of it selfe, to have and to hold the sayd Tract of land and premises with all and singular their appurtenances together, with the priviledges and Immunities and franchies herein given and granted unto the sayd John Bishop, Richard law, Capt. Jonathan Silleck, Capt. John Silleck, Lnt. francis Bell, Lnt. Jonathan Bell, Ens. John Bates, Mr. Abraham Ambler; Mr. peter ferris & Mr. Joshua Hoyte and other the present proprietors Inhabitants of Standford their heirs successors and assigns forever and to the only proper use & behoofe of the sayd Mr. John Bishop, Richard law, Capt. Jonathan Silleck, Capt. John Silleck, Lnt. Francis Bell, Lnt. Jonathan Bell, Ens. John Bates, Mr. Abraham Ambler, Mr. peter ferris & Mr. Joshua Hoyte

And other proprietors Inhabitants of Standford their heirs, successors and assigns forever, according to the tenor of East Greenwich in Kent in free & comon soccage & not in capitee nor by knight service—

They to make improvent of the same as they are capable according to the customs of the country, yielding, rendering and paying therefore to our sovereign lord the king his heirs and successors his dues according to charter: In WITNESS whereof we have cause the seale of the colony to be here unto affixed this Twenty sixth of May One Thousand Six Hundred eighty-five in the first year of the reign of our souereign lord king James the second of England, scotland france & Ireland, defender of the fayth.

per order of the General Court, signed per me, John Allyn Sec'y.

B.

A list of graduates and professionally educated men, natives of Stamford, or belonging to Stamford families. This list embraces only those who have not been already indicated in the preceding pages.

ADAMS, BENJAMIN, son of Sands, a Methodist preacher.

BISHOP, JAMES W., son of Kitchel, of Darien, now city missionary in Brooklyn, N. Y.

BARTON, Rev. J. G., a student of St. Paul's, N. Y., and received his diploma at St. James', Md., in 1843. He was chosen Professor of Belles lettres and English literature in the Free Academy, since named the "College of the City of New York," in 1852, and since 1853, has lived in Stamford. He still holds his chair in the college.

BETTS, SYLVESTER M., son of James. in Yale, class of 1864, was obliged to leave from failure of sight. He is now a publisher in Hartford.

BETTS, WILLIAM J., second son of James, member of Yale, class of 1870.

BETTS, ALSOP L., third son of James, member of Yale, class of 1872.

CLASON, SOLOMON, a native of Stamford, who became a physician, having studied with Dr. Close. Taught school and went west, where he has been a successful physician.

COMSTOCK, DAVID C., a native of New Canaan. Graduated at Yale in 1830, where he was tutor. Studied theology and was settled in the ministry, (Congregational), in Redding, 1840–'45. Came to Stamford in 1851, and taught a school for young ladies. He still lives here. He married Elizabeth Ann Tompkins of New York city, and has had six children.

COMSTOCK, WM. S., a native of Redding, and son of the above. Graduated at Yale, 1865, with honor. He is now engaged revising and correcting surveys for local maps in the vicinity of New York city.

COMSTOCK, DAVID, son of Rev. David C., and born in Redding. Was in the Union service during the war, mainly in the Hospital department. Is now, 1868, a medical student at Ann Arbor, Mich.

COCKROFT, WILLIAM, graduated at Columbia College, N. Y., in 1834, and at the Medical College in 1837. He purchased, in 1863, the beautiful place on Elm Hill, which he has made one of the most attractive residences in town.

DAVENPORT, JOHN, son of Rev. James, graduated at Princeton, N. J., 1769, became a minister and settled in Southold, L. I., and at Bedford, N. Y. and Deerfield, N. J. He died at Lysander, N. Y., July 13, 1825, at 73 years of age, leaving no children.

DAVENPORT, JOHN ALFRED. son of John, graduated at Yale, 1802, and soon went into business in New York. After a successful business career of some fifty years, he moved to New Haven in 1853, where he died, Oct. 14, 1864, in the 82d year of his age.

DAVENPORT, GEORGE F., son of Rufus, graduated at University of New York, 1830, and was a lawyer in New York city.

DAVENPORT, JOHN SIDNEY, son of John A., above, born in Stamford, Sept. 26, 1808, became an Episcopal minister and was settled at Oswego, N. Y., and after going abroad, returned and accepted a charge in Boston.

DAVENPORT, JAMES RADCLIFFE, brother of John S., graduated at Yale, 1830; became an Episcopal minister, and was settled in Albany, N. Y. He now resides in New York City.

DAVENPORT, JAMES, son of deacon Theodore, entered Yale in 1861, but left his class at the end of the junior year to go into business.

DEAN, HENRY, son of Samuel, began teaching early, and became a Congregational minister. He removed to Brooklyn, where he taught, and where for years he has been clerk of the board of education.

DEAN, GEORGE W., son of Col. John, of North Stamford, graduated at Columbia College and became an Episcopal minister. He was settled at Ballston, N. Y., and is now professor of Latin and Greek at Racine College.

FERRIS, SAMUEL P., son of Joshua B., graduated at West Point in 1861; and is now a captain in the U. S. A.

FERGUSON, JOHN DAY, son of John and Helen G. [Morewood] Ferguson—the family having moved to Stamford in 1842—graduated at Trinity College, Hartford, in 1851. He studied law, and has had an office in New York city.

FERGUSON, Samuel, brother of the above, graduated at Trinity in 1857. He and his brother Henry were on board the Hornet, a clipper which left New York for San Francisco in Jan. 1866, and which was burned on the Pacific, May 3d. For forty-three days they were in a little open boat with fourteen others. They were reduced to the verge of starvation, when they drifted into a port of Hawaii, just in time to avoid a horrible death. The journal which he managed to write is one of intensest interest. He died in San Francisco, Oct. 1, 1866.

FERGUSON, EDMUND M., third brother of this family was in Trinity College, class of 1857, but left from sickness.

FERGUSON, WALTON, fourth member of this family was also in Trinity College, class of 1863, but was obliged to leave from sickness.

FERGUSON, HENRY, fifth and youngest son of John, graduated at Trinity College the present year, 1868, one of the prize students.

FESSENDEN, SAMUEL C., graduated at Bowdoin College in 1834, and at the Bangor Theological Seminary in 1837. He was also admitted to the bar in 1856. He is now in the government service in Washington. He has resided, since 1866, in Stamford.

FINCH, SHERMAN, a native of the town; graduated at Yale, 1828, studied law and settled in Ohio.

FUERTES, E. A., a native of Porto Rico; graduated B. Ph. and M. D. in Porto Rico, and civil engineer in Troy, N. Y. He has lived here since 1864.

HOLLY, WM. WELLES, son of Alfred A., was three years at Trinity; studied law at Yale; admitted to orders in the Episcopal Church; was first assistant to the rector of St. John's church, New Haven, and now rector of church at Elton, Long Island.

HOLLY, CHARLES F., son of Isaac, educated at Kenyon, Ohio; became a lawyer and settled in Nebraska. He was appointed assistant Judge of the Territory of Colorado. During the recent war he raised and commanded a company of volunteers.

HOLLY, FRANCIS MANTON, son of Wm. Welles, graduated in medicine at Yale, 1855, and is now in Texas, a surgeon in the United States Army.

HOYT, SHERMAN, son of Dea. John, a Congregational minister, now settled at Pleasant Plains, Fishkill, N. Y.

HOYT, JOHN BENEDICT, graduated at Yale, 1814.

HOYT, PHILIP, son of Enoch and Hannah [Lockwood] Hoyt, is a Methodist preacher.

HOYT, WILLIAM C., brother of Philip, received the degree of A. M. at the Wesleyan University; became a Methodist minister, and, in 1860 was appointed presiding elder of the Bridgeport district. He resides in Stamford, and is engaged in the Methodist Book House in New York city.

HUMPHREY, H. M., graduated at the Jefferson Medical College, in Philadelphia, in 1842, and practiced medicine in Philadelphia and New York city. He removed to Stamford in 1855, where he has been connected with our banks, as cashier of the Stamford Bank, and as president of the First National Bank of Stamford.

LOCKWOOD, RUFUS A., son of Daniel, graduated at Yale, 1831, became a minister, and settled in Tennessee, where he died in 1835.

LOCKWOOD, JOHN D., son of Rev. Peter and Matilda [Davenport], born in Stamford, Oct. 9, 1825, died while a member of Yale College in 1844. [Memoirs of J. D. Lockwood].

LORD, JOHN, L. L. D, graduated at Dartmouth College, 1833, and studied theology. He has devoted his life, mainly to lecturing on historical topics, in which he has been very successful. He has resided in Stamford since 1853.

LYMAN, JOSEPH B., graduated at Yale, 1850. He came to Stamford, in 1865, exiled from the South, and is now the agricultural editor of the New York *World*.

MINOR, CHARLES WM., son of Gov. Wm. T., now a student in Germany.

MINOR, ISRAEL, jr., graduated at Yale, 1862, studied law at the Columbia Law School, was admitted to the bar in 1864, and is now practicing law in New York city.

MINOR, JOHN CRANNEL, son of Israel Minor, graduated at the College of Physicians and Surgeons in New York city, in 1865. Was appointed professor of chemistry and natural science in East Tennessee University in 1866, and also state assayer of Tennessee. Resigned these posts, and in 1863, resumed the practice of medicine in New York city. He was, during the war, also in the service of the government as Act. Ass. Surgeon, U. S. A.

MEAD, J. D., a successful physician, for years in New York city. Has lived, retired, for several years on Long Ridge.

PRIOR, ISRAEL, jr., son of Capt. Prior, graduated in medicine, New York Bellevue Hospital Medical College, 1865 ; married Mary F., daughter of Philip H. Brown, Esq., and is now in the practice of his profession in Catlin, Ill.

RITCH, THOMAS GARDINER, son of Welles R., graduated at Yale, 1854, became a lawyer, and has his office in New York city.

ROCKWELL, HENRY, graduated in New York, 1862. He is a surgeon in the U. S. A., now stationed west of St. Paul, Minn.

SCOFIELD, AZARIAH, son of Uriah, born in Feb., 1776, graduated at Yale 1801, and became a teacher and merchant.

SCOFIELD, JAMES, a physician, went to Danbury.

SCOFIELD, JARED, son of Reuben, graduated at Yale, 1801, and was a teacher in Philadelphia.

SCOFIELD, JOHN O., son of Dea. Alfred, born Sept. 18, 1846, graduated M. D. 1866, at the Bellevue Hospital Med. Coll. He is now practicing medicine in Bedford, N. Y.

SCOFIELD, WALTER, son of Dea. Alfred, born in Stamford, April 28, 1839 and grad. M. D. at the New York College of Physicians and Surgeons, 1861. Commissioned Ass. Surgeon, U. S. Navy, June 20, 1861, promoted Surgeon, June, 1866. He accompanied the U. S. Squadron to Russia, in 1866, and now has his headquarters in Boston.

SELLECK, CHARLES G., son of Charles, of Darien, grad. at Yale, 1827, licensed to preach by Fairfield West association, and settled in Ridgefield from 1831 to 1837. He went to Illinois and preached at Alton. He then opened a school for young ladies in Jacksonville, which was quite successful. He afterwards went to Plaquemine, La., where he also established a flourishing school for young ladies, in which he was engaged, when, in 1861, the local authorities, finding him too thoroughly a "Union man," gave him five hours to leave the place. He is now in Hopedale, near De Soto, Ill.

SEELEY, EBENEZER, graduated at Yale, 1841, became a physician, and settled in Oyster Bay, L. I.

SELLECK, JOHN, graduated at Harvard in 1690.

SKELDING, THOMAS, son of Henry K., graduated M. D., in New York, 1865 ;

and was physician to the New York City Hospital. He is now at the General Hospital in Vienna, Austria.

SMITH, ARTHUR, son of Charles E. and Mary [Waring] Smith, born in Stamford in 1843; graduated M. D. at the Bellevue Hospital Medical College, New York city, in 1866; and has since been in the office of Dr. Wood in the city.

SMITH, Rev. JOHN, a native of Wethersfield, graduated at Yale, 1821, and was licensed to preach by the Fairfield East Association, in 1824. From 1839 to 1848 he was settled as pastor over the Congregational Church in Wilton. Since 1850, he has resided in Stamford. His wife died here. He has three sons, James D., Charles S., and Walter M., all in successful business in New York, and all residing with their families in Stamford. He has, also, three daughters, Susan W., Esther M., and Maria L.

WEBB, HENRY W., son of Dr. Samuel, was a physician in New York city.

WEBB, BENJAMIN, graduated at Yale, 1856; studied theology, and became an Episcopal minister. He is now in the service of the Pacific Coast Associate Mission, and is located at San Jose, Cal.

WEED, BENJAMIN, was a preacher, and during the revolutionary war, he had his Bible taken from him by a party of the British.

WEED, THOMAS A., son of Philo, studied in Oberlin and at Lane Seminary, and was settled in the ministry at Mexico, N, Y.

WEED, C. MILTON, son of Charles A., a member of Harvard, class of 1772.

WEED, HARVEY, son of Nathaniel, graduated at Columbia College, 18—, with the honors of his class. He practiced law in New York city until, his health failing, he retired to the family home in Darien.

WELCH, MICHAEL, a missionary of the American and Foreign Christian Union. Has lived here several years.

WHEELOCK, RALPH, son of Rev. Eleazer D. and Sarah Davenport, graduated at Yale, 1765.

WHELPLEY, JAMES DAVENPORT, son of Rev. Philip M. and Abigail F. [Davenport], graduated at Yale, 1837, and in medicine in 1842.

WILLIAMS, STEPHEN, son of Rev. Stephen, D. D. and Abigail [Davenport], graduated, 1742, and was settled in Woodstock, Conn., in 1747. He preached nearly fifty years.

WILLIAMS, WARHAM, brother of Stephen above, graduated at Yale 1745, and was settled in Northford, Conn. He preached about forty years.

WILLIAMS NATHAN, brother of the two above, graduated at Yale, 1756, and settled in the ministry at Tolland, Conn. He preached about sixty-six years.

WOOD, GEORGE INGERSOLL, a native of the town, son of Joseph, graduated at Yale in 1832, and has been a successful minister. He is now preaching in St. Cloud, Mich.

WOOD, OLIVER E., son of the above, is now at the West Point Military Academy.

WOODBURY, W. H., author of works in modern languages, on the Ollendorff system. Located at Springdale in Stamford in 1867.

C.

OFFICIAL LISTS.

1. REPRESENTATIVES AND SENATORS FROM STAMFORD.

The following list contains all the names which can now be recovered of the representatives and senators of Stamford in the state legislature. Down to 1665 they represented the town in the general court of New Haven; afterwards in the general court or legislature of the colony and state of Connecticut. The omission of names between 1644 and 1653 was occasioned by the loss of the New Haven colony records of that period, a loss probably not to be supplied. There will also be found occasional omissions of the regular meeting of the legislature, occasioned by the fact that no representatives appeared from the town at those meetings. The omission for October 1687, the two sessions of 1688 and for April 1889, is due to the assumption of the government by Sir Edmund Andross for that period. Our list contains also the representatives for Darien from the incorporation of that town in 1820. The thanks of the author are due to the kindness of J. Hammond Trumbull, for his cheerful aid in completing the catalogue.

1641—Andrew Ward and Francis Bell.
1642—Matthew Mitchell and John Whitmore.
1643—John Underhill, Richard Gildersleeve and John Chapman.
1644—Andrew Ward and Robert Coe.
1653—Richard Law and Francis Bell.
1654— „ „ and John Holly,
1655— „ „ „ „
1656— „ „
1657— „ John Waterbury and George Slawson.
1658— „ and Francis Bell.
1659— „ „ „
1661— „ „ „
1663— „ John Holly and George Slawson.
1664— „ and Francis Bell.
1665— „ Peter Disbrow and Francis Brown.
1666— „
1667—Robert Usher and Francis Brown.
1668—Francis Brown and John Green.
1669—Ensign Francis Brown, John Green and Richard Law.
1670—Lieut. Jonathan Selleck and John Green.
„ —Oct. John Holly and Jonathan Bell.
1671—May, Lieut. Jonathan Selleck and John Green.
„ —Oct., John Green and Joseph Theale.
1672—Richard Law and Jonathan Selleck.
1673—John Green and Joseph Theale.
1674—May, Lieut. Jonathan Bell and Abram Ambler.
„ —Oct., Joseph Theale and John Green.
1675—May, Jonathan Selleck and Joseph Theale.
„ —Oct., Lieut. Jonathan Bell and „
1776—May, Capt. Jonathan Selleck and Lieut. Jonathan Bell.
„ —Oct., Lieut. Jonathan Bell and Joseph Theale.
1677—May, „ „ Abram Ambler.

1677—Oct.. Joseph Theale, Abram Ambler and Jon. Reynolds.
1678—May, " "
" —Oct., " "
1679—May, " "
" —Oct., "
1680—May, Jonathan Bell and Joseph Theale.
" —Oct.,—Joseph Theale.
1681—May, " and Abram Bell.
" —Oct., Lieut. Jonathan Bell and Joshua Hoyt.
1682—May, Abram Ambler and Joseph Theale.
" —Oct., Lieut. Jonathan Bell and Joshua Hoyte.
1683—May, Lieut. Jonathan Bell and Capt. Jonathan Selleck.
" —Oct., " Joshua Hoyte.
1684—May, " "
" —Oct., " "
1685—May, Capt. Jonathan Selleck and Lieut. Jonathan Bell.
" —Oct., Jonathan Bell and Joshua Hoyt.
1686—May, Capt. Jonathan Selleck and Lieut. Jonathan Bell.
" —Oct., Jonathan Bell and Joshua Hoyt.
1687—May, Capt. Jonathan Selleck and Lieut. Jonathan Bell.
1689—Aug., Ens. John Bates, abs.
" —Oct., Samuel Hoyt.
1690—May, "
" —Oct., Abram Ambler.
1691—May, Jonathan Bell and Abram Ambler.
" —Oct., Abram Ambler and Daniel Wescott.
1692—May, Samuel Hoyt "
" —Oct., Abram Ambler "
1693—May, Samuel Hoyt and David Waterbury.
" —Oct., David Waterbury.
1694—May, " and Daniel Westcott.
" —Oct., Daniel Wescott and Daniel Weed.
1695—Oct., David Waterbury. "
1696—May, Lieut. Jonathan Bell.
" —Oct., Sergt. David Waterbury.
1697—Oct., " Samuel Hoyt.
1698—Oct., Lieut. David Waterbury.
1699—May, " and Ens. Samuel Hoyt.
" —Oct., Samuel Hoyt and Jonathan Bell.
1700—May, Elisha Holly.
" —Oct., Lieut. David Waterbury and Stephen Bishop.
1701—May, " Elisha Holly.
" —Oct., " "
1702—May, Samuel Webb.
" —Oct., Lieut. David Waterbury and Samuel Webb.
1703—May, " Capt. John Clock.
" —Oct.. Samuel Hoyt.
1704—May, " Elisha Holly.
" —Oct., " "
1705—May, Capt. Jonathan Selleck and Lieut. David Waterbury.
" — Lieut. David Waterbury.
1706—May, Capt. Jonathan Selleck and Lieut. David Waterbury.
" —Oct., Lieut. David Waterbury and Jonathan Selleck.

1707—May, Capt. Jonathan Selleck and Elisha Holly.
" —Oct., Stephen Bishop "
1708—May, Capt. Jonathan Selleck "
" —Oct., Stephen Bishop "
1709—May, " "
" —Oct., " "
1710—May, Jonathan Bates.
" —Oct., Elisha Holly.
1711—May, " John Ambler.
" —Oct., "
1712—May, Jonathan Bates and John Stone.
" —Oct., Jonathan Bell.
1713—May, Elisha Hawley and Jonathan Bell.
" —Oct., "
1714—May, Jonathan Bell and Jonathan Bates.
" —Oct., " John Stone.
1715—May, " "
" —Oct., Jonathan Bates and John Hoyt.
1716—May, John Hoyt and John Stone.
" —Oct., John Stone and Samuel Hoyt.
1717—May, John Hoyt and Jonathan Bell.
" —Oct., John Stone and John Hoyt.
1718—May, Samuel Weed and Jonas Weed.
" —Oct., John Stone "
1719—May, John Hoyt and John Stone.
" —Oct., " and John Bell.
1720—May, " John Stone.
1721—May, " Samuel Weed.
" —Oct., " John Stone.
1722—May, " "
" —Oct., " "
1723—May, " "
1724—May, " "
" —Oct., Capt. Jonathan Hoyt and Jonathan Bates.
1725—May, " "
" —Oct., " "
1726—May, " "
" —Oct., " "
1727—May, " "
" —Oct., Capt. Samuel Hoyt and Samuel Weed.
1728—May, Capt. Jonathan Hoyt and Capt. Samuel Hoyt
" —Oct., Capt. Jonathan Bates and Capt. Jonathan Hoyt
1729—May, Capt. Jonathan Hoyt and Capt. Samuel Hoyt.
" —Oct., Capt. Jonathan Bates and Capt. Jonathan Hoyt.
1730—Oct., Capt. John Bell "
1731—May, Capt. Jonathan Hoyt and John Bell.
" —Oct., John Hoyt and Jonathan Bates.
1732—May, " "
" —Oct., Capt. Jonathan Hoyt and John Bell.
1733—May, " Jonathan Bates.
" —Oct., " Samuel Hoyt.
1734—May, "
" —Oct., " Samuel Hoyt.
1735—May, " Jonathan Maltby.

1735—Oct.,	Capt. Jonathan Hoyt and	Jonathan Bates.
1736—May,	"	Jonathan Maltby.
" —Oct.,	"	"
1737—May,	"	"
" —Oct.,	"	"
1738—May,	"	"
" —Oct.,	"	"
1739—May,	"	"
" —Oct.,	"	"
1740—May,	Col. "	"
" —Oct.,	"	"
1741—May,	"	"
" —Oct.,	"	"
1742—May,	"	"
" —Oct.,	"	"
1743—May,	Col. "	Jonathan Bates.
" —Oct.,	"	"
1744—May,	Col. "	Jonathan Maltby.
" —Oct.,	"	"
1745—May,	"	
" —Oct.,	Col. "	Jonathan Bates.
1746—May,	"	Jonathan Maltby.
" —Oct.,	"	Capt. "
1747—May,	"	"
" —Oct.,	Capt. Nathaniel Weed and	Abraham Davenport.
1748—May,	Jonathan Hoyt	"
" —Oct.,	Col. "	"
1749—May,	"	"
" —Oct.,	Col. "	"
1750—May,	"	"
" —Oct.,	"	"
1751—May,	"	"
" —Oct.,	"	"
1752—May.,	"	"
" —Oct.,	"	"
1753, May,	"	"
" —Oct.,	"	"
1754—May,	"	Jonathan Maltby
" —Oct.,	"	"
1755—May,	"	"
" —Oct.,	"	"
1756—May,	John Holly.	
" —Oct.,	Col. Jonathan Hoyt	"
1757—May,	"	Jonathan Selleck.
" —Oct.,	"	Abraham Davenport.

1758—May, Charles Webb and Jonathan Dibble.
" —Oct,, Jonathan Dibble and Charles Webb.
1759—May, Charles Webb and Abraham Davenport.
" —Oct., Abraham Davenport and Charles Webb.
1760—May, Col. Jonathan Hoyt and Abraham Davenport.
" —Oct., Abraham Davenport and Capt. Charles Webb.
1761—May, Capt. Charles Webb and Abraham Davenport.
" —Oct., Abraham Davenport and Col. Jonathan Hoyt.
1762—May, Col. Jonathan Hoyt and Abraham Davenport.

1762—Oct., Abraham Davenport and Col. Jonathan Hoyt.
1763—May, Col. Jonathan Hoyt and Abraham Davenport.
" —Oct., Abraham Davenport and Col. Jonathan Hoyt.
1764—May, Col. Jonathan Hoyt and Abraham Davenport.
" —Oct., Abraham Davenport and Col. Jonathan Hoyt.
1765—May, Col. Jonathan Hoyt and Abraham Davenport.
" —Oct., Abraham Davenport and Col. Jonathan Hoyt.
1766—May, Capt. Charles Webb and Abraham Davenport.
" —Oct., Charles Webb and Col. Jonathan Hoyt.
1767—May, Capt. Charles Webb and Col. Jonathan Hoyt.
" —Oct., Charles Webb.
1768—May, Capt. Charles Webb and Benj. Weed.
" —Oct., Charles Webb "
1769—May, Capt. Charles Webb and Maj. David Waterbury.
" —Oct., David Waterbury and Benj. Weed.
1770—May, Capt. Chas. Webb and Maj. David Waterbury.
" —Oct., Benjamin Weed.
1771—May, Chas. Webb and Benj. Weed.
" —Oct., " "
1772—May, "
" —Oct., " "
1773—May, " "
" —Oct., " "
1774—May, David Waterbury and Thos. Young.
" —Oct., Chas. Webb and David Waterbury.
1775—May, Col. Charles Webb and Col. David Waterbury.
" —Oct., Benjamin Weed and Thos. Young.
1776—May, " Col. David Waterbury.
" —Oct., " John Davenport.
1777—May, John Davenport and John Hoyt, Jr.
" —Oct., Capt. Sylvester Knapp and Capt. Isaac Lockwood.
1778—May, Maj. John Davenport and Col. Charles Webb.
" —Oct., Capt. Daniel Bouton and Capt. Isaac Lockwood.
1779—May, Col. Charles Webb and Capt. Daniel Bouton.
" —Oct., Capt. Daniel Bouton and Charles Webb.
1780—May, Col. Charles Webb.
" —Oct., Charles Weed and Charles Webb.
1781—May, Only record, in private journal of Gov. Trumbull.
" —Oct., Charles Weed.
1782—May, Maj. John Davenport and Charles Weed.
" —Oct., Charles Weed and Maj. John Davenport.
1783—May, Gen. D. Waterbury and Charles Weed.
" —Oct., Charles Weed and Gen. D. Waterbury.
1784—May, Maj. John Davenport and Charles Weed.
" —Oct., Charles Weed and Maj. John Davenport.
1785—May, Maj. John Davenport and Charles Weed.
" —Oct., Charles Weed and James Davenport.
1786—May, James Davenport and Charles Weed.
" —Oct., "
1787—May, James Davenport and Charles Weed.
" —Oct., " "
1788—May, " John Davenport.
" —Oct., John Davenport and James Davenport.
1789—May, James Davenport and Col. Joseph Hoyt.

1789—Oct., John Davenport and James Davenport.
1790—May, Maj. 〃
〃 —Oct., 〃 Benj. Scofield.
1791—May, Maj. 〃 William Fitch.
〃 —Oct., 〃 〃
1792—May, Maj 〃 Thaddeus Weed.
〃 —Oct., 〃 〃
1793—May, Maj. 〃 Benjamin Scofield.
〃 —Oct., 〃 〃
1794—May, David Waterbury and Thaddeus Weed.
〃 —Oct., John Davenport 〃
1795—May, David Waterbury 〃
〃 —Oct., John Davenport and George Mills.
1796—May, *Joshua King and William Forrester.
〃 —Oct., John Davenport and George Mills.
1797—May, George Mills and Noyes Mather.
〃 —Oct., Noyes Mather and George Mills.
1798—May, George Mills and Noyes Mather.
〃 —Oct., Noyes Mather and Isaiah Tiffany.
1799—May, Isaiah Tiffany and Isaac Lockwood.
〃 —Oct., Isaac Lockwood and Nathan Weed, Jr.
1800—May, 〃 〃
〃 —Oct., 〃 〃
1801—May, 〃 Edward McLaughlin.
〃 —Oct., 〃 Wm. Waterbury 4th.
1802—May, 〃 〃
〃 —Oct., Nathan Weed and Noyes Mather.
1803—May, Isaac Lockwood and John Wm. Holly.
〃 —Oct., Nathan Weed and Isaac Lockwood.
1804—May, 〃 and Jas. Stephens.
〃 —Oct., Jas. Stephens and Thaddeus Bell, Jr.
1805—May, 〃 〃
〃 —Oct., 〃 Nathan Weed.
1806—May, Isaac Lockwood and Thaddeus Bell, Jr.
〃 —Oct., Josiah Smith and Nathan Weed.
1807—Oct., Thaddeus Bell and Ezra Lockwood.
1808—May, Wm. Waterbury 4th and Isaac Lockwood Jr.
〃 —Oct., Isaac Lockwood and Jas. Stephens.
1809—May, Jas. Stephens and Isaac Lockwood, Jr.
〃 —Oct., Smith Weed and Jas. Stevens.
1810—May, Jas. Stevens and Nathan Weed.
〃 —Oct., Thaddeus Bell and Jas. Stevens.
1811—May, 〃 Isaac Lockwood, Jr.
〃 —Oct., Henry Hoyt, Jr. and John Weed, Jr.
1812—May, John Weed, Jr. and Henry Hoyt, Jr.
〃 —Oct., Nathan Weed and Simeon H. Minor.
1813—May, John Weed, Jr. 〃
〃 —Oct., Isaac Lockwood and John Augur.
1814—May, Jas. Stephens 〃
〃 —Oct., Isaac Lockwood and Henry Close.
1815—May, Jas. Stevens and Thaddeus Bell.

*Said, in pencil, to be from Ridgefield. Both names are probably by mistake credited to Stamford.

		DARIEN.
1815—Oct.,	Isaac Lockwood and John Weed, Jr.	
1816—May,	John Brown, Jr. and Solomon Clason.	
" —Oct.,	Isaac Lockwood and John Brown, Jr.	
1817—May,	Jas. Stevens and Simeon H. Minor.	
" —Oct.,	" "	
1818—May,	" , Thaddeus Bell.	
" —Oct.,	" "	
1819—May,	Thad. Bell and Isaac Lockwood.	
1820— "	" John Augur.	
1821— "	Joseph Wood and Chas. Hawley.	Thaddeus Bell.
1822— "	" Daniel Lockwood.	Henry Bates.
1823— "	Chas. Hawley "	John Weed, Jr.
1824— "	" "	John Bell.
1825— "	Isaac Lockwood and T. Davenport.	Abraham Clock.
1826— "	Chas. Hawley and Jotham Hoyt.	Thaddeus Bell.
1827— "	" Abel Reynolds.	John Bell.
1828— "	" "	"
1829— "	" Simeon H. Minor.	Jonathan Bates.
1830— "	S. H. Minor and Wm. Waterbury, Jr.	John Bell.
1831— "	Wm. Waterbury and Sol. Clason.	Holly Bell.
1832— "	" Selleck Scofield.	"
1833— "	Selleck Scofield and Royal L. Gay.	Edward Scofield.
1834— "	" "	John Weed, Jr.
1835— "	" "	Edward Scofield.
1836— "	Royal L. Gay and Joshua B. Ferris.	Holly Bell.
1837— "	Selleck Scofield "	Nathl. H. Wildman.
1838— "	Joshua B. Ferris and Seth Clason.	Edward Scofield.
1839— "	Selleck Scofield and S. Lockwood.	Wm. Andreas.
1840— "	Andrew Perry.	
1841— "	Wm. T. Minor and Josephus Brush.	Edward Scofield.
1842— "	Selleck Scofield and Wm. T. Minor.	Gil. G. Waterbury.
1843— "	Wm. T, Minor and Josephus Brush.	"
1844— "	Selleck Scofield and Wm. T. Minor.	"
1845— "	" Royal L. Gay.	"
1846— "	" Wm. T. Minor.	Isaac L. Hoyt.
1847— "	Amzi Scofield "	"
1848— "	Heth Stevens and S. Lockwood, Jr.	Benj. S. Reed.
1849— "	" Henry J. Sanford.	Ira Scofield.
1850— "	Steph'n. B. Provost and Josiah Smith.	Benj. S. Reed.
1851— "	Seth Miller and John Clason.	Lester St. John.
1852— "	Wm. T. Minor and S. B. Provost.	Benj. S. Reed.
1853— "	James H. Hoyt and Chas. Brown.	G. G. Waterbury.
1854— "	Wells R. Ritch and John Clason.	"
1855— "	J. D. Warren and Hickford Marshall.	Thomas Reed.
1856— "	Chas. A. Weed and E. P. Whitney.	Holly Bell.
1857— "	Wm. W. Holly and Geo. Lounsbury.	Nathan Roberts.
1858— "	Chas. H. Leeds and Wm. W. Scofield.	"
1859— "	" George Scofield.	"
1860— "	H. M. Humphrey and I. S. Jones.	Chas. Brown.
1861— "	W. R. Ritch aad I. S. Jones.	Holly Bell.
1862— "	Morgan Morgans, and I. S. Jones.	Benjamin Weed.
1863— "	Selleck Scofield and J. D. Warren.	W. A. Cummings.
1864— "	J. B. Hoyt and Alfred Hoyt.	"
1865— "	" "	Henry Morehouse.

60

1866—May, J. D. Ferguson and Seth S. Cook.	Henry Morehouse.
1867— " " H. G. Scofield.	"
1868— " W. T. Minor and H. G. Scofield.	Ira Scofield.

STATE SENATORS FROM STAMFORD.

1643 & 4—Thurston Raynor.
1646—Andrew Ward.
1647—Richard Law.
1695-1701—Maj. Jonathan Selleck.
1766-1784—Abraham Davenport.
1790-1797—James Davenport.
1830—Charles Hawley.
1850—Joshua B. Ferris
James H. Hoyt.
1859—Matthew F. Merrit.
1863—Morgan Morgans.
1865—Charles W. Ballard.

2. TOWNSMEN OR SELECTMEN OF STAMFORD.

The following catalogue of "townsmen," or Selectmen, is as complete as the town records enabled the author to make it. From 1642 to 1666 there are no records to show who were appointed ; and in 1673 the records which are otherwise full, make no mention of the choice of townsmen. The other years for which there is no record of a choice, are, 1681, 2 & 3, 1685 and 1699. Instead of copying the list, as chosen, I have simply indicated the year when each one was first chosen, and the number of years he served.

1640—Rev. Richard Denton, 1
" Matthew Mitchel, 2
" Andrew Ward, 2
" Thurston Raynor, 2
" Richard Crabb, 2
1641—John Whitmore, 1
" Richard Law, 6

The most of the above served probably through the next twenty years, of which there is no record.

1666—Lieut. Francis Bell, sen., 5
" John Holly, 4
" William Newman, 2
" Richard Hardy, 3
" Joseph Garnsey, 1
" Richard Ambler, 2
1667—Peter Ferris, 7
" Richard Webb, 2
" Abraham Ambler, 13
1668—Robert Usher, 1
" Jonathan Bell, 14
1669—John Green, 3
" Francis Brown, 1
1670—Jonathan Selleck, 1
1671—George Slawson, sen., 3
" John Pettit, 1
" John Holmes, 2
" Joshua Hait, 6
" John Slawson, 2
1674—John Bates, 3
1676—Samuel Hoyt, 8
" Daniel Weed, 5
" Daniel Westcott, 5
1677—Joseph Theal, 3
1680—Samuel Dean, 1
" James Weed, 1
" Jonas Weed, 11
1684—Steven Bishop, 5
" John Waterbury, 6
1686—Joseph Hoyt, 2
1687—David Waterbury, 11
1689—Daniel Scofield, 20
" John Scofield, 2
" John Bates, jr., 9
1690—Eleazer Slason, 1
" Benjamin Hoyt, 1
1694—Increase Holly, 1
1695—Elisha Holly, 6
1696—Jonathan Selleck, 1
" John Holly, sen., 1
1700—Richard Scofield, 1
" Samuel Holly, 1
1701—Benjamin Green, 2
" Jonathan Bell, 19
" Joseph Ferris, 7
1703—Deacon Sam'l Hoyt, 6
1704—Capt. Joseph Bishop, 10
1709—John Ambler, 2
" Lieut. Sam'l Weed, 14
1713—John Bell, 1
1714—John Slason, sen., 4
" Deac. John Hoyt, 13
" Sam'l Blachley, 4
1716—Capt. John Knapp, 1
" Capt. Sam'l Hoyt, jun., 17
1717—Deac. Jonathan Hoyt, 1

1719—Lieut. Joseph Webb, 9
" Serg't John Scofield, 1
" Jonas Weed, 9
" Benj. Hoyt, jr., 4
1725—Samuel Scofield, 3
1728—Capt. Jonathan Hoyt, 29
" Maj. Jonathan Maltby, 20
1734—Lieut. John Waterbury, 4
1735—Lieut. Samuel Weed, 3
1738—Joseph Bishop, 8
1740—Serg't Jonathan Clason, 7
1741—Serg't Samuel Scofield, 5
1742—Capt. Nathaniel Weed, 8
1746—Col. Abraham Davenport, 31
1747—Lieut. Jonathan Bell, 9
1750—Ensign John Holly, 21
1754—Serg't Stephen Ambler, 2
" Capt. David Waterbury, 1
" Lieut. Eliphalet Seeley, 22
1756—Lieut. Jonathan Selleck, 4
" Capt. Stephen White, 1
1757—Col. Charles Webb, 20
1760—Samuel Broker, 1
1761—Serg't Samuel Bishop, 4
1763—Joseph Husted, 2
" Abraham Hoyt, 10
1769—Thomas Youngs, 2
" Benjamin Weed, 2
1771—Gen. David Waterbury, 7
1775—Lieut. Samuel Hutton, 2
" David Webb, 2
1776—John Bell, 3
" Capt. Isaac Lockwood, 19
" Thomas June, 1
1777—Deac. Joshua Ambler, 10
1777—Daniel Bouton, 2
" Ebenezer Ferris, 2
" Capt. Sylvanus Knapp, 23
1778—Capt. Charles Smith, 12
1779—Capt. Gershom Scofield, 6
" Capt. Reuben Scofield, 1
1780—Charles Weed, 5
" Capt. Amos Smith, 2
1781—Isaac Weed, 2
" Samuel Richards, 2
" Serg't Jonathan Waring, 2
" Jesse Bell, 2
1786—Lieut. Seth Weed, jr., 10
1789—Hon. James Davenport, 6
1790—Thaddeus Hoyt, 1
1791—Capt. Nathaniel Webb, 5
" Capt. Thaddeus Weed, 2
1792—Nathan Weed, jr., 8
1794—David Maltby, 1
1794—Stephen Rockwell, 1
" Frederick Hoyt, 1
1795—Hon. John Davenport, 1
1796—Josiah Smith, 12
" Benjamin Weed, 1
1799—Amos Weed, 11
" Alexander Mills, 1
1800—Carey Leeds, 1
" Isaac Penoyer, 2
1801—Ezra Lockwood, 3
" Wm. Waterbury, 4th, 9
1802—Thaddeus Bell, jr., 8
" George Mills, 4
1807—Isaac Wardwell, 6
" David Smith, 3d, 1
1809—Smith Weed, 1
" Simeon H. Minor, Esq., 1
" Carey Bell, 4
" Seth Smith, 6
1810—John Weed, jr., 8
" Henry Hoyt, jr., 1
" Jeremiah Andreas, 1
" Abishai Weed, 5
1811—Timothy Reynolds, 4
" John Browning, 2
1812—Jonathan Brown, 3
1813—Daniel Lockwood, jr., 8
1814—Isaac Lockwood, jr., 3
1815—James Stevens, Esq., 3
" Philo Weed, 3
1817—John Bell, 2
" Solomon Clason, 3
1818—Epenetus Hoyt, 5
1819—Nathaniel Webb, 1
" Luther Weed, 1
" Isaac Holly, 1

From this date there have been but three Selectmen.

1810—Dr. Lockwood, 1
1821—Joseph Wood, Esq., 3
" Abishai Scofield, 3
1824—Jotham Hoyt, 6
" Abel Reynolds, 6
1825—Theodore Davenport, 3
1828—David Hoyt, 1
1829—Ezra Knapp, 1
1830—Wm. Waterbury, 2
" Selleck Scofield, 20
" John Brown, 1
1831—Royal L. Gay, 20
1832—Benj. M. Weed, 8
1839—Heth Stevens, 6
1841—Edwin S. Holly, 1
" Amzi Scofield, 1

1842—Ebenezer Lockwood, 5
1847—Abishai Weed, 1
" Nehemiah Hoyt, 1
1851—Charles Brush, 1
" Nathaniel Lockwood, 1
1852—Philip H. Brown, 2
" Isaac Jones, 1
" Nelson W. Smith, 1
1853—Edwin Scofield, jr., 1
" Walter Searls, 1
1854—Seth Miller, 1
" Lorenzo Meeker, 1
" Hickford Marshall, 3
1855—Wells R. Ritch, 12
" Edward Gay, 1
1856—Geo. Lounsbury, 1
" Charles Brown, 1
1857—Stephen B. Provost, 1
1858—Floyd T. Palmer, 2
" Josiah Smith, 1
1859—Wm. Wallace Scofield, 6
1861—Cephas Stevens, 4
1866—Charles Gaylor, 1
" Wm. R. Lockwood, 3
" Lewis Raymond, 2
1868—Erastus E. Scofield, 1

DARIEN.

1820—John Bell, 1
" John Weed, 2
" Henry Bates, 12
1821—John Bell, jr., 2
1822—John Weed, jr., 8
1826—Enos Wilmot, 8
1830—Wm. H. Bates, 3
1831—Jeremiah Andreas, 2
1832—Abraham Clock, 4
" Holly Bell, 5
1837—Wm. Andreas, 13
" Jacob Lockwood, 4
" John Holmes, 10
1839—Daniel Beers, 1
" Elisha Seeley, 1
1840—Edward Scofield, 3
1844—Joseph Mather, 4
1849—Benj. S. Reed, 6
1850—Nathaniel A. Bouton, 1
1851—G. G. Waterbury, 1
" Isaac Weed, 1
1852—Henry Gorham, 4
" Richard Bates, 1
" Henry Morehouse, 3
1854—George Mather, 1
1855—George R. Stevens, 5
" Chas. A. Bates, 1
1856—Chas. Hoyt, 1
1757—Nathan Roberts, 1
" John N. Scofield, 4
1858—Walter H. Bates, 2
1860—Isaac L. Hoyt, 1
1861—John D. Farrington, 1
1862—Legrand Winters, 1
1863—Ira Scofield, 6
1864—Edward O. Page, 1
1867—Holly Bell, 4
1868—Sam'l Sands, M. D., 2

3. TOWN CLERKS.

Richard Law, 1641-1664.
Jona. Selleck, 1664-1668.
John Holly, sen., 1668-1670.
Abram Ambler, 1670-1686.
Jona. Bell, 1687-1699.
Samuel Holly, sen., 1699-1708.
Elisha Holly, 1708-1709.
Stephen Bishop, sen., 1709-1722.
Lieut. Sam'l Weed, 1722-1738.
Joseph Bishop, 1738-1760.
Samuel Jarvis, 1760-1775.
John Hoyt, jr., 1775-1806.
Samuel Hoyt, jr., 1806-1819.
Seymour Jarvis, 1819-1843.
Wm. H. Holly, 1843.
Roswell Hoyt, 1843-1844.
Edwin Scofield, jr., 1844-1868.

DARIEN.

1820—Joshua Morehouse.
1822—Darius K. Scofield.
1828—Joshua Scofield.
1831—Edward Scofield.
1838—Abram Clock.
1839—Geo. H. Wallace.
1840—Chas. H. Waterbury.
1842—Jas. N. Gorham.
1844—Ira Scofield.
1856—Henry Gorham.
1857—John S. Waterbury.

4. TREASURERS.

John Stone, 1713.
Samuel Weed, 1733.
Abraham Davenport, 1779.
Ebenezer Weed, 1779-1790.
John Hoyt, jr., 1790-1802.
Alex. Mills, 1802-1807.
Samuel Hoyt, 1807-1819.
Seymour Jarvis, 1819-1843.
Royal L. Gay, 1844-1857.
Welles R. Ritch, 1857-1861.
Stephen B. Provost, 1861-1862.
Welles R. Ritch, 1862-1868.

5. POSTMASTERS IN STAMFORD.

Abraham Davenport, down to 1820.
Hon. James Stevens.
John Brown.
William Hoyt, jr.
Sands Seeley, twice.
Roswell Hoyt, twice.
Theodore J. Daskam, since 1861.

D.

STAMFORD BUSINESS,* 1868.

This list will show how early any of the parties indicated were in business in the town, and is as full and accurate, as the time allowed the author to make it.

Adams, Nathaniel E., architect and builder,	1827
Arnold, A. C., do do	1860
Alphonse, John W., fruit and confectionery, police,	1863
Alphonse, Charles, police,	1865
Avery, Horace, blacksmith, three hands.	
Brown, Philip H., mason, eighteen men,	1840
Billard & Nichols, sash and blinds, nine hands,	1861
Barker & Avery, blacksmith at Ring's End,	1860
Barber, Mrs., boarding house,	1867
Buxton & Webb, builders, eight hands,	1844
Brown, Samuel C., livery,	1862
Benjamin, Ralph, billiards.	
Bates, Mrs. Fred., fancy goods,	1863
Birchard, James, cabinet, at Darien depot,	1865
Brooks, Wm. H., barber,	1860
Bouton, Samuel M., carman,	1865
Bunten, Cornelian, blacksmith and carriage maker, eight men,	1844
Bunten, Aurelian, do. do. do., four men,	1847
Bostwick, John, jr., carpenter.	
Bates, Chas. E., coal and fuel, at Ring's End,	1864
Bernhard, T. & Bro., fancy dry goods and millinery,	1868
Benas, Maurice, cigars and tobacco,	1865
Boettger, Mrs. Clara, millinery,	1868
Barret, Isaac, carman.	
Briggs, S., Union House, (built 1844,) successor to Theodore Searls,	1864
Beers, Miss S. A., fancy goods, at Darien depot,	1868
Broadway, W. H., grocer, Quintard's Block,	1868
Brown, Francis H., music conservatory,	1867
Bostwick & Waterbury, grocers, four hands,	1865

* Excepting such as is already recorded in the preceding pages.

Butler, J. K., telegraph at depot, two assistants, 1867
Buxton, Edwin, shoes, at Turn of River, 1833
Buxton, Nelson, do. do. do., 1836
Buxton, John H., do. do. do., 1838
Clark, David H., insurance and real estate agent and auctioneer, 1860
Crabe, Allen L., cooper in North Stamford.
Cook, M. L., fancy goods, 1865
Cook, Mrs. C., hairdresser, 1866
Christie & Clancy, Misses, milliners, 1867
Card & Hill, painters, 1856
Crawford, James S., photographer, 1861
Crombie, Richard, tailor, 1854
Cohen, W., tailor, three hands, 1862
Curtis, Hiram, baskets, 1850
Combs & Provost, carriage makers, eight hands, 1846
Daskam, B. J., grocer, 1835
Daskam, T. J., insurance agent and deputy assessor, 1861
Dibble, Wm. H., boarding-house, Strawberry Hill, 1847
Dayton, George, cooper in North Stamford.
Dann, Seth, do.
Dixon, G. H., grocer at New Hope, 1868
Dean, Geo. W., marble yard, 1858
Daniel, James, painter, seven hands, 1851
Dammyer, John C., painter, four hands, 1864
Davis, Theodore, sash and blind, 1855
Dix & Cousin, shoes, at Darien depot, thirty-six hands, 1856
Dean, Isaac, shoes, at Deanville.
Dean, Seth, cooper, at North Stamford.
Ells & Gogan, painters, 1845
Fairchild, Robert, builder, 1861
Finney, Henry & Bros., blacksmiths, West Stamford.
Fox, Jacob, clothing merchant and tailor, 1659
Ficket, John B., carpenter, in Darien.
Ferris, De Forest, carman.
Gifford, carriages, at Long Ridge, four hands, 1853
Goldy, Henry, builder, ten men.
Guernsey, William.
Gardner, jr., Thomas.
Gorham & Garland, grocers, in Darien, 1850
Goff & Ellwood, soda and sarsaparilla, 1863
Hicks, John H., billiard saloon, 1867
Holly, Alexander N., hardware and lumber, 1842
Hoyt, jr., Wm., dry goods, 1826
Hoyt & Leeds, grocers, 1826
Hoyt, Lyman, cabinet, seven hands, 1837
Hoyt, James H., carpenter.
Hoyt, George, ticket agent at depot, 1855
Hoyt & Ayres, grocers, 1862
Hoyt, John W., restaurant, Cornucopia. 1866
Hoyt, J. A., shoes, two men. 1860
Hobbie, Chas. A., carriage and blacksmithing, five men, Darien, 1850
Harper, Robert, music.
Hay, William, carman.
Hathaway, B. F., civil engineer, 1857

Hubbard & Holly, dry goods and tailoring, 1855
Hurlbutt, W. P. & L. H., merchant tailors, fifteen hands, 1861
Hallock, Wm. H. H., mason.
Hendricks, Wm., photography, 1867
Johnson, Lewis, boating. 1840
Johnson, Sam'l H., boating. 1861
Jerman, W. H., shoes, six men, 1851
Jessup & Lockwood, builders.
Jones, Thaddeus, carman, 1840
Jennings, W. H., dyeing.
Jennings, Mrs. L. A., dressmaking, Madam Demorest's agent.
Jones, Charles & Co., dry goods, five hands, 1858
June, Hanford, carpenter.
Jones, Lewis, flour and feed at mill, High Ridge.
Jacobs, P. S.. grocer, 1865
Jones, N. D. & Co., fish market, 1863
Jones, Daniel H., carman.
Keeler, J. H., carman, successor to his father, who was here in 1841
Knapp, Charles H., mason.
Knappe & Crossner, barbers, succeed Andrew Schmidt. 1862
Knapp, Sylvester L., grocery and dry goods, at Roxbury.
Knapp, David H., shoes, at North Stamford.
Knapp, John B., harnesses, 1865
Ketcham, Oliver & John, oyster trade.
Kirk & Scofield, builders, four hands, 1857
Kennedy & Burke, restaurant, 1867
Lehigh, John, stair builder, 1862
Leeds, E. A., livery, successor to his father, 1845
Lounsbury, H. I., shoes, four men, 1857
Lownds, Geo. L. & Son, builders, ten men, 1847
Lockwood, James L., stoves and tinware, nine hands, 1847
Lockwood & Haight, druggists, successors of the Drs. Lockwood, 1848
Lockwood, Wm. W., news office, books and stationery.
Lockwood, Wm. A., blacksmith, four men, 1852
Lockwood, Sylvester, blacksmith, at Long Ridge, 1844
Lockwood, Edward R., cooper, at Long Ridge.
Lockwood, Samuel, dentist, 1840
Leeds, R. A., gate fixtures, inventor and manufacturer, 1867
Lockwood, V. B., grocer, 1863
Lounsbury, C. W., stoves and tinware, at Darien depot, 1867
Lum, H. B.., stoves and tinware, seven hands, 1851
Mather, M. S. & J. C., successors of George, Darien depot, 1830
Merritt, Mrs. H. V., dressmaker, eighteen hands, 1856
McCoun, Samuel, billiards, Quintard's Block, 1864
McQuhae, George, blacksmith, three hands, 1862
Miller, C. O. & Co., dry goods, four hands, 1868
Matthews, Jas. L., flour and feed, mill at River Bank.
Miller, R. S., grocer, 1855
Morgan, O. A., shoes, 1860
Morgan, O. B., grocer, 1867
Moore, Hampton, plastic slate, 1864
Moore, John, harness, 1868
Morris, Mrs. E. F., millinery, succeeds Mrs. N. A. Weed, four hands, 1859
Monroe & Thompson, painters.

Morgan, Alonzo B., carman.	
Newman, John, carriage and blacksmith, at High Ridge,	1849
Nichols, Charles H., carpenter.	
Nichols, Wm. B., livery,	1856
Nichols, Emma C., millinery,	1863
Payne, E. T., dentist,	1863
Provost, William, blacksmith, West Stamford,	1818
Price, William, grocer, three hands,	1852
Peck, J. A. & Co., grocers, at River Side.	
Provost & Drew, grocers,	1868
Palmer, W. & Son, grocers, at Long Ridge.	
Powelson, C. G., watch work and sewing machines,	1840
Palmer, Hannah, milliner,	1860
Prior, A. M., oyster trade.	
Playford, Thomas, fresco work.	
Reed, J. W., hats and furs,	1835
Renoude, Jarvis, cabinet,	1846
Richards, Ambrose, carpenter, in Darien.	
Read, Jane R., dressmaker, nine hands,	1858
Rockwell, James R., grocer, at Long Ridge,	1866
Reardon, Mrs., harness,	1864
Scofield, Erastus E., flour and feed,	1857
Scofield, John A., painter, seven hands,	1854
Scofield, Charles H., dry goods, five clerks,	1851
Scofield, Henry, carpenter.	
Scofield, M. S., carpenter.	
Scofield, Oliver & Son, coal, fuel and building materials,	1848
Scofield, S. N., cooper, North Stamford.	
Scofield, D. L., civil engineer and railroad contractor,	1848
Scofield, H. G., civil engineer,	1866
Scofield, Chas. W., mason.	
Scofield, Edward, miller, North Stamford.	
Scofield, S. W., house furnishing goods,	1861
Scofield, H. L., meat market,	1660
Schlocker, Geo. P., landscape gardening and rustic work,	1850
Silliman & Morrison, drnggists, succeed S. O. Silliman,	1857
Saunders, Wm. H., blacksmith and carriage making, N. Stamford,	1849
Shaw, W. F., grocer,	1857
Shaw, James, carpenter, in Darien.	
Shaw, Fred., do. do.	
Slater, Charles, cooper, North Stamford.	
Smith, Wm. L., grocer,	1859
Seeley, Albert, Stamford House, (built 1810,)	1837
Smith, A. T. & Son, millers, Long Ridge,	1857
Smith, Wm. H., carpenter.	
Smith, Wm. D., coal, fuel and building materials,	1867
Smith, James, grocery, at River Bank.	
Smith, Frank., grocer, at Darien depot,	1864
Smith & Dayton, house furnishing goods,	1863
Smith, S. H., watchmaker and jeweler,	1859
Sherwood, Samuel, cooper, Hunting Ridge,	1840
Smith, J. H., shoes,	1825
Smith, Geo. W., blacksmith, at Cove.	
Smith, T. F., blacksmith, at Cove.	

Studwell, Edgar, builder.
Spaulding, Gilbert, real estate.
Stottlar, John, fish market, 1868
Stevens, Samuel, shoes, at High Ridge.
Stevens, Cephas, baskets.
Stevenson, R. J., boarding-house, Henry street.
Taylor Brothers, grocers, 1868, successors to A. G. Clark & Co., 1830
Taylor, ——, shoes, at River Bank.
Turkinton, John, shoes, twelve men, 1852
Todd, C. J., grocer, 1855
Toucey, Wm. B., clothing, 1850
Triaca & Co., soap manufacturers, West Stamford.
Trinka, M., cigar manufacturer, five hands, 1868
Uncles, John, shoes, seven men, 1862
Valentine, Chas. W., meat market, 1855
Voorhies, A. W., baker. 1867
Waterbury, David & Wm. T., steamboat, 1839
Wardwell, Rufus, coal and fuel, 1848
Waterbury, J. S., grocer, successor to Ira Scofield, Darien, 1856
Waterbury, S. C. & Co., meat market, 1863
Waterbury, Geo. H. & Son, florist and gardener, 1844
Waterbury, C. H., cooper, North Stamford.
Wicks, H. W., bakery, 1860
White, Elbert, manufactures, insurance and real estate, 1840
Weed, Augustus, watchmaker and jeweler, 1848
Whitney, C. S. & W. S., grocers, at Darien depot, 1867
Webb, Wm., carpenter.
Webb, Mary, millinery, 1830
Whitney, Wm. M., carpenter, in Darien.
Whitney, James, shoes, three hands, 1866
Williams, Mrs., boarding, Clark's Hill.
Weed, A. G. & Bro., grocers, 1862
Weed, Alvan, groceries and dry goods, North Stamford. 1841
Weed, C. L., groceries and dry goods, High Ridge, 1865
Weed, Wm. A. & Co., meat market, 1853
Wood, John, cooper, Hunting Ridge.
Woodman, I. & H., builders, 1849
Weed & Ensley, stoves and tinware, four hands, 1867
Webb, J. N., harnesses, three hands, 1847
Williams, A. W., restaurant, near depot, 1853
Williams, Andrew T., auctioneer.
White, Wheeler & Bulkely, restaurant, at depot, 1867
Woeltge, Albert, music, 1853

NAMES REPRESENTED IN BUSINESS, ELSEWHERE.

Adams, John, Frank & James J.
Betts, Wm. G. & Charles E.
Bliss, Ira
Brantingham, Charles
Brown, Capt. Chas. H., George L., Samuel & Belden B.
Brooks, Horace
Burgess, C. A.
Candee, Julius A. & G. W.
Canfield, D. W.
Crane, Thomas & Albert.
Daskam, James W. & Eugene B.
Davenport, Amzi B., James J., John & James B.
Dewing, Hiram
De Forest, C. T.
Dodge, J. Smith
Dowe, John J.

Dunn, J.
Elder, Geo., Geo., jr., & Rob't, jr.
Faulkner, James C.
Fair. Robert
Fosdick, Wm. R.
Flint, J. T.
Frost, M. S.
Genung, E. W.
Gardner, Thomas, jr.
Gillespie, Fred. R.
Gorham, Edwin
Gwynne, John A.
Haldeman, John
Hawley, Francis M.
Hale, J.
Hall, Thomas S.
Hobby, Moses M., Louis & George
Holly, Edward
Holmes, Samuel, Samuel H., Luke & Frederick
Hoyt, Joseph B., Oliver, William, George A , Frank L., Edgar & Rufus
Hook, Gulian
Hubbard, Alexander & John W.
Hyde, Samuel N.
Haight, Jas. P.
Ingraham, Charles W.
Inslee, Gage
Jacquelin, Charles
Jones, Wm. P. & Wm. P., jr.
Jenkins, G. W. A.
Ketcham, J seph,
Lockwood, John R. & Munson
McKenzie, Alexander
Milne, Alexander
Merritt, M. F.
Moffatt, E M.
Marsden, F. A.
Mowbray, Oliver
Munn, Benj.
Nesbitt, George F.
Paradise, Andrew W.
Pitt, Charles & Charles, jr.
Porter, Eleazer
Quintard, Charles R.
Redding, George
Rhodes, Fr nk
Rickard, R. H.
Riker, Thaddeus
Robins, David
Sackett, J. L. & J. W.,
Scofield, C. E.
Seely, Sands
Skiddy, Wm. W.
Sloan, John & Wm. J.
Smith, Truman, James D., Chas. L., Walter M., Charles Edgar, W. H., Charles Edwin, & Theophilus
Snelling, J. G.
Skelding, William F. & Francis E.
Stebbins, Jared N.
Stickney, C. L. & Charles
Swartwout, Robert Satterlee & Robert D.
Starr, Charles J.
Strowbridge, Wm. C.
Taylor, Frank
Talmadge, Wm. H.
Trowbridge, Dudley L.
Van Name, C.
Vinton, Gen. D. H.
Voorhies, Abraham
Wardell, Charles W.
Warner, B.
Warren, James. James R., Joseph C. & George E.
Weed, Addison
Weston, C. W. & C. W., jr.
Wilcox, James & Charles H.
Wheeler, Frederick G.
White, John M.
Whiting, Lieut. Wm. B.
Wright, John
Young, T. S. & F. H.

E.

HOYT FAMILY MEETING.*

This meeting was the result of a circular issued in May, 1865, over the names of the following Hoyt's: Rev. Wm. C., of Stamford; James A., of Norwalk; Henry, of Boston; Wm. H., of Burlington, Vt.; Rev. Ralph New York city; Rev. James, Orange, N. Y.; F. A., Philadelphia; David W.,

* This record accidentally dropped out of its place in Chapter XXV, but is of too great historic interest to be omitted.

Providence, R. I.; Rev. C. A., Oberlin, O; and Alfred Hoitt, of Durham, N. H. The time and place of the meeting were fixed at a meeting held at the residence of Seymour Hoyt, Atlantic street, Stamford, March 19, 1866; and the meeting itself was held in the Congregational Church of Stamford, June 20 and 21, 1866. Its organization was as follows:

President—Oliver Hoyt, of Stamford.

Vice Presidents—Henry, of Boston; Wm. H., of Vermont; Hon. Joseph G., of Maine; James H., of Connecticut; Wm. C., of Michigan; Dr. John P., of Penn.; Edwin, of New York; Rev. J. Chester, of New York; Rev. Cornelius A., of Ohio; and Jas. L., of Illinois.

Secretaries—Rev. Jas., of N. J.; Henry E., of Michigan, and David W., of R. I.

David W. Hoyt, of Providence, the author of the Hoyt Family, and who has since then been arranging the descendants of the Connecticut Hoyts for an addition to the former work, was the orator of the meeting, and the speeches made were many and interesting. The entire meeting was a very delightful one.

A permanent organization of the Hoyts was made, under the name of THE HOYT FAMILY UNION, whose officers are:

President—Joseph B. Hoyt, of Stamford, Conn.

Secretary—David W. Hoyt, Providence, R. I.

Permanent Committee—Hon. Joseph G. Hoyt, Farmington, Me.; Aaron B. Hoyt, Sandwich, N. H.; Wm. Henry Hoyt, Burlington, Vt.; Dr. Enos Hoyt, Framingham, Mass.; David W. Hoyt, Providence, R. I.; Joseph B. Hoyt, Stamford, Conn.; Dr. Wm. Henry Hoyt, Syracuse, N. Y.; Rev. Jas. Hoyt, Orange, N. J.; Gen. Henry M. Hoyt, Wilkesbarre, Pa.; Rev. Prof. Cornelius A. Hoyt, Oberlin, Ohio; Prof. Benj. T. Hoyt, Greencastle, Ind.; James L. Hoyt, Woodstock, Ill.; Wm. C. Hoyt, Esq., Detroit, Mich.; John W. Hoyt, Madison, Wis.; Gould R. Hoyt, Lake City, Minn.; Chas. Hoyt, South English, Iowa; Rev. Prof. James W. Hoyt, Nashville, Tenn.; Ira G. Hoitt, San Francisco, Cal.; Leopold A. Hoyt, Hillsborough, New Brunswick; Jesse Hoyt, New Glasgow, Nova Scotia.

A full report of the meeting was issued in pamphlet form by the Historian of the family, D. W. Hoyt, of Providence, in 1866, and the complete genealogy of this numerous family will soon be ready for publication.

F.

POPULATION AND GROWTH OF STAMFORD.

Year.	Populat'n.	Year.	Populat'n.	Year.	Populat'n.
1665	420	1745	1510	‡1820	3284
1676	405	1756	2648	1830	3705
1687	410	*1760	2580	1840	3516
1700	585	1800	4465	¶1850	4965
1714	905	†1810	4440	1860	7185

In 1868, including Darien and the part of New Canaan once in the town, the population would not be less than 11000.

The following facts will show the relative growth of Stamford, and leave us with a promise of what we may hope for, when the History of the town shall be revised and enlarged at some future day.

* The first official census.
† A part of New Canaan had been cut off.
‡ Darien had just been cut off.
¶ N. Y. & N. H. R. R. just built.

In 1665, of 20 towns in Connecticut, Stamford ranked the tenth in wealth.

In 1678, of 23, it was the eleventh in wealth and twelfth in population.

In 1687, of 24, it was the fourteenth in wealth and twelfth in population.

In 1829, of 130, it stood the twentieth in wealth and twenty-sixth in population.

In 1850, of 160, it was the eighth in wealth and ninth in population.

In 1857, it ranked the third town in the State, in INCREASE OF WEALTH during the ten preceding years. The entire State had increased 60 per cent.; fourteen towns only had increased 100 per cent.; while Stamford had gone forward 200 per cent. The only two towns whose increase had been greater than that of Stamford, were Waterbury and Meriden.

This note on the population and growth of Stamford, accidentally final, will yet furnish a pleasant and hopeful introduction to the history of the Stamford yet to be. We leave these studies of this ancient town with the strongest conviction, that in no New England town can be found the elements of a surer growth or of a more stable prosperity.

RESIDENCE OF J. WILCOX, Esq., STAMFORD.

OUR WOOD CUTS.

For the beautiful cuts of Stamford residences with which our History is so well illustrated, the author is happy to acknowledge his great indebtedness to James Wilcox, Esq., whose own residence is a perpetual witness to his interest in the locality which he chose, and which his taste has done so much to adorn.

The following brief description of these residences will be of sufficient historical interest to justify ins rtion in our record of the town.

ECHO LAWN.

This place, now owned by James Wilcox, Esq., of the firm of Wilcox & Gibbs, New York, embraces about fifty acres of land on the western slope of the Noroton Hill. It furnishes a delightful view of the village to the south-west; of Clark and Richmond and the more distant Greenwich hills, to the west; and of Strawberry Hill to the north-west; with pleasant glimpses of the Sound and Island to the south. From one of our roughest hill-sides, falling off abruptly into one of our rockiest and most impracticable marshes, Echo Lawn now presents to the visitor a picture which even our beautiful cut does not flatter. It shows what good taste and liberal expenditures can do in the hands of adequate enterprise.

JOSEPH B. HOYT'S RESIDENCE.

In 1858, Mr. Hoyt, after a successful business career as the oldest of the Hoyt Brothers, built this elegant and substantial Home, a little west of the summit of the hill where Main street crosses it. A little east of north, across Main street, lie the beautiful grounds of his brother Oliver, crowned with their showy residence, and to the north-east, about a hundred rods, stands the massive brick residence of his brother William, on the old home lot of the family.

A. B. DAVENPORT'S RESIDENCE.

This showy structure occupies a most commanding view from the west slope of Davenport Ridge. It is about five miles north by east from the Stamford depot. The panorama stretching around it is, at any season of the year, well worth a study, and in summer is very beautiful.

This locality was voted to the Rev. John Davenport, of Stamford, by the proprietors of the town, in January, 1705-6, in consideration of his hundred pounds interest in the "Long Lots," as agreed upon at the time of his settlement in the ministry here in 1693. By his will, January 20, 1728, he gave it to his eldest son, John, who built his home upon it, and died there in 1742. The property passed next into the hands of the third John, who died in 1756, leaving it to the fourth John, a deacon in the North Stamford Church, who died in 1820. A portion of this land was bought of the heirs, by Amzi B. Davenport, a grandson of this deacon John, in 1857, and on it he built the residence represented in our cut. It occupies the site of an old residence removed about eighty years ago.

"SPRING HILL."

This is one of the most expensive, as it is one of the most attractive and showy residences of the town. It is built of granite, and shows to admirable advantage from the summit of the gently rounded elevation on which it stands. The lawn in front, to the west, and the undulating surface towards the south and east, are very beautiful. In 1864, Mr. E. A. Quintard purchased this tract of Mr. Z. B. Nichols, and removed the building in which Mr. Nichols had carried on his boarding-school for years, and substituted for it the fine structure, with which we are happy to illustrate one feature of our town prosperity.

SOUND VIEW.

This elegant retreat, owned since 1854 by Benjamin L. Waite, Esq., is at the present terminus of our Westcott road, about a mile and a half east of the village. It overlooks a stretch of beautiful fields, sloping gracefully towards the south, until they meet the waters of the Sound. These, and the added beauty of the Island beyond, constitute a very charming view.

OUR CHURCHES.

We are sure we need no apology for introducing into their appropriate places the two elegant cuts of our Congregational and Baptist churches. Our only regret is that we could not get as good ones of the other churches of the town.

NOTE.—While these last sheets have been printing, the old "Washington House," referred to as "Webb's Tavern," page 252, has been removed. The ground has been thoroughly explored by Charles Alphonse, Esq., and the many coins, both silver and copper, together with various other relics found there, indicate it to have been as noted a place as our local tradition supposes it to have been.

Errors and Additions.

Page	line		
Page 18,	line 24,	for	Lucretia, read Susan.
19,	30,		Marshall, read Morehouse.
20,	32,		Whitman, read Whitmore.
33,	32,		1851, read 1856.
34,	6,		1.8, read 6.8.
154,	25,		1860, read 1801.
"	26,		1830, read 1820.
200,	15,		Wooster, read Waterbury, 2d.
221,	20,		following chapter, read Chapters XVI and XVII.
235,	31,		32, read 82.
259,	29,		Mrs., read Miss Lucretia.
262,	17,		Lavinia, read Lucretia.
267,	15,		Gorman, read Gorham.
377,	31,		Stamford, read Stratford.
406,	27,		Shay, read Shaw.
427,	28,		honest, read earnest.

On page 434 occurs an error of the author, arising from a verbal mistake made in the "Wetmore Family." The sermon which called forth the "Vindication" from Rev. James Wetmore, was that of Noah Hobart, of Fairfield, not of Stamford. The sermon was preached in Stamford on the occasion of Dr. Welles' ordination; and in the hurry of the author to vindicate the truth of our local history, he committed an error greater than the one he would correct.

Page 454, line 34, for draws, read drawers.

" 456, " 27, " and Africa, read Africa and.

To the list of graduates, page 459, add:

Davenport, William, son of William of North Stamford, a member of Amherst College, class, 1870.

Sloan, Wm. J., a surgeon in the U. S. A., whose residence is in Stamford, and who will be reported in the Soldier's Memorial.

INDEX TO SURNAMES.

The reader will notice the abbreviations in the reference to the pages. A dash indicates that all of the intervening pages are included in the reference.